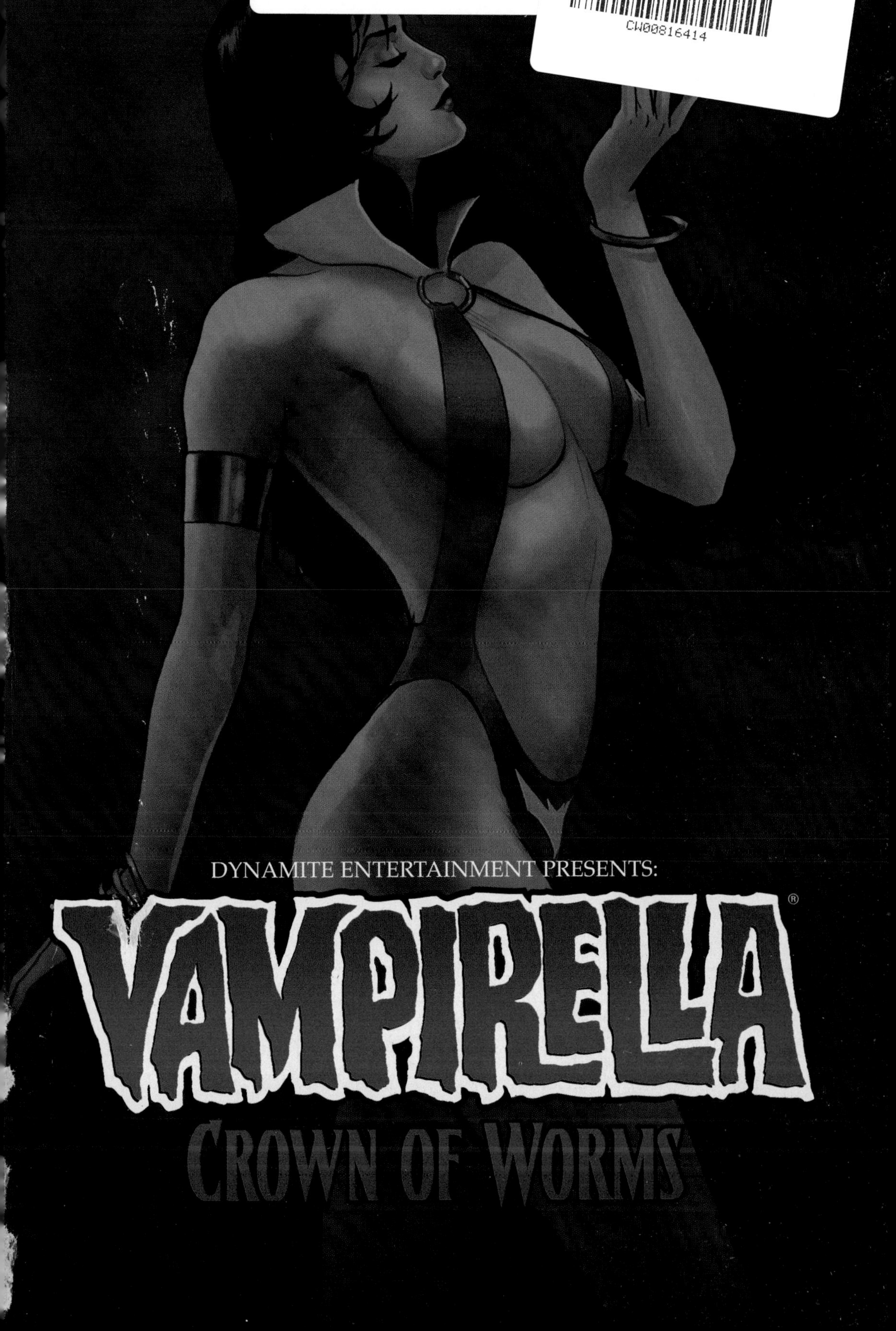

DYNAMITE ENTERTAINMENT PRESENTS:

VAMPIRELLA®

CROWN OF WORMS

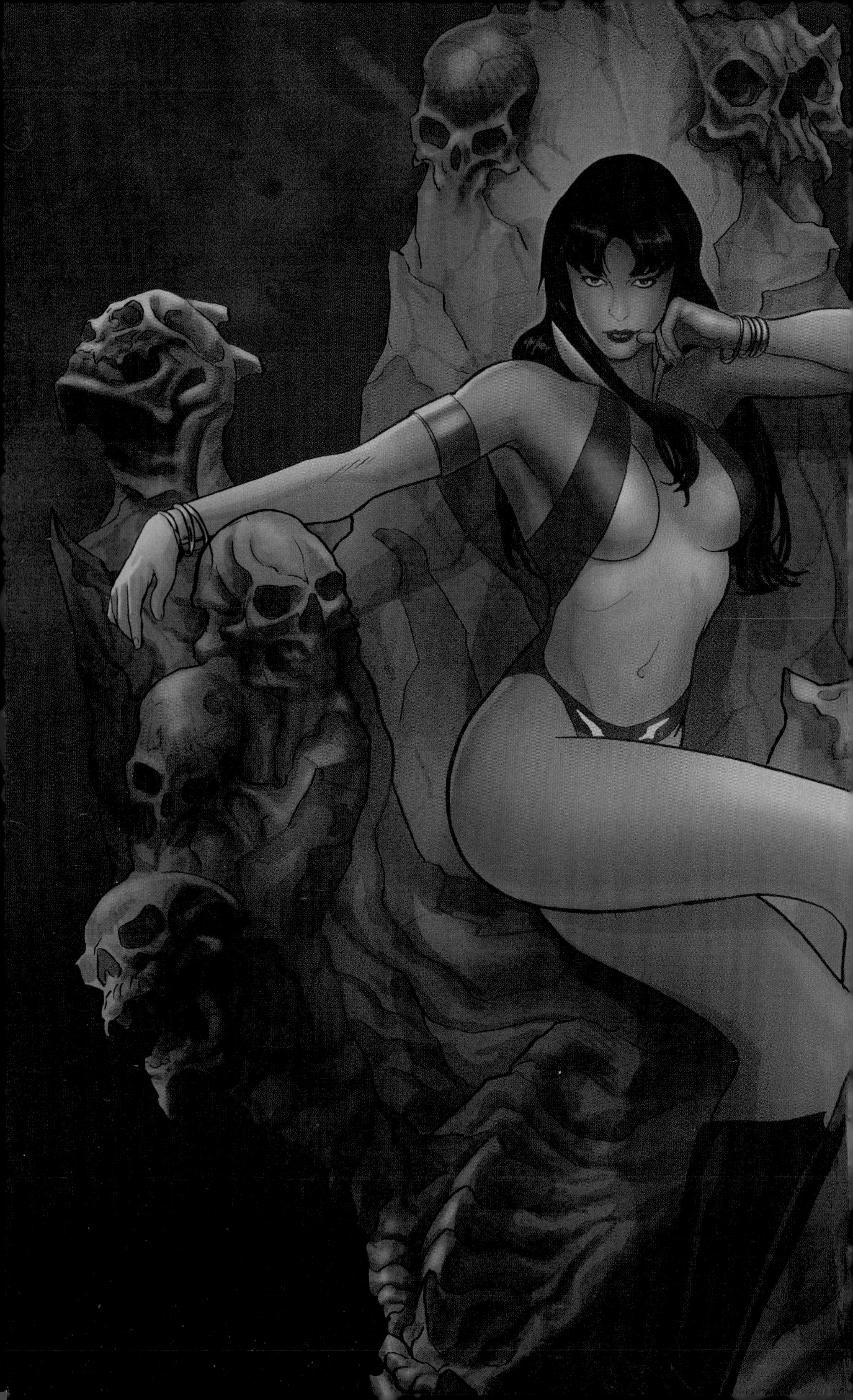

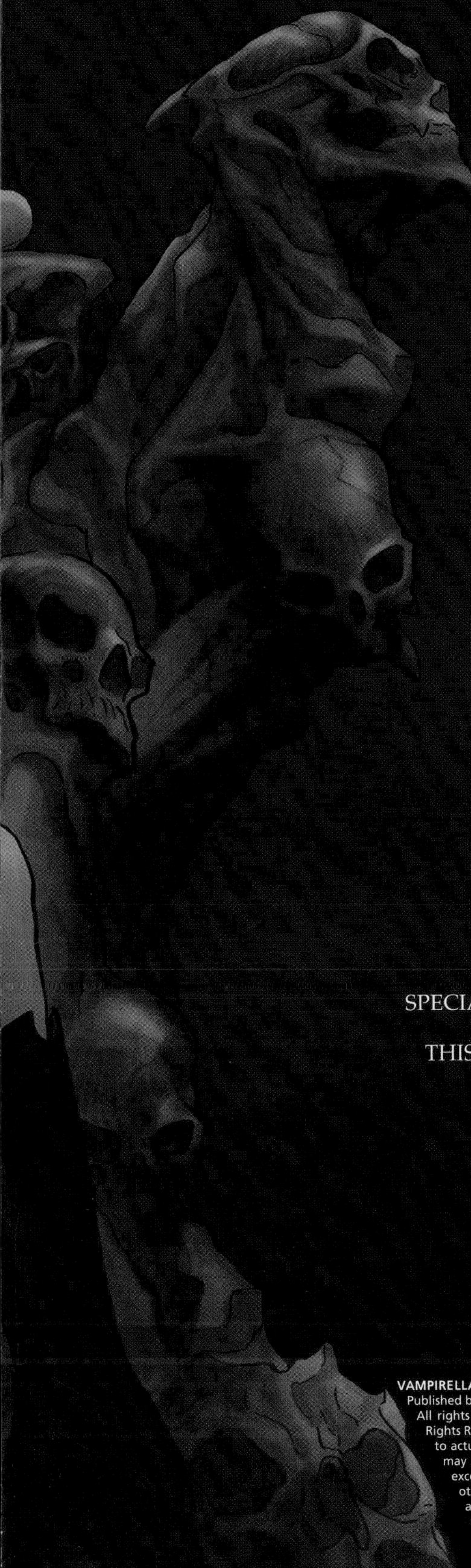

CROWN OF WORMS

WRITTEN BY

ERIC TRAUTMANN

ILLUSTRATED BY

WAGNER REIS issues 1-6
FABIANO NEVES issues 1-6
WALTR GEOVANI issue 7

LETTERED BY

MARCHALL DILLON

COLORS BY

INLIGHT STUDIO issues 1-6
IVAN NUNES issue 7

COLLECTION COVER BY

J. SCOTT CAMPBELL

COLLECTION DESIGN BY

JASON ULLMEYER

SPECIAL THANKS TO JANA WRIGHT AND BRANNON BOREN

THIS VOLUME COLLECTS VAMPIRELLA #1-7 ORIGINALLY
PUBLISHED BY DYNAMITE ENTERTIANMENT

VISIT US ONLINE AT: WWW.DYNAMITE.NET

NICK BARRUCCI • PRESIDENT
JUAN COLLADO • CHIEF OPERATING OFFICER
JOSEPH RYBANDT • EDITOR
JOSH JOHNSON • CREATIVE DIRECTOR
RICH YOUNG • DIRECTOR OF BUSINESS DEVELOPMENT
JASON ULLMEYER • SENIOR DESIGNER
JOSH GREEN • TRAFFIC COORDINATOR
CHRIS CANIANO • PRODUCTION ASSISTANT

ISBN10: 1-60690-212-1   ISBN13: 978-1-60690-212-7   First Printing   10 9 8 7 6 5 4 3 2 1

"PART OF YOU HAS ALWAYS BEEN INNOCENT. REMEMBER THAT PART, AS YOU WRITE YOUR TALE."

Introduction by Jen Van Meter

1973. This cabin is old. It was old when my great-grandparents purchased it in the 1950s, and in the summers it is full of their clan, smaller family groups escaping the heat of California's central valley to form a sort of cheerfully scruffy herd in the shade of the redwoods.

In the one-room main floor there's a wood stove, a table with mismatched chairs and benches for fourteen or so, and a couple double beds with faded chenille spreads wedged into the far corners. At night, this is where the big kids play Crazy Eights, Hearts and Spoons, laughing sharp and giddy, up much later than they would ever be permitted at home.

On the porch, the grownups play cribbage and listen to Henry Mancini on a record player that folds up like a suitcase. Their laughter is subdued and warm, throaty. My uncle's return from service in Vietnam is already a dim memory to me, but they are out there counting blessings, grateful to be together and safe in a world that the last few years has shown them is full of stark, sudden, bewildering horror and tragedy.

Up the narrow stairs, there's another single room, this one crammed full of twin beds made up with sheets worn soft and nearly transparent over the years, and quilts of flannel and scritchy wool that play hell with even the slightest sunburn. The only other piece of furniture is a bulky dresser, the bottom drawer of which has been accumulating comic books for at least 30 years.

I am the youngest and have been sent to bed. I have a flashlight and an issue of *Vampirella*. This is my earliest memory of reading by myself.

Why did I choose her? Maybe the issue was on top, maybe Frazetta's subdued palette caught my eye, I don't know. What I do know is that I flipped to the lettercol, "Vampi's Scarlet Letters," and saw that she answered her own mail. I knew she was a fiction but I liked that little smiling picture of her next to each response, and there, in the tone some anonymous staffer took while answering Vampi's fan mail, I found the heart of the character: she was kind. As scary as her stories looked, and as intimidatingly sexual and adult as *she* looked, her responses to readers were warm, almost sisterly in their gentle friendliness. She was perfect for that moment in time, perfect for me; her stories acknowledged the scary world I too knew was out there, but as a window on it—and as a capable, dynamic agent in it —she was safe to be around. Because she wanted to be. Her narrative was about her will to be decent overriding the dark forces acting against—and within—her.

A lot of years have passed and I'm a grown woman, eyes and ears wide open. There's plenty I could write about 'dark forces acting within' women in fiction, about the trope of the bad girl with a heart of gold, about subversive and repressive modes in the horror genre. I could write a whole separate essay just about the tensions surrounding Vampi's iconic costume; it is undeniably exploitative, fabulously mod, and designed by Trina Robbins, a woman with more feminist cred than I could ever hope to have. All of those topics would be valid; one of the things that has made the character and her stories endure is that they are hard to dismiss as inconsequential or insubstantial. There's always been a lot more going on with Vampirella than simple shock or lurid objectification; her point of view has always been a crucial part of her stories, and it's the key to the book now in your hands.

In the story collected here—the first seven issues of Eric Trautmann's run on the title— Vampirella looks and acts very little like the character as I knew her all those years ago, not because he doesn't value the same things I do about her, but because he *does*. When his chance came to write her, Vampirella had lost Adam van Helsing, the great love of her unlife, and Trautmann steadfastly refuses to let that be irrelevant. You'll turn the page in a minute and meet a Vampi who is angrier than we've ever seen her, not sure if she cares anymore whether she's safe to be around. Grieving for Adam, she's rejected the light-hearted flirtation—and the costume—that used to offset the horror of her surroundings; all grim vengeance now, she starts "Crown of Worms" wanting to deny almost everything she associates with her happier past.

Artists Wagner Reis, Fabiano Neves and Walter Geovani work wonderfully with the story Trautmann's telling; the world we're looking at is gritty, a little grainy, very dark and often claustrophobic. The violence feels as unforgiving and raw as Vampirella's emotional state, and, especially at first, there's not a lot of focus on her legendary beauty.

It's a little unsettling for a long-time fan, and it's supposed to be.

Trautmann, Reis and Neves want it to seem they're telling one of those 'radical reinvention' stories in which a character with roots and a long history becomes nearly unrecognizable, but I'm not giving away the trick when I tell you "Crown of Worms" is really about Vampirella quite literally wrestling with herself over who she was, who she's going to be, and whether she can retrieve the joy and hope she thinks she's lost. They tell us up front we're going to see a lady sawn in half; the pleasure of this story is in watching as they mix magic words and ink and she comes back together, stepping—whole and familiar—out of the box.

Get your flashlight. You're in for a treat.

May, 2011
Portland, Oregon

Jen Van Meter is best known for her Hopeless Savages *comics and graphic novels from Oni Press. She has also written* Red Sonja: Break the Skin, Black Lightning: Year One, Amazing Spider-Man Presents: Black Cat (Trophy Hunters), *and numerous other comics. She lives in Portland, Oregon with her family.*

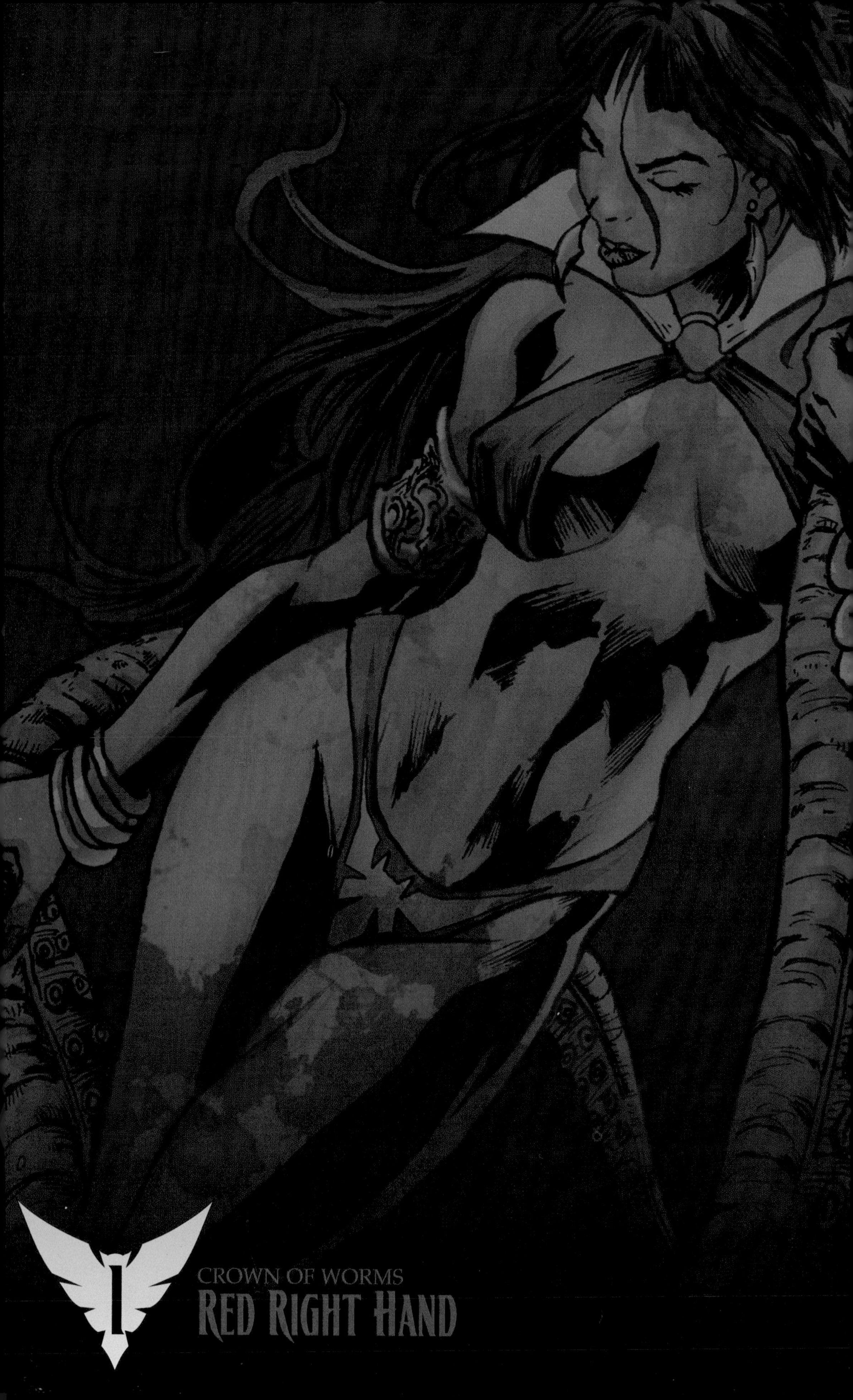

CROWN OF WORMS

RED RIGHT HAND

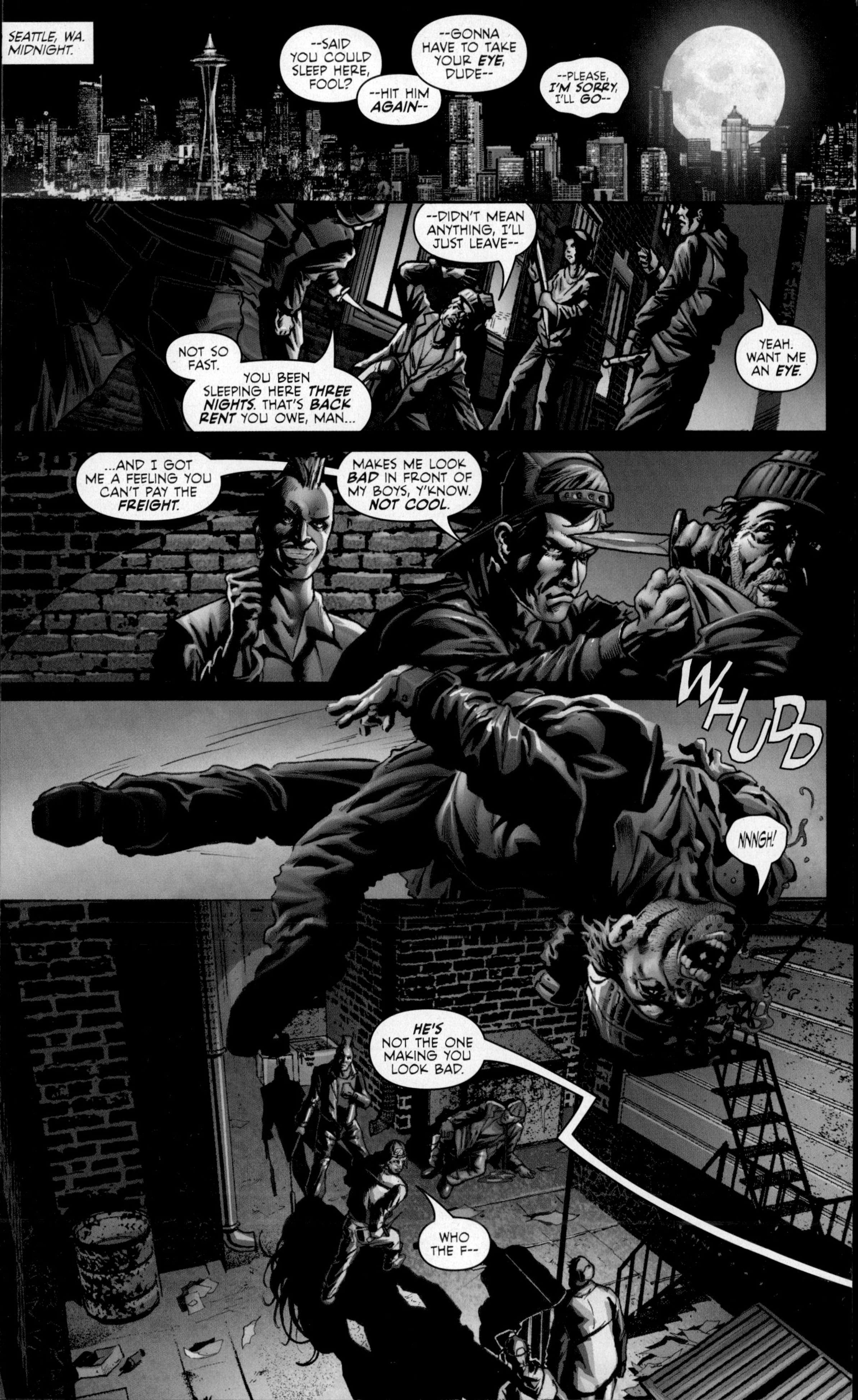
SEATTLE, WA. MIDNIGHT.
--SAID YOU COULD SLEEP HERE, FOOL?
--HIT HIM AGAIN--
--GONNA HAVE TO TAKE YOUR EYE, DUDE--
--PLEASE, I'M SORRY, I'LL GO--
--DIDN'T MEAN ANYTHING, I'LL JUST LEAVE--
NOT SO FAST.
YOU BEEN SLEEPING HERE THREE NIGHTS. THAT'S BACK RENT YOU OWE, MAN...
YEAH. WANT ME AN EYE.
...AND I GOT ME A FEELING YOU CAN'T PAY THE FREIGHT.
MAKES ME LOOK BAD IN FRONT OF MY BOYS, Y'KNOW. NOT COOL.
WHUDD
NNNGH!
HE'S NOT THE ONE MAKING YOU LOOK BAD.
WHO THE F--

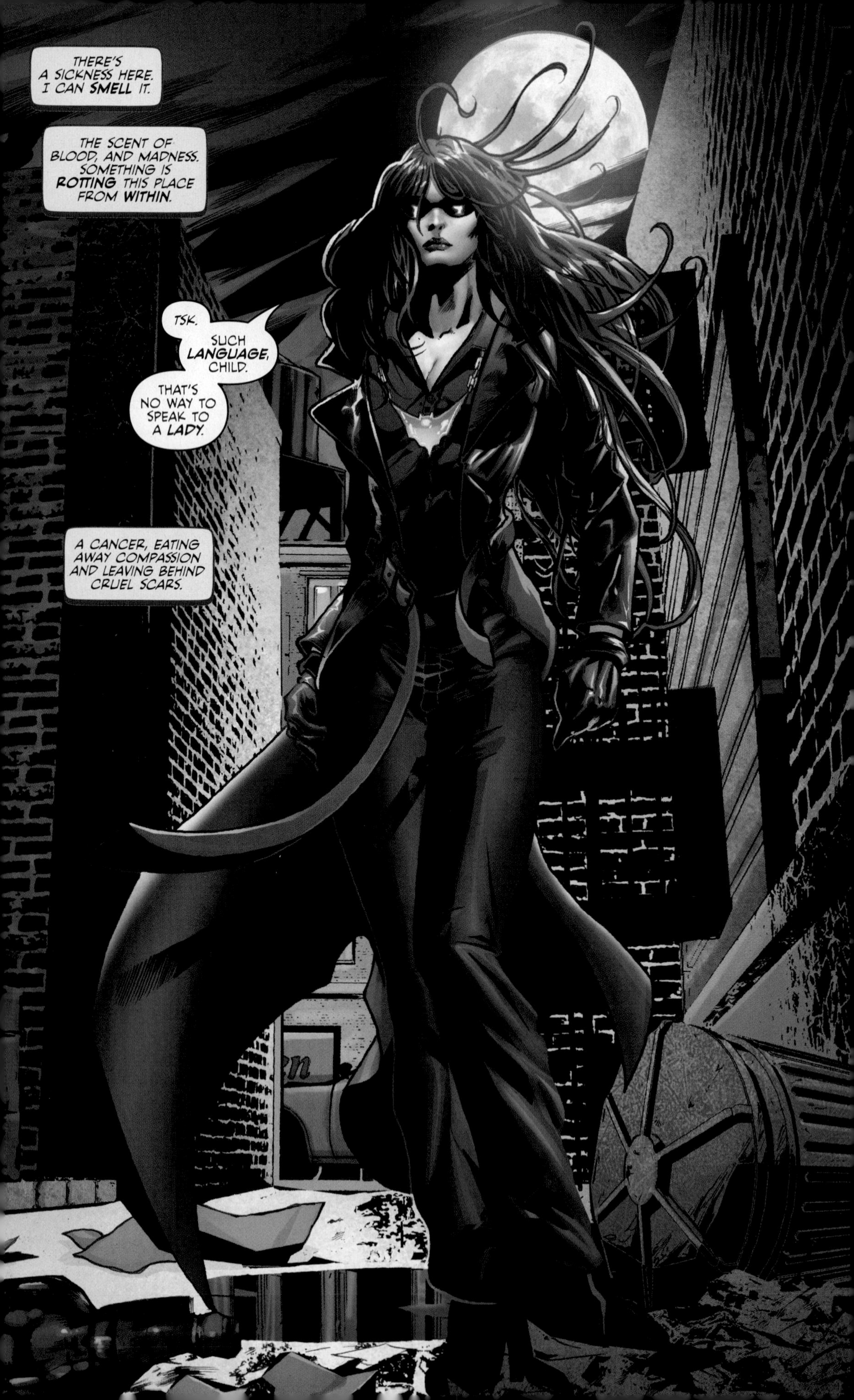
THERE'S A SICKNESS HERE. I CAN SMELL IT.
THE SCENT OF BLOOD, AND MADNESS. SOMETHING IS ROTTING THIS PLACE FROM WITHIN.
TSK.
SUCH LANGUAGE, CHILD.
THAT'S NO WAY TO SPEAK TO A LADY.
A CANCER, EATING AWAY COMPASSION AND LEAVING BEHIND CRUEL SCARS.

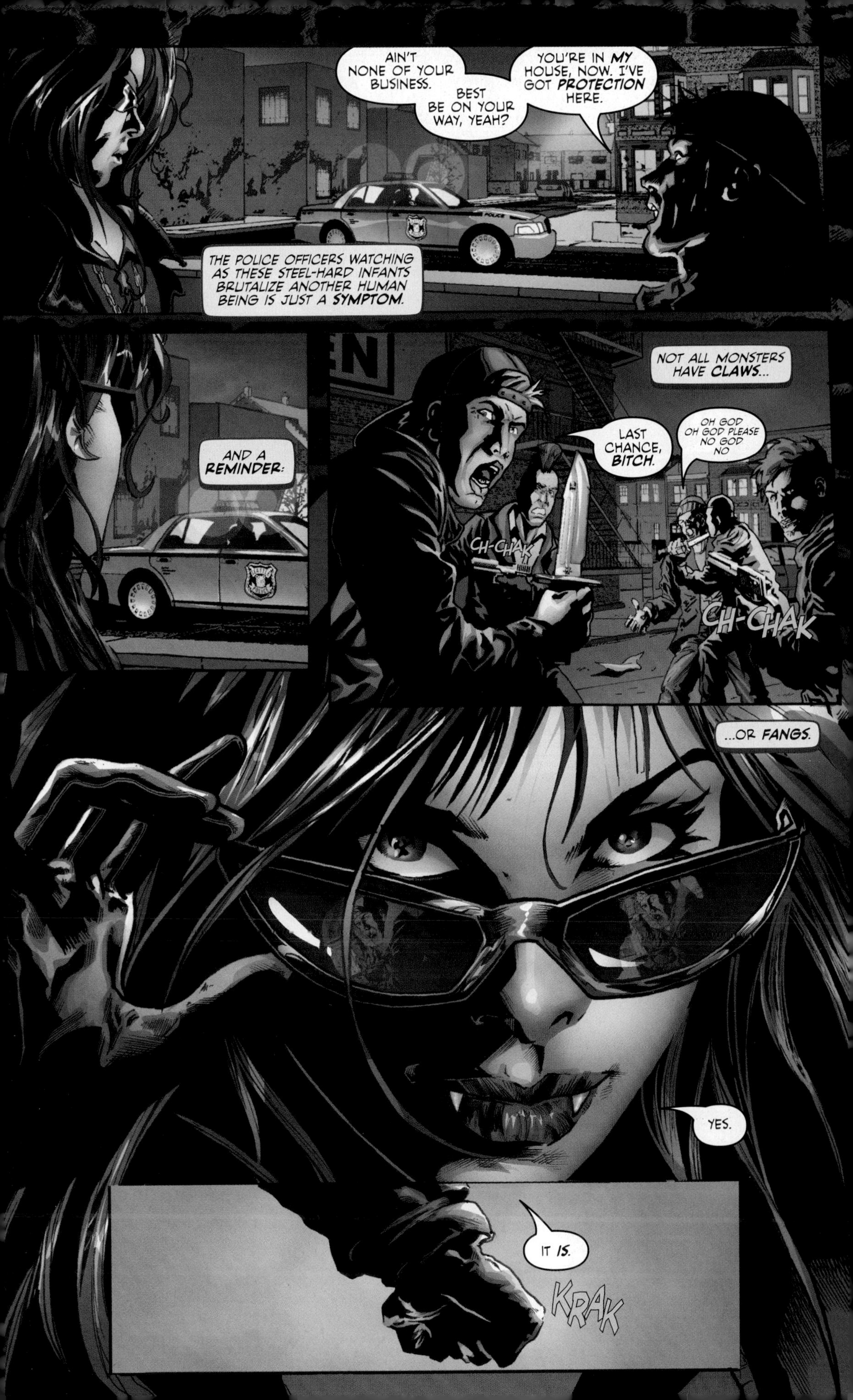
AIN'T NONE OF YOUR BUSINESS.
BEST BE ON YOUR WAY, YEAH?
YOU'RE IN MY HOUSE, NOW. I'VE GOT PROTECTION HERE.
THE POLICE OFFICERS WATCHING AS THESE STEEL-HARD INFANTS BRUTALIZE ANOTHER HUMAN BEING IS JUST A SYMPTOM.
AND A REMINDER:
NOT ALL MONSTERS HAVE CLAWS...
LAST CHANCE, BITCH.
OH GOD OH GOD PLEASE NO GOD NO
CH-CHAK
CH-CHAK
...OR FANGS.
YES.
IT IS.
KRAK

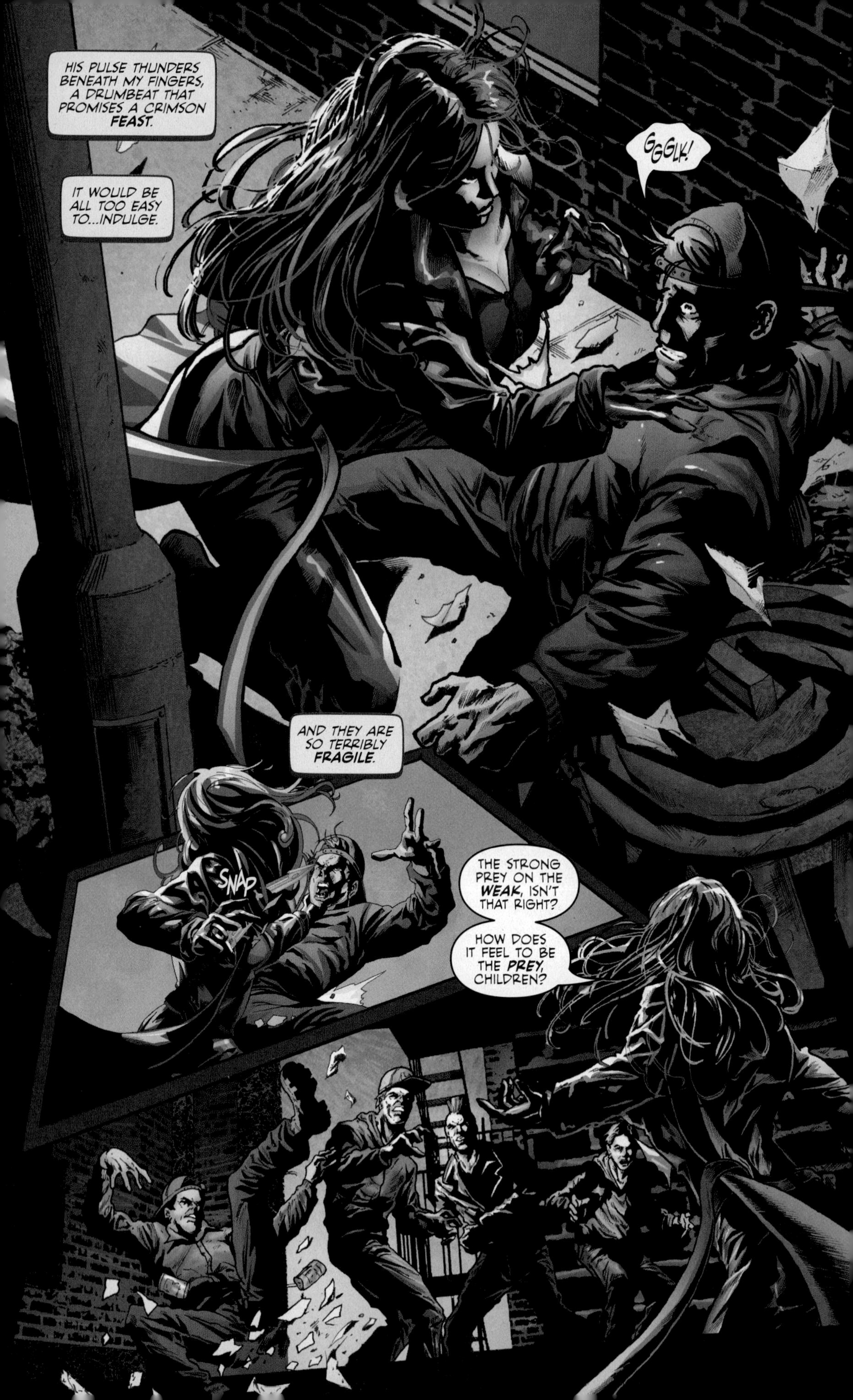
HIS PULSE THUNDERS BENEATH MY FINGERS, A DRUMBEAT THAT PROMISES A CRIMSON FEAST.
GGGLK!
IT WOULD BE ALL TOO EASY TO...INDULGE.
AND THEY ARE SO TERRIBLY FRAGILE.
SNAP
THE STRONG PREY ON THE WEAK, ISN'T THAT RIGHT?
HOW DOES IT FEEL TO BE THE PREY, CHILDREN?

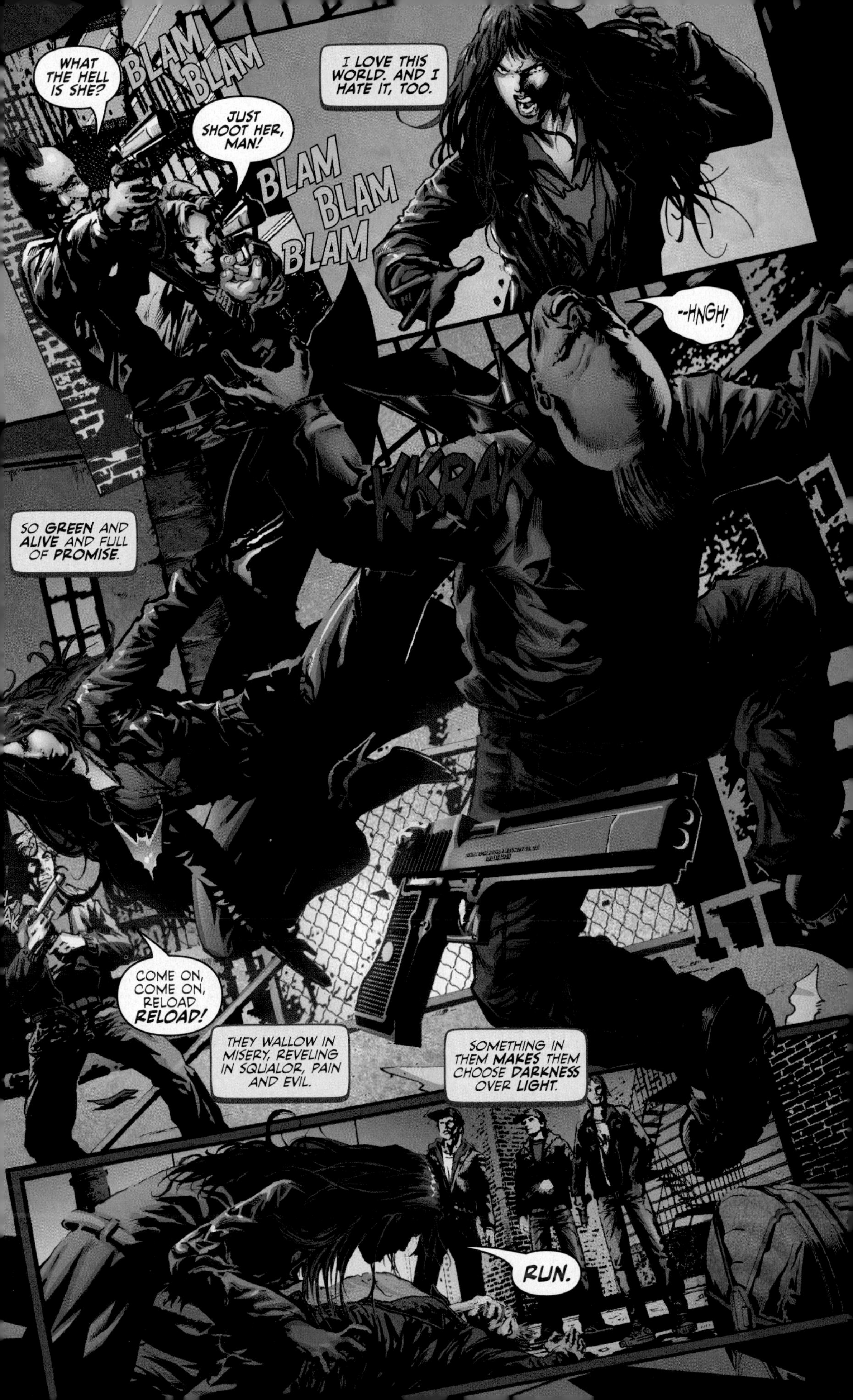
WHAT THE HELL IS SHE?
BLAM BLAM
I LOVE THIS WORLD. AND I HATE IT, TOO.
JUST SHOOT HER, MAN!
BLAM BLAM BLAM
--HNGH!
KKRAK
SO GREEN AND ALIVE AND FULL OF PROMISE.
COME ON, COME ON, RELOAD RELOAD!
THEY WALLOW IN MISERY, REVELING IN SQUALOR, PAIN AND EVIL.
SOMETHING IN THEM MAKES THEM CHOOSE DARKNESS OVER LIGHT.
RUN.

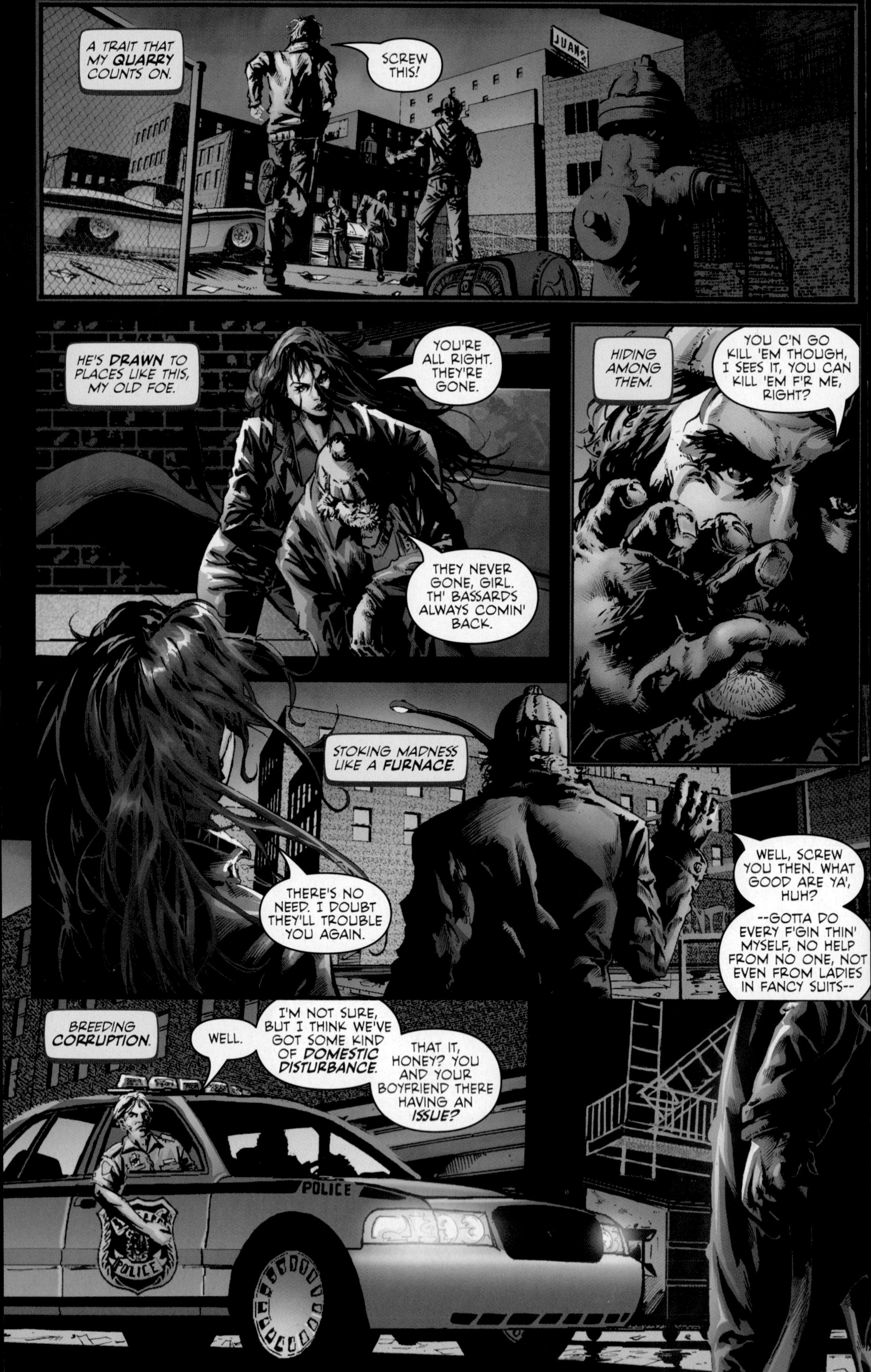
A TRAIT THAT MY QUARRY COUNTS ON.
SCREW THIS!
JUAN
HE'S DRAWN TO PLACES LIKE THIS, MY OLD FOE.
YOU'RE ALL RIGHT. THEY'RE GONE.
THEY NEVER GONE, GIRL. TH' BASSARDS ALWAYS COMIN' BACK.
HIDING AMONG THEM.
YOU C'N GO KILL 'EM THOUGH, I SEES IT, YOU CAN KILL 'EM F'R ME, RIGHT?
STOKING MADNESS LIKE A FURNACE.
THERE'S NO NEED. I DOUBT THEY'LL TROUBLE YOU AGAIN.
WELL, SCREW YOU THEN. WHAT GOOD ARE YA', HUH?
--GOTTA DO EVERY F'GIN THIN' MYSELF, NO HELP FROM NO ONE, NOT EVEN FROM LADIES IN FANCY SUITS--
BREEDING CORRUPTION.
WELL.
I'M NOT SURE, BUT I THINK WE'VE GOT SOME KIND OF DOMESTIC DISTURBANCE.
THAT IT, HONEY? YOU AND YOUR BOYFRIEND THERE HAVING AN ISSUE?
POLICE
POLICE

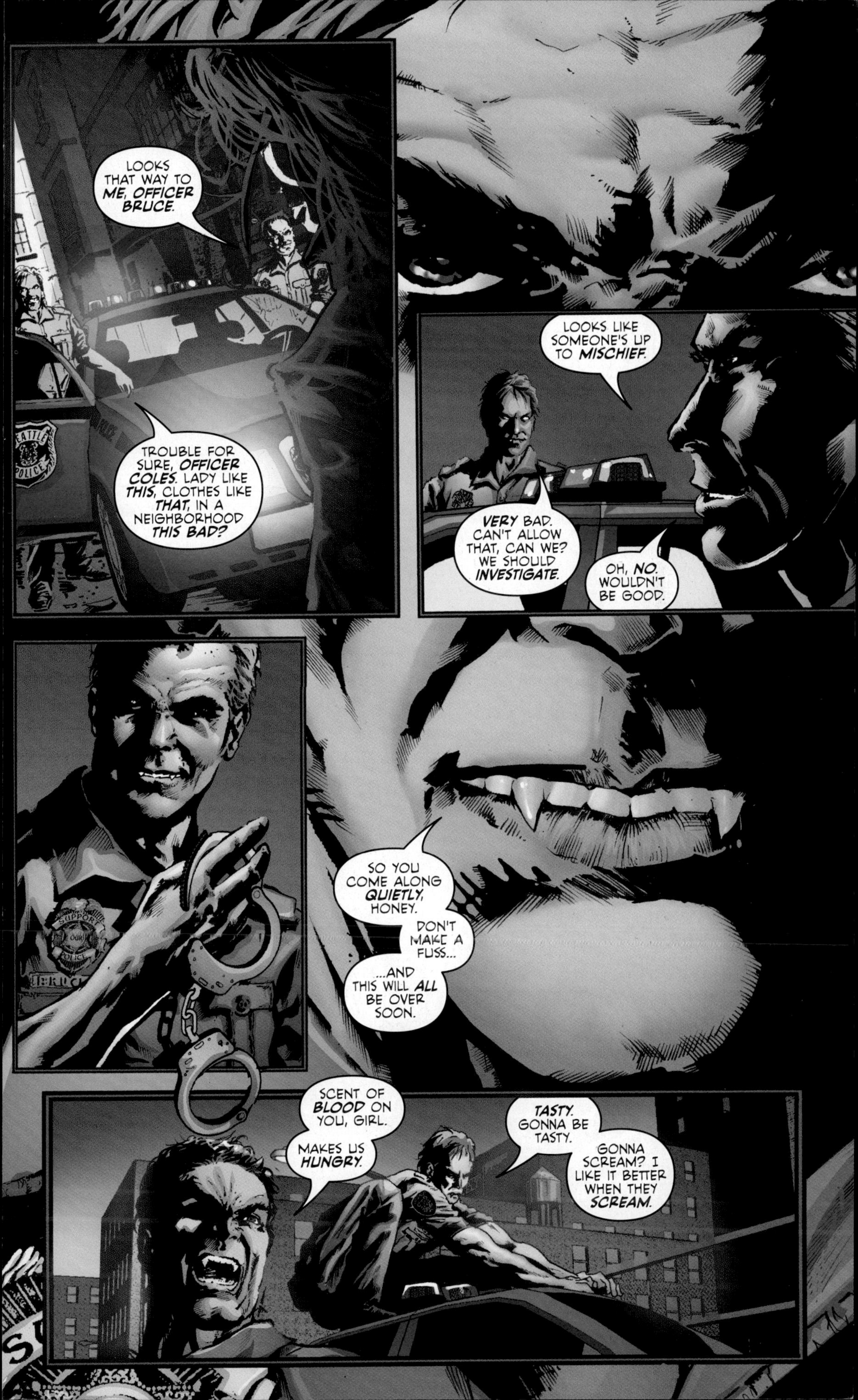
LOOKS THAT WAY TO ME, OFFICER BRUCE.
TROUBLE FOR SURE, OFFICER COLES. LADY LIKE THIS, CLOTHES LIKE THAT, IN A NEIGHBORHOOD THIS BAD?
LOOKS LIKE SOMEONE'S UP TO MISCHIEF.
VERY BAD. CAN'T ALLOW THAT, CAN WE? WE SHOULD INVESTIGATE.
OH, NO. WOULDN'T BE GOOD.
SO YOU COME ALONG QUIETLY, HONEY.
DON'T MAKE A FUSS...
...AND THIS WILL ALL BE OVER SOON.
SCENT OF BLOOD ON YOU, GIRL.
MAKES US HUNGRY.
TASTY. GONNA BE TASTY.
GONNA SCREAM? I LIKE IT BETTER WHEN THEY SCREAM.

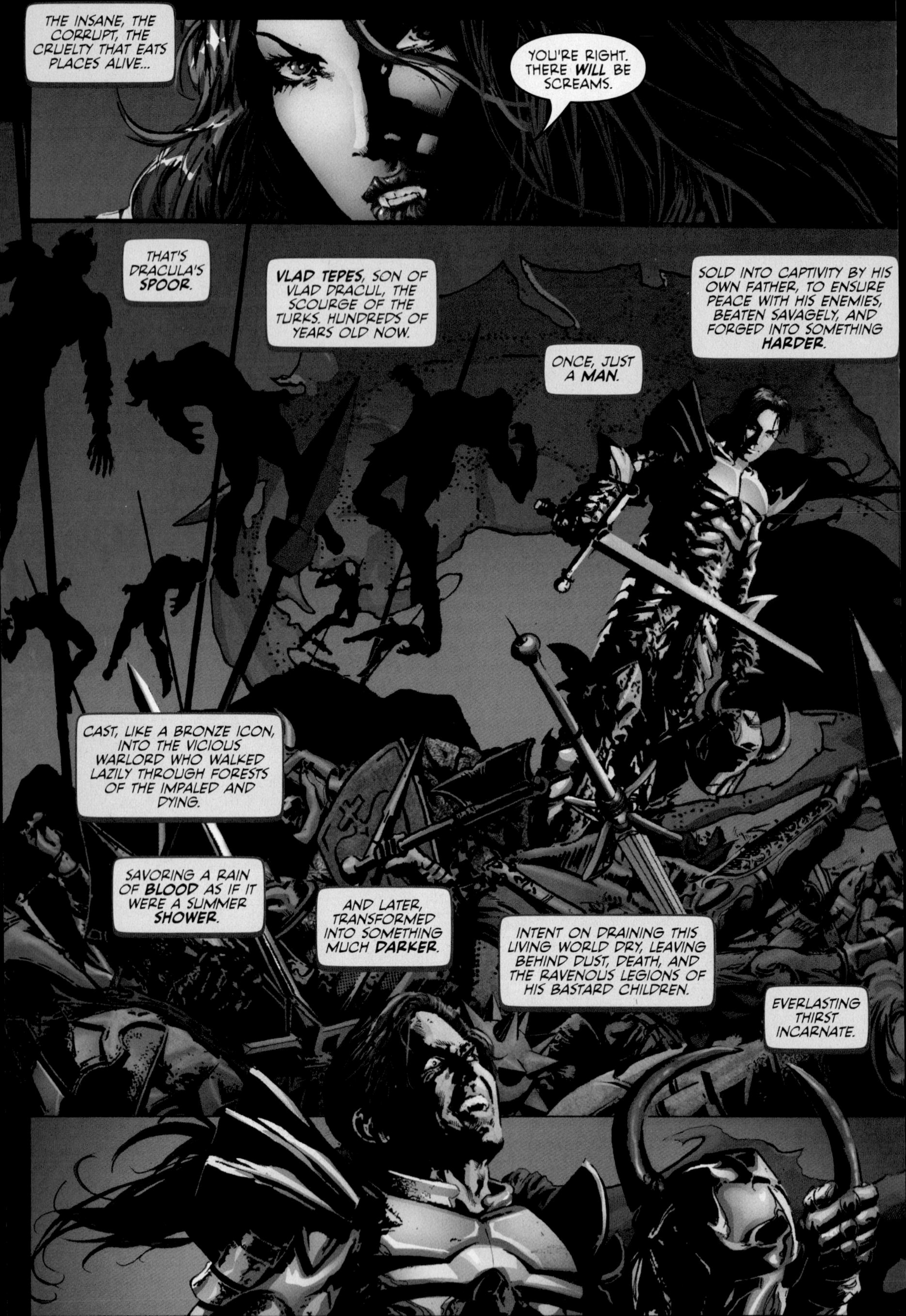
THE INSANE, THE CORRUPT, THE CRUELTY THAT EATS PLACES ALIVE...
YOU'RE RIGHT. THERE **WILL** BE SCREAMS.
THAT'S DRACULA'S **SPOOR**.
VLAD TEPES, SON OF VLAD DRACUL, THE SCOURGE OF THE TURKS. HUNDREDS OF YEARS OLD NOW.
ONCE, JUST A **MAN**.
SOLD INTO CAPTIVITY BY HIS OWN FATHER, TO ENSURE PEACE WITH HIS ENEMIES, BEATEN SAVAGELY, AND FORGED INTO SOMETHING **HARDER**.
CAST, LIKE A BRONZE ICON, INTO THE VICIOUS WARLORD WHO WALKED LAZILY THROUGH FORESTS OF THE IMPALED AND DYING.
SAVORING A RAIN OF **BLOOD** AS IF IT WERE A SUMMER **SHOWER**.
AND LATER, TRANSFORMED INTO SOMETHING MUCH **DARKER**.
INTENT ON DRAINING THIS LIVING WORLD DRY, LEAVING BEHIND DUST, DEATH, AND THE RAVENOUS LEGIONS OF HIS BASTARD CHILDREN.
EVERLASTING THIRST INCARNATE.

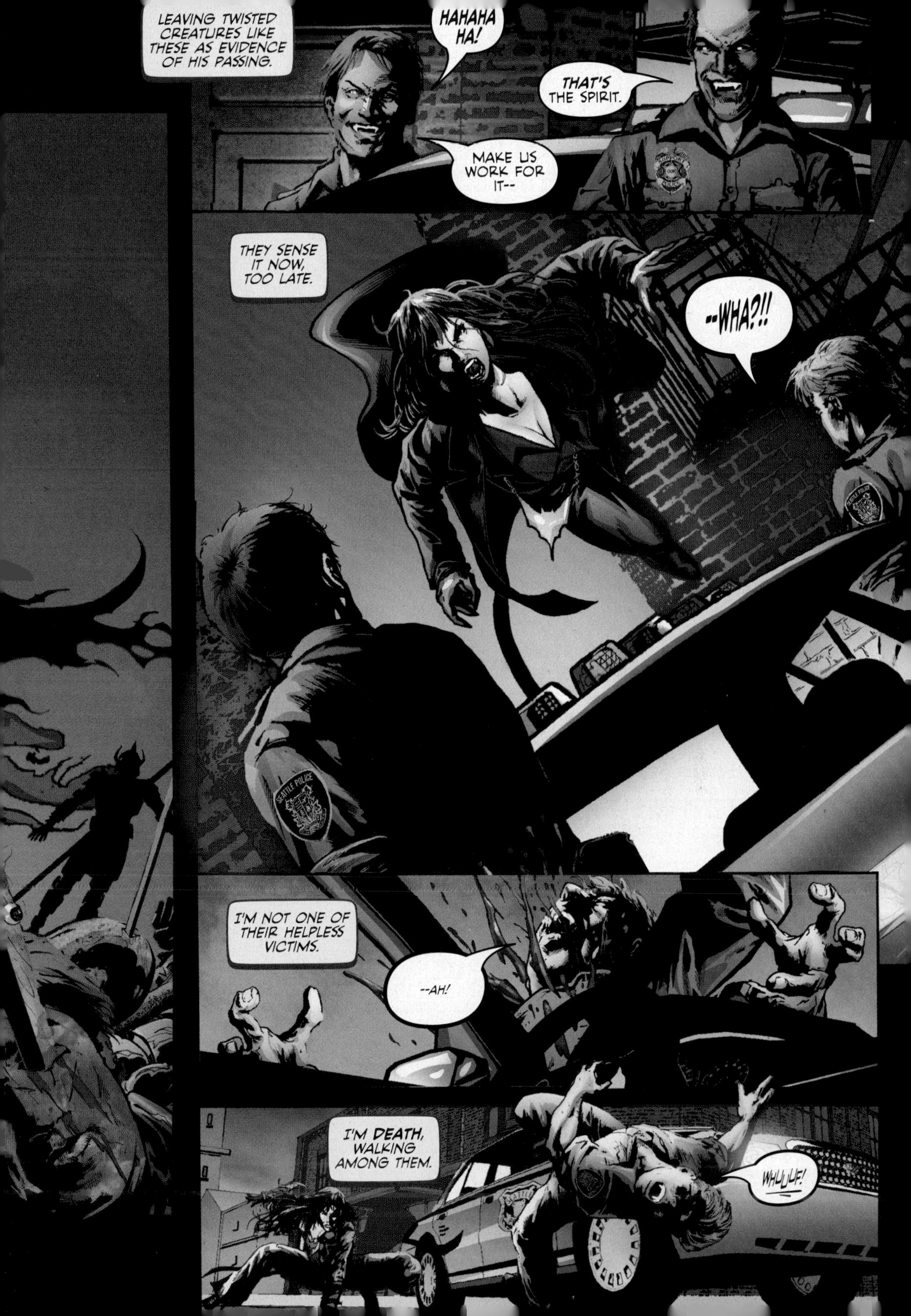

LEAVING TWISTED CREATURES LIKE THESE AS EVIDENCE OF HIS PASSING.
HAHAHA HA!
THAT'S THE SPIRIT.
MAKE US WORK FOR IT--
THEY SENSE IT NOW, TOO LATE.
--WHA?!!
I'M NOT ONE OF THEIR HELPLESS VICTIMS.
--AH!
I'M DEATH, WALKING AMONG THEM.
WHUUUF!

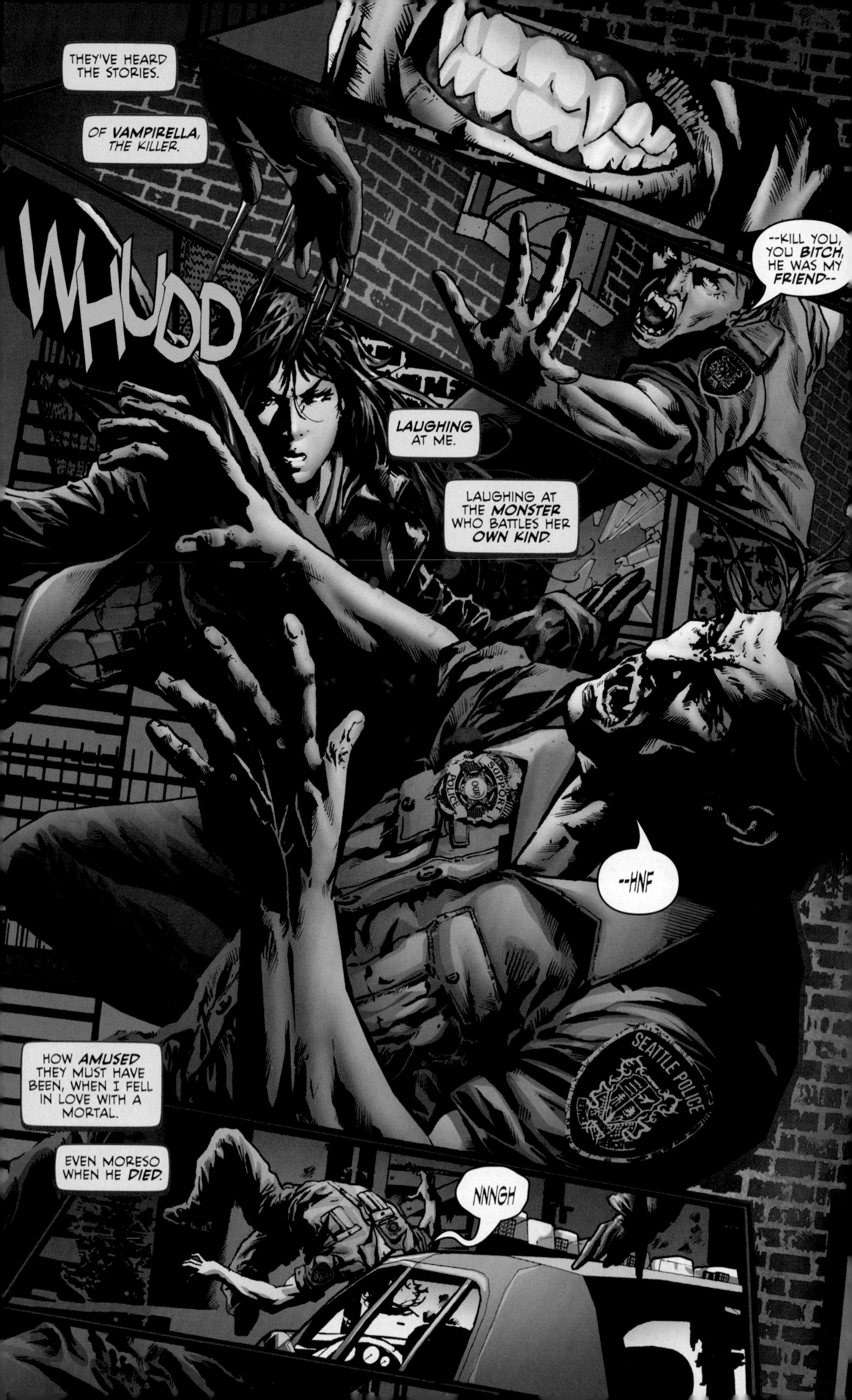
THEY'VE HEARD THE STORIES.
OF VAMPIRELLA, THE KILLER.
WHUDD
--KILL YOU, YOU BITCH, HE WAS MY FRIEND--
LAUGHING AT ME.
LAUGHING AT THE MONSTER WHO BATTLES HER OWN KIND.
--HNF
SEATTLE POLICE
HOW AMUSED THEY MUST HAVE BEEN, WHEN I FELL IN LOVE WITH A MORTAL.
EVEN MORESO WHEN HE DIED.
NNNGH

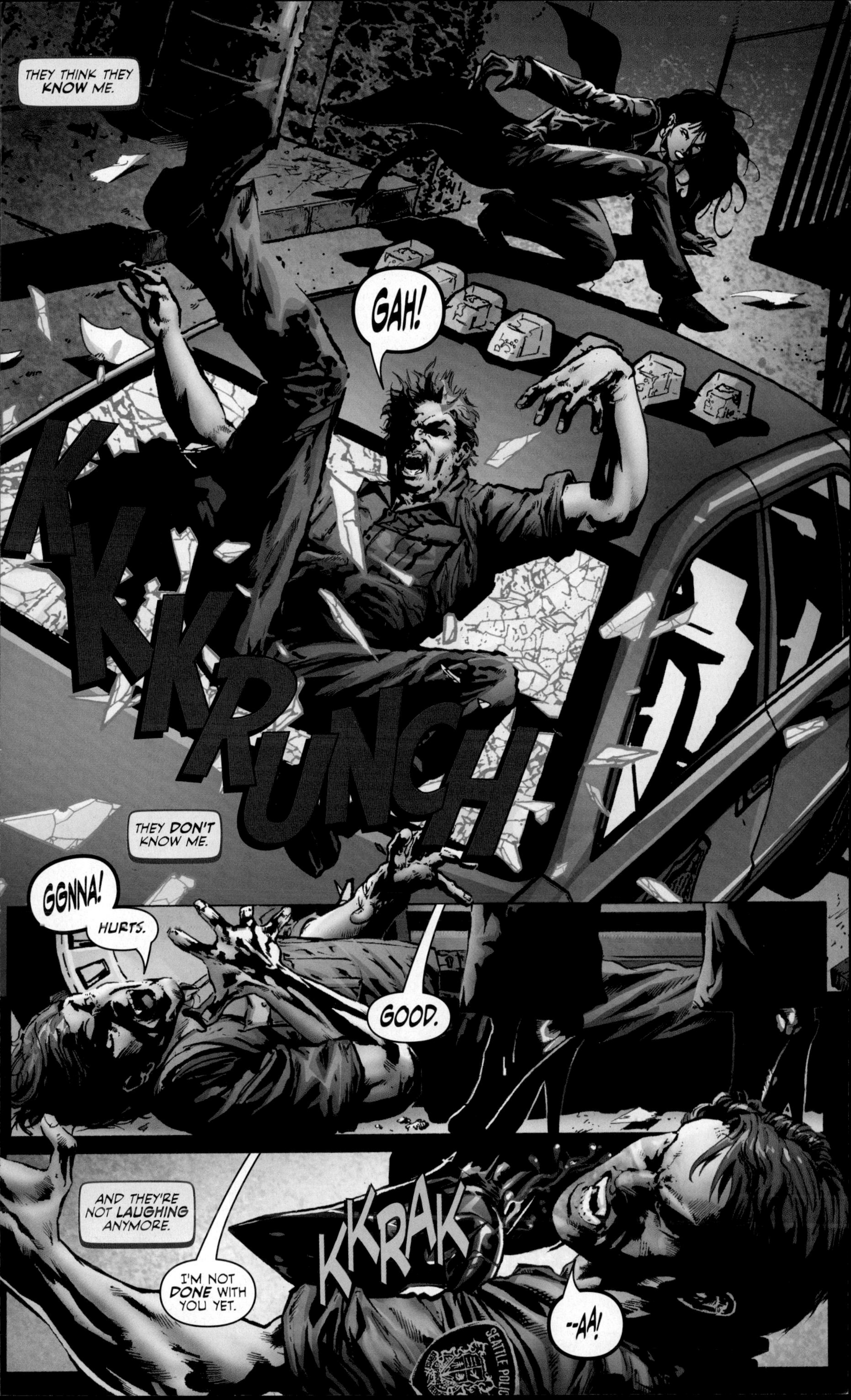
THEY THINK THEY KNOW ME.
GAH!
KKKRUNCH!
THEY DON'T KNOW ME.
GGNNA!
HURTS.
GOOD.
AND THEY'RE NOT LAUGHING ANYMORE.
I'M NOT DONE WITH YOU YET.
KKRAK
--AA!

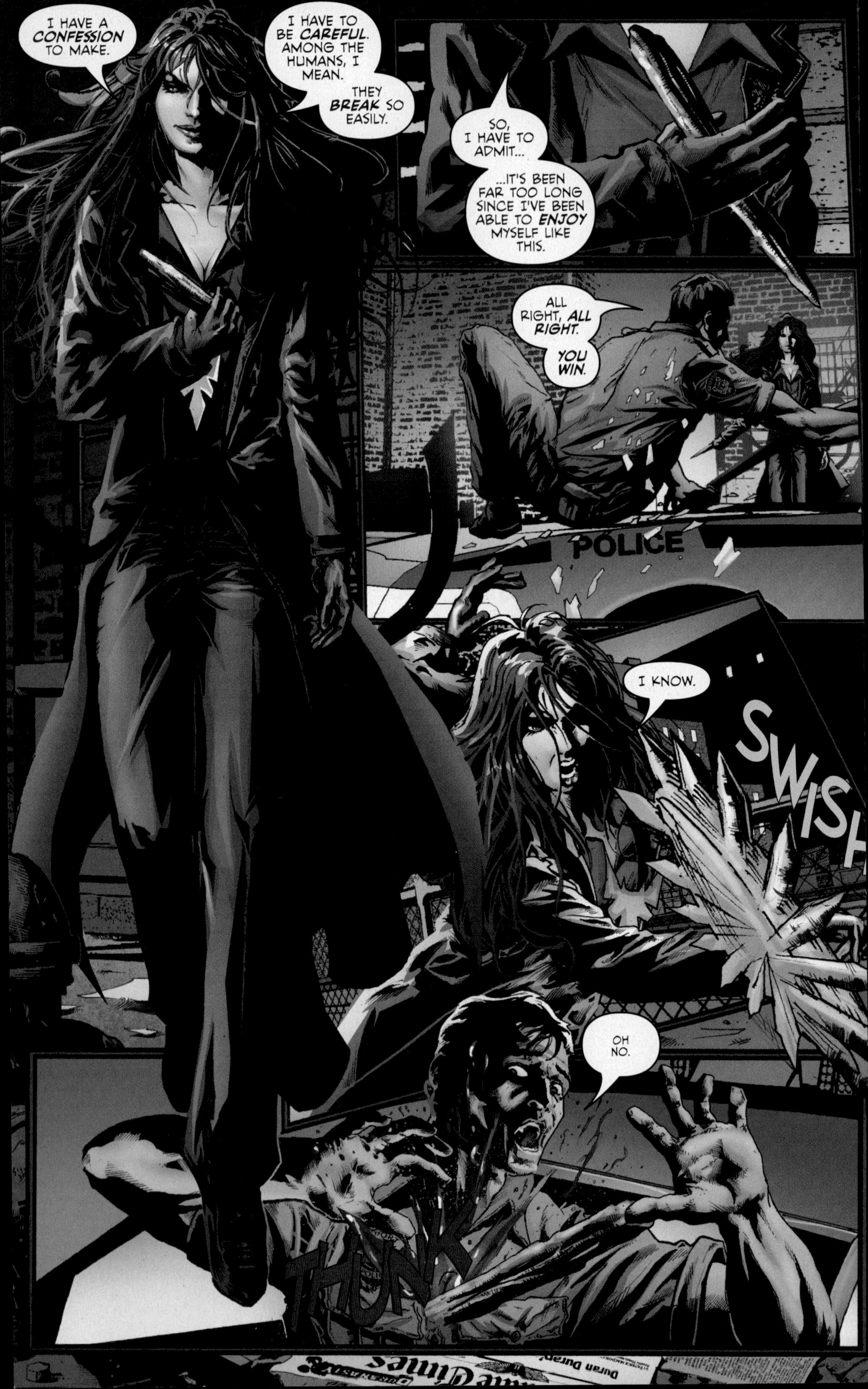
I HAVE A CONFESSION TO MAKE.
I HAVE TO BE CAREFUL. AMONG THE HUMANS, I MEAN.
THEY BREAK SO EASILY.
SO, I HAVE TO ADMIT...
...IT'S BEEN FAR TOO LONG SINCE I'VE BEEN ABLE TO ENJOY MYSELF LIKE THIS.
ALL RIGHT, ALL RIGHT.
YOU WIN.
POLICE
I KNOW.
SWISH
OH NO.

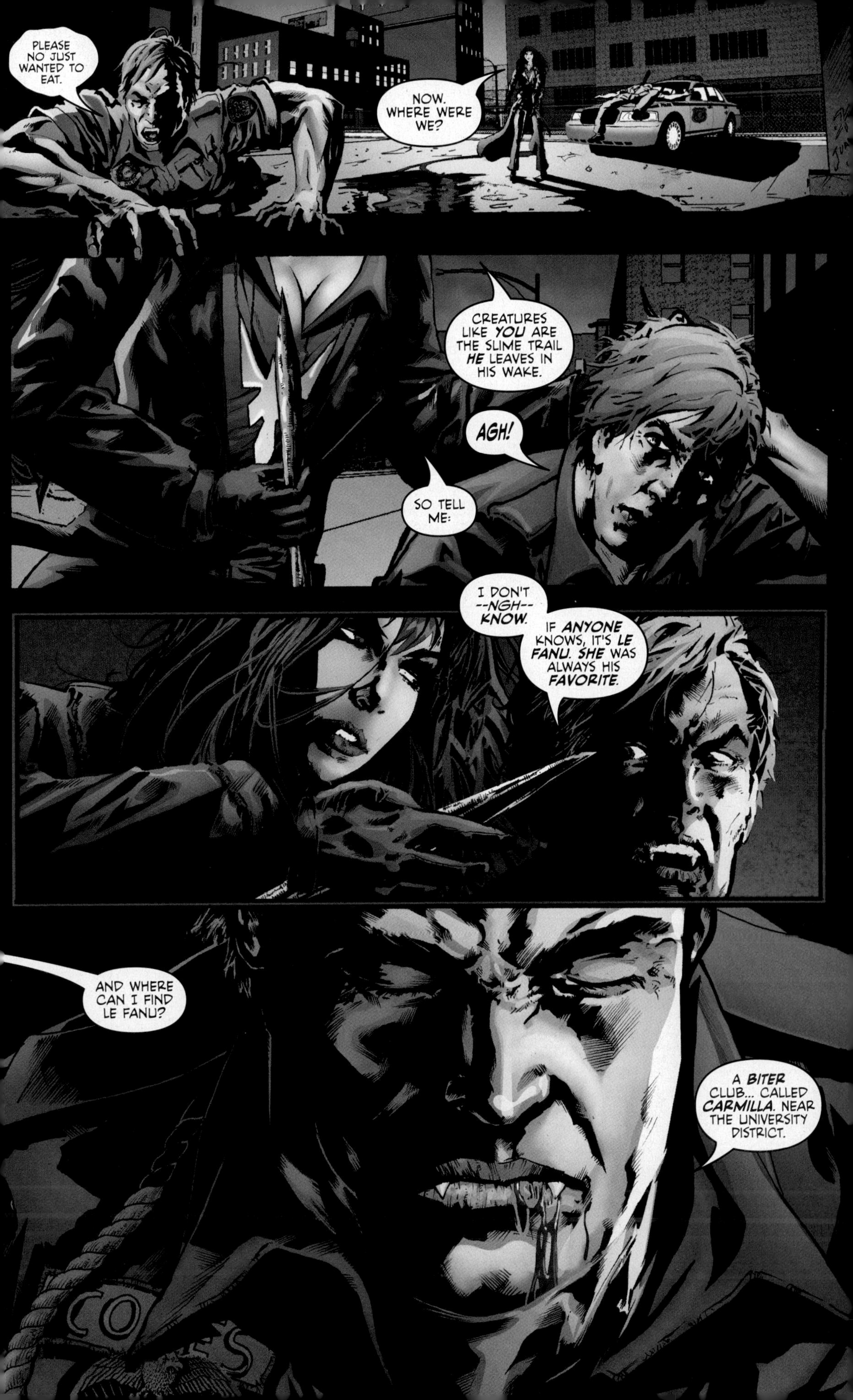
PLEASE NO JUST WANTED TO EAT.
NOW. WHERE WERE WE?
CREATURES LIKE YOU ARE THE SLIME TRAIL HE LEAVES IN HIS WAKE.
AGH!
SO TELL ME:
I DON'T --NGH-- KNOW.
IF ANYONE KNOWS, IT'S LE FANU. SHE WAS ALWAYS HIS FAVORITE.
AND WHERE CAN I FIND LE FANU?
A BITER CLUB... CALLED CARMILLA. NEAR THE UNIVERSITY DISTRICT.

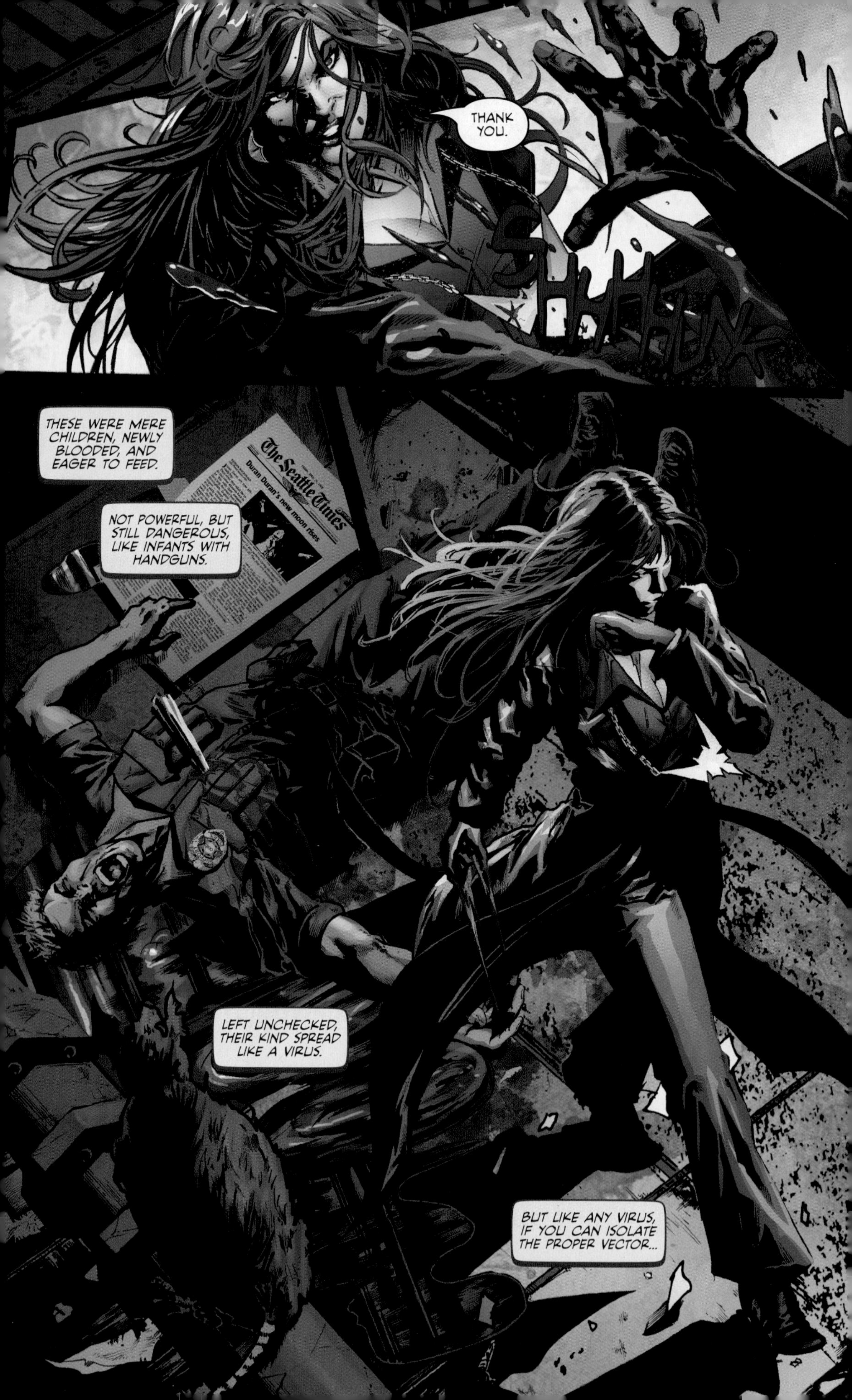
THANK YOU.
SHHHHUNK
THESE WERE MERE CHILDREN, NEWLY BLOODED, AND EAGER TO FEED.
The Seattle Times
Duran Duran's new moon rises
NOT POWERFUL, BUT STILL DANGEROUS, LIKE INFANTS WITH HANDGUNS.
LEFT UNCHECKED, THEIR KIND SPREAD LIKE A VIRUS.
BUT LIKE ANY VIRUS, IF YOU CAN ISOLATE THE PROPER VECTOR...

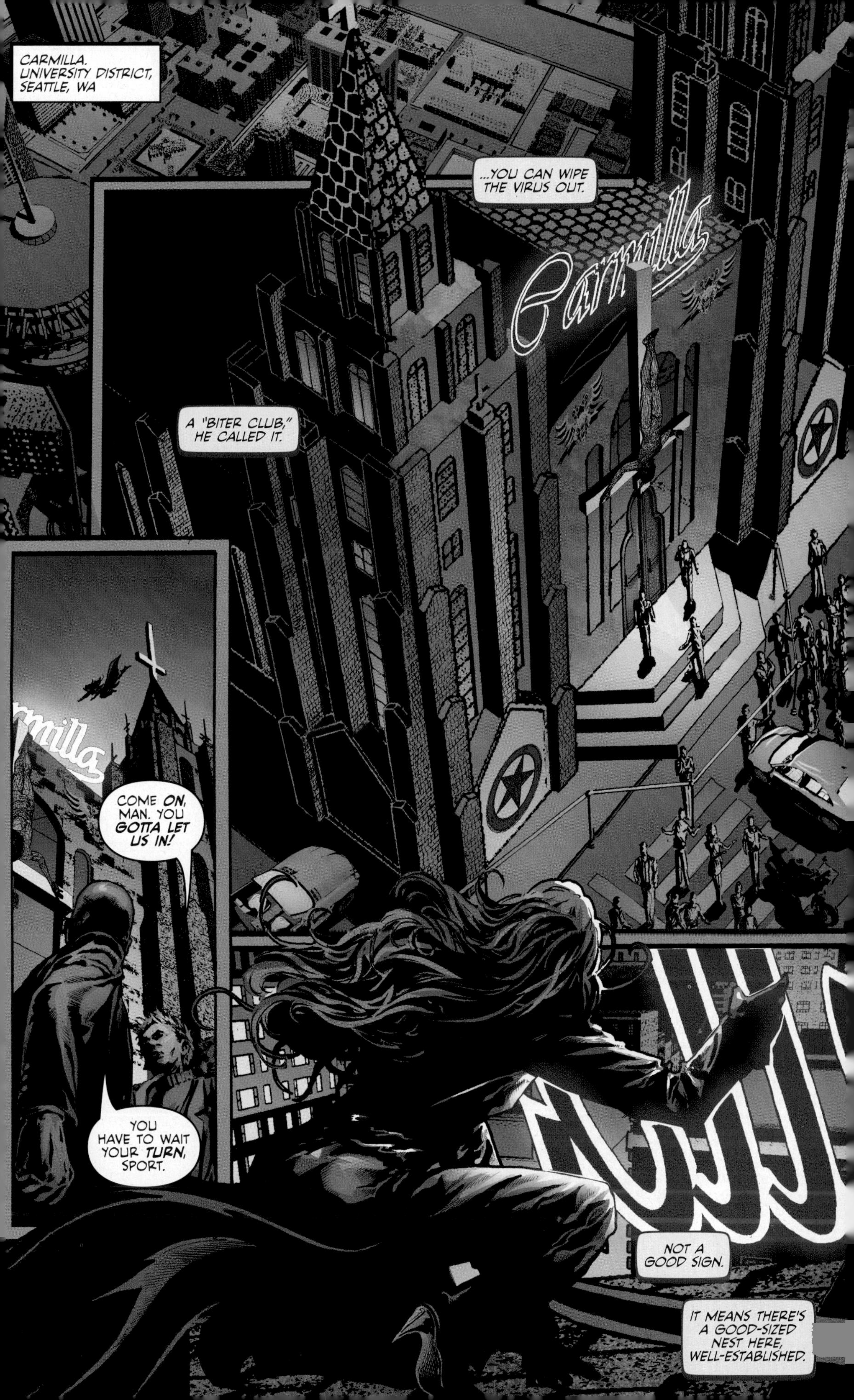
CARMILLA. UNIVERSITY DISTRICT, SEATTLE, WA
...YOU CAN WIPE THE VIRUS OUT.
A "BITER CLUB," HE CALLED IT.
Carmilla
COME ON, MAN. YOU GOTTA LET US IN!
YOU HAVE TO WAIT YOUR TURN, SPORT.
NOT A GOOD SIGN.
IT MEANS THERE'S A GOOD-SIZED NEST HERE, WELL-ESTABLISHED.

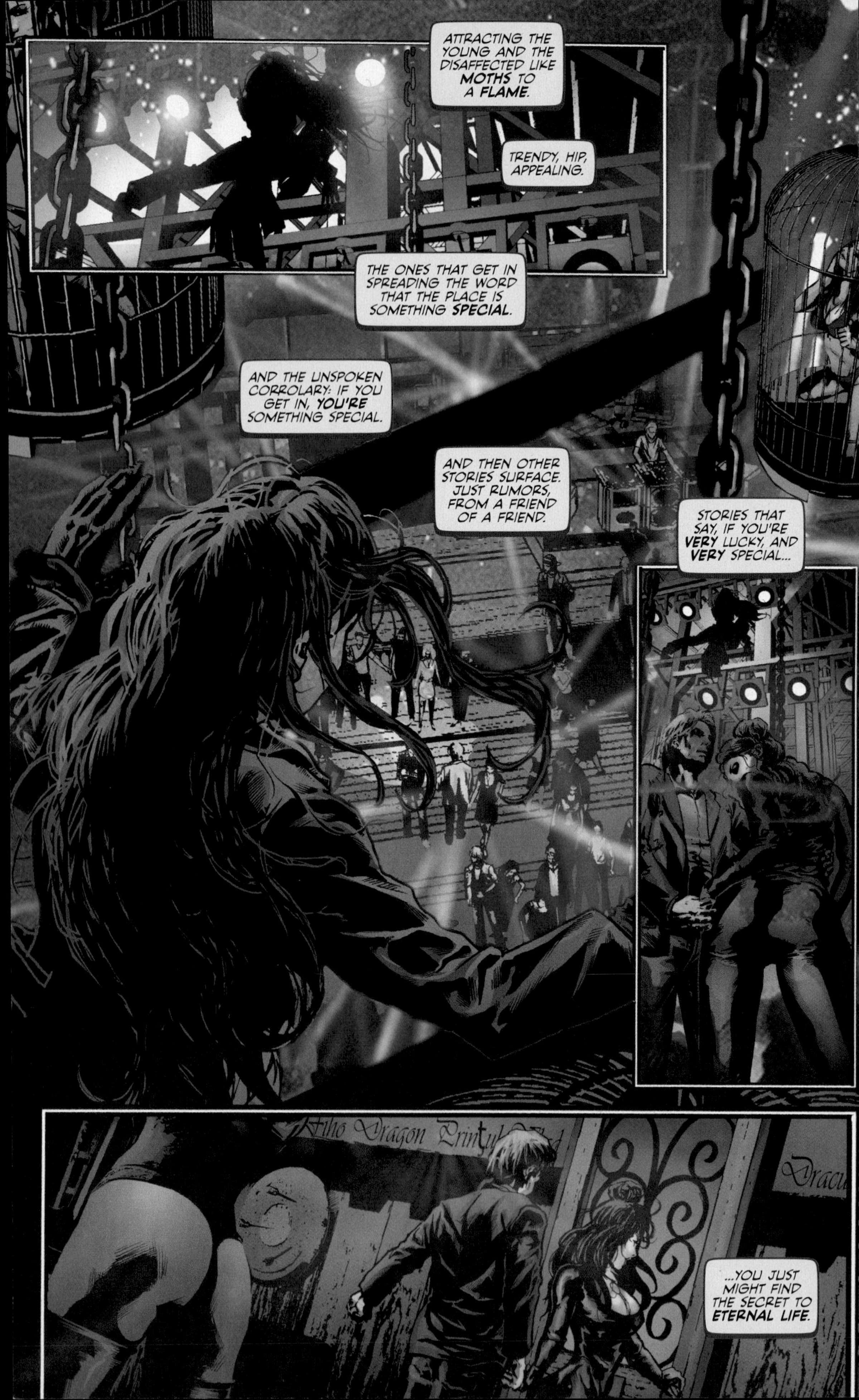
ATTRACTING THE YOUNG AND THE DISAFFECTED LIKE MOTHS TO A FLAME.
TRENDY, HIP, APPEALING.
THE ONES THAT GET IN SPREADING THE WORD THAT THE PLACE IS SOMETHING SPECIAL.
AND THE UNSPOKEN CORROLARY: IF YOU GET IN, YOU'RE SOMETHING SPECIAL.
AND THEN OTHER STORIES SURFACE. JUST RUMORS, FROM A FRIEND OF A FRIEND.
STORIES THAT SAY, IF YOU'RE VERY LUCKY, AND VERY SPECIAL...
...YOU JUST MIGHT FIND THE SECRET TO ETERNAL LIFE.

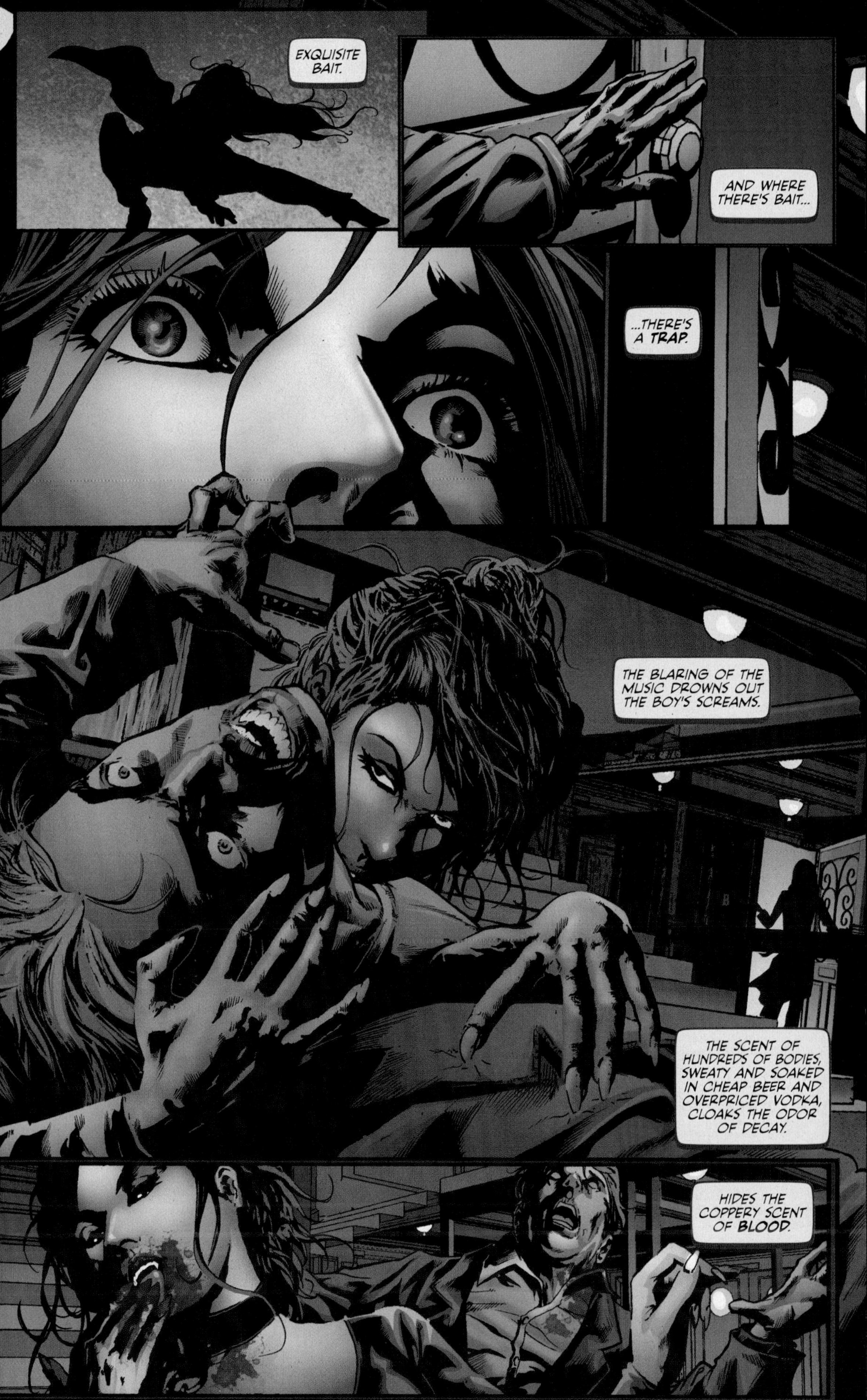
EXQUISITE BAIT.
AND WHERE THERE'S BAIT...
...THERE'S A TRAP.
THE BLARING OF THE MUSIC DROWNS OUT THE BOY'S SCREAMS.
THE SCENT OF HUNDREDS OF BODIES, SWEATY AND SOAKED IN CHEAP BEER AND OVERPRICED VODKA, CLOAKS THE ODOR OF DECAY.
HIDES THE COPPERY SCENT OF BLOOD.

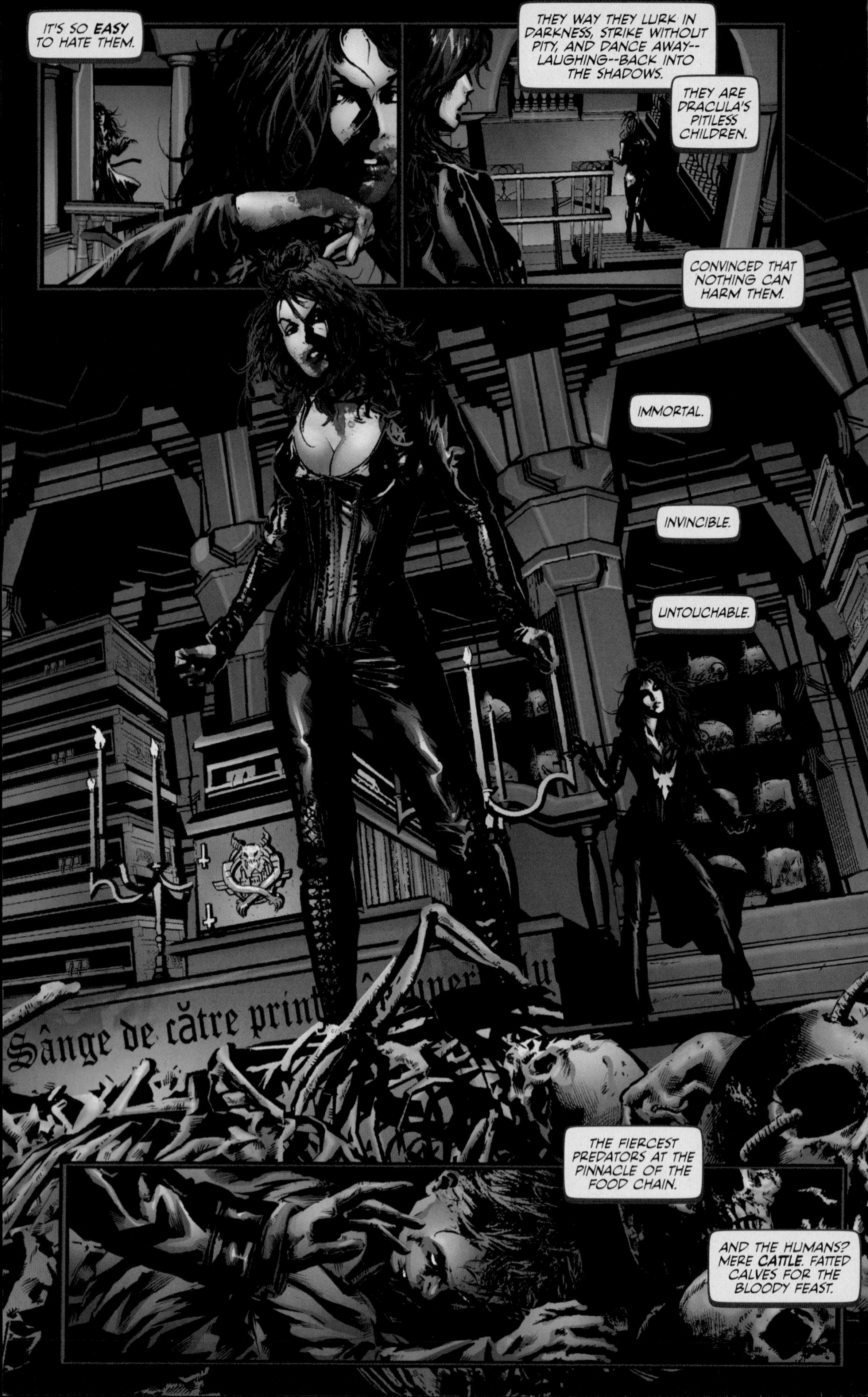
IT'S SO **EASY** TO HATE THEM.
THEY WAY THEY LURK IN DARKNESS, STRIKE WITHOUT PITY, AND DANCE AWAY--LAUGHING--BACK INTO THE SHADOWS.
THEY ARE DRACULA'S PITILESS CHILDREN.
CONVINCED THAT NOTHING CAN HARM THEM.
IMMORTAL.
INVINCIBLE.
UNTOUCHABLE.
Sânge de către
THE FIERCEST PREDATORS AT THE PINNACLE OF THE FOOD CHAIN.
AND THE HUMANS? MERE **CATTLE**. FATTED CALVES FOR THE BLOODY FEAST.

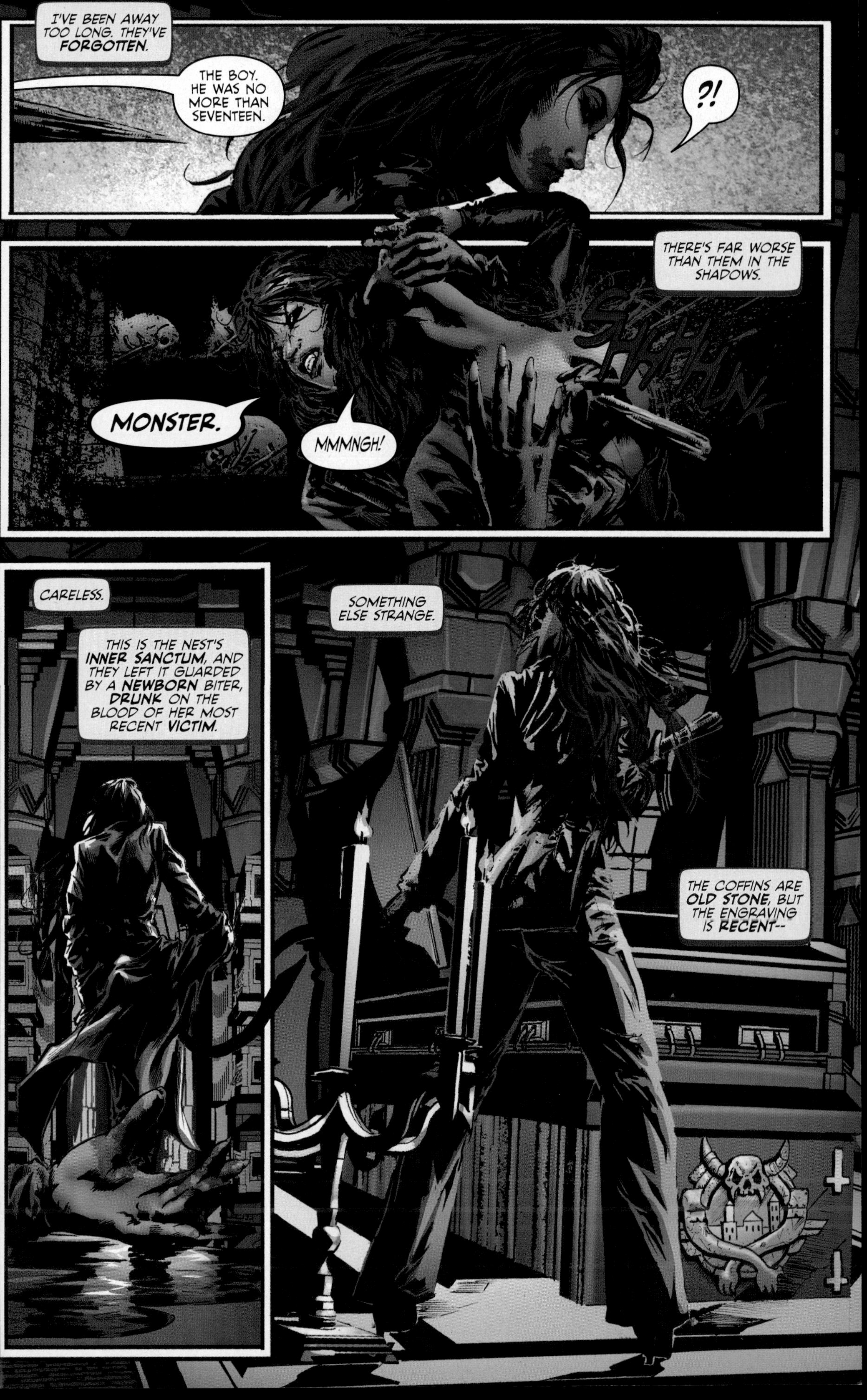

I'VE BEEN AWAY TOO LONG. THEY'VE FORGOTTEN.
THE BOY. HE WAS NO MORE THAN SEVENTEEN.
?!
THERE'S FAR WORSE THAN THEM IN THE SHADOWS.
MONSTER.
MMMNGH!
CARELESS.
THIS IS THE NEST'S INNER SANCTUM, AND THEY LEFT IT GUARDED BY A NEWBORN BITER, DRUNK ON THE BLOOD OF HER MOST RECENT VICTIM.
SOMETHING ELSE STRANGE.
THE COFFINS ARE OLD STONE, BUT THE ENGRAVING IS RECENT--

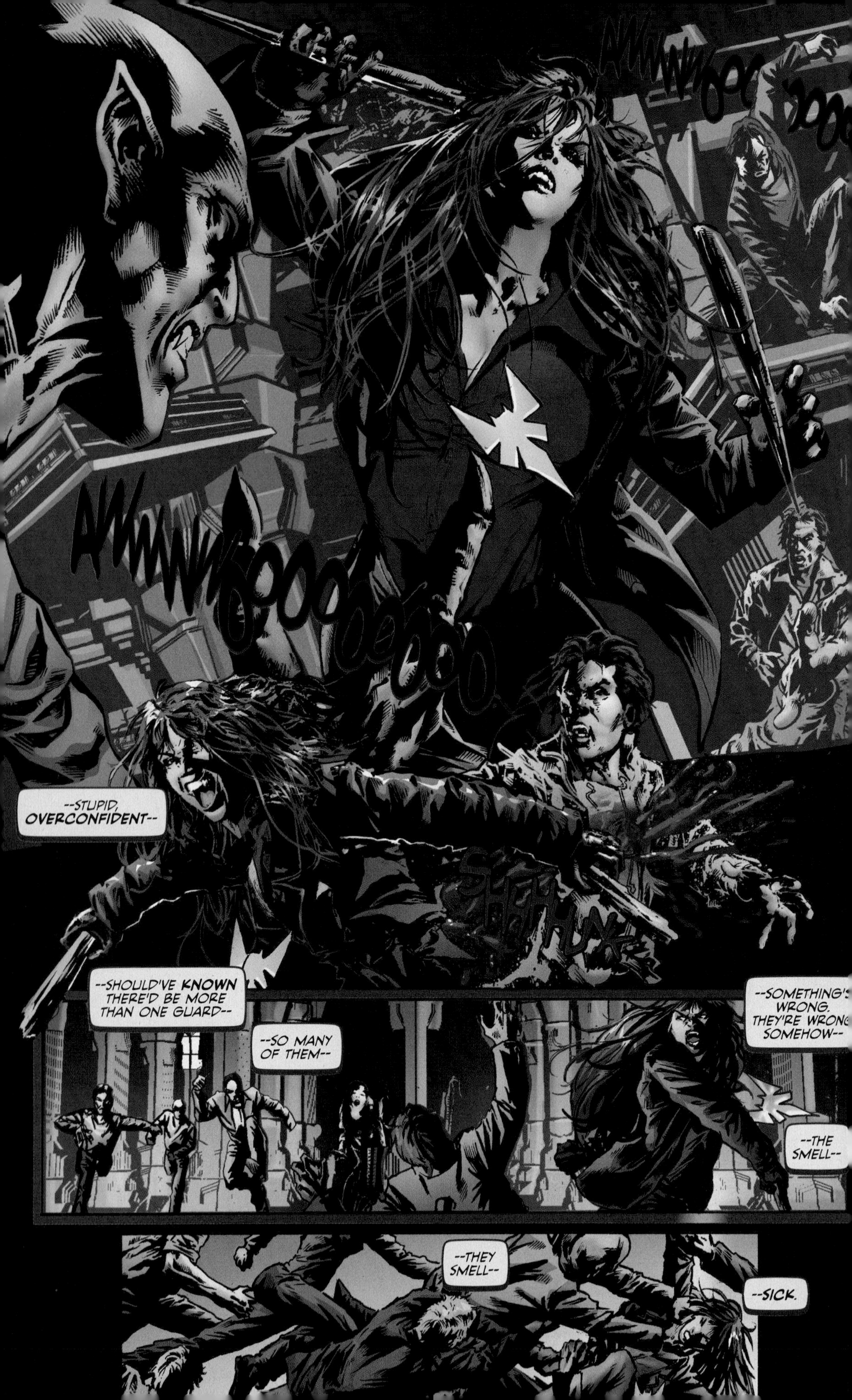

AWWWWOOO OOOO
AWWWWOOOOOOOOOOO
--STUPID, OVERCONFIDENT--
SHHHUNK
--SHOULD'VE KNOWN THERE'D BE MORE THAN ONE GUARD--
--SO MANY OF THEM--
--SOMETHING'S WRONG. THEY'RE WRONG SOMEHOW--
--THE SMELL--
--THEY SMELL--
--SICK.

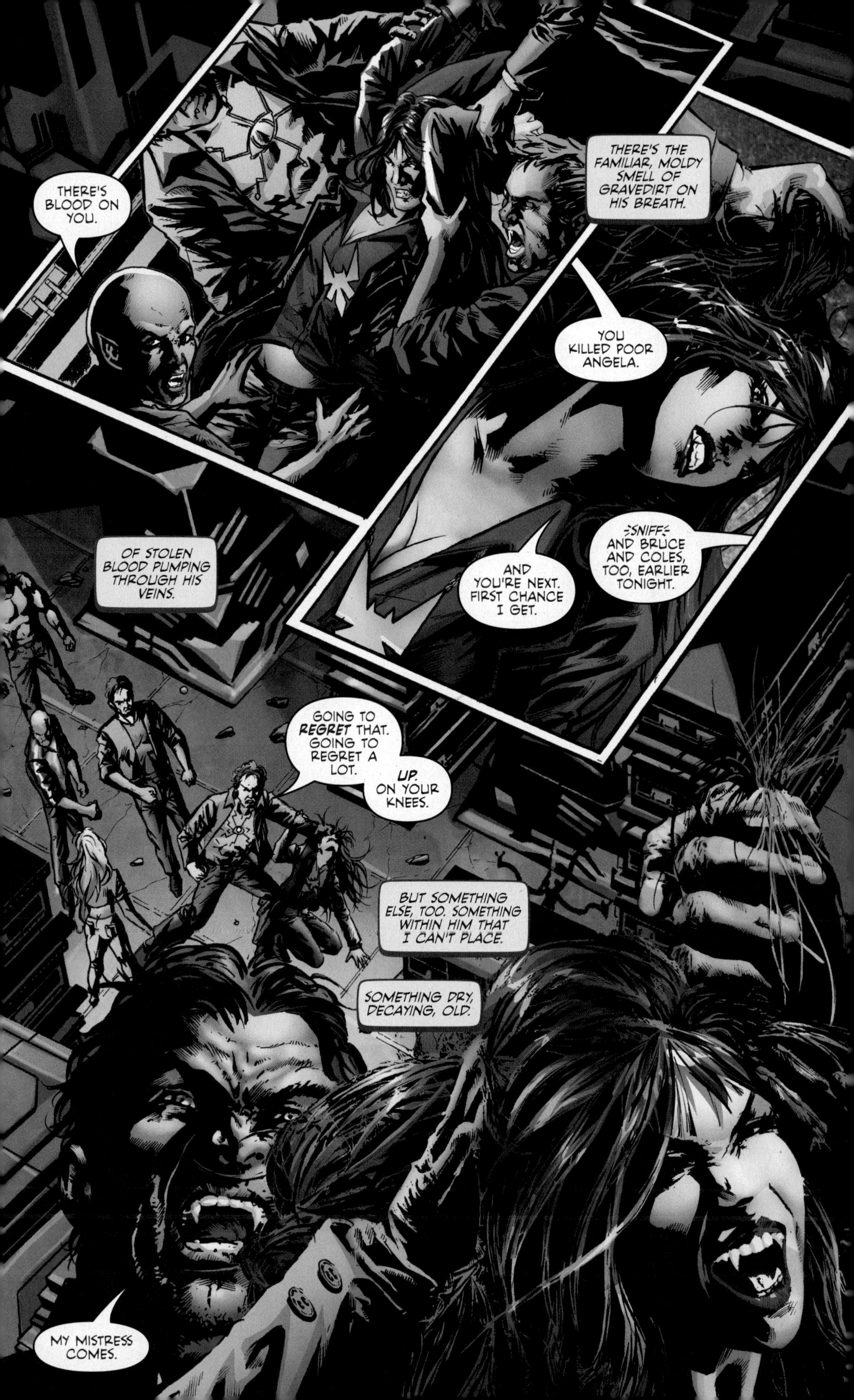
THERE'S BLOOD ON YOU.
THERE'S THE FAMILIAR, MOLDY SMELL OF GRAVEDIRT ON HIS BREATH.
YOU KILLED POOR ANGELA.
OF STOLEN BLOOD PUMPING THROUGH HIS VEINS.
AND YOU'RE NEXT. FIRST CHANCE I GET.
=SNIFF= AND BRUCE AND COLES, TOO, EARLIER TONIGHT.
GOING TO REGRET THAT. GOING TO REGRET A LOT.
UP. ON YOUR KNEES.
BUT SOMETHING ELSE, TOO. SOMETHING WITHIN HIM THAT I CAN'T PLACE.
SOMETHING DRY, DECAYING, OLD.
MY MISTRESS COMES.

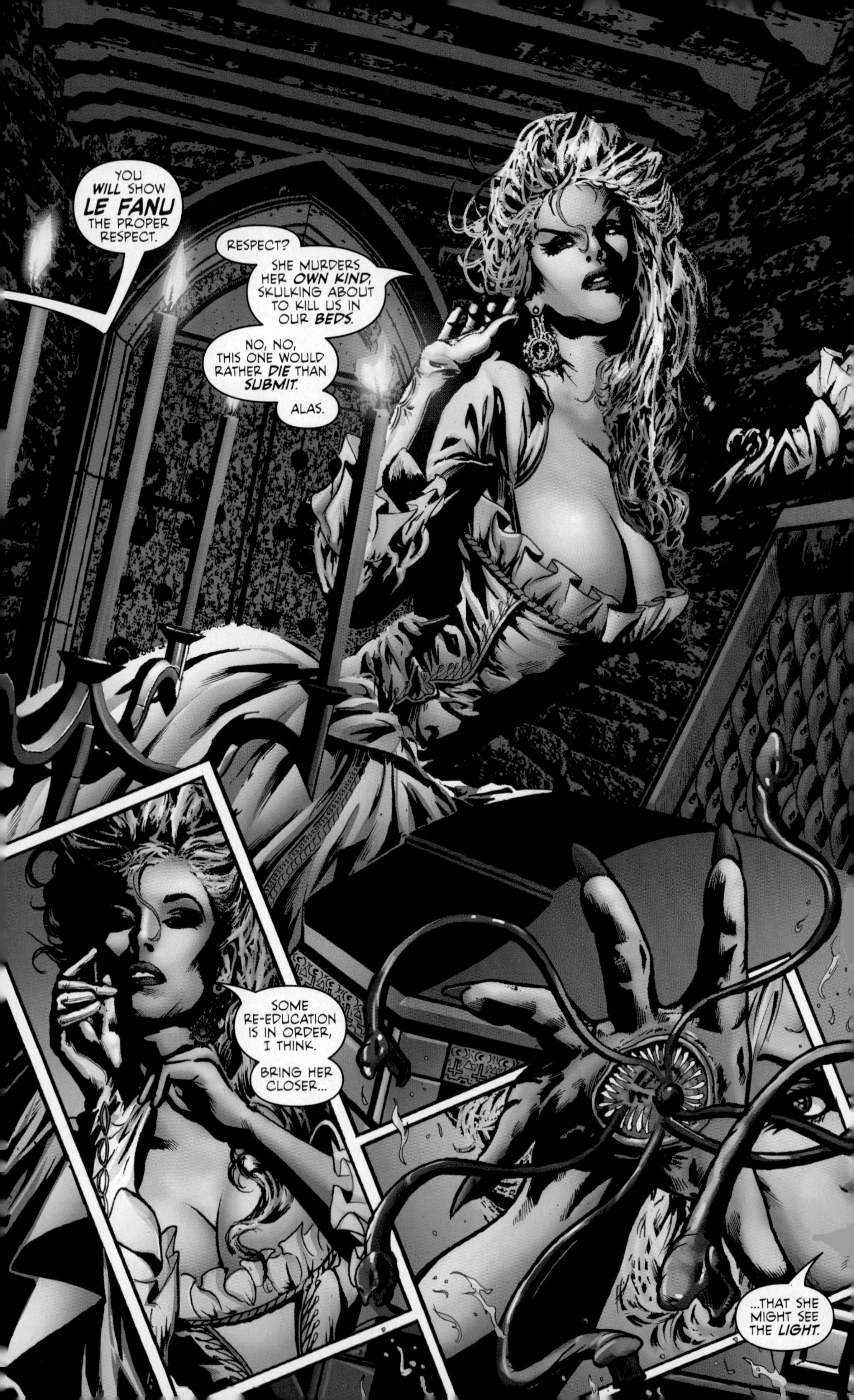
YOU WILL SHOW LE FANU THE PROPER RESPECT.
RESPECT?
SHE MURDERS HER OWN KIND, SKULKING ABOUT TO KILL US IN OUR BEDS.
NO, NO, THIS ONE WOULD RATHER DIE THAN SUBMIT.
ALAS.
SOME RE-EDUCATION IS IN ORDER, I THINK.
BRING HER CLOSER...
...THAT SHE MIGHT SEE THE LIGHT.

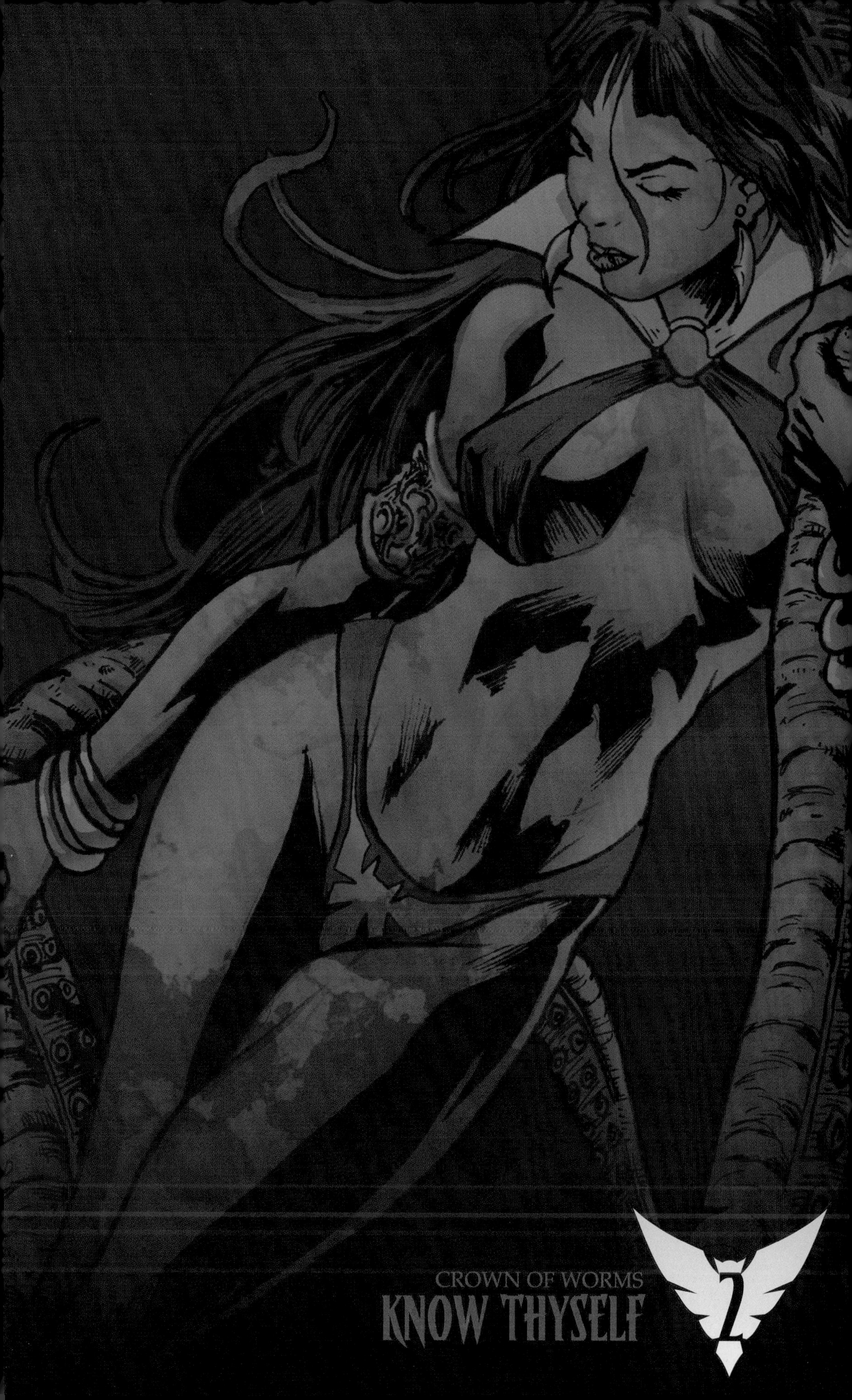
CROWN OF WORMS
KNOW THYSELF
7

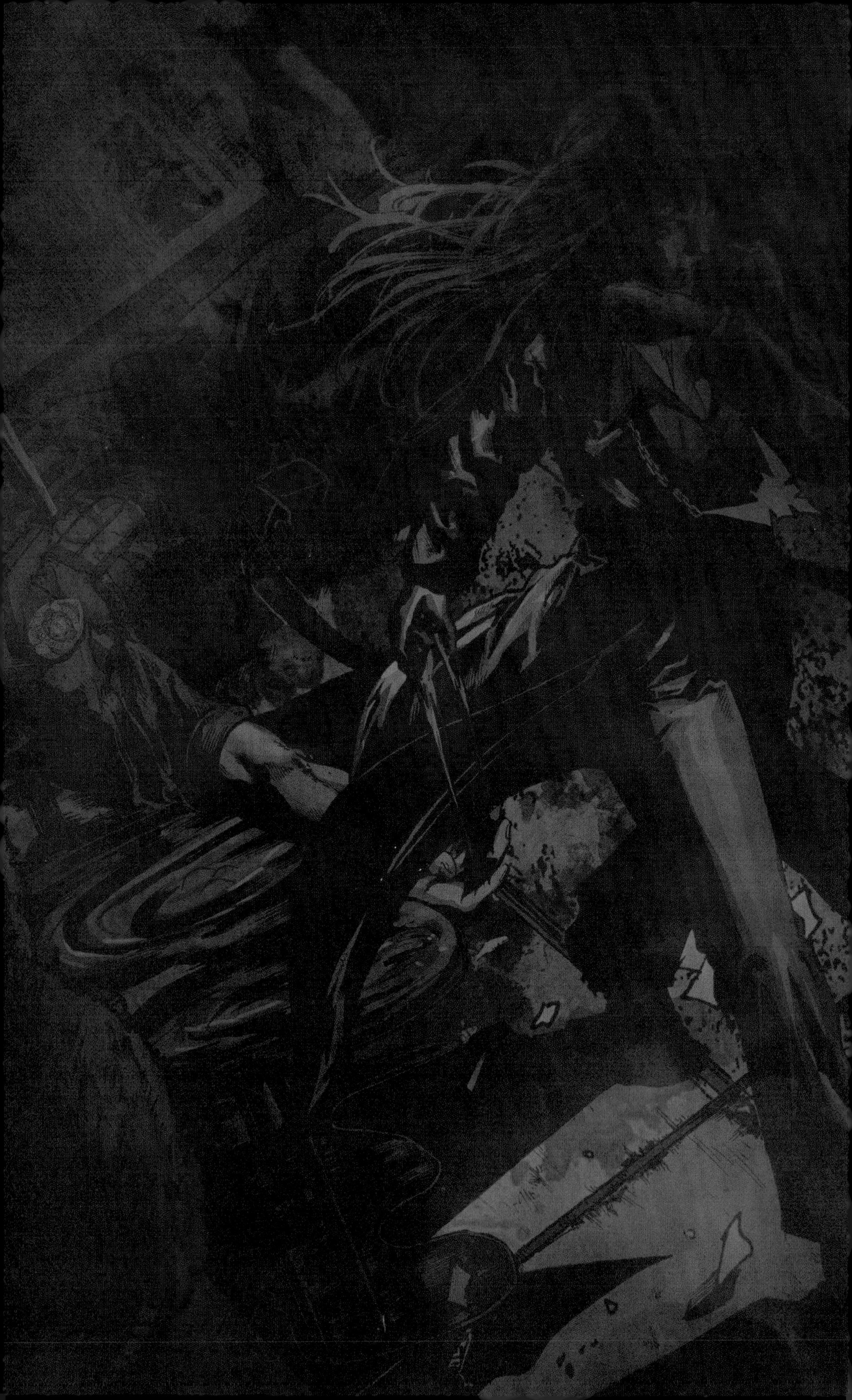

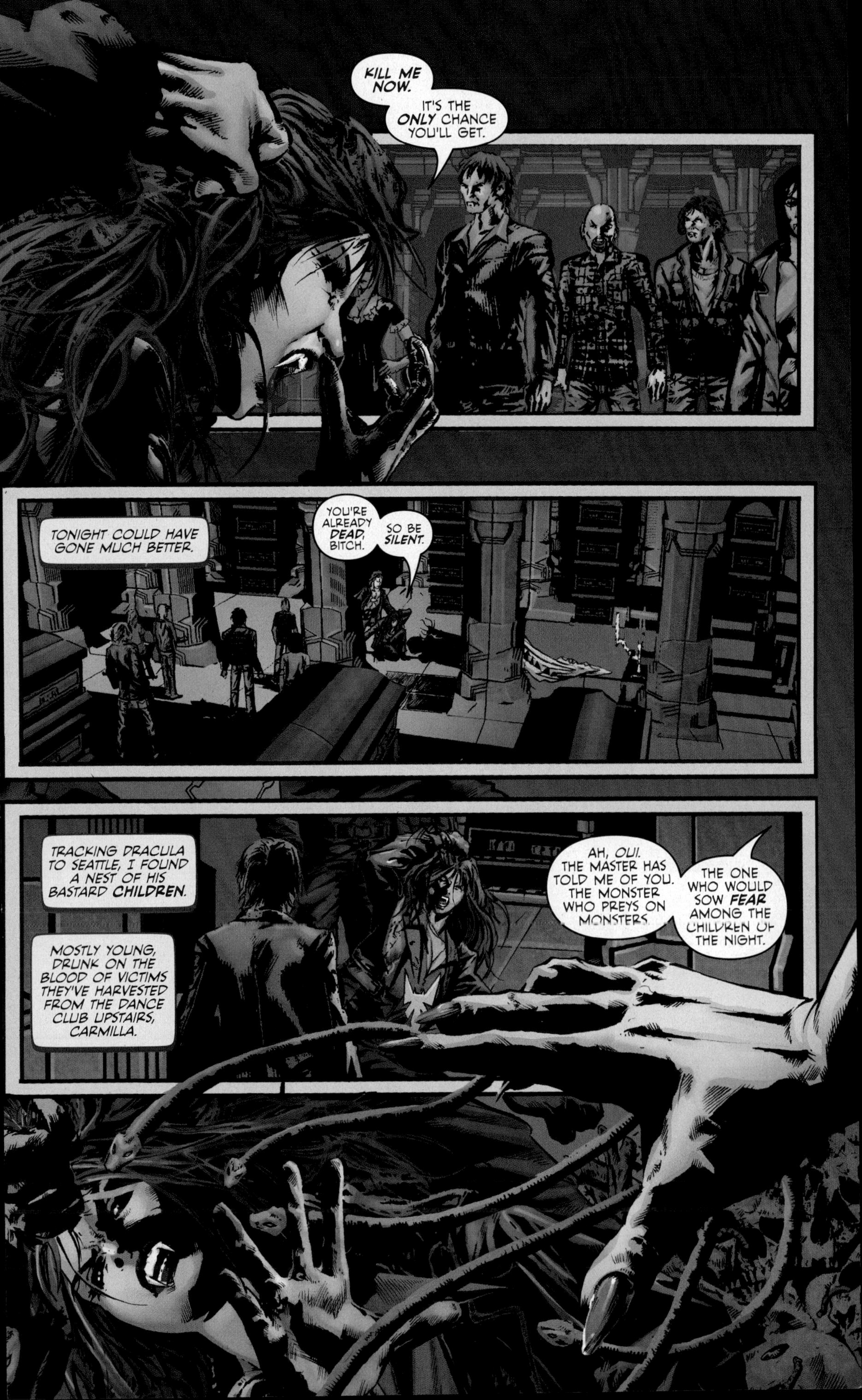
KILL ME NOW.
IT'S THE ONLY CHANCE YOU'LL GET.
TONIGHT COULD HAVE GONE MUCH BETTER.
YOU'RE ALREADY DEAD, BITCH.
SO BE SILENT.
TRACKING DRACULA TO SEATTLE, I FOUND A NEST OF HIS BASTARD CHILDREN.
MOSTLY YOUNG, DRUNK ON THE BLOOD OF VICTIMS THEY'VE HARVESTED FROM THE DANCE CLUB UPSTAIRS, CARMILLA.
AH, OUI. THE MASTER HAS TOLD ME OF YOU. THE MONSTER WHO PREYS ON MONSTERS.
THE ONE WHO WOULD SOW FEAR AMONG THE CHILDREN OF THE NIGHT.

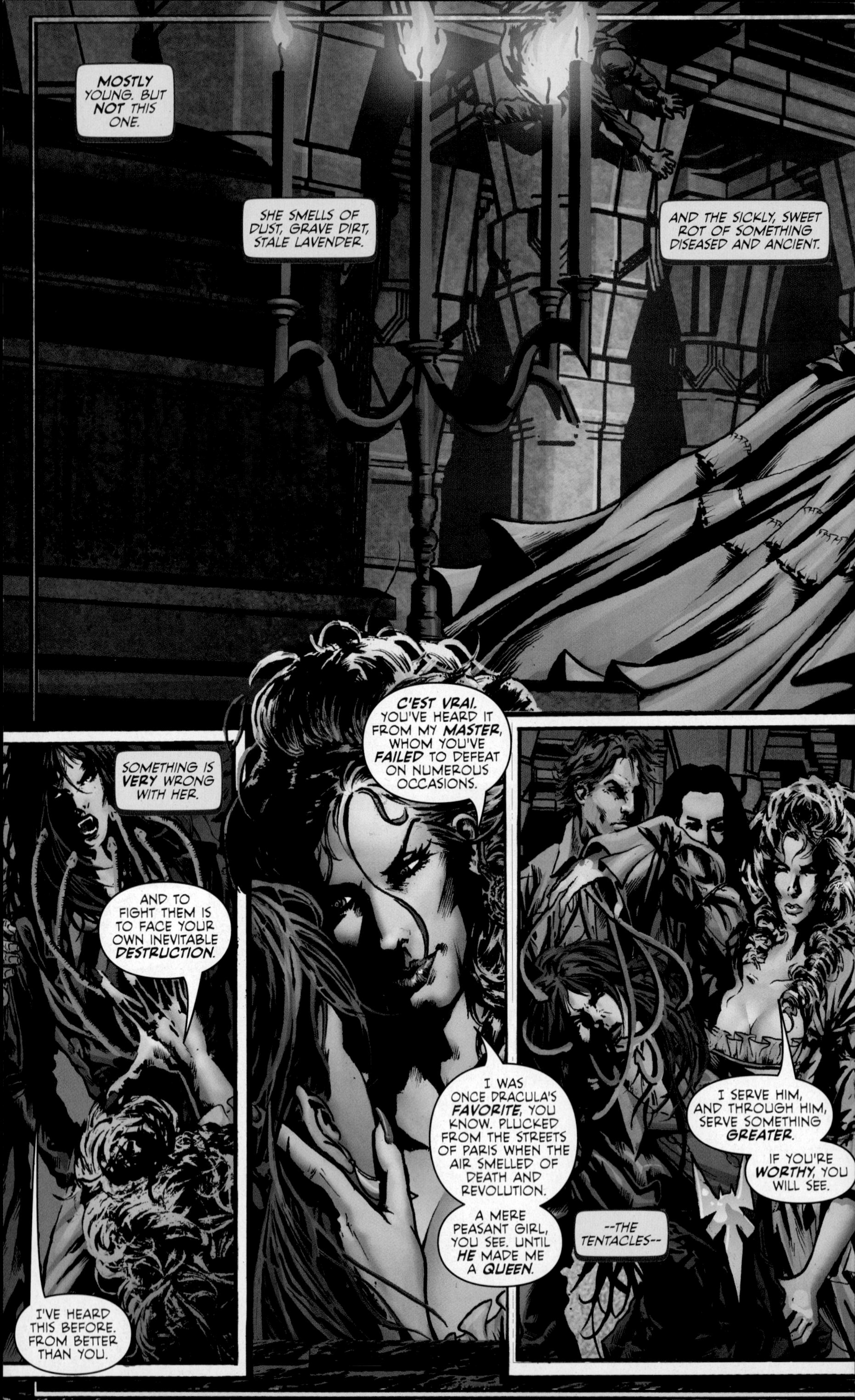
MOSTLY YOUNG. BUT NOT THIS ONE.
SHE SMELLS OF DUST, GRAVE DIRT, STALE LAVENDER.
AND THE SICKLY, SWEET ROT OF SOMETHING DISEASED AND ANCIENT.
SOMETHING IS VERY WRONG WITH HER.
AND TO FIGHT THEM IS TO FACE YOUR OWN INEVITABLE DESTRUCTION.
I'VE HEARD THIS BEFORE. FROM BETTER THAN YOU.
C'EST VRAI. YOU'VE HEARD IT FROM MY MASTER, WHOM YOU'VE FAILED TO DEFEAT ON NUMEROUS OCCASIONS.
I WAS ONCE DRACULA'S FAVORITE, YOU KNOW. PLUCKED FROM THE STREETS OF PARIS WHEN THE AIR SMELLED OF DEATH AND REVOLUTION.
A MERE PEASANT GIRL, YOU SEE. UNTIL HE MADE ME A QUEEN.
--THE TENTACLES--
I SERVE HIM, AND THROUGH HIM, SERVE SOMETHING GREATER.
IF YOU'RE WORTHY, YOU WILL SEE.

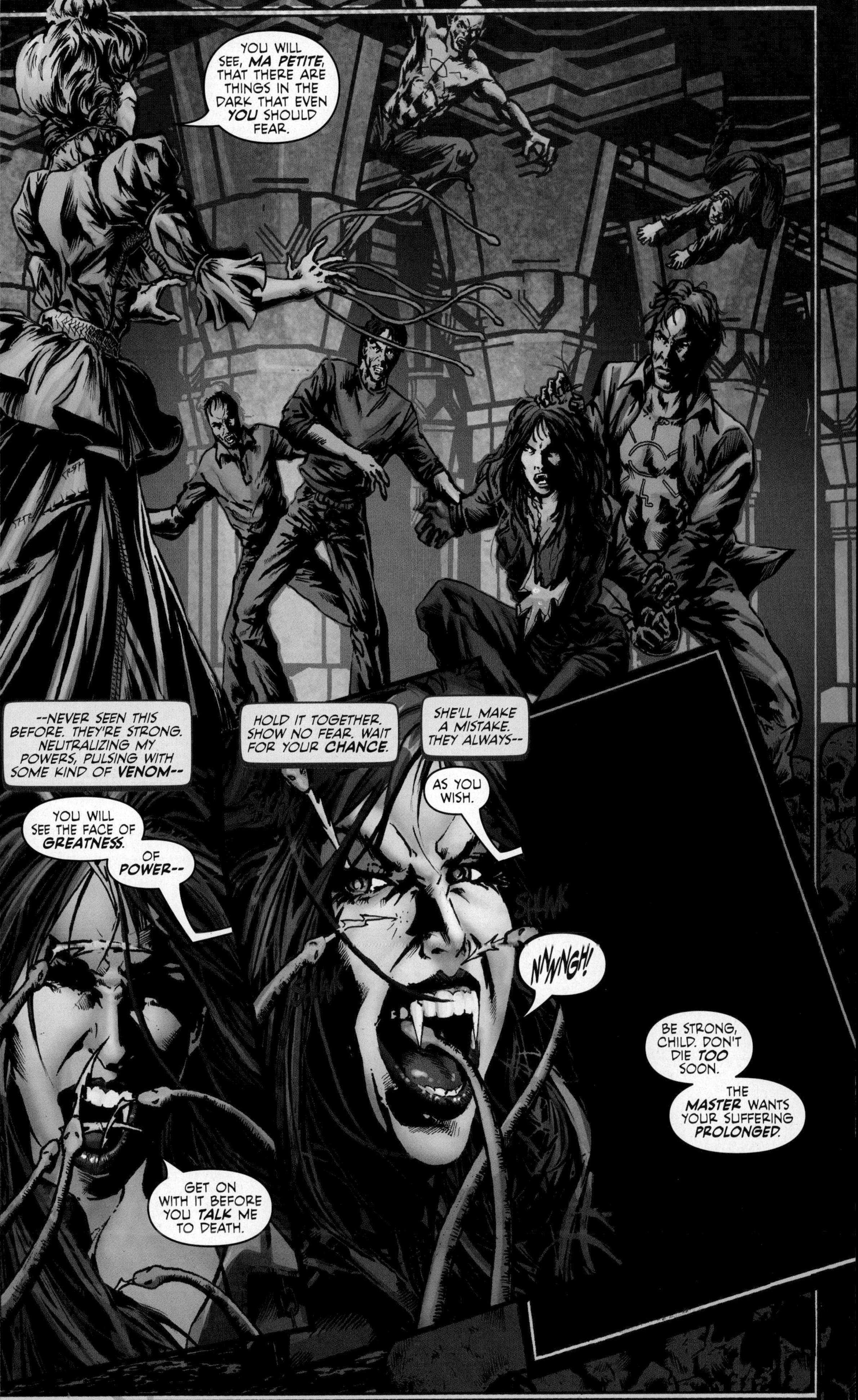
YOU WILL SEE, MA PETITE, THAT THERE ARE THINGS IN THE DARK THAT EVEN YOU SHOULD FEAR.
--NEVER SEEN THIS BEFORE. THEY'RE STRONG. NEUTRALIZING MY POWERS, PULSING WITH SOME KIND OF VENOM--
HOLD IT TOGETHER. SHOW NO FEAR. WAIT FOR YOUR CHANCE.
SHE'LL MAKE A MISTAKE. THEY ALWAYS--
YOU WILL SEE THE FACE OF GREATNESS.
OF POWER--
AS YOU WISH.
NNNNGH!
GET ON WITH IT BEFORE YOU TALK ME TO DEATH.
BE STRONG, CHILD. DON'T DIE TOO SOON.
THE MASTER WANTS YOUR SUFFERING PROLONGED.

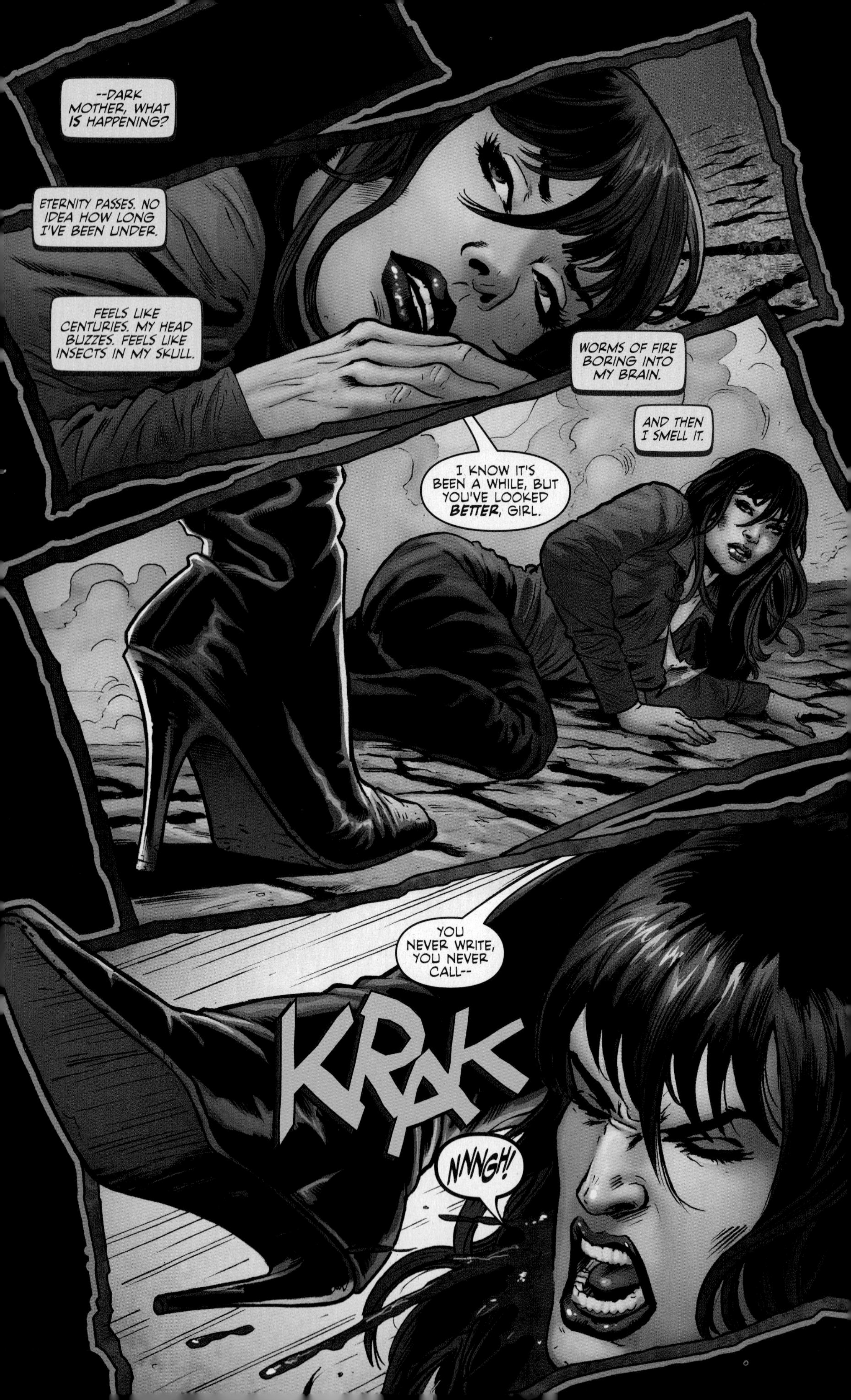
--DARK MOTHER, WHAT IS HAPPENING?
ETERNITY PASSES. NO IDEA HOW LONG I'VE BEEN UNDER.
FEELS LIKE CENTURIES. MY HEAD BUZZES. FEELS LIKE INSECTS IN MY SKULL.
WORMS OF FIRE BORING INTO MY BRAIN.
AND THEN I SMELL IT.
I KNOW IT'S BEEN A WHILE, BUT YOU'VE LOOKED BETTER, GIRL.
YOU NEVER WRITE, YOU NEVER CALL--
KRAK
NNNGH!

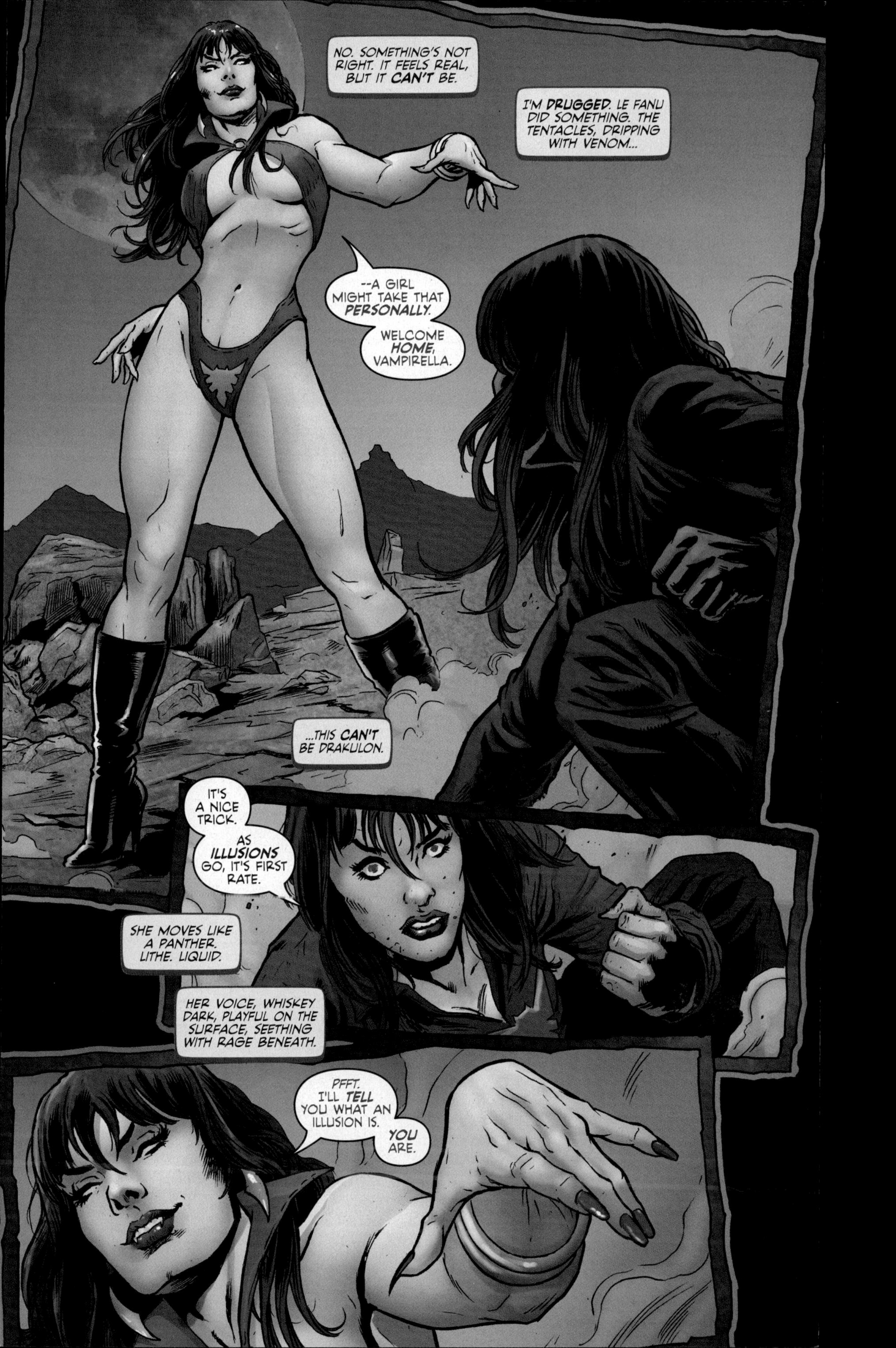
NO. SOMETHING'S NOT RIGHT. IT FEELS REAL, BUT IT CAN'T BE.
I'M DRUGGED. LE FANU DID SOMETHING. THE TENTACLES, DRIPPING WITH VENOM...
--A GIRL MIGHT TAKE THAT PERSONALLY.
WELCOME HOME, VAMPIRELLA.
...THIS CAN'T BE DRAKULON.
IT'S A NICE TRICK.
AS ILLUSIONS GO, IT'S FIRST RATE.
SHE MOVES LIKE A PANTHER. LITHE. LIQUID.
HER VOICE, WHISKEY DARK, PLAYFUL ON THE SURFACE, SEETHING WITH RAGE BENEATH.
PFFT. I'LL TELL YOU WHAT AN ILLUSION IS.
YOU ARE.

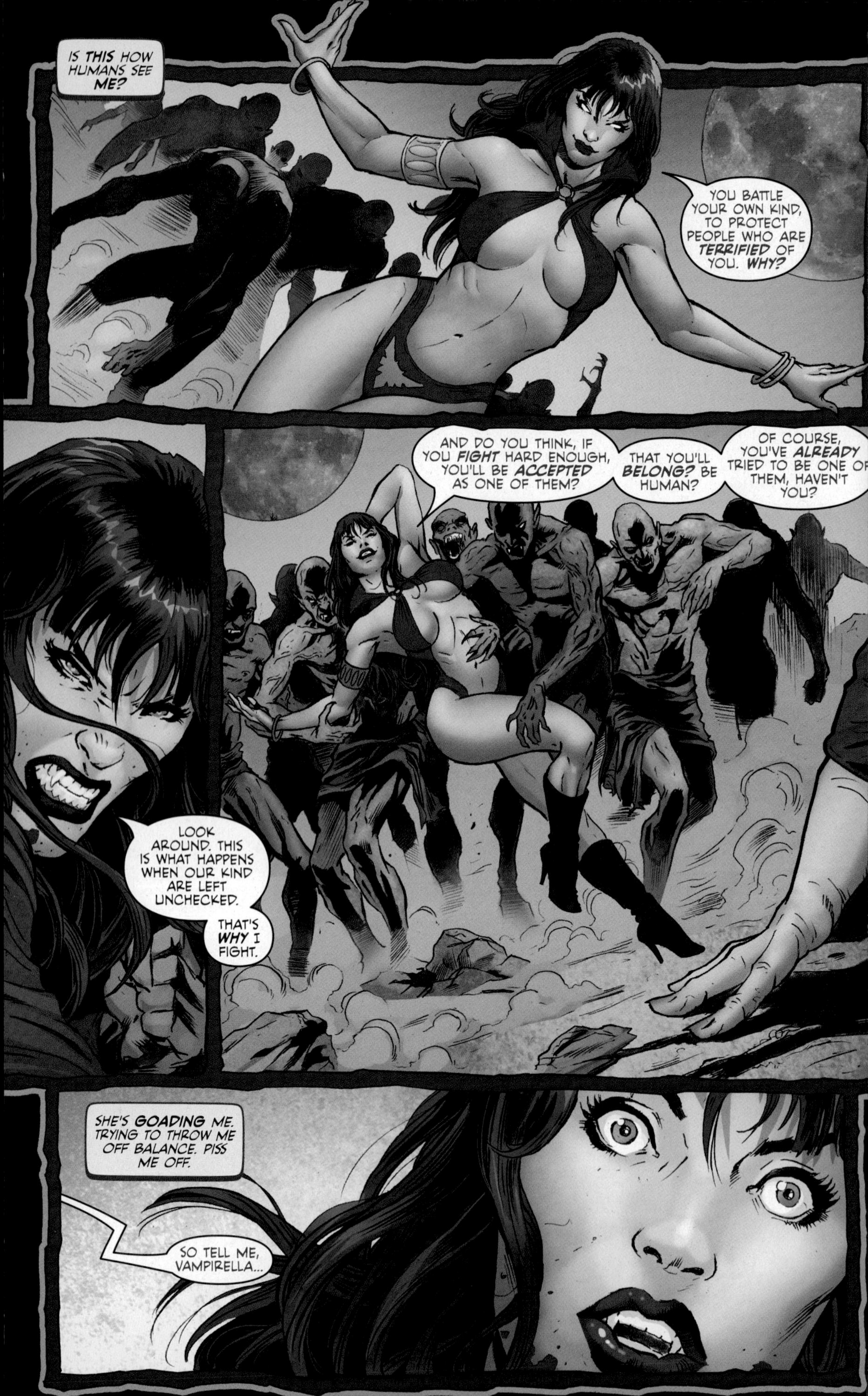

IS THIS HOW HUMANS SEE ME?
YOU BATTLE YOUR OWN KIND, TO PROTECT PEOPLE WHO ARE TERRIFIED OF YOU. WHY?
AND DO YOU THINK, IF YOU FIGHT HARD ENOUGH, YOU'LL BE ACCEPTED AS ONE OF THEM?
THAT YOU'LL BELONG? BE HUMAN?
OF COURSE, YOU'VE ALREADY TRIED TO BE ONE OF THEM, HAVEN'T YOU?
LOOK AROUND. THIS IS WHAT HAPPENS WHEN OUR KIND ARE LEFT UNCHECKED.
THAT'S WHY I FIGHT.
SHE'S GOADING ME. TRYING TO THROW ME OFF BALANCE. PISS ME OFF.
SO TELL ME, VAMPIRELLA...

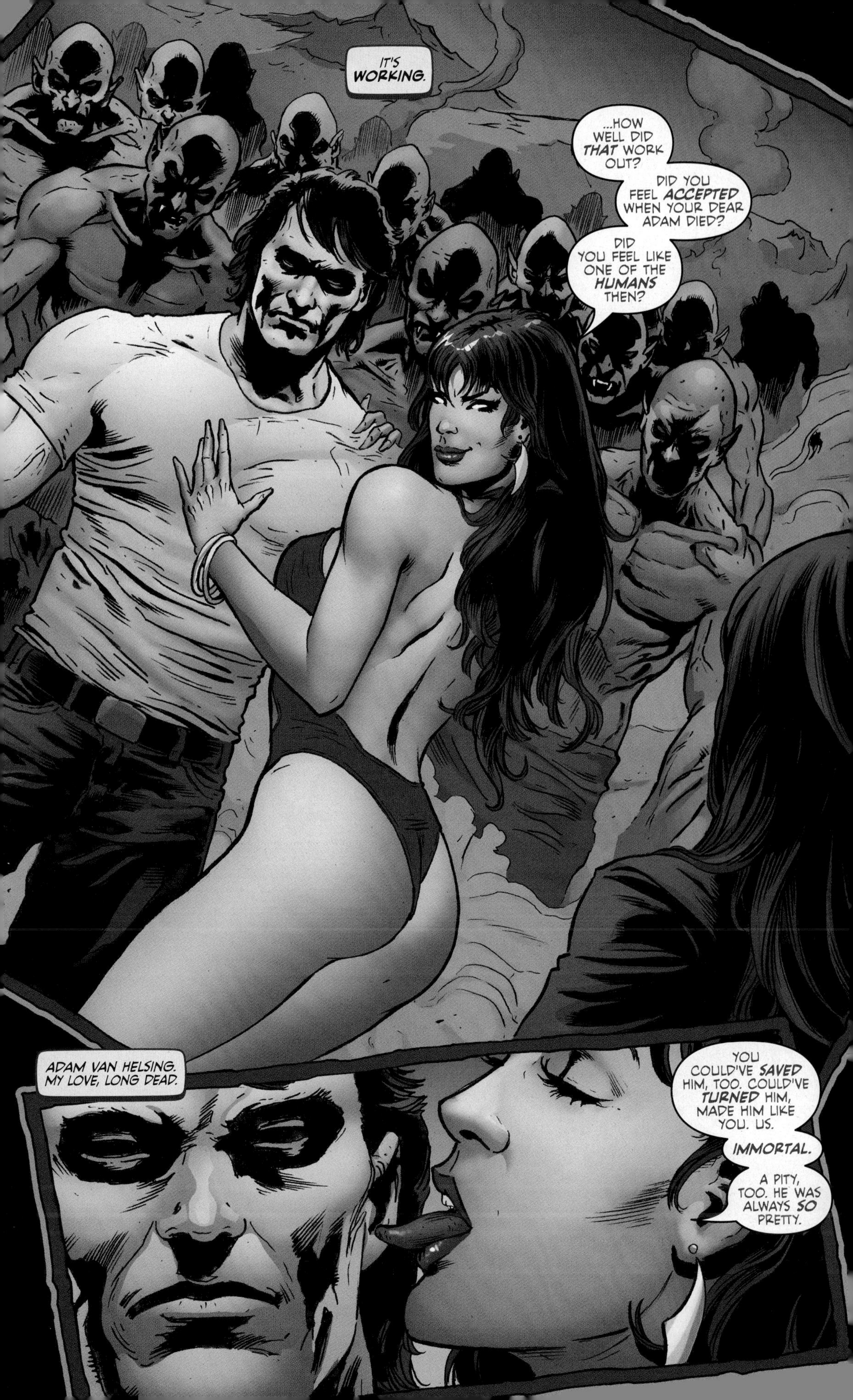
IT'S WORKING.
...HOW WELL DID THAT WORK OUT?
DID YOU FEEL ACCEPTED WHEN YOUR DEAR ADAM DIED?
DID YOU FEEL LIKE ONE OF THE HUMANS THEN?
ADAM VAN HELSING. MY LOVE, LONG DEAD.
YOU COULD'VE SAVED HIM, TOO. COULD'VE TURNED HIM, MADE HIM LIKE YOU. US.
IMMORTAL.
A PITY, TOO. HE WAS ALWAYS SO PRETTY.

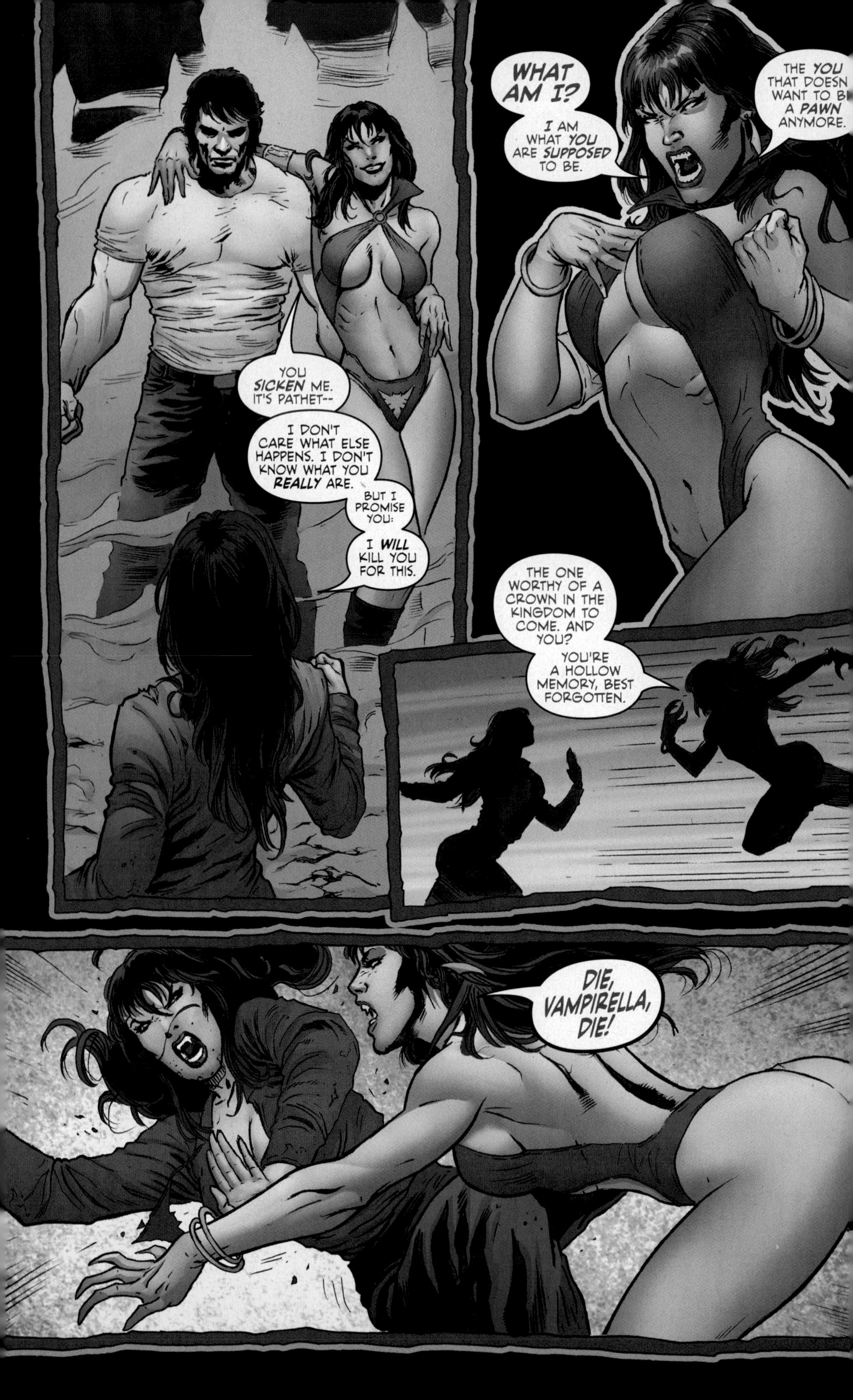
YOU SICKEN ME. IT'S PATHET--
I DON'T CARE WHAT ELSE HAPPENS. I DON'T KNOW WHAT YOU REALLY ARE.
BUT I PROMISE YOU:
I WILL KILL YOU FOR THIS.
WHAT AM I?
I AM WHAT YOU ARE SUPPOSED TO BE.
THE YOU THAT DOESN WANT TO B A PAWN ANYMORE.
THE ONE WORTHY OF A CROWN IN THE KINGDOM TO COME. AND YOU?
YOU'RE A HOLLOW MEMORY, BEST FORGOTTEN.
DIE, VAMPIRELLA, DIE!

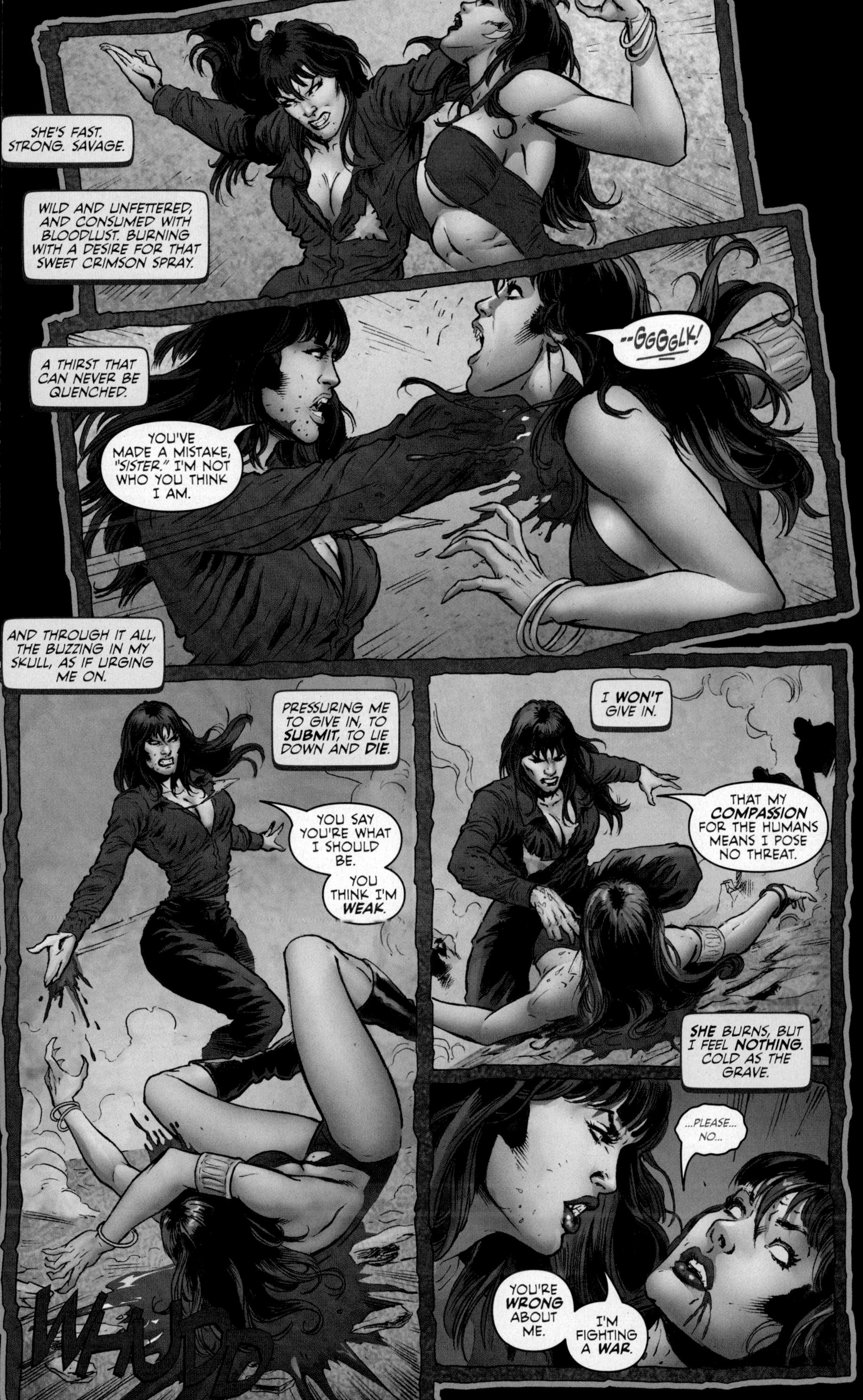
SHE'S FAST. STRONG. SAVAGE.
WILD AND UNFETTERED, AND CONSUMED WITH BLOODLUST. BURNING WITH A DESIRE FOR THAT SWEET CRIMSON SPRAY.
A THIRST THAT CAN NEVER BE QUENCHED.
--GGGGLK!
YOU'VE MADE A MISTAKE, "SISTER." I'M NOT WHO YOU THINK I AM.
AND THROUGH IT ALL, THE BUZZING IN MY SKULL, AS IF URGING ME ON.
PRESSURING ME TO GIVE IN, TO SUBMIT, TO LIE DOWN AND DIE.
YOU SAY YOU'RE WHAT I SHOULD BE.
YOU THINK I'M WEAK.
I WON'T GIVE IN.
THAT MY COMPASSION FOR THE HUMANS MEANS I POSE NO THREAT.
SHE BURNS, BUT I FEEL NOTHING. COLD AS THE GRAVE.
...PLEASE... NO...
YOU'RE WRONG ABOUT ME.
I'M FIGHTING A WAR.

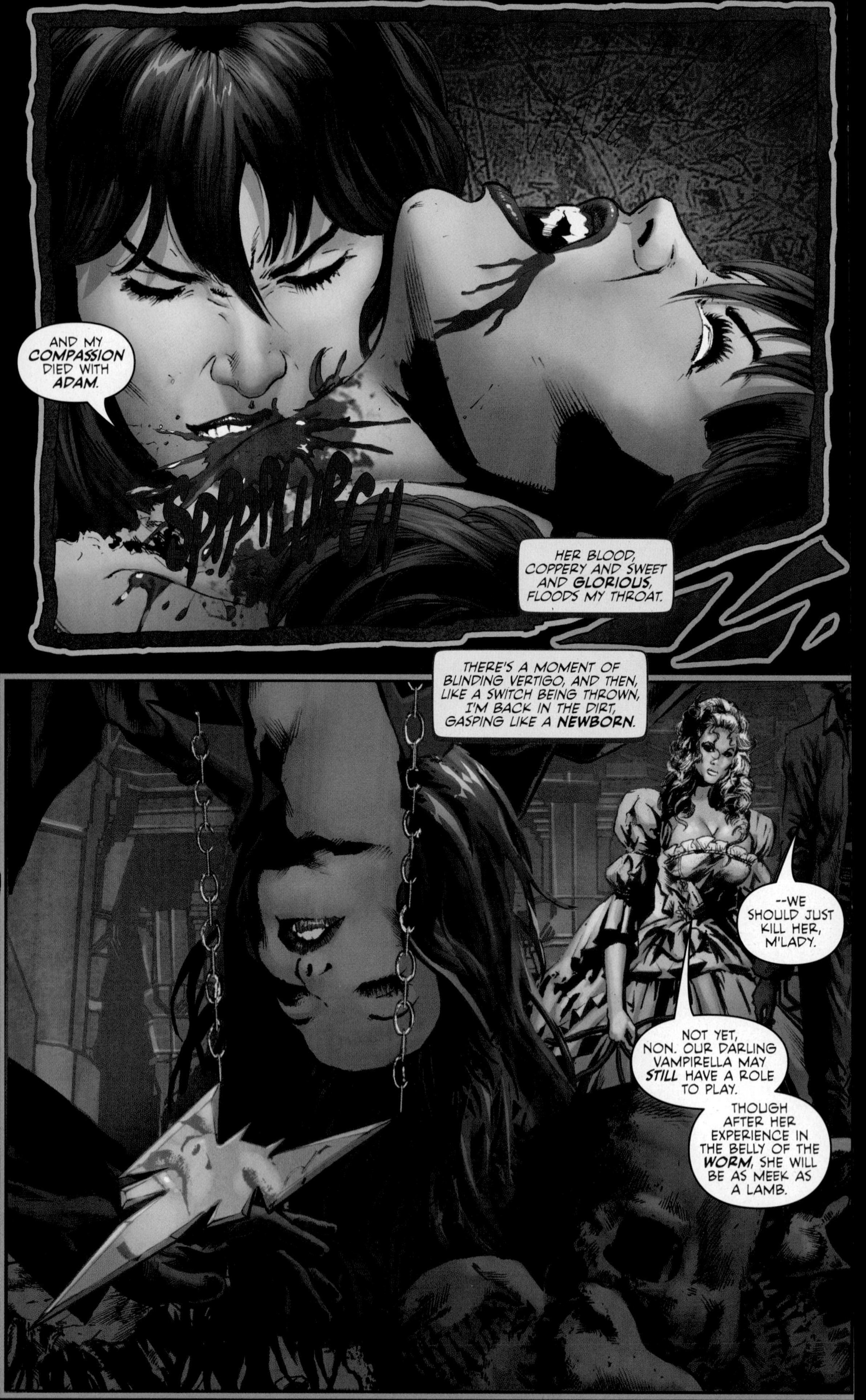
AND MY COMPASSION DIED WITH ADAM.
SPPPLURCH
HER BLOOD, COPPERY AND SWEET AND GLORIOUS, FLOODS MY THROAT.
THERE'S A MOMENT OF BLINDING VERTIGO, AND THEN, LIKE A SWITCH BEING THROWN, I'M BACK IN THE DIRT, GASPING LIKE A NEWBORN.
--WE SHOULD JUST KILL HER, M'LADY.
NOT YET, NON. OUR DARLING VAMPIRELLA MAY STILL HAVE A ROLE TO PLAY.
THOUGH AFTER HER EXPERIENCE IN THE BELLY OF THE WORM, SHE WILL BE AS MEEK AS A LAMB.

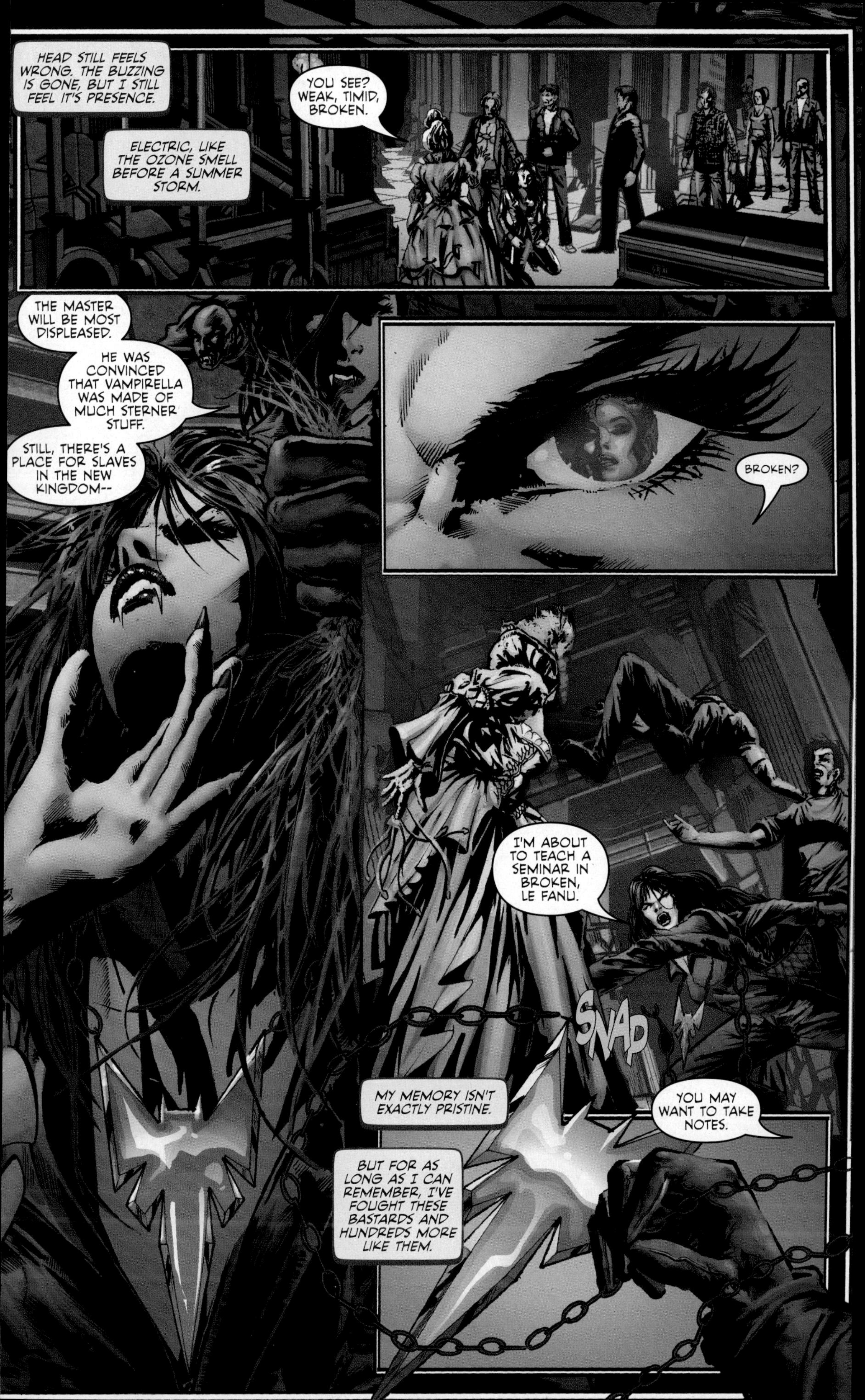
HEAD STILL FEELS WRONG. THE BUZZING IS GONE, BUT I STILL FEEL IT'S PRESENCE.
ELECTRIC, LIKE THE OZONE SMELL BEFORE A SUMMER STORM.
YOU SEE? WEAK, TIMID, BROKEN.
THE MASTER WILL BE MOST DISPLEASED.
HE WAS CONVINCED THAT VAMPIRELLA WAS MADE OF MUCH STERNER STUFF.
STILL, THERE'S A PLACE FOR SLAVES IN THE NEW KINGDOM--
BROKEN?
I'M ABOUT TO TEACH A SEMINAR IN BROKEN, LE FANU.
SNAP
MY MEMORY ISN'T EXACTLY PRISTINE.
BUT FOR AS LONG AS I CAN REMEMBER, I'VE FOUGHT THESE BASTARDS AND HUNDREDS MORE LIKE THEM.
YOU MAY WANT TO TAKE NOTES.

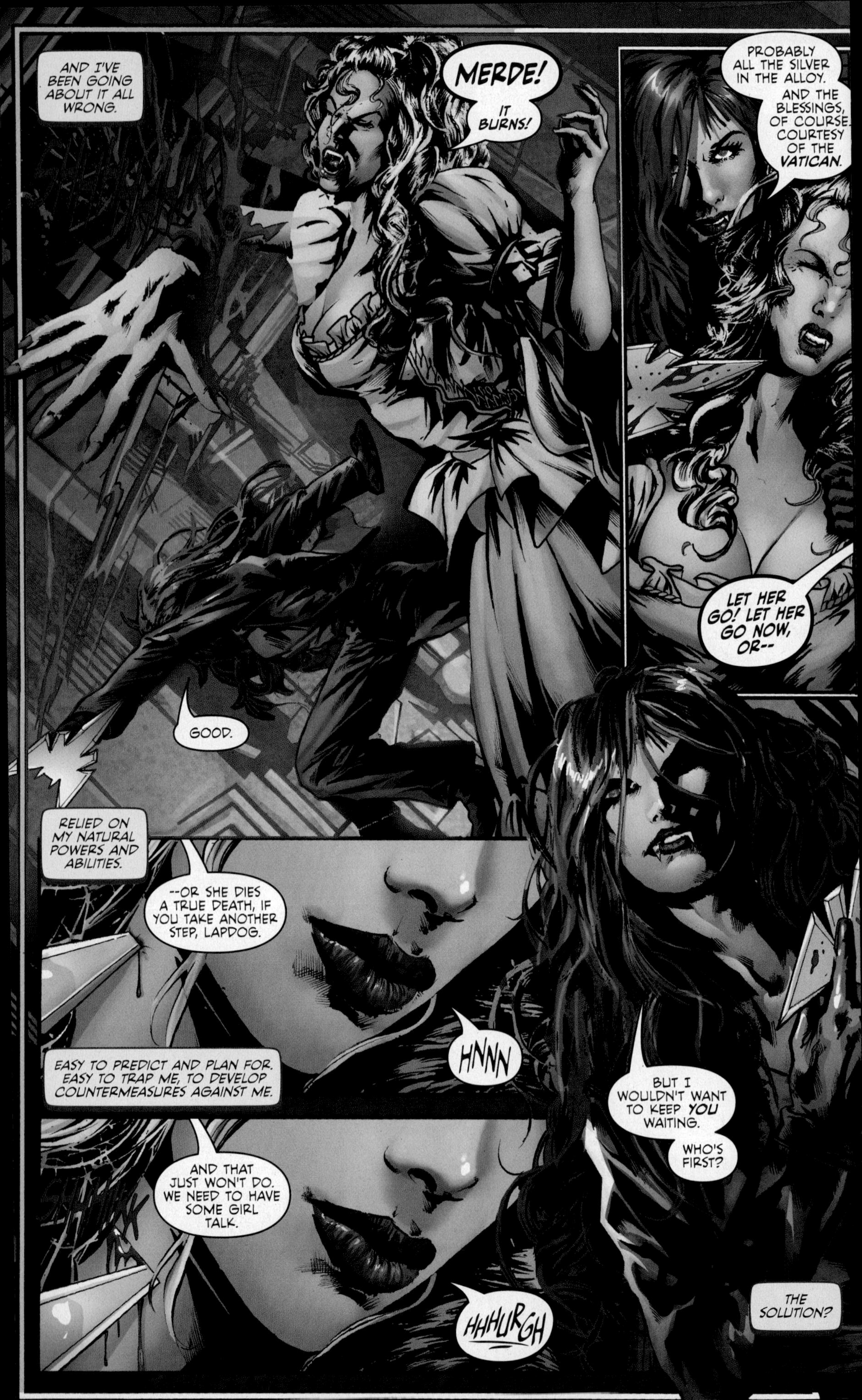
AND I'VE BEEN GOING ABOUT IT ALL WRONG.
MERDE!
IT BURNS!
PROBABLY ALL THE SILVER IN THE ALLOY.
AND THE BLESSINGS, OF COURSE. COURTESY OF THE VATICAN.
LET HER GO! LET HER GO NOW, OR--
GOOD.
RELIED ON MY NATURAL POWERS AND ABILITIES.
--OR SHE DIES A TRUE DEATH, IF YOU TAKE ANOTHER STEP, LAPDOG.
HNNN
EASY TO PREDICT AND PLAN FOR. EASY TO TRAP ME, TO DEVELOP COUNTERMEASURES AGAINST ME.
BUT I WOULDN'T WANT TO KEEP YOU WAITING.
WHO'S FIRST?
AND THAT JUST WON'T DO. WE NEED TO HAVE SOME GIRL TALK.
HHHURGH
THE SOLUTION?

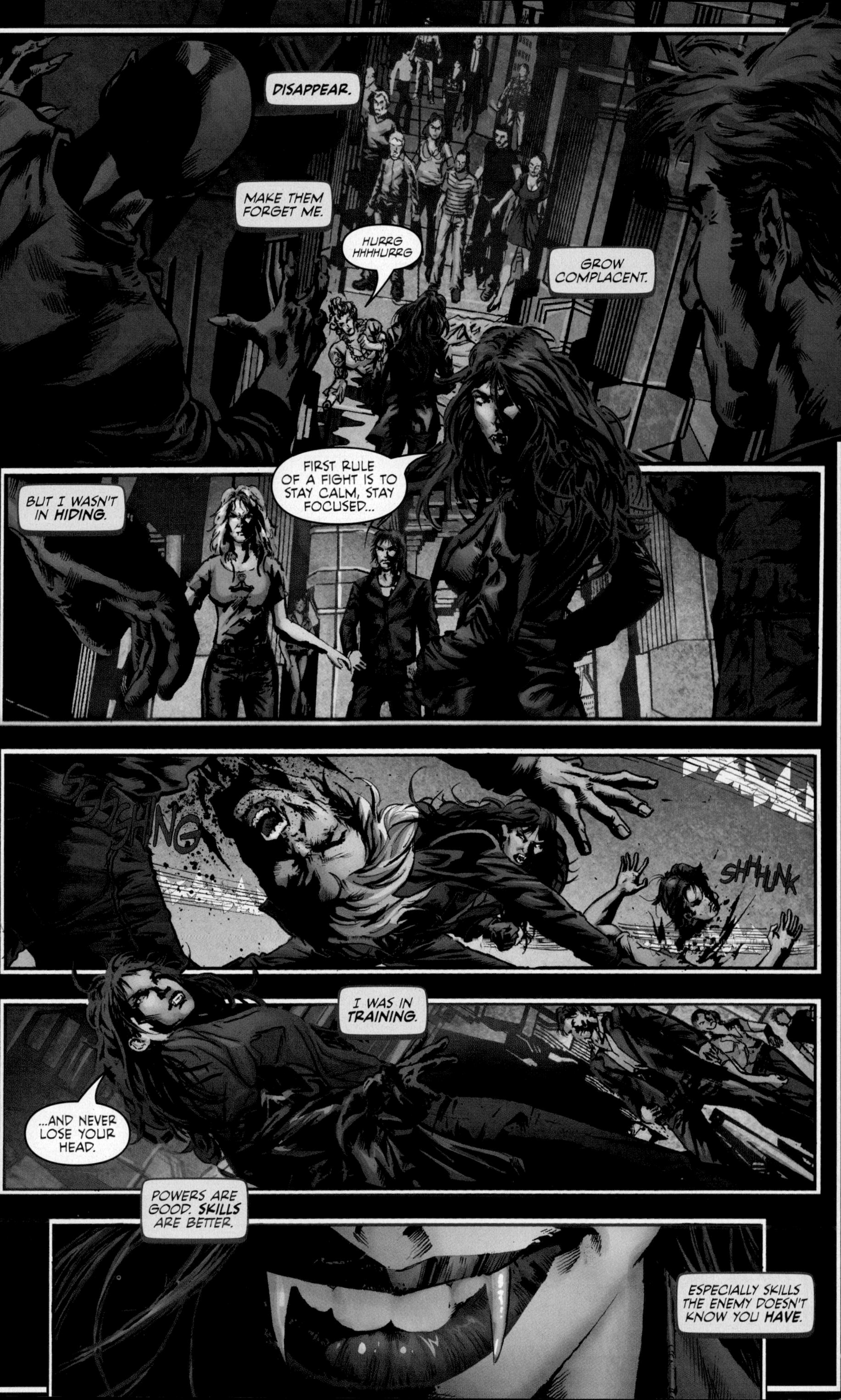

DISAPPEAR.
MAKE THEM FORGET ME.
HURRG HHHHURRG
GROW COMPLACENT.
BUT I WASN'T IN HIDING.
FIRST RULE OF A FIGHT IS TO STAY CALM, STAY FOCUSED...
SHHHUNK
I WAS IN TRAINING.
...AND NEVER LOSE YOUR HEAD.
POWERS ARE GOOD. SKILLS ARE BETTER.
ESPECIALLY SKILLS THE ENEMY DOESN'T KNOW YOU HAVE.

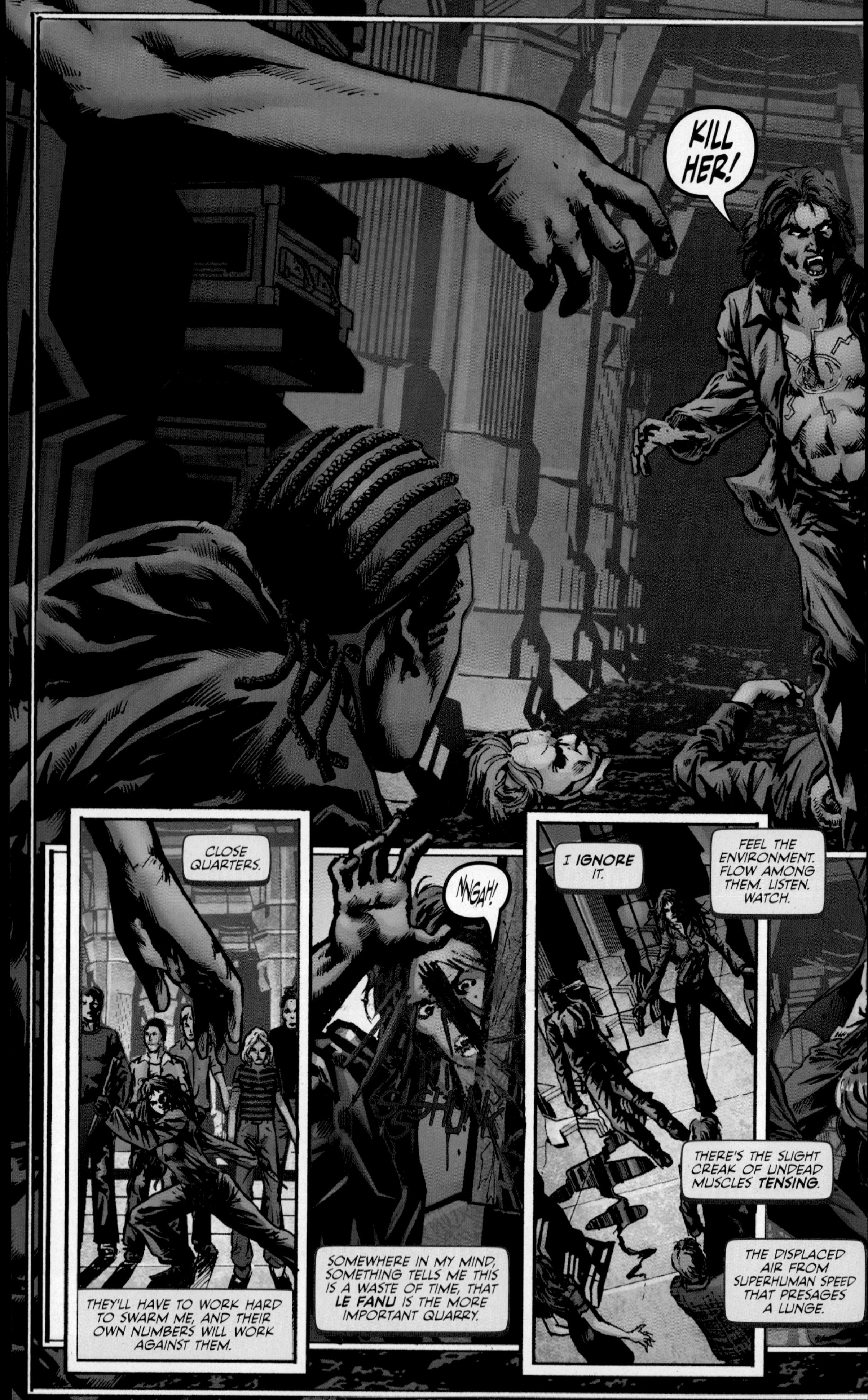
KILL HER!
CLOSE QUARTERS.
THEY'LL HAVE TO WORK HARD TO SWARM ME, AND THEIR OWN NUMBERS WILL WORK AGAINST THEM.
NNGAH!
SHUNK
SOMEWHERE IN MY MIND, SOMETHING TELLS ME THIS IS A WASTE OF TIME, THAT LE FANU IS THE MORE IMPORTANT QUARRY.
I IGNORE IT.
FEEL THE ENVIRONMENT. FLOW AMONG THEM. LISTEN. WATCH.
THERE'S THE SLIGHT CREAK OF UNDEAD MUSCLES TENSING.
THE DISPLACED AIR FROM SUPERHUMAN SPEED THAT PRESAGES A LUNGE.

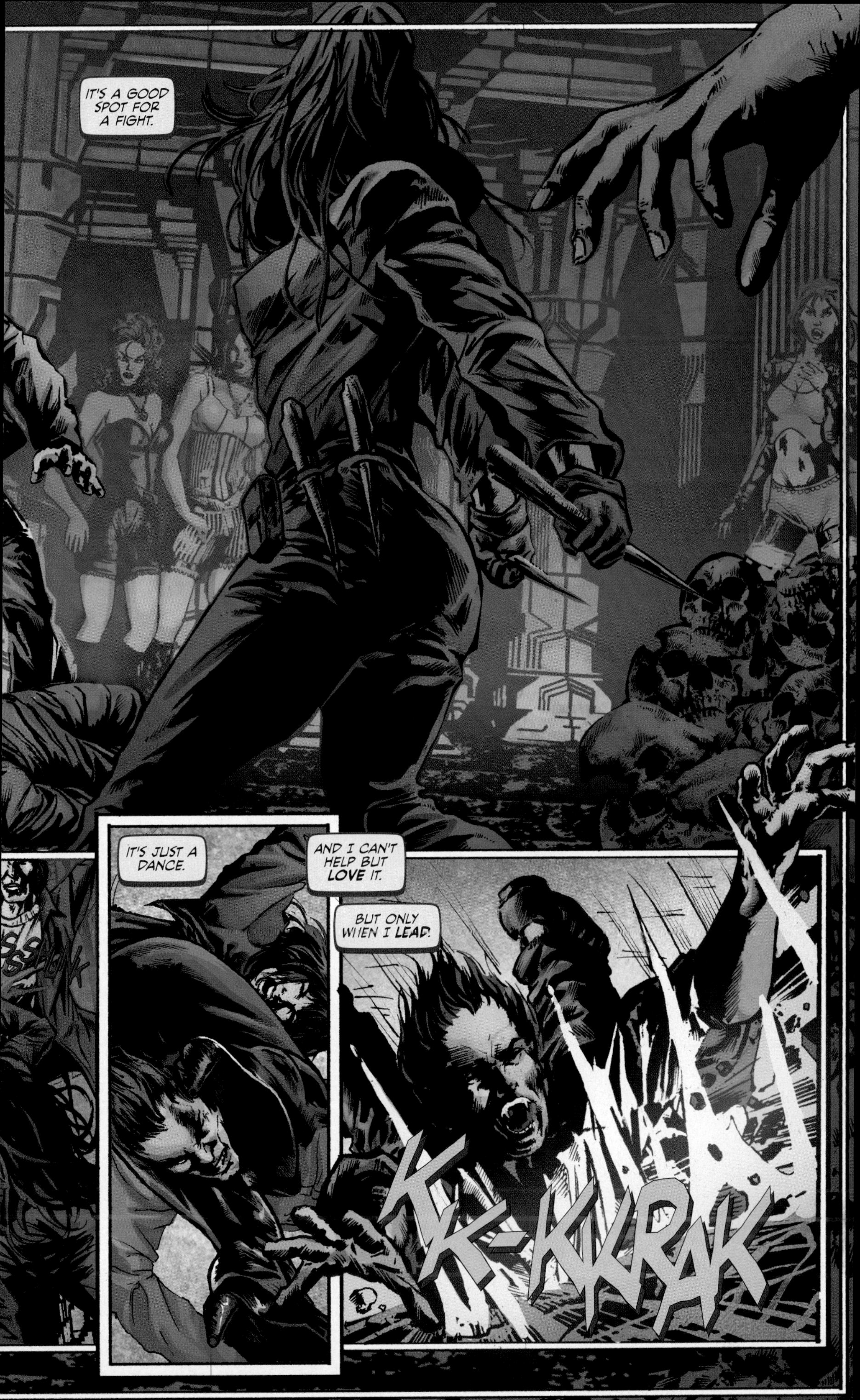
IT'S A GOOD SPOT FOR A FIGHT.
IT'S JUST A DANCE.
AND I CAN'T HELP BUT **LOVE** IT.
BUT ONLY WHEN I **LEAD**.
KK-KKRAK

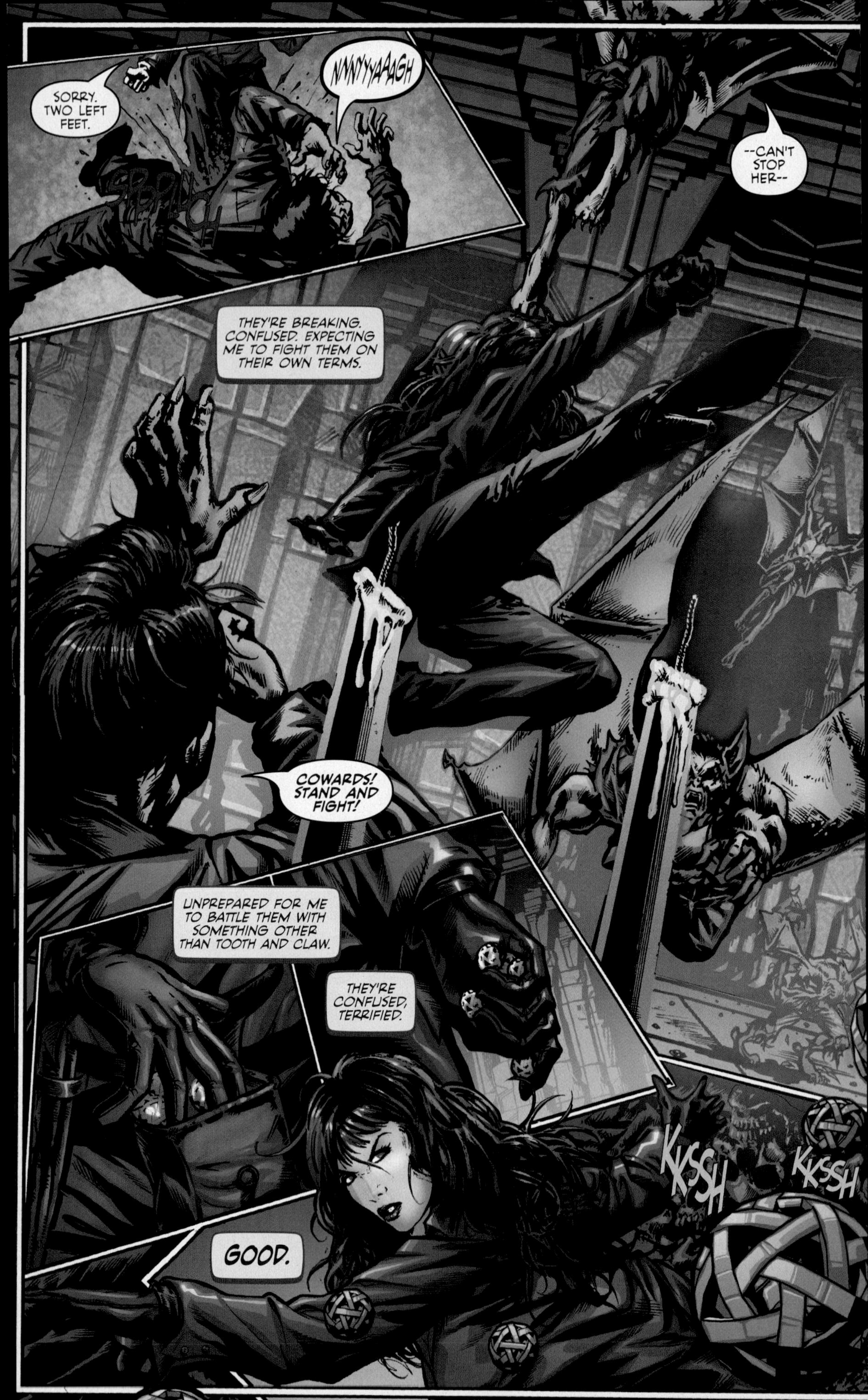
SORRY. TWO LEFT FEET.
NNNYYYAAAGH
SPPPLUCH
--CAN'T STOP HER--
THEY'RE BREAKING. CONFUSED. EXPECTING ME TO FIGHT THEM ON THEIR OWN TERMS.
COWARDS! STAND AND FIGHT!
UNPREPARED FOR ME TO BATTLE THEM WITH SOMETHING OTHER THAN TOOTH AND CLAW.
THEY'RE CONFUSED, TERRIFIED.
KKSSH
KKSSH
GOOD.

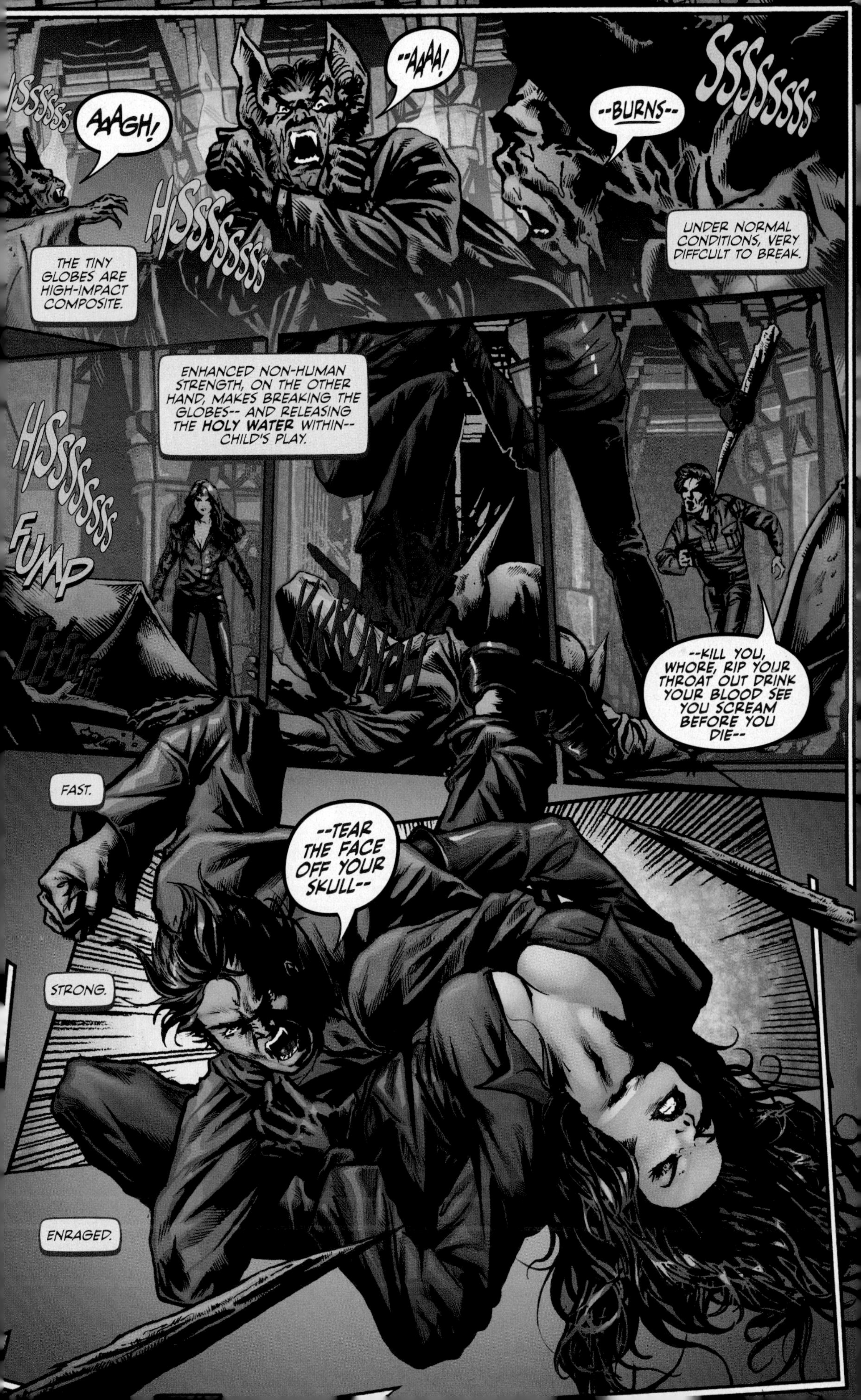
HISSSSSS
AAAGH!
--AAAA!
SSSSSSSS
--BURNS--
HISSSSSSSSS
THE TINY GLOBES ARE HIGH-IMPACT COMPOSITE.
UNDER NORMAL CONDITIONS, VERY DIFFCULT TO BREAK.
ENHANCED NON-HUMAN STRENGTH, ON THE OTHER HAND, MAKES BREAKING THE GLOBES-- AND RELEASING THE HOLY WATER WITHIN-- CHILD'S PLAY.
HISSSSSSSS
FUMP
KKRUNCH
--KILL YOU, WHORE, RIP YOUR THROAT OUT DRINK YOUR BLOOD SEE YOU SCREAM BEFORE YOU DIE--
FAST.
--TEAR THE FACE OFF YOUR SKULL--
STRONG.
ENRAGED.

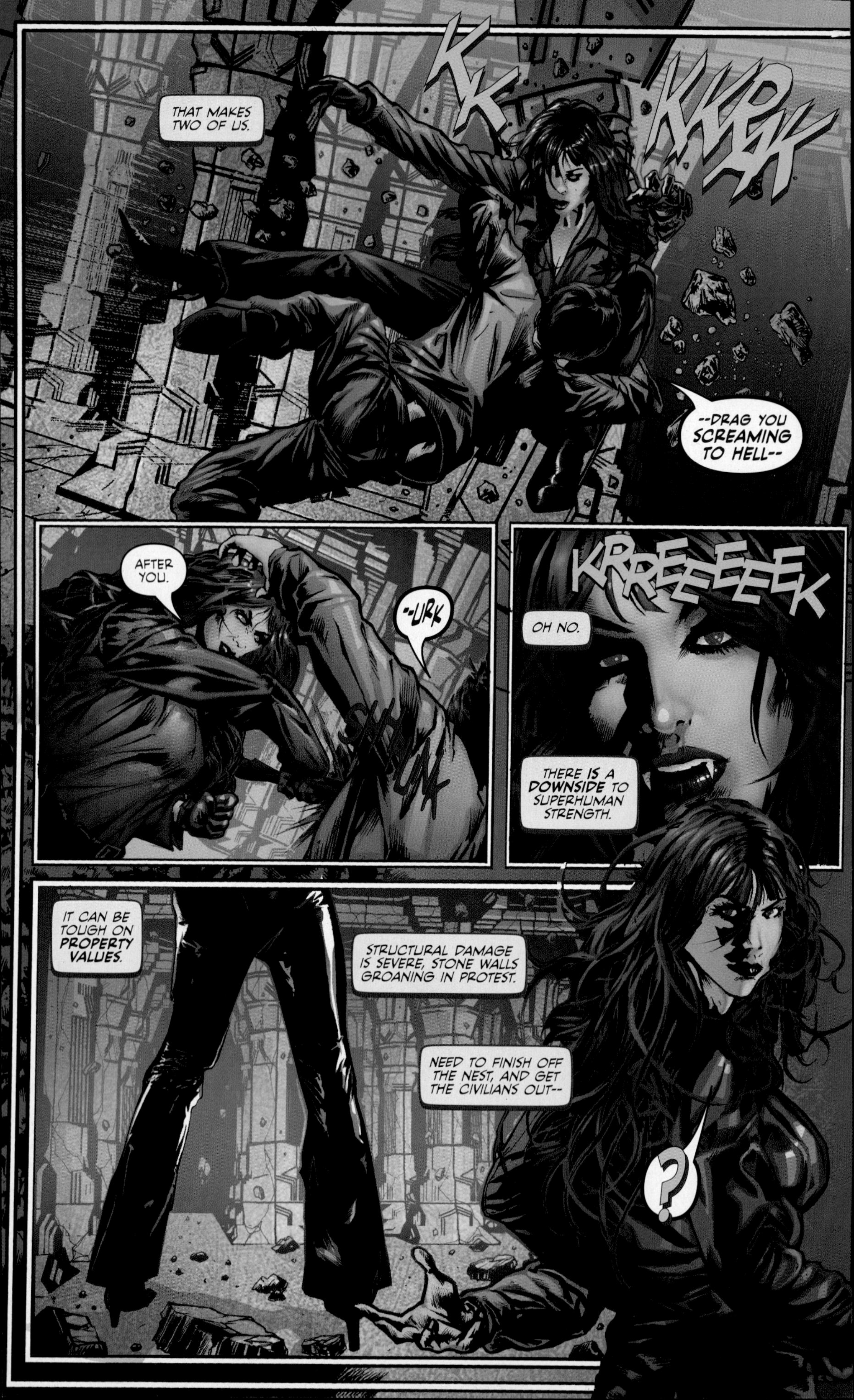

KK
KKRK
THAT MAKES TWO OF US.
--DRAG YOU SCREAMING TO HELL--
AFTER YOU.
--URK
SHHUNK
KRREEEEEK
OH NO.
THERE IS A DOWNSIDE TO SUPERHUMAN STRENGTH.
IT CAN BE TOUGH ON PROPERTY VALUES.
STRUCTURAL DAMAGE IS SEVERE, STONE WALLS GROANING IN PROTEST.
NEED TO FINISH OFF THE NEST, AND GET THE CIVILIANS OUT--
?

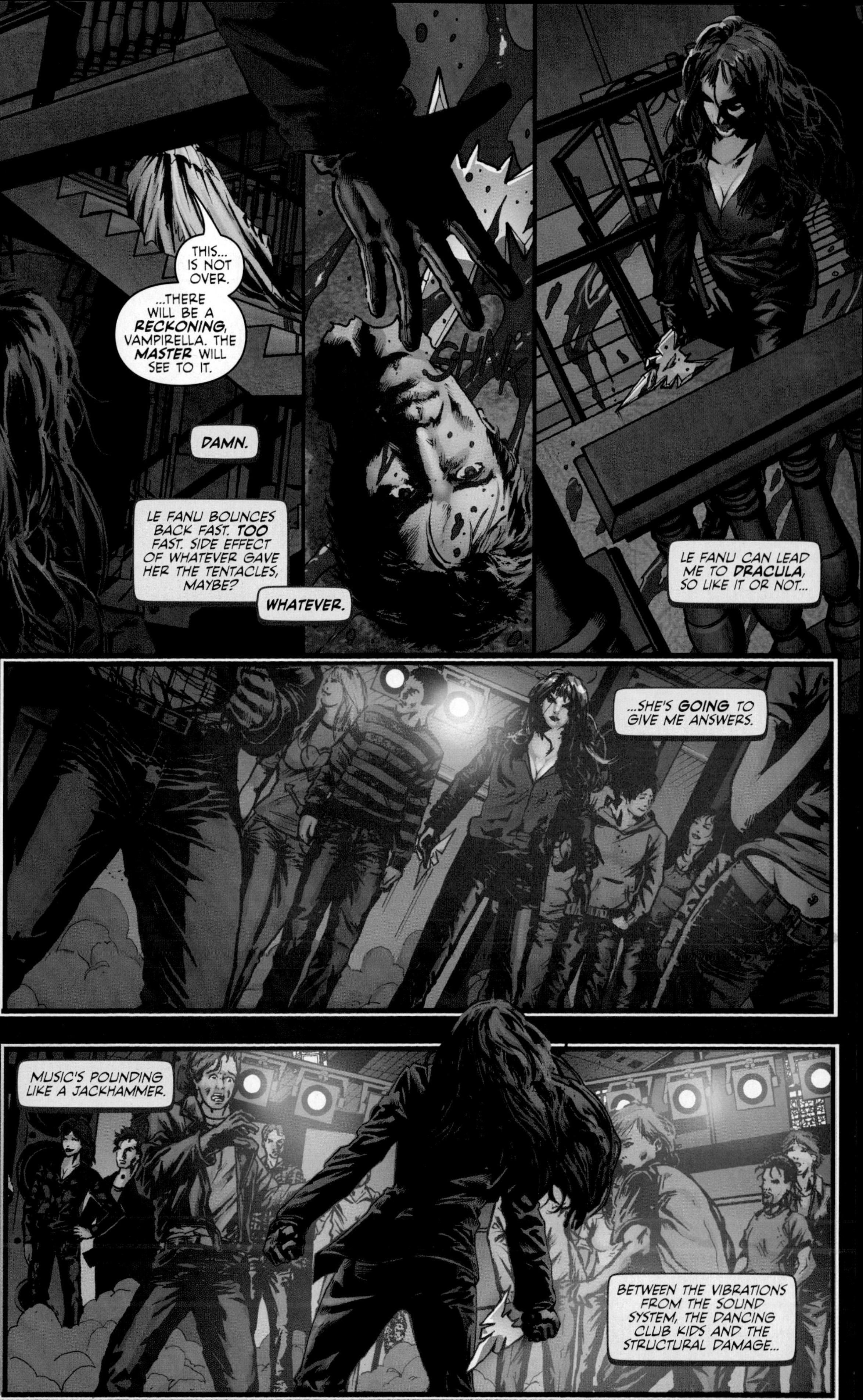
THIS... IS NOT OVER.
...THERE WILL BE A RECKONING, VAMPIRELLA. THE MASTER WILL SEE TO IT.
DAMN.
LE FANU BOUNCES BACK FAST. TOO FAST. SIDE EFFECT OF WHATEVER GAVE HER THE TENTACLES, MAYBE?
WHATEVER.
LE FANU CAN LEAD ME TO DRACULA, SO LIKE IT OR NOT...
...SHE'S GOING TO GIVE ME ANSWERS.
MUSIC'S POUNDING LIKE A JACKHAMMER.
BETWEEN THE VIBRATIONS FROM THE SOUND SYSTEM, THE DANCING CLUB KIDS AND THE STRUCTURAL DAMAGE...

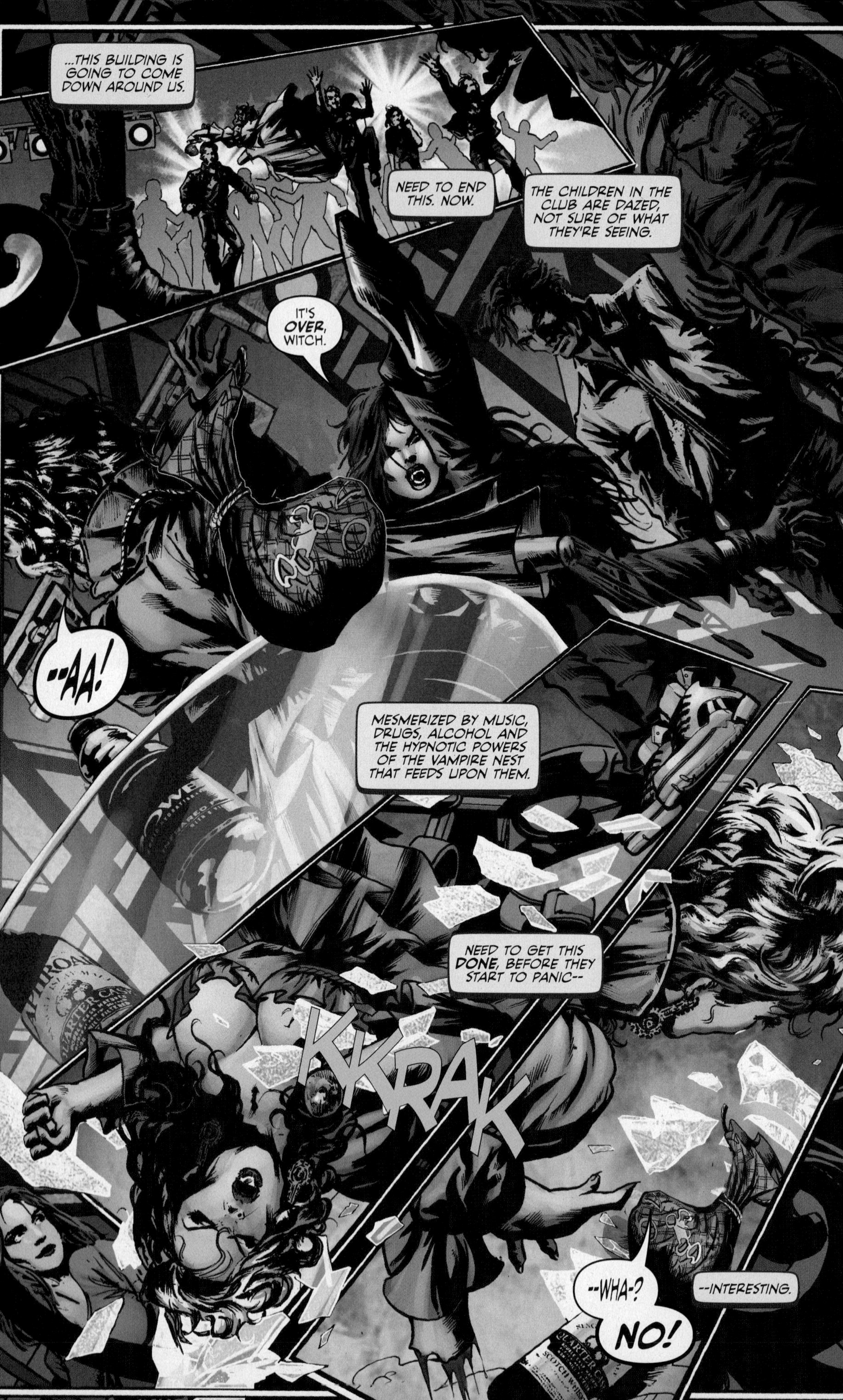
...THIS BUILDING IS GOING TO COME DOWN AROUND US.
NEED TO END THIS. NOW.
THE CHILDREN IN THE CLUB ARE DAZED, NOT SURE OF WHAT THEY'RE SEEING.
IT'S OVER, WITCH.
--AA!
MESMERIZED BY MUSIC, DRUGS, ALCOHOL AND THE HYPNOTIC POWERS OF THE VAMPIRE NEST THAT FEEDS UPON THEM.
NEED TO GET THIS DONE, BEFORE THEY START TO PANIC--
KKRAK
--WHA-?
NO!
--INTERESTING.

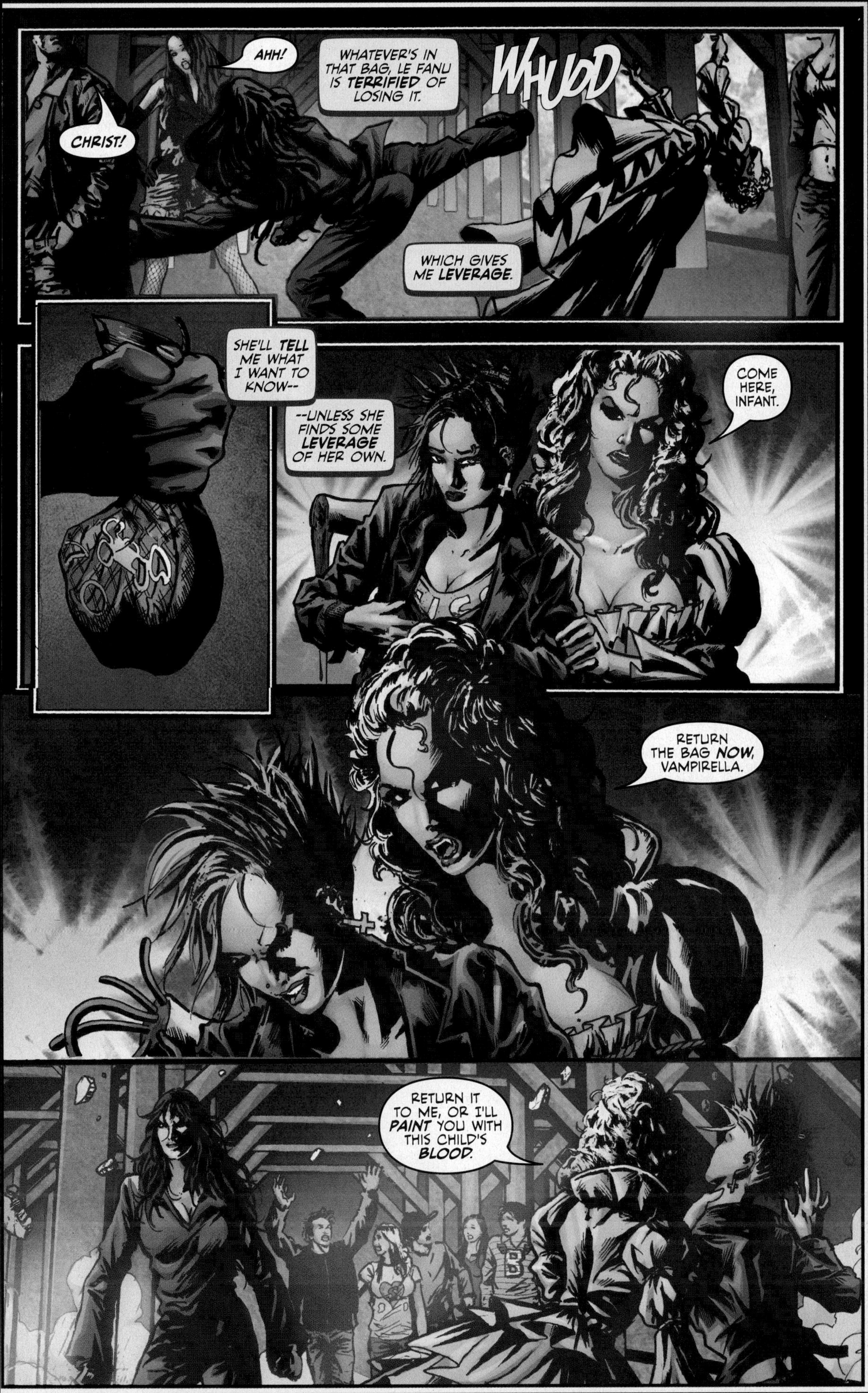
AHH!
CHRIST!
WHATEVER'S IN THAT BAG, LE FANU IS TERRIFIED OF LOSING IT.
WHUDD
WHICH GIVES ME LEVERAGE.
SHE'LL TELL ME WHAT I WANT TO KNOW--
--UNLESS SHE FINDS SOME LEVERAGE OF HER OWN.
COME HERE, INFANT.
RETURN THE BAG NOW, VAMPIRELLA.
RETURN IT TO ME, OR I'LL PAINT YOU WITH THIS CHILD'S BLOOD.

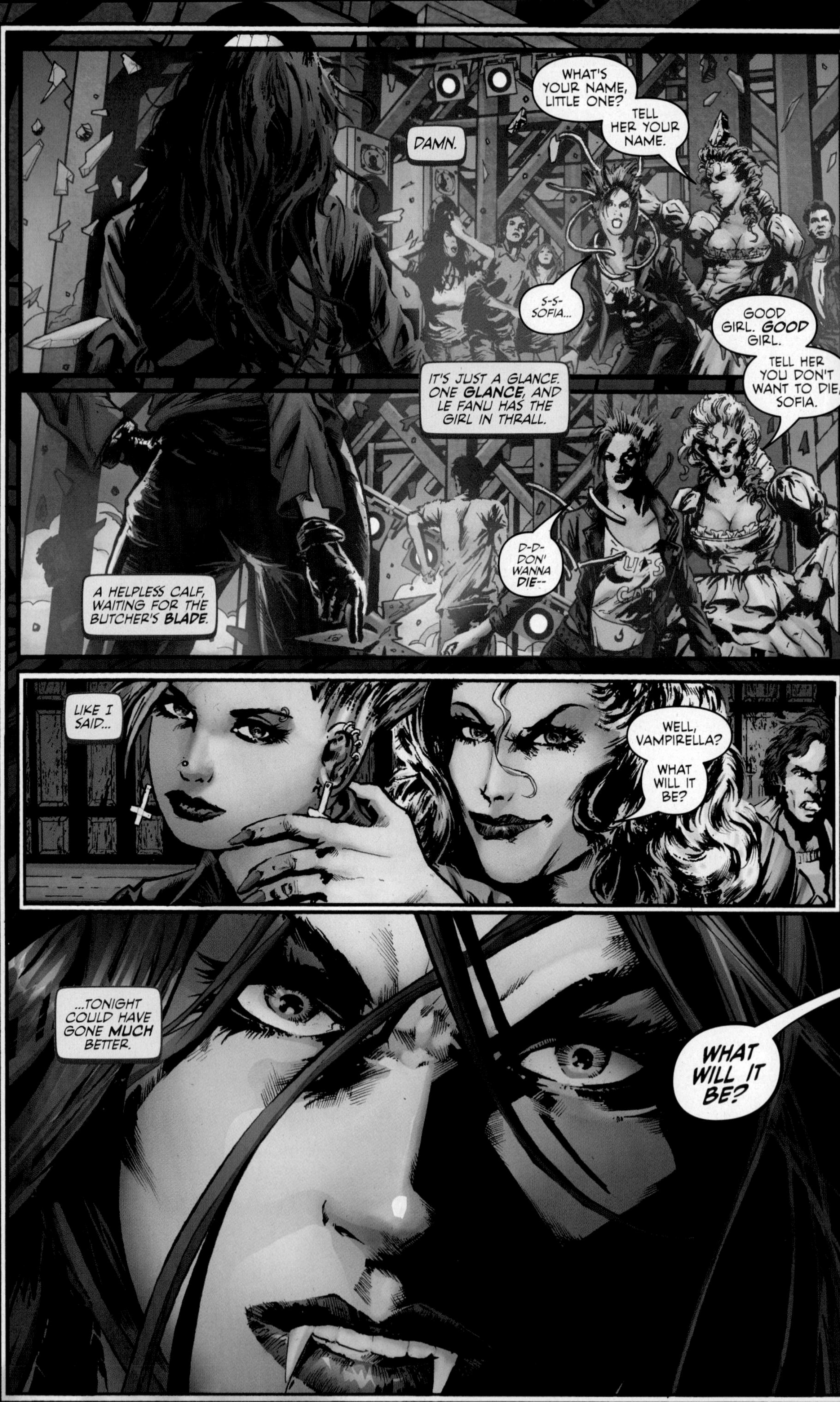
DAMN.
WHAT'S YOUR NAME, LITTLE ONE?
TELL HER YOUR NAME.
S-S-SOFIA...
GOOD GIRL. GOOD GIRL.
TELL HER YOU DON'T WANT TO DIE, SOFIA.
IT'S JUST A GLANCE. ONE GLANCE, AND LE FANU HAS THE GIRL IN THRALL.
A HELPLESS CALF, WAITING FOR THE BUTCHER'S BLADE.
D-D-DON' WANNA DIE--
LIKE I SAID...
WELL, VAMPIRELLA?
WHAT WILL IT BE?
...TONIGHT COULD HAVE GONE MUCH BETTER.
WHAT WILL IT BE?

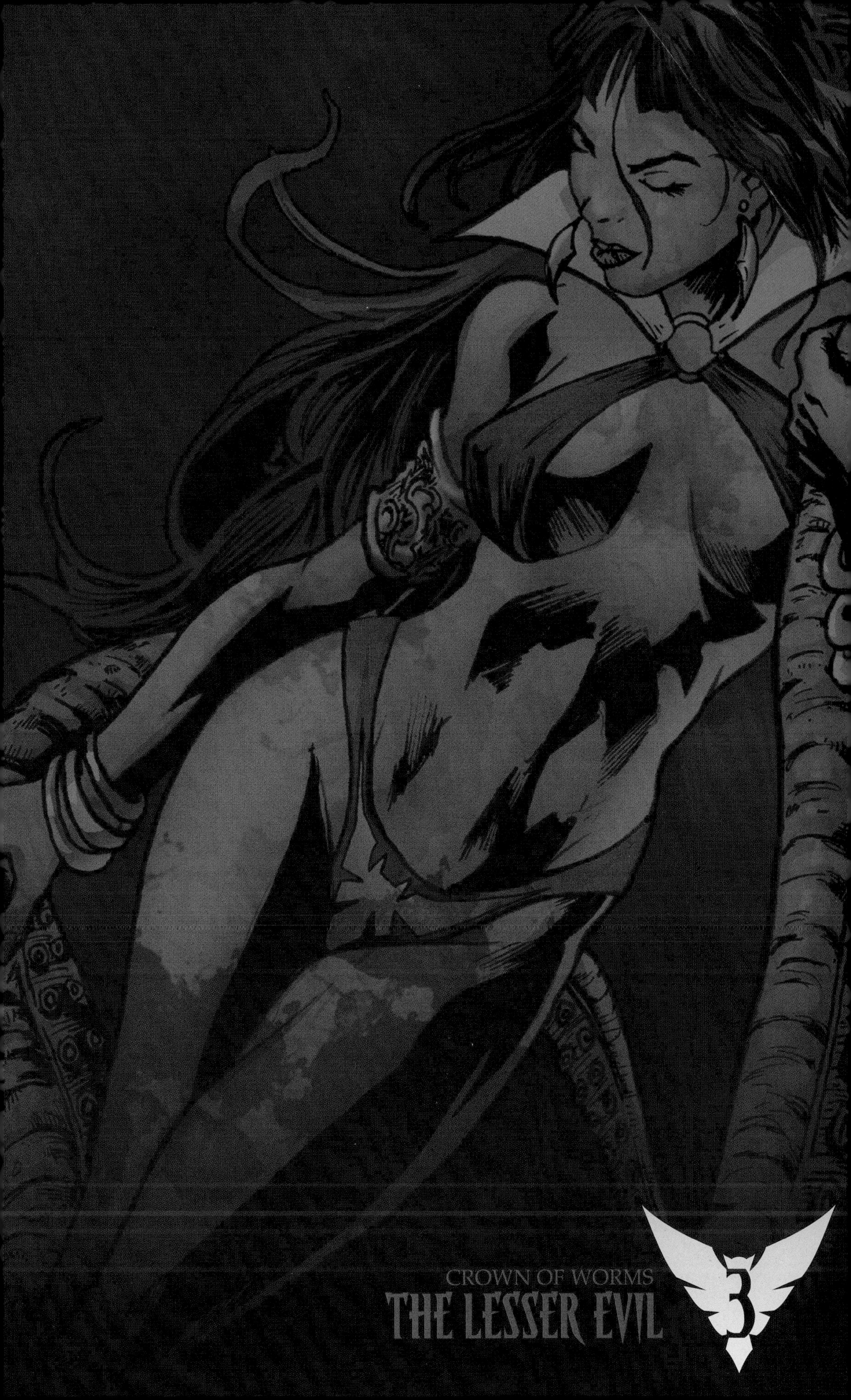
CROWN OF WORMS
THE LESSER EVIL
3

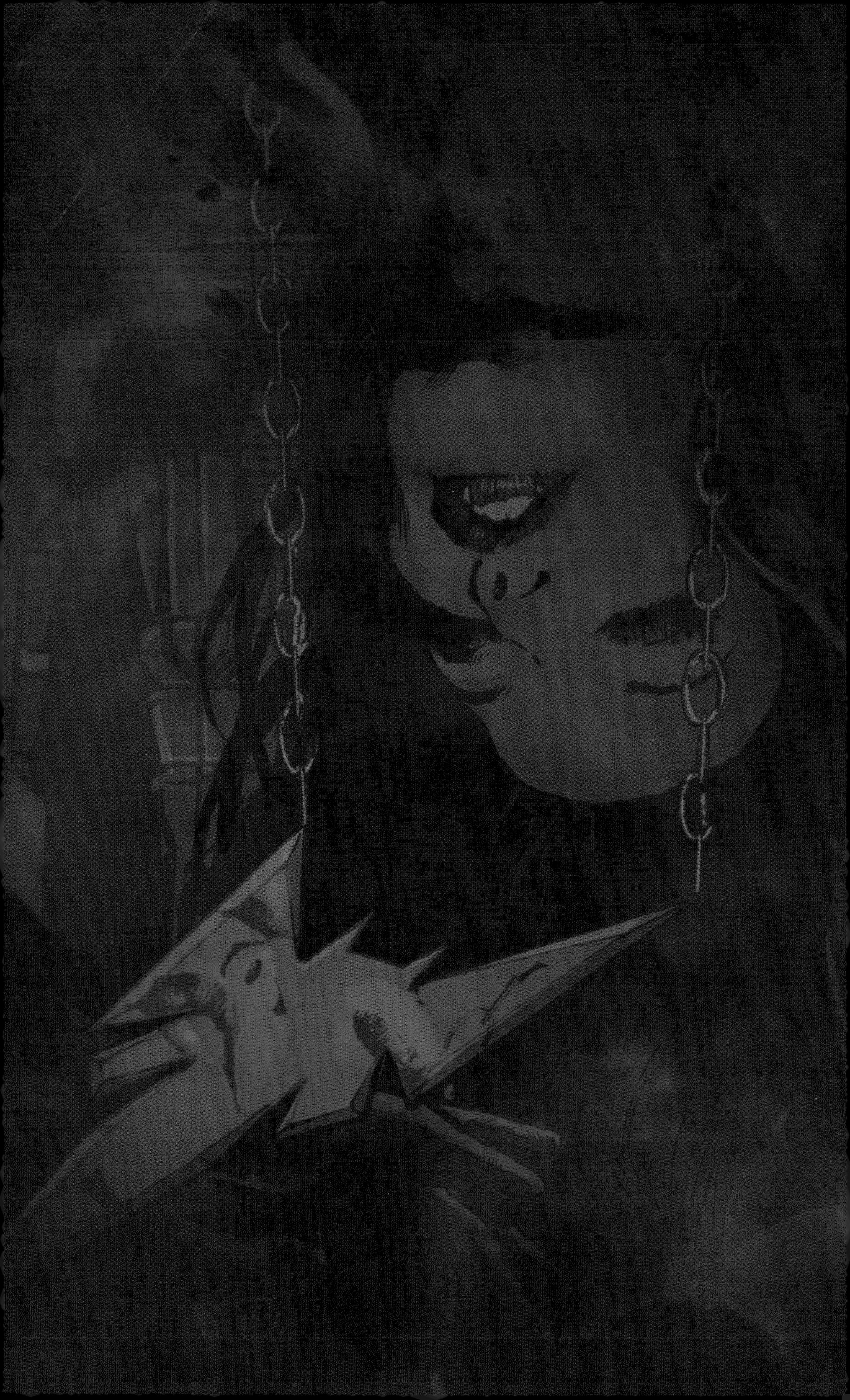

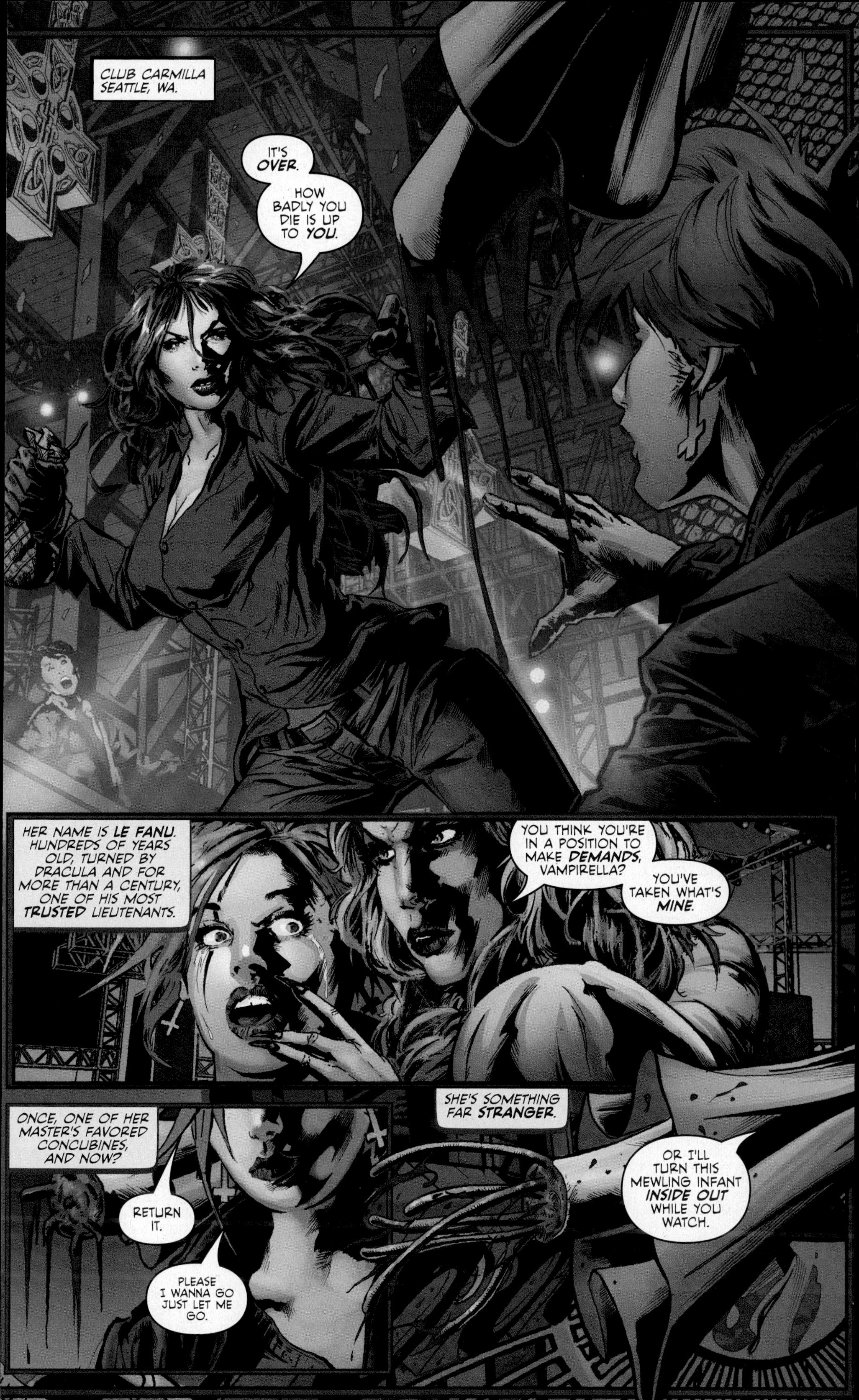
CLUB CARMILLA
SEATTLE, WA.
IT'S **OVER**.
HOW BADLY YOU DIE IS UP TO **YOU**.
HER NAME IS **LE FANU**. HUNDREDS OF YEARS OLD, TURNED BY DRACULA AND FOR MORE THAN A CENTURY, ONE OF HIS MOST **TRUSTED** LIEUTENANTS.
YOU THINK YOU'RE IN A POSITION TO MAKE **DEMANDS**, VAMPIRELLA?
YOU'VE TAKEN WHAT'S **MINE**.
ONCE, ONE OF HER MASTER'S FAVORED CONCUBINES, AND NOW?
SHE'S SOMETHING FAR **STRANGER**.
RETURN IT.
OR I'LL TURN THIS MEWLING INFANT **INSIDE OUT** WHILE YOU WATCH.
PLEASE I WANNA GO JUST LET ME GO.

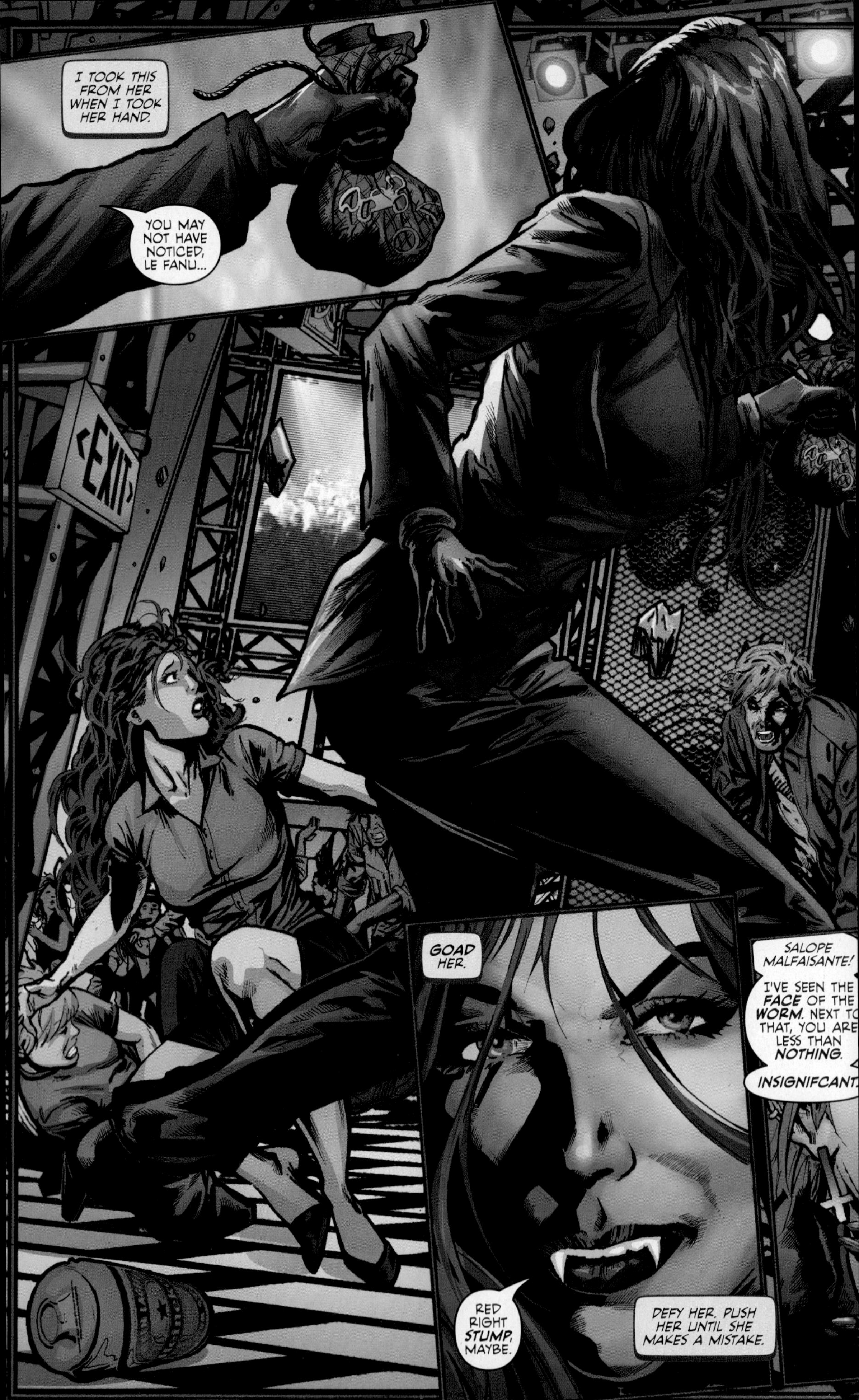
I TOOK THIS FROM HER WHEN I TOOK HER HAND.
YOU MAY NOT HAVE NOTICED, LE FANU...
<EXIT>
GOAD HER.
SALOPE MALFAISANTE!
I'VE SEEN THE FACE OF THE WORM. NEXT TO THAT, YOU ARE LESS THAN NOTHING.
INSIGNIFCANT.
RED RIGHT STUMP, MAYBE.
DEFY HER. PUSH HER UNTIL SHE MAKES A MISTAKE.

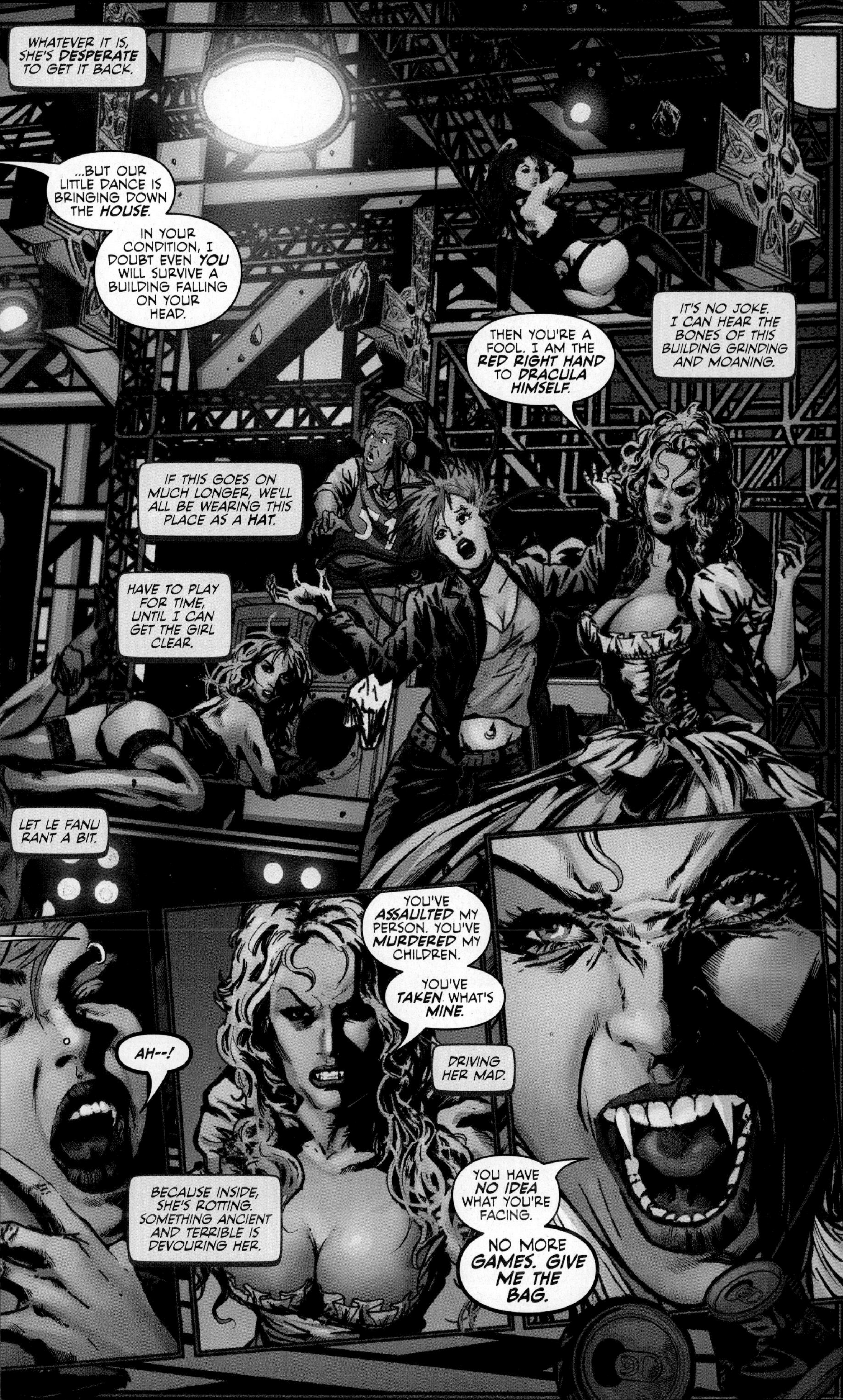
WHATEVER IT IS, SHE'S DESPERATE TO GET IT BACK.
...BUT OUR LITTLE DANCE IS BRINGING DOWN THE HOUSE.
IN YOUR CONDITION, I DOUBT EVEN YOU WILL SURVIVE A BUILDING FALLING ON YOUR HEAD.
THEN YOU'RE A FOOL. I AM THE RED RIGHT HAND TO DRACULA HIMSELF.
IT'S NO JOKE. I CAN HEAR THE BONES OF THIS BUILDING GRINDING AND MOANING.
IF THIS GOES ON MUCH LONGER, WE'LL ALL BE WEARING THIS PLACE AS A HAT.
HAVE TO PLAY FOR TIME, UNTIL I CAN GET THE GIRL CLEAR.
LET LE FANU RANT A BIT.
AH--!
YOU'VE ASSAULTED MY PERSON. YOU'VE MURDERED MY CHILDREN.
YOU'VE TAKEN WHAT'S MINE.
DRIVING HER MAD.
BECAUSE INSIDE, SHE'S ROTTING. SOMETHING ANCIENT AND TERRIBLE IS DEVOURING HER.
YOU HAVE NO IDEA WHAT YOU'RE FACING.
NO MORE GAMES. GIVE ME THE BAG.

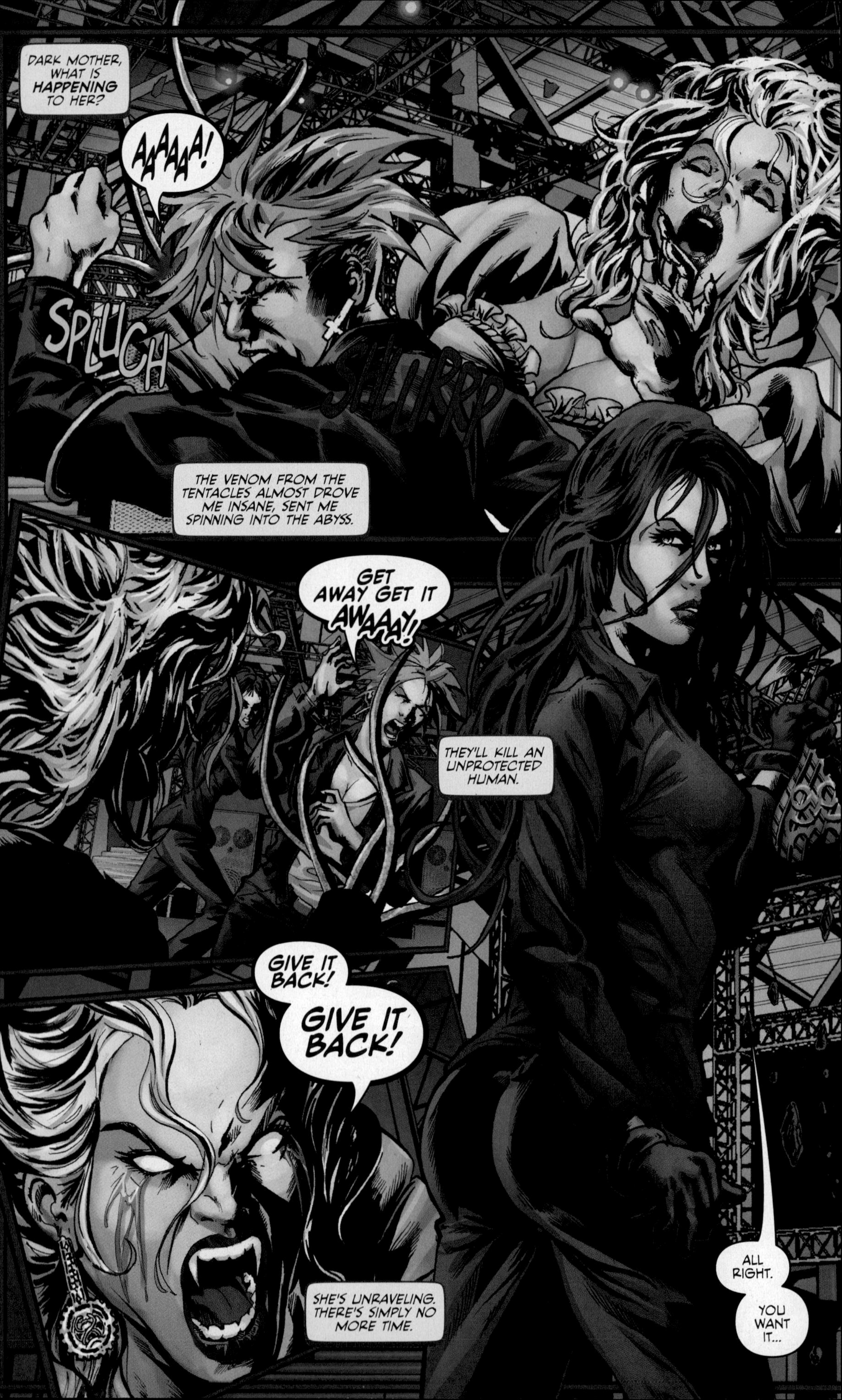

DARK MOTHER, WHAT IS HAPPENING TO HER?
AAAAAA!
SPLUCH
SHLURRP
THE VENOM FROM THE TENTACLES ALMOST DROVE ME INSANE, SENT ME SPINNING INTO THE ABYSS.
GET AWAY GET IT AWAAAY!!
THEY'LL KILL AN UNPROTECTED HUMAN.
GIVE IT BACK!
GIVE IT BACK!
SHE'S UNRAVELING. THERE'S SIMPLY NO MORE TIME.
ALL RIGHT.
YOU WANT IT...

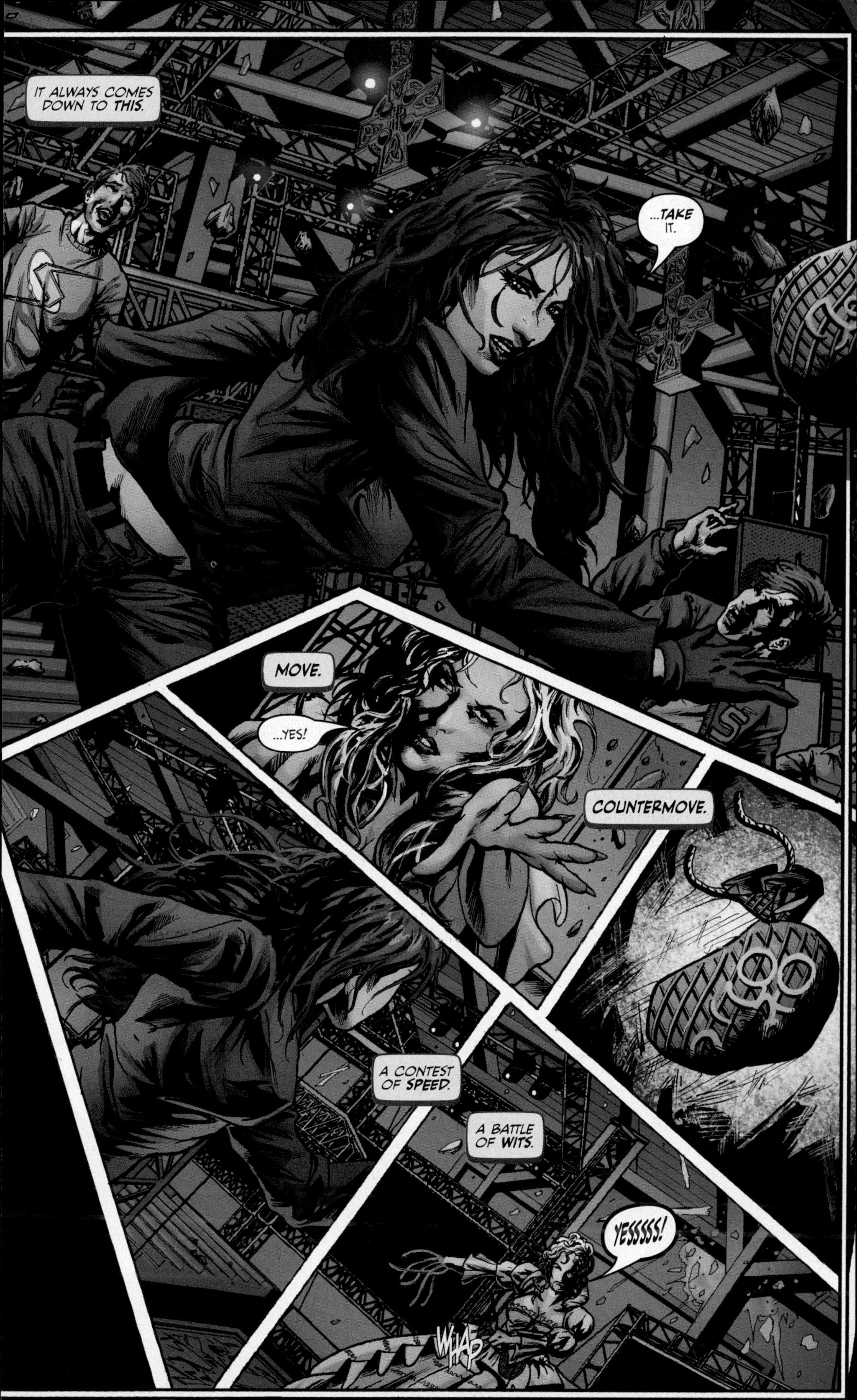
IT ALWAYS COMES DOWN TO THIS.
...TAKE IT.
MOVE.
...YES!
COUNTERMOVE.
A CONTEST OF SPEED.
A BATTLE OF WITS.
YESSSSS!
WHAP

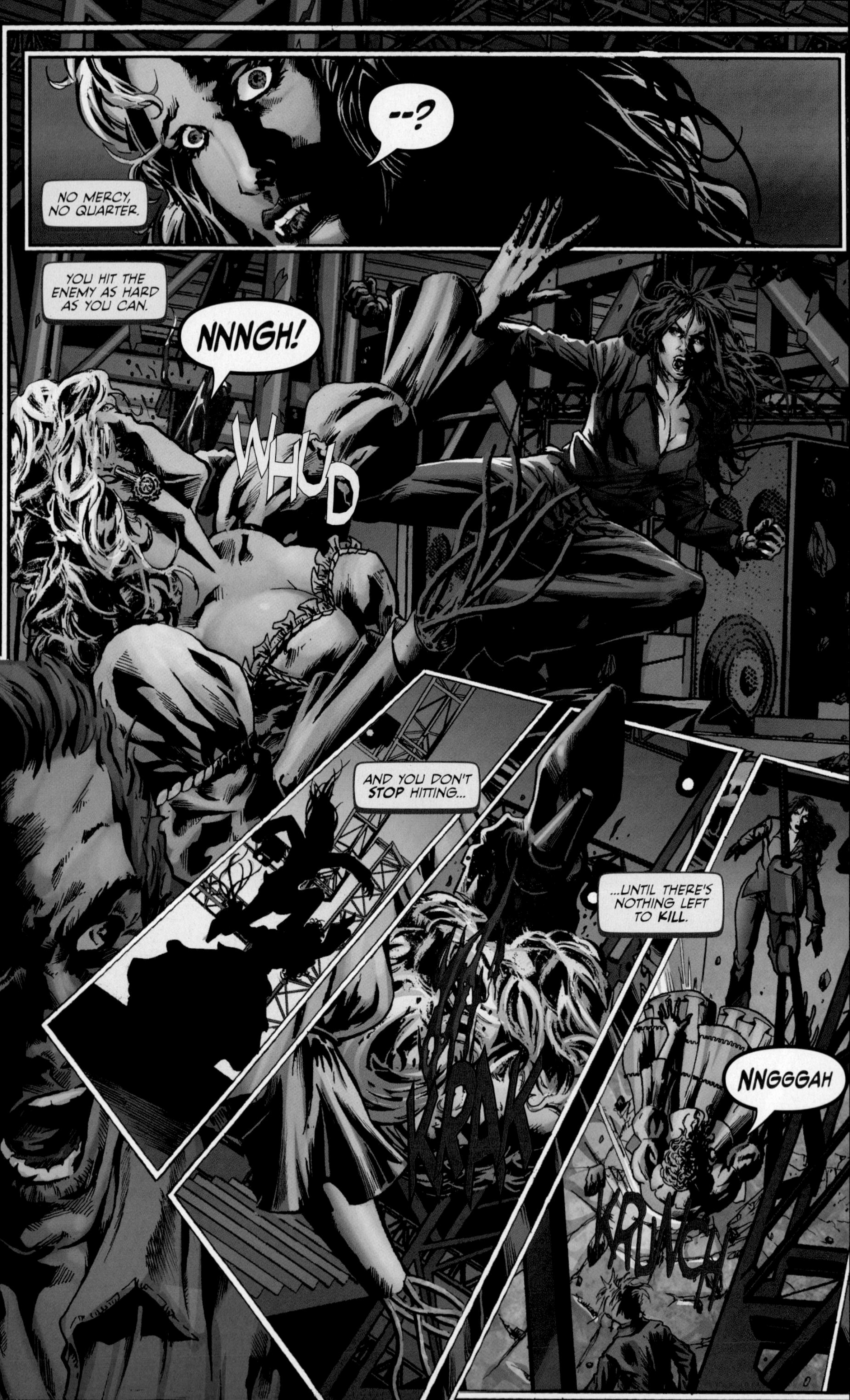
--?
NO MERCY, NO QUARTER.
YOU HIT THE ENEMY AS HARD AS YOU CAN.
NNNGH!
WHUD
AND YOU DON'T STOP HITTING...
...UNTIL THERE'S NOTHING LEFT TO KILL.
KRAK
NNGGGAH
KRUNCH

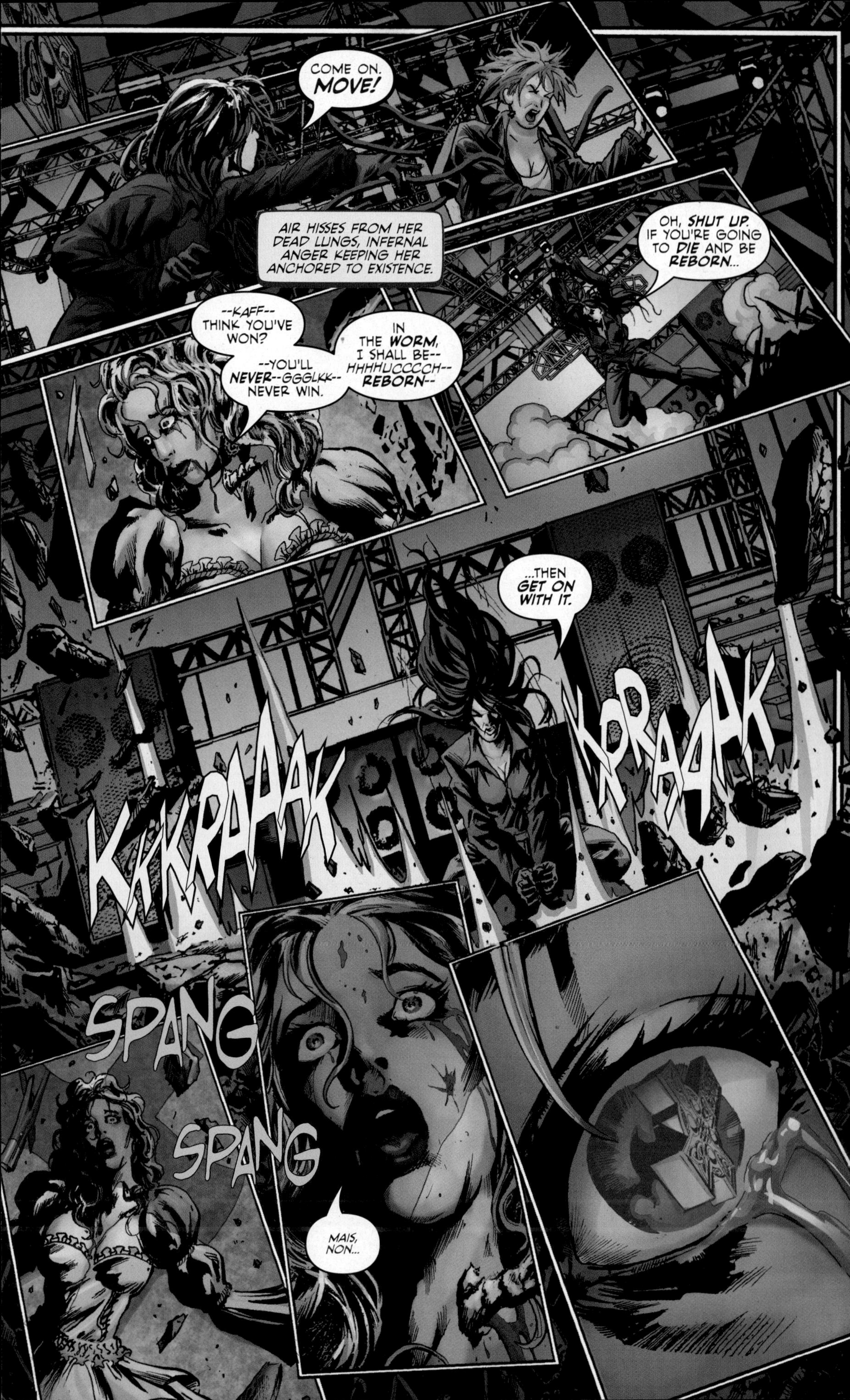
COME ON. MOVE!
AIR HISSES FROM HER DEAD LUNGS, INFERNAL ANGER KEEPING HER ANCHORED TO EXISTENCE.
OH, SHUT UP. IF YOU'RE GOING TO DIE AND BE REBORN...
--KAFF-- THINK YOU'VE WON?
--YOU'LL NEVER--GGGLKK-- NEVER WIN.
IN THE WORM, I SHALL BE-- HHHHUCCCCH-- REBORN--
...THEN GET ON WITH IT.
KKKRAAAK
KRRAAAK
SPANG
SPANG
MAIS, NON...

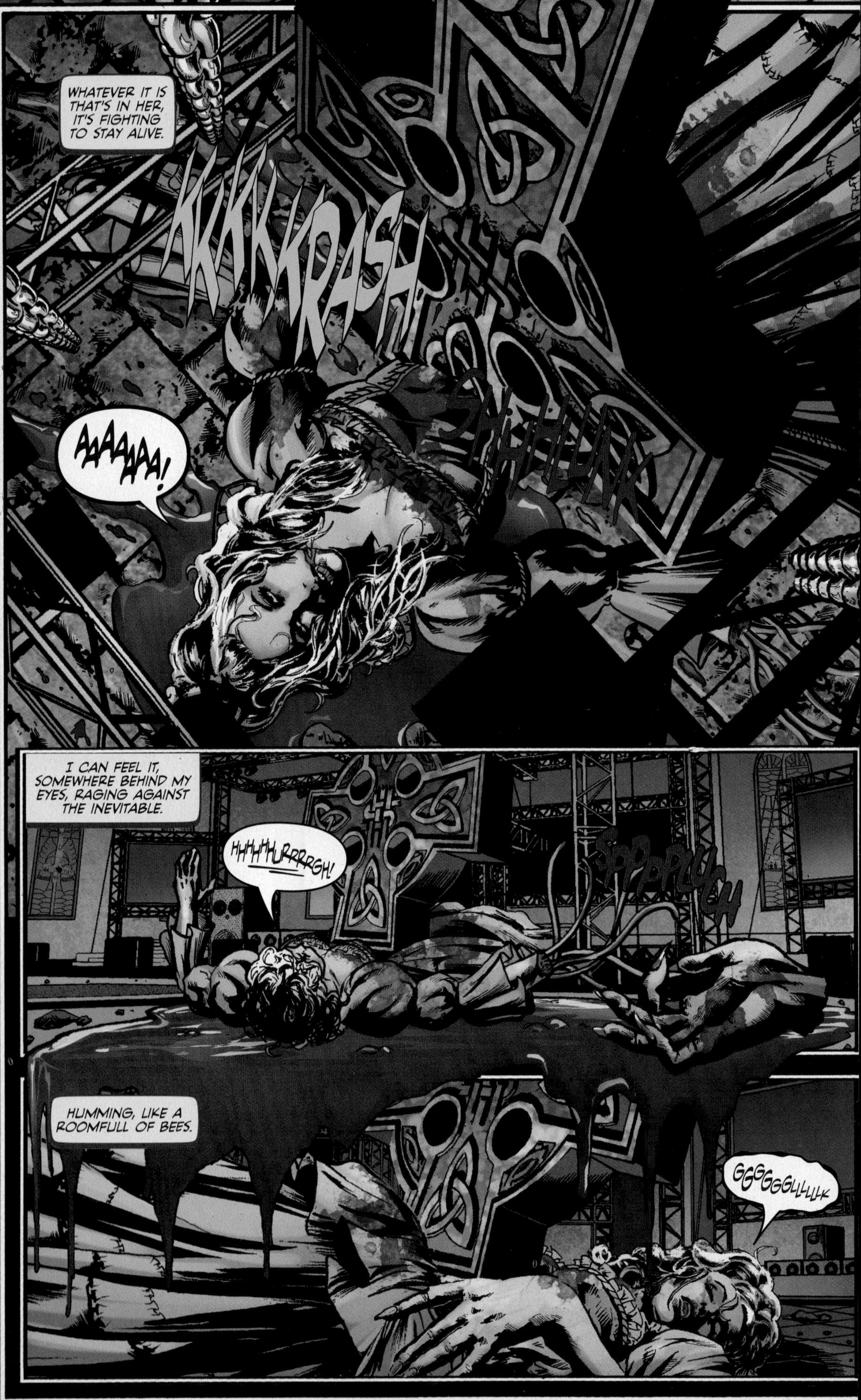
WHATEVER IT IS THAT'S IN HER, IT'S FIGHTING TO STAY ALIVE.
KKKKKRASH
AAAAAAA!
SHHHLUNK
I CAN FEEL IT, SOMEWHERE BEHIND MY EYES, RAGING AGAINST THE INEVITABLE.
HHHHHURRRRGH!
SPPPLUCH
HUMMING, LIKE A ROOMFULL OF BEES.
GGGGGGLLLLLK

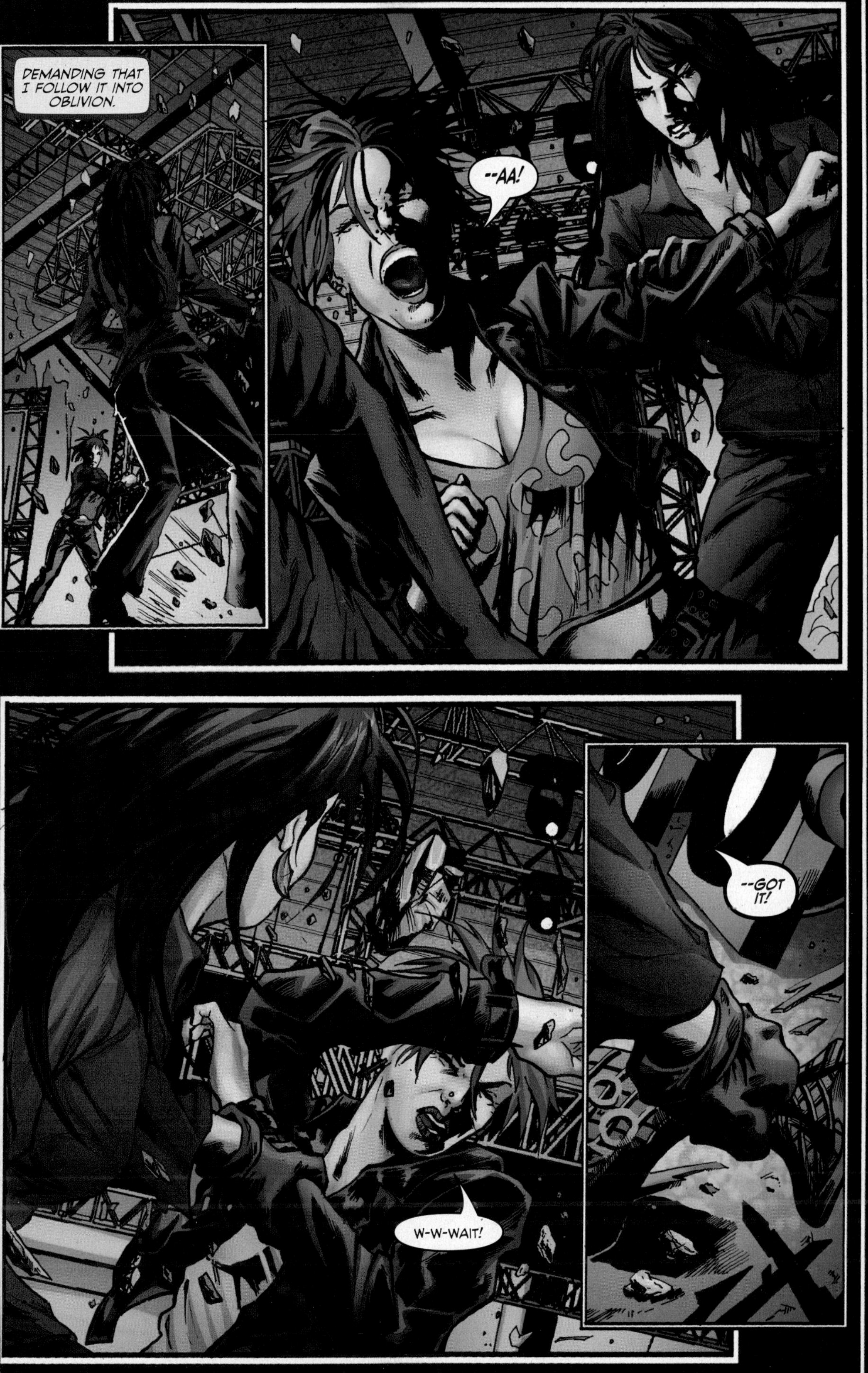
DEMANDING THAT I FOLLOW IT INTO OBLIVION.
--AA!
--GOT IT!
W-W-WAIT!

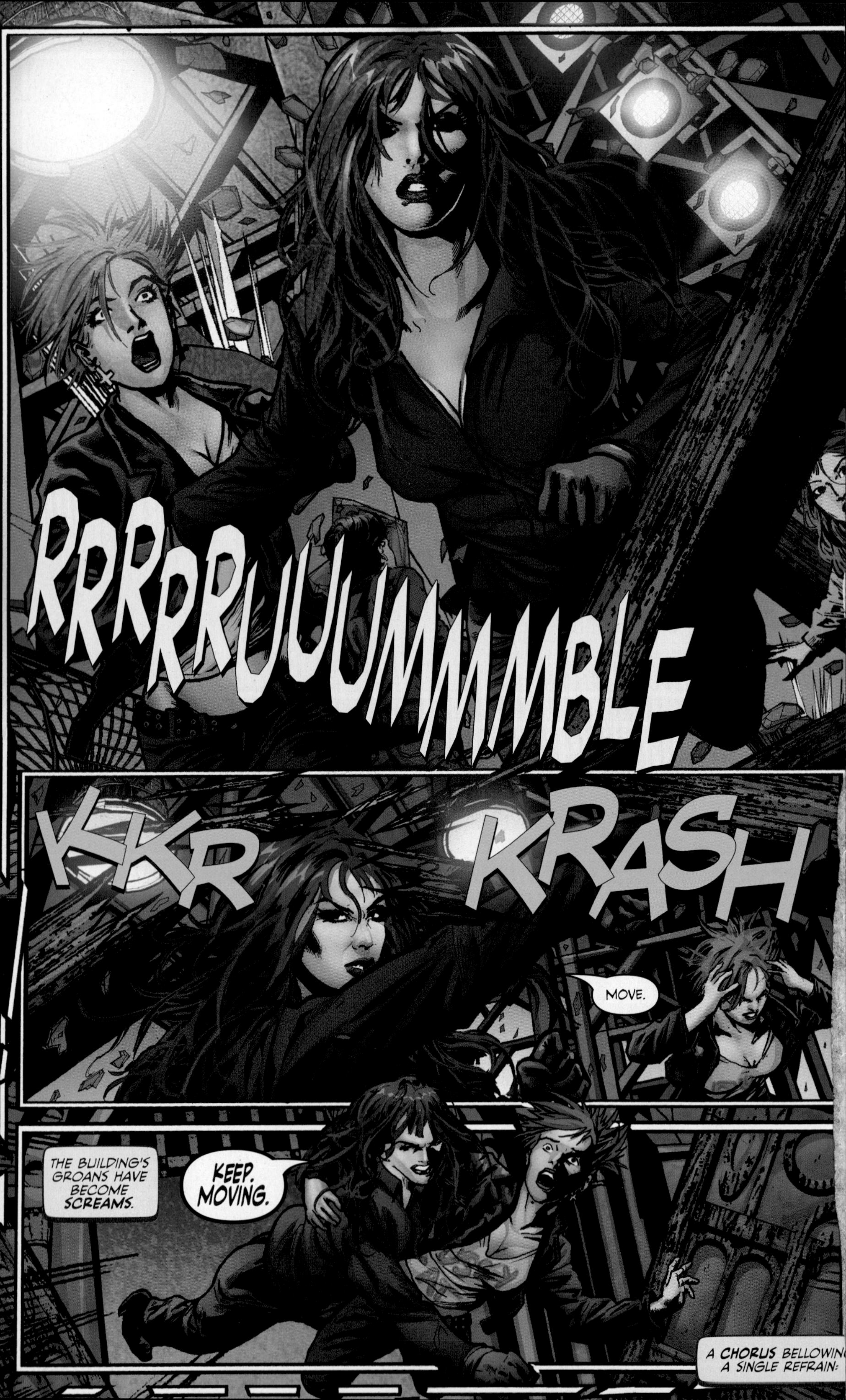
RRRRRUUUMMMBLE
KKR KRASH
MOVE.
THE BUILDING'S GROANS HAVE BECOME SCREAMS.
KEEP. MOVING.
A CHORUS BELLOWING A SINGLE REFRAIN:

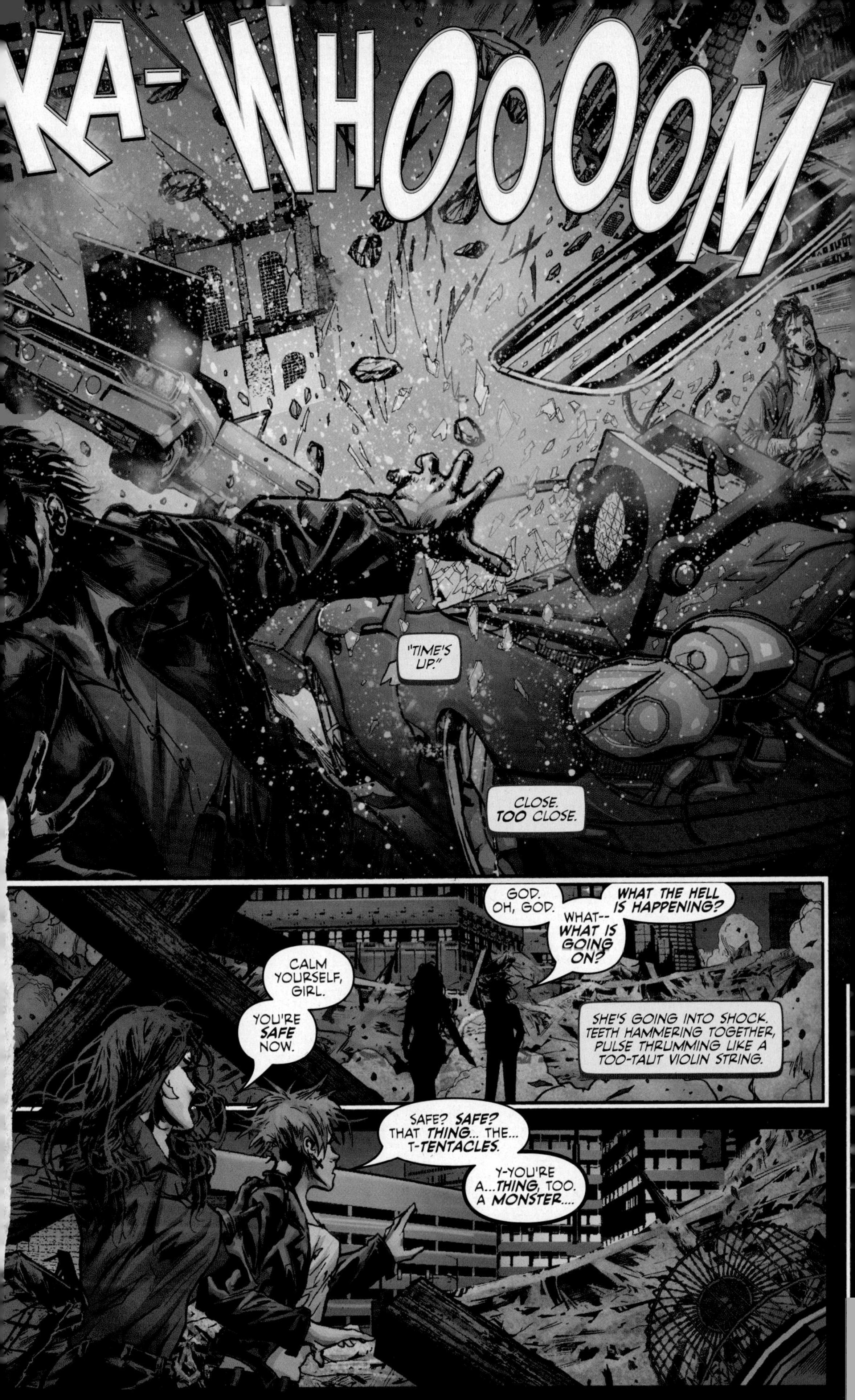
KA-WHOOOOM
"TIME'S UP."
CLOSE. TOO CLOSE.
GOD. OH, GOD.
WHAT THE HELL IS HAPPENING?
WHAT-- WHAT IS GOING ON?
CALM YOURSELF, GIRL.
YOU'RE SAFE NOW.
SHE'S GOING INTO SHOCK. TEETH HAMMERING TOGETHER, PULSE THRUMMING LIKE A TOO-TAUT VIOLIN STRING.
SAFE? SAFE? THAT THING... THE... T-TENTACLES.
Y-YOU'RE A...THING, TOO. A MONSTER....

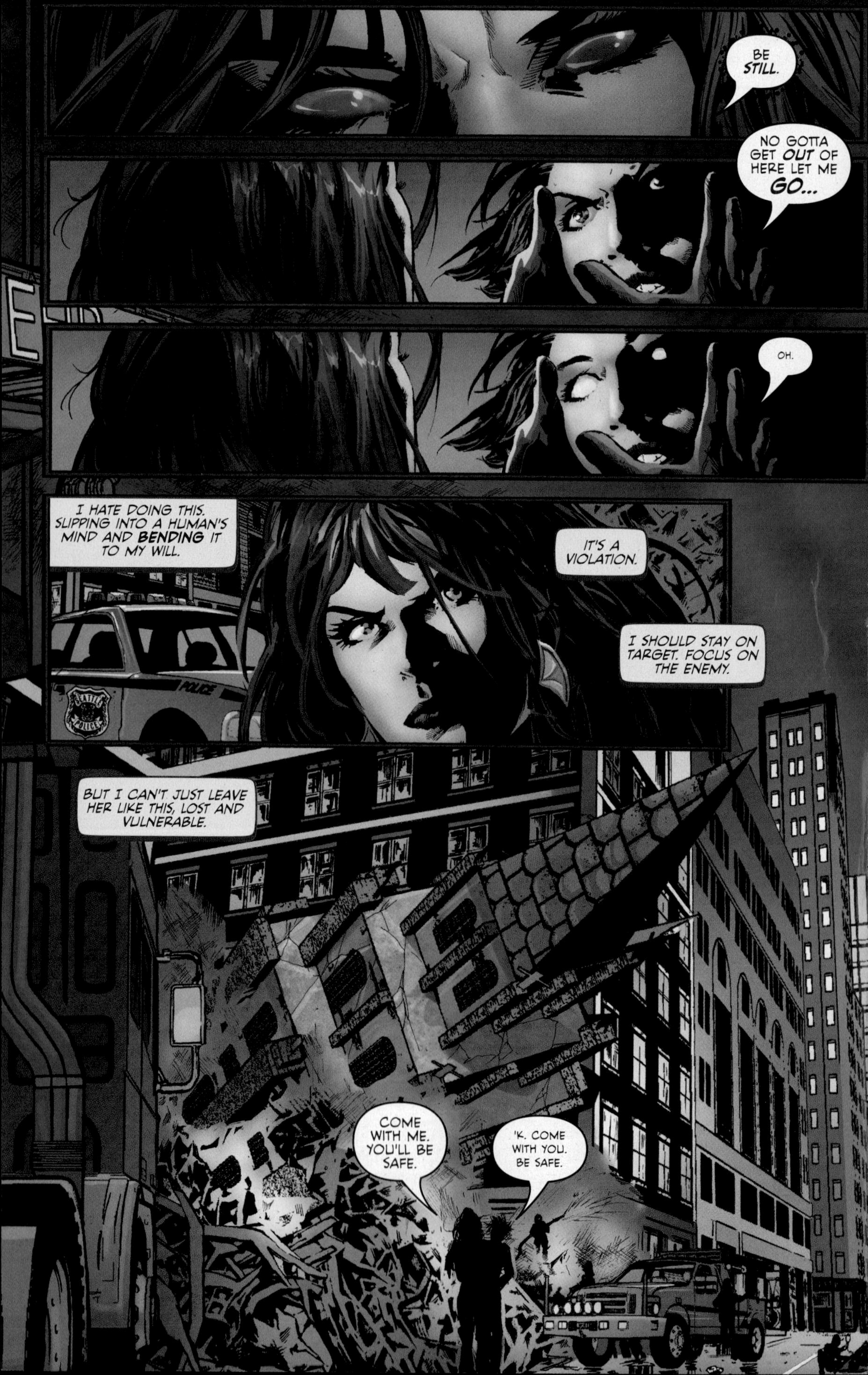

BE STILL.
NO GOTTA GET OUT OF HERE LET ME GO...
OH.
I HATE DOING THIS. SLIPPING INTO A HUMAN'S MIND AND BENDING IT TO MY WILL.
IT'S A VIOLATION.
I SHOULD STAY ON TARGET. FOCUS ON THE ENEMY.
POLICE
BUT I CAN'T JUST LEAVE HER LIKE THIS, LOST AND VULNERABLE.
COME WITH ME. YOU'LL BE SAFE.
'K. COME WITH YOU. BE SAFE.

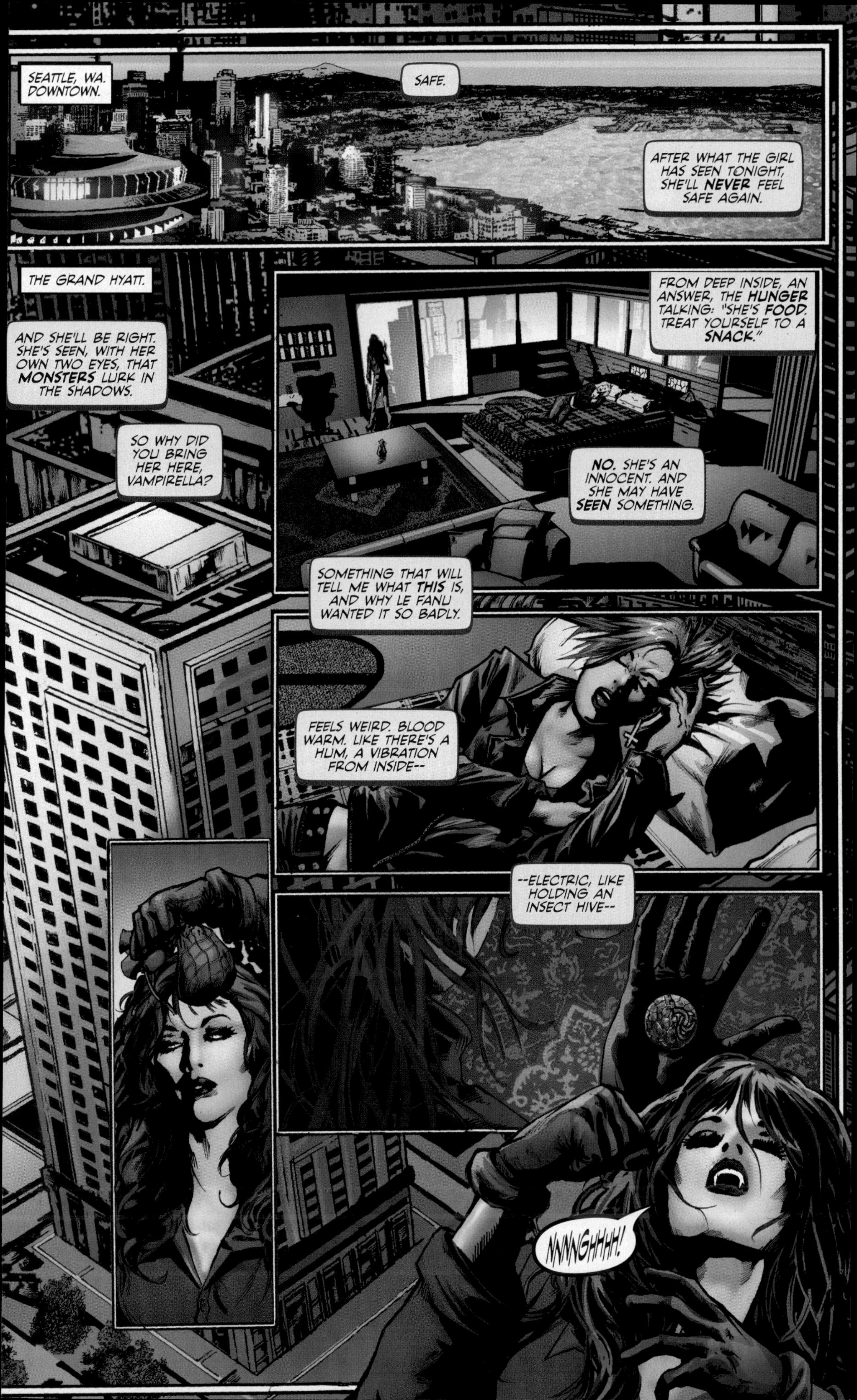
SEATTLE, WA. DOWNTOWN.
SAFE.
AFTER WHAT THE GIRL HAS SEEN TONIGHT, SHE'LL NEVER FEEL SAFE AGAIN.
THE GRAND HYATT.
AND SHE'LL BE RIGHT. SHE'S SEEN, WITH HER OWN TWO EYES, THAT MONSTERS LURK IN THE SHADOWS.
SO WHY DID YOU BRING HER HERE, VAMPIRELLA?
FROM DEEP INSIDE, AN ANSWER, THE HUNGER TALKING: "SHE'S FOOD. TREAT YOURSELF TO A SNACK."
NO. SHE'S AN INNOCENT. AND SHE MAY HAVE SEEN SOMETHING.
SOMETHING THAT WILL TELL ME WHAT THIS IS, AND WHY LE FANU WANTED IT SO BADLY.
FEELS WEIRD. BLOOD WARM. LIKE THERE'S A HUM, A VIBRATION FROM INSIDE--
--ELECTRIC, LIKE HOLDING AN INSECT HIVE--
NNNNGHHHH!

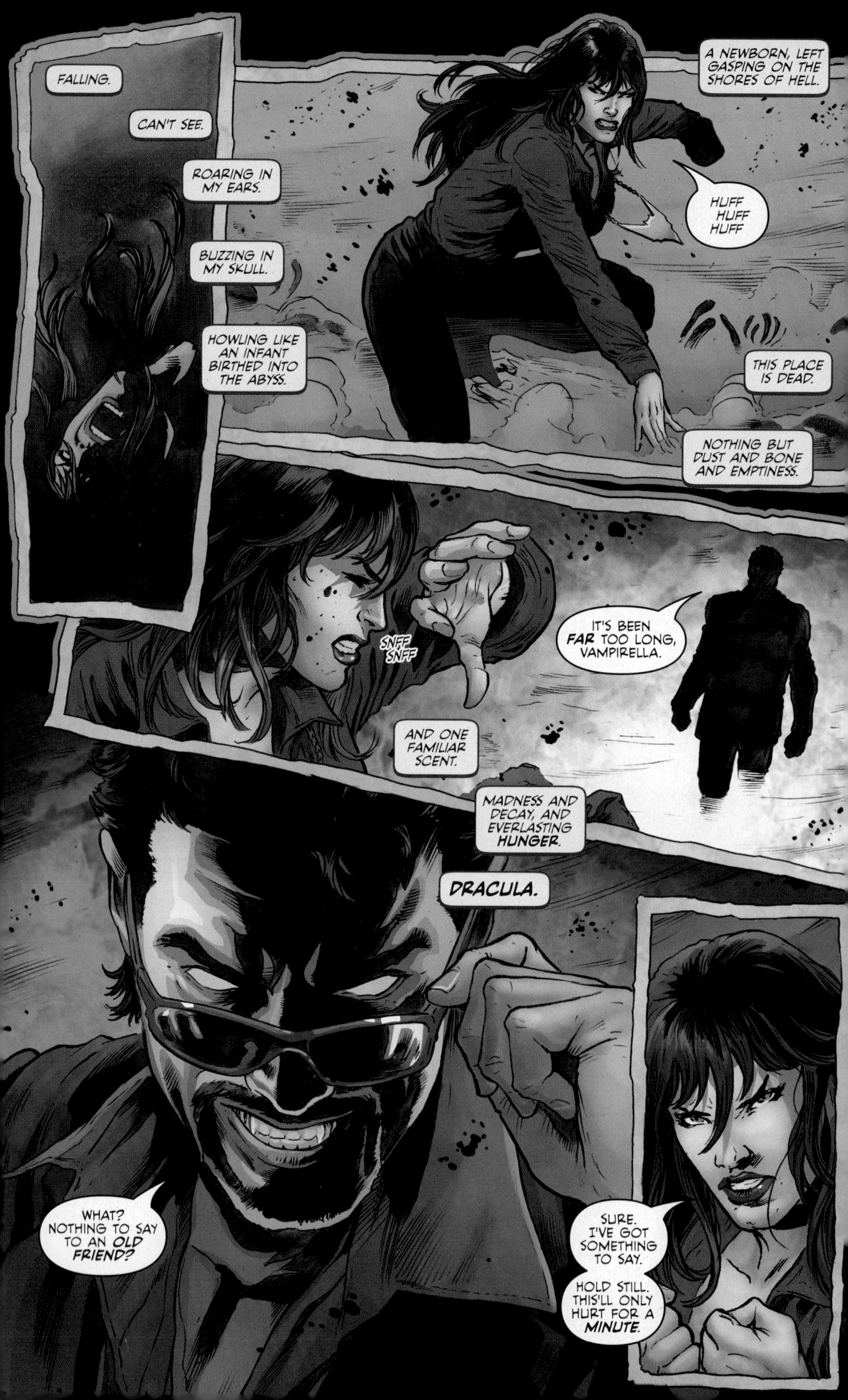
FALLING.
CAN'T SEE.
ROARING IN MY EARS.
BUZZING IN MY SKULL.
HOWLING LIKE AN INFANT BIRTHED INTO THE ABYSS.
A NEWBORN, LEFT GASPING ON THE SHORES OF HELL.
HUFF HUFF HUFF
THIS PLACE IS DEAD.
NOTHING BUT DUST AND BONE AND EMPTINESS.
SNFF SNFF
IT'S BEEN FAR TOO LONG, VAMPIRELLA.
AND ONE FAMILIAR SCENT.
MADNESS AND DECAY, AND EVERLASTING HUNGER.
DRACULA.
WHAT? NOTHING TO SAY TO AN OLD FRIEND?
SURE. I'VE GOT SOMETHING TO SAY.
HOLD STILL. THIS'LL ONLY HURT FOR A MINUTE.

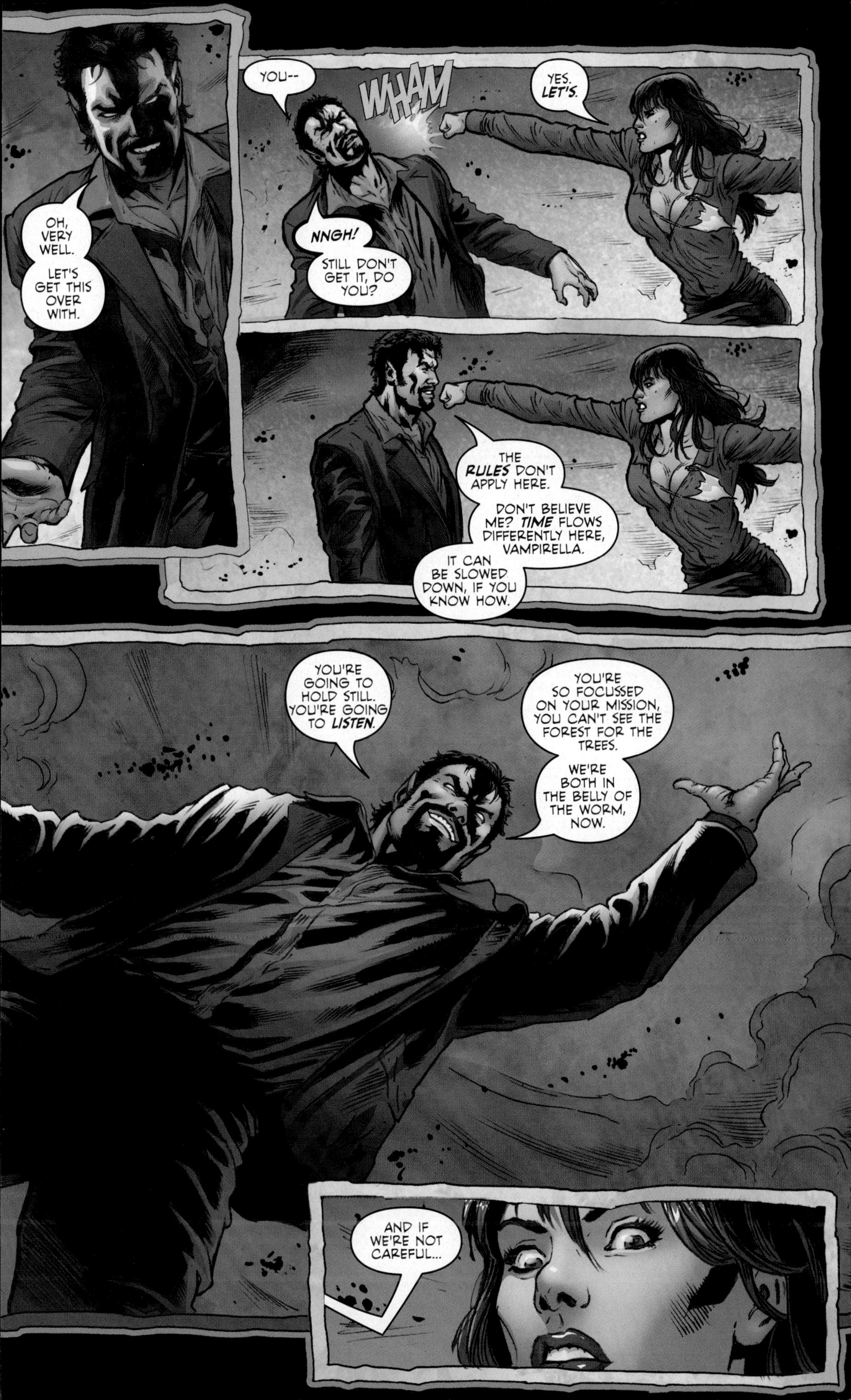
OH, VERY WELL.
LET'S GET THIS OVER WITH.
YOU--
WHAM
YES. LET'S.
NNGH!
STILL DON'T GET IT, DO YOU?
THE RULES DON'T APPLY HERE.
DON'T BELIEVE ME? TIME FLOWS DIFFERENTLY HERE, VAMPIRELLA.
IT CAN BE SLOWED DOWN, IF YOU KNOW HOW.
YOU'RE GOING TO HOLD STILL. YOU'RE GOING TO LISTEN.
YOU'RE SO FOCUSSED ON YOUR MISSION, YOU CAN'T SEE THE FOREST FOR THE TREES.
WE'RE BOTH IN THE BELLY OF THE WORM, NOW.
AND IF WE'RE NOT CAREFUL...

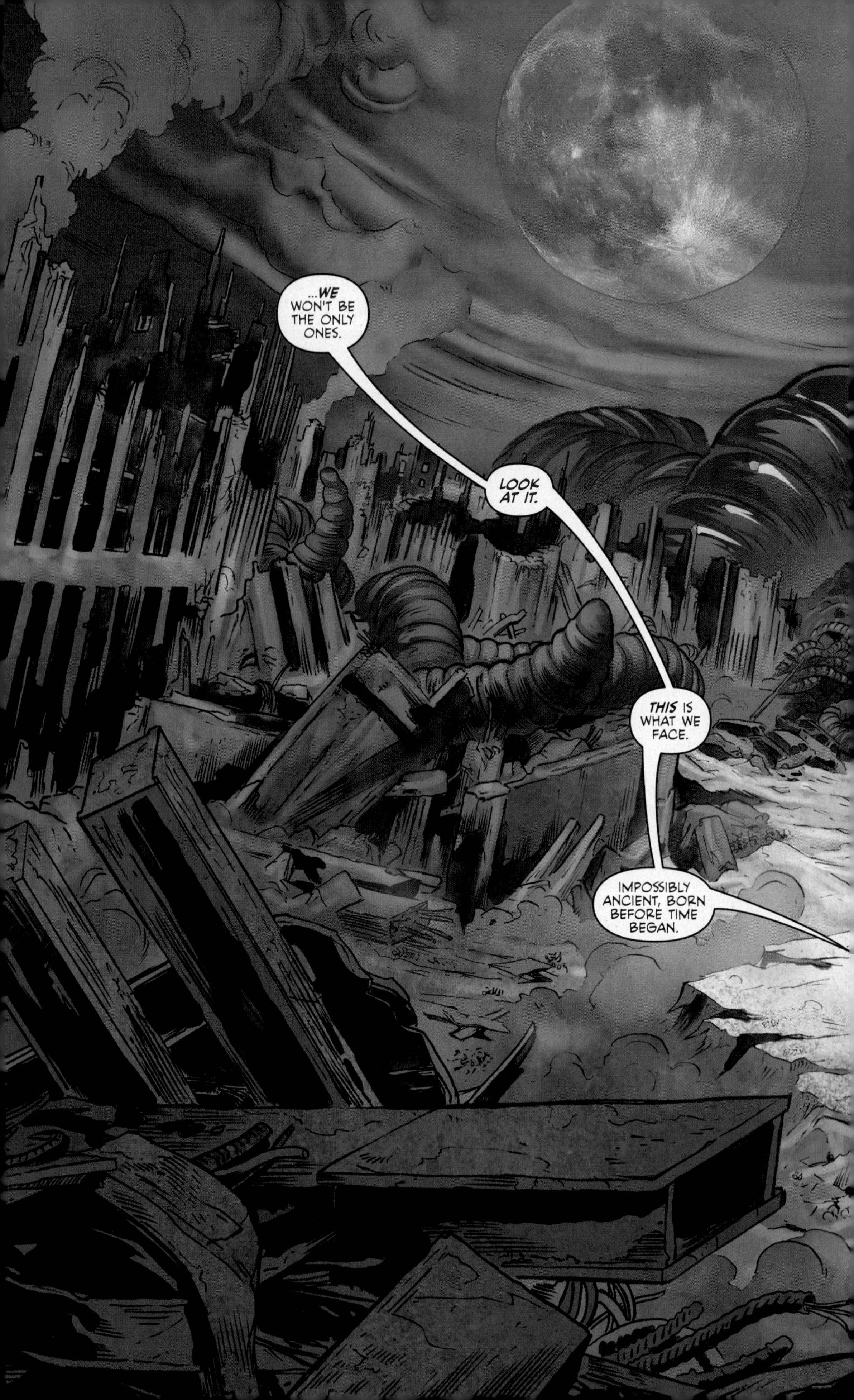
...WE WON'T BE THE ONLY ONES.
LOOK AT IT.
THIS IS WHAT WE FACE.
IMPOSSIBLY ANCIENT, BORN BEFORE TIME BEGAN.

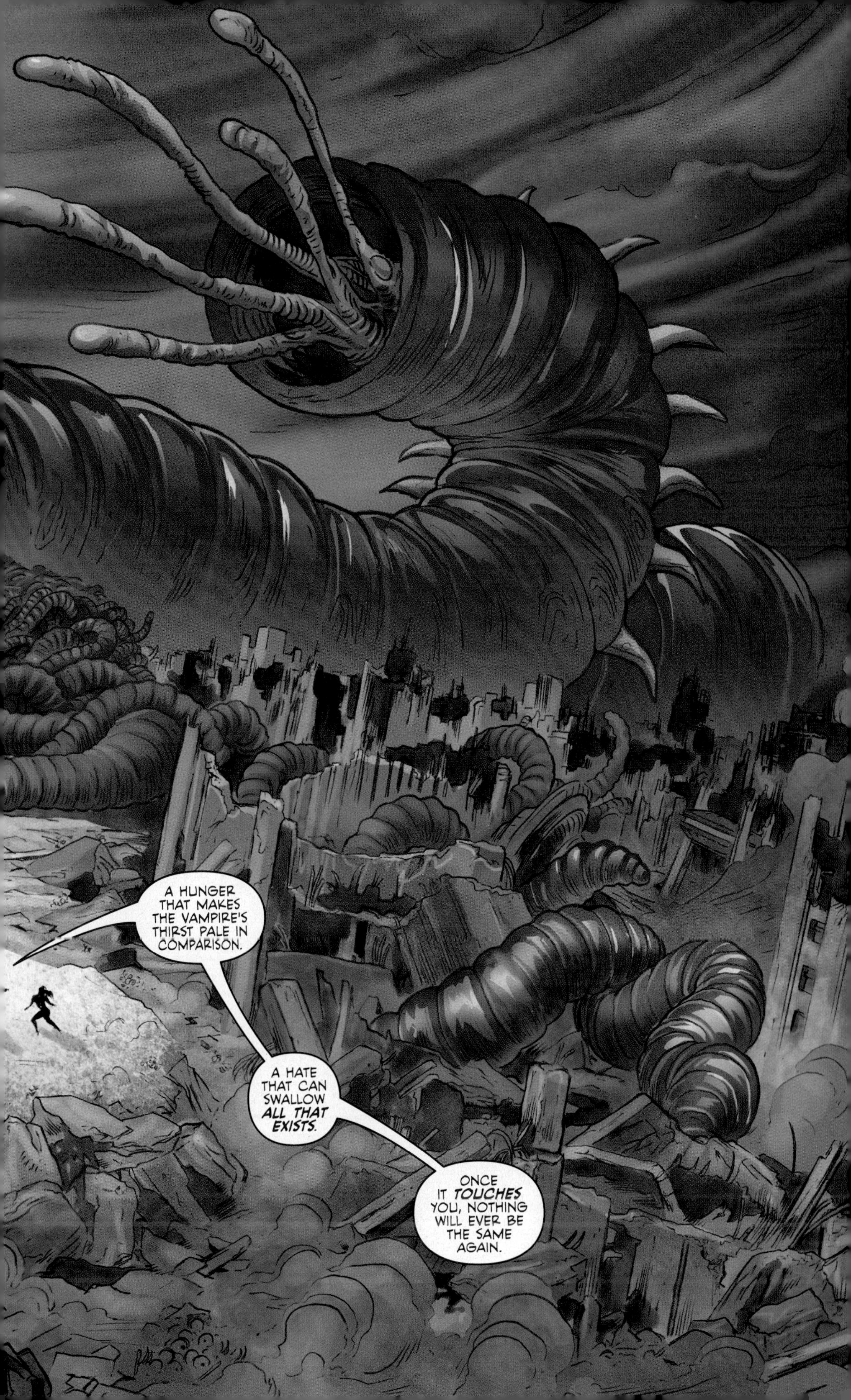
A HUNGER THAT MAKES THE VAMPIRE'S THIRST PALE IN COMPARISON.
A HATE THAT CAN SWALLOW ALL THAT EXISTS.
ONCE IT TOUCHES YOU, NOTHING WILL EVER BE THE SAME AGAIN.

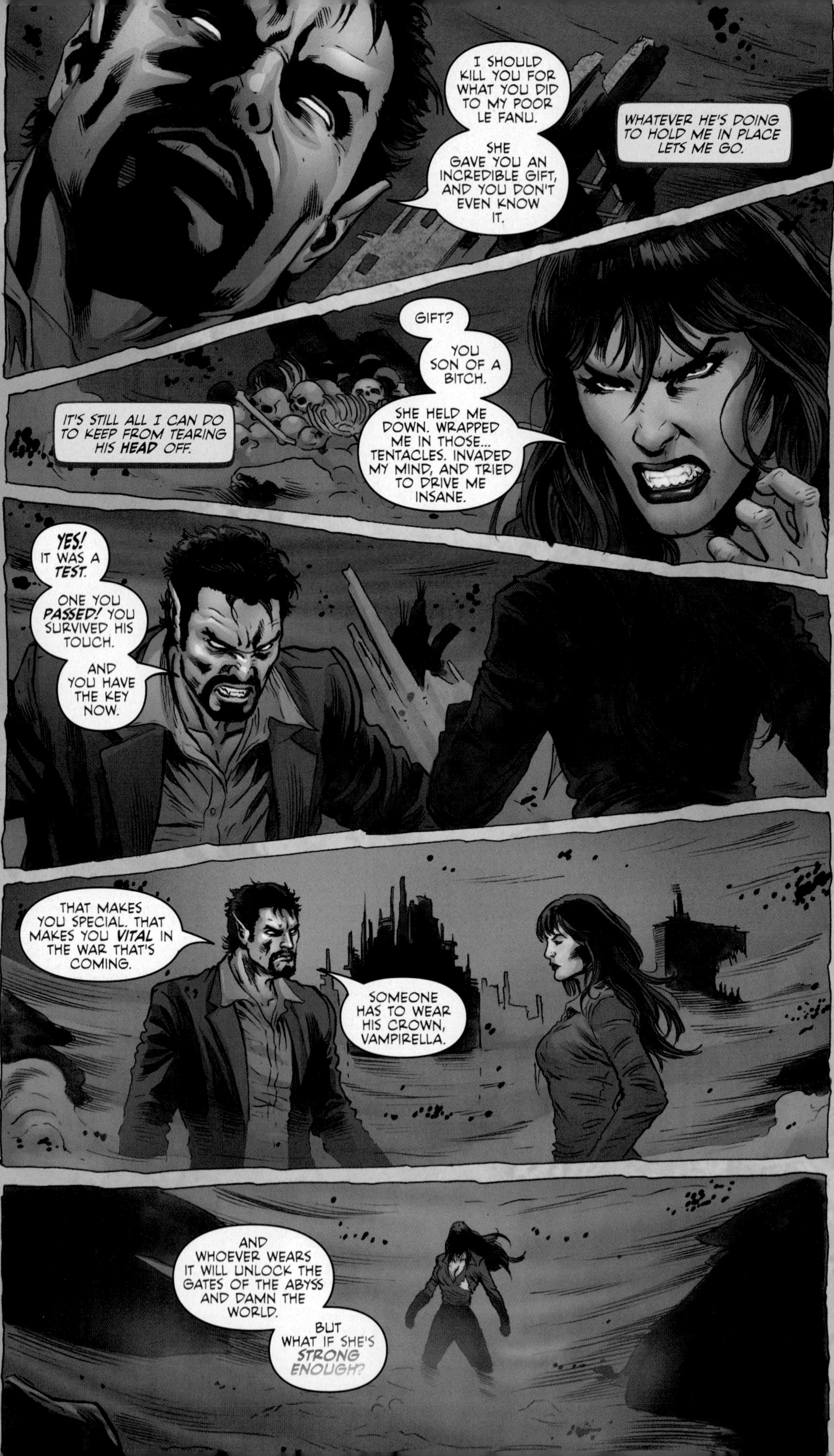
I SHOULD KILL YOU FOR WHAT YOU DID TO MY POOR LE FANU.
SHE GAVE YOU AN INCREDIBLE GIFT, AND YOU DON'T EVEN KNOW IT.
WHATEVER HE'S DOING TO HOLD ME IN PLACE LETS ME GO.
GIFT?
YOU SON OF A BITCH.
SHE HELD ME DOWN. WRAPPED ME IN THOSE... TENTACLES. INVADED MY MIND, AND TRIED TO DRIVE ME INSANE.
IT'S STILL ALL I CAN DO TO KEEP FROM TEARING HIS **HEAD** OFF.
YES! IT WAS A **TEST.**
ONE YOU **PASSED!** YOU SURVIVED HIS TOUCH.
AND YOU HAVE THE KEY NOW.
THAT MAKES YOU SPECIAL. THAT MAKES YOU **VITAL** IN THE WAR THAT'S COMING.
SOMEONE HAS TO WEAR HIS CROWN, VAMPIRELLA.
AND WHOEVER WEARS IT WILL UNLOCK THE GATES OF THE ABYSS AND DAMN THE WORLD.
BUT WHAT IF SHE'S **STRONG ENOUGH?**

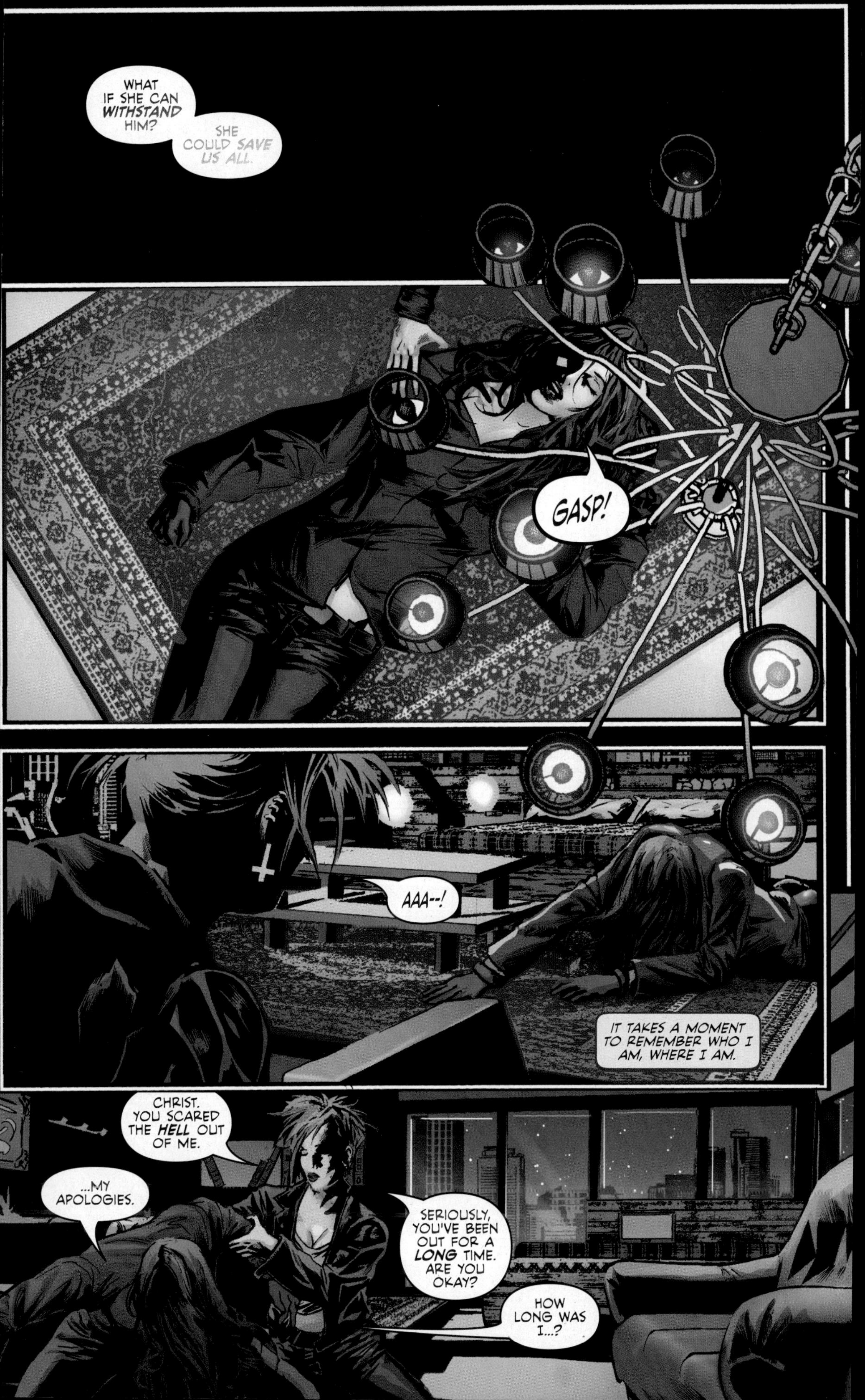
WHAT IF SHE CAN WITHSTAND HIM?
SHE COULD SAVE US ALL.
GASP!
AAA--!
IT TAKES A MOMENT TO REMEMBER WHO I AM, WHERE I AM.
CHRIST. YOU SCARED THE HELL OUT OF ME.
...MY APOLOGIES.
SERIOUSLY, YOU'VE BEEN OUT FOR A LONG TIME. ARE YOU OKAY?
HOW LONG WAS I...?

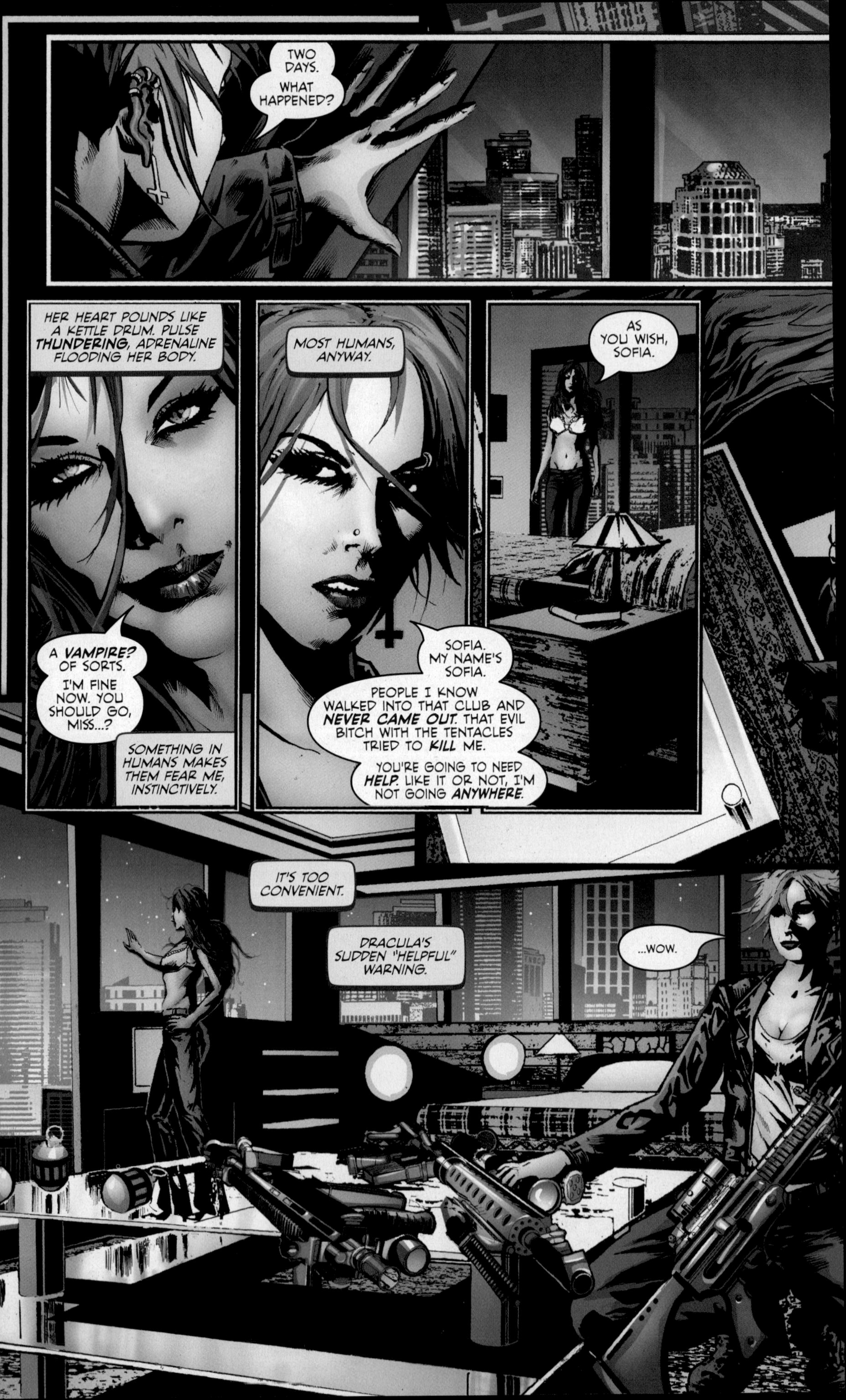
TWO DAYS.
WHAT HAPPENED?
HER HEART POUNDS LIKE A KETTLE DRUM. PULSE THUNDERING, ADRENALINE FLOODING HER BODY.
A VAMPIRE? OF SORTS.
I'M FINE NOW. YOU SHOULD GO, MISS...?
SOMETHING IN HUMANS MAKES THEM FEAR ME, INSTINCTIVELY.
MOST HUMANS, ANYWAY.
SOFIA. MY NAME'S SOFIA.
PEOPLE I KNOW WALKED INTO THAT CLUB AND NEVER CAME OUT. THAT EVIL BITCH WITH THE TENTACLES TRIED TO KILL ME.
YOU'RE GOING TO NEED HELP. LIKE IT OR NOT, I'M NOT GOING ANYWHERE.
AS YOU WISH, SOFIA.
IT'S TOO CONVENIENT.
DRACULA'S SUDDEN "HELPFUL" WARNING.
...WOW.

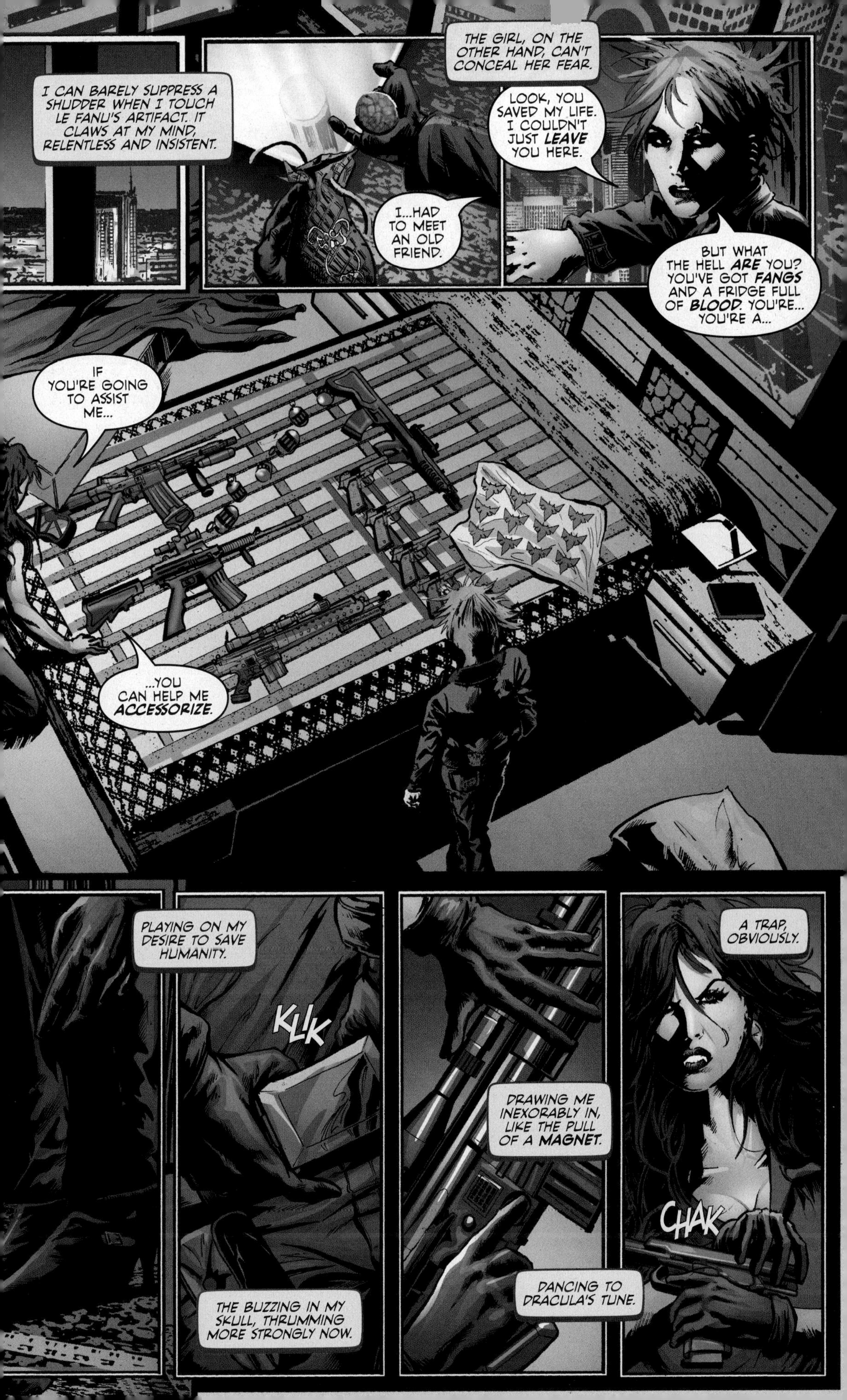
I CAN BARELY SUPPRESS A SHUDDER WHEN I TOUCH LE FANU'S ARTIFACT. IT CLAWS AT MY MIND, RELENTLESS AND INSISTENT.
THE GIRL, ON THE OTHER HAND, CAN'T CONCEAL HER FEAR.
LOOK, YOU SAVED MY LIFE. I COULDN'T JUST LEAVE YOU HERE.
I...HAD TO MEET AN OLD FRIEND.
BUT WHAT THE HELL ARE YOU? YOU'VE GOT FANGS AND A FRIDGE FULL OF BLOOD. YOU'RE... YOU'RE A...
IF YOU'RE GOING TO ASSIST ME...
...YOU CAN HELP ME ACCESSORIZE.
PLAYING ON MY DESIRE TO SAVE HUMANITY.
KLIK
THE BUZZING IN MY SKULL, THRUMMING MORE STRONGLY NOW.
DRAWING ME INEXORABLY IN, LIKE THE PULL OF A MAGNET.
DANCING TO DRACULA'S TUNE.
A TRAP, OBVIOUSLY.
CHAK

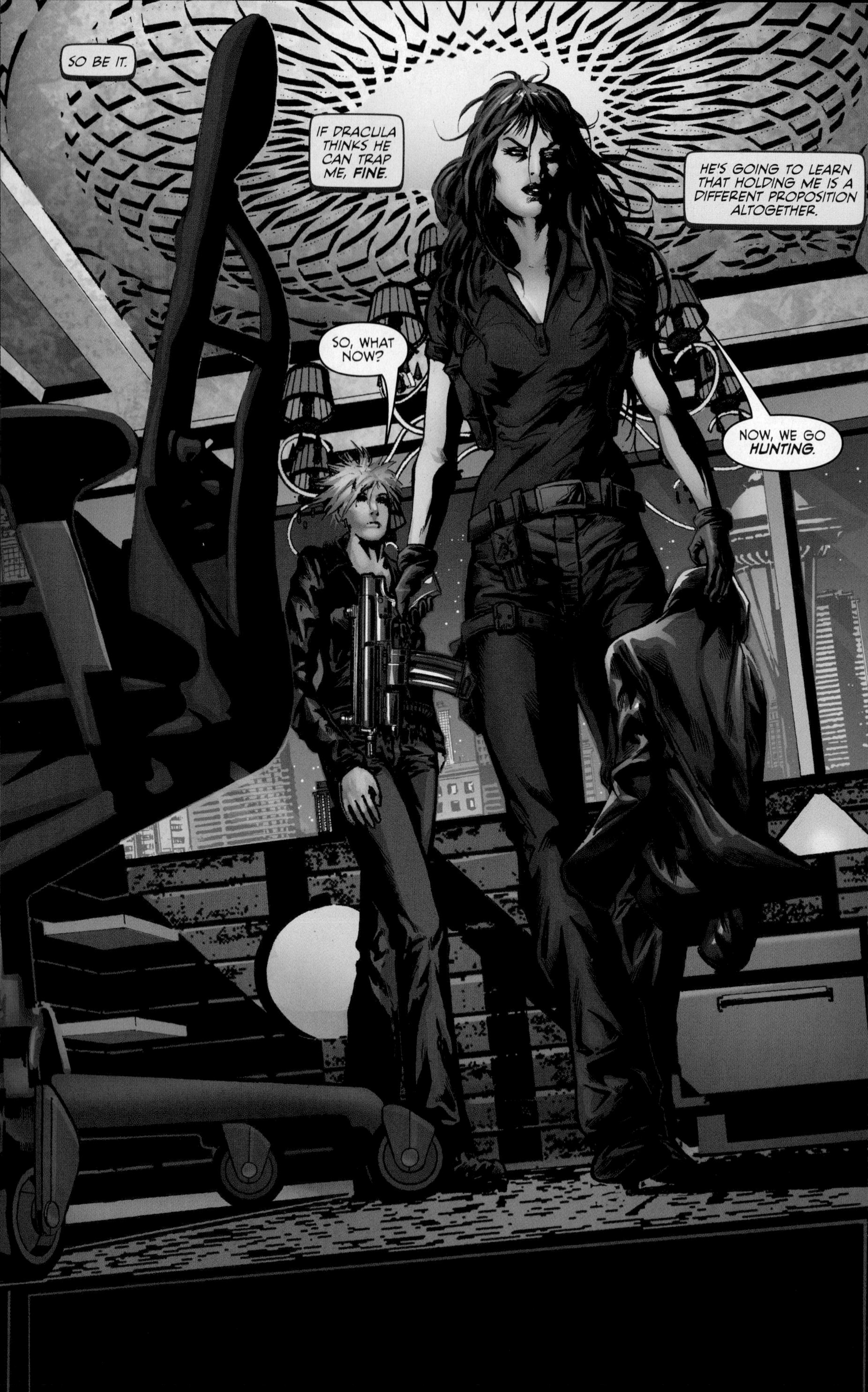
SO BE IT.
IF DRACULA THINKS HE CAN TRAP ME, FINE.
HE'S GOING TO LEARN THAT HOLDING ME IS A DIFFERENT PROPOSITION ALTOGETHER.
SO, WHAT NOW?
NOW, WE GO HUNTING.

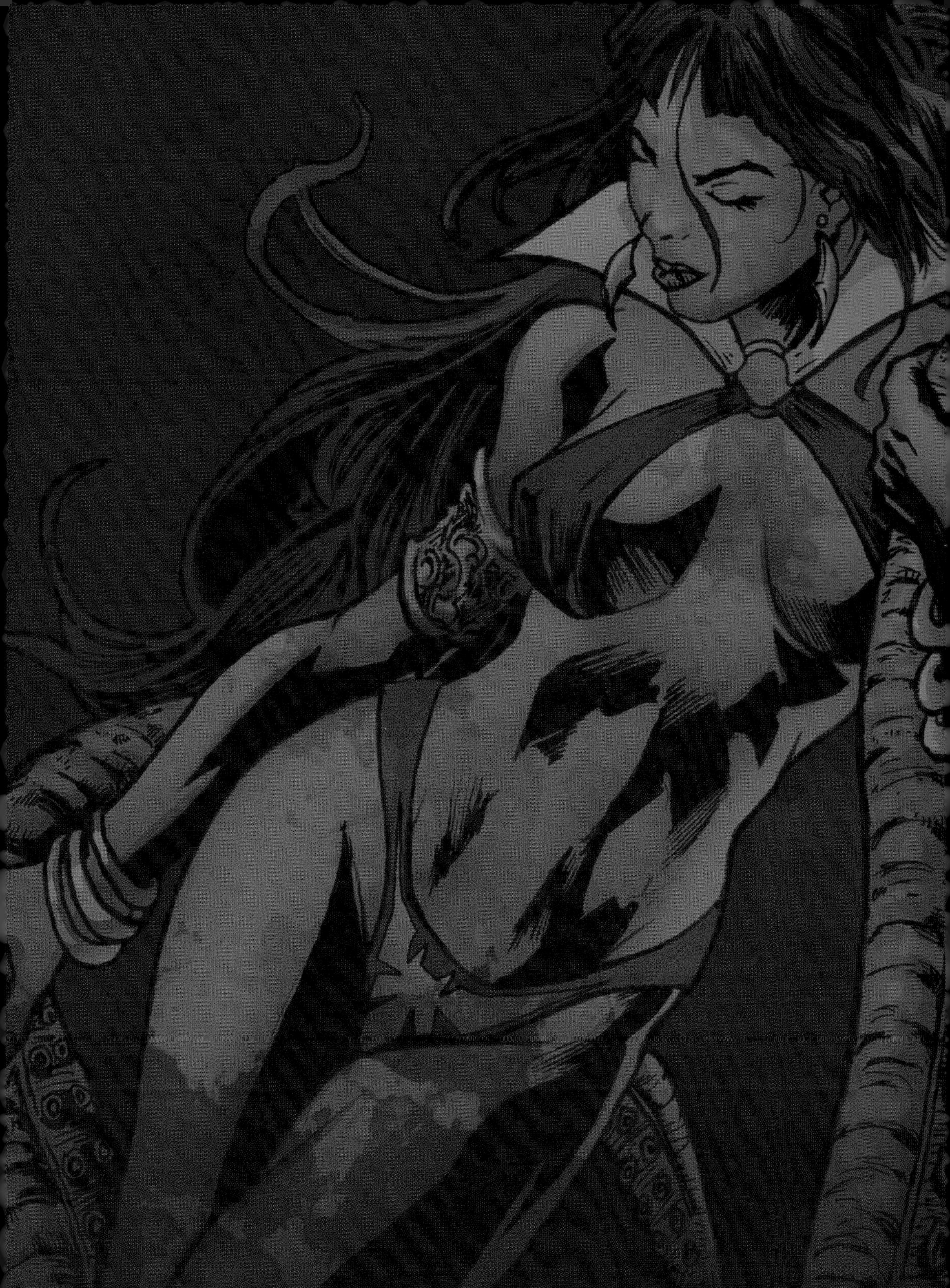

CROWN OF WORMS

DOWN IN THE GROUND WITH DEAD THINGS

4

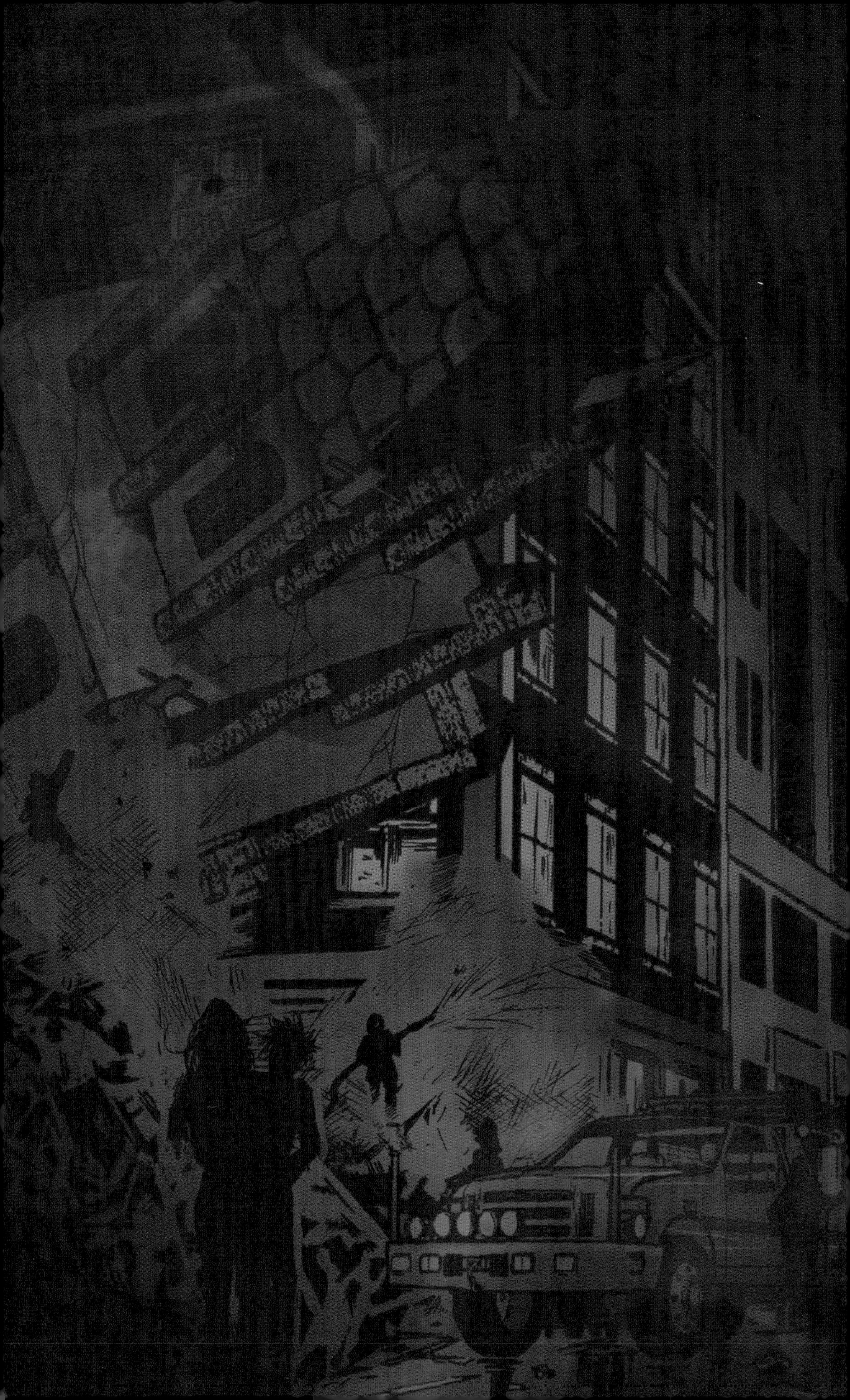

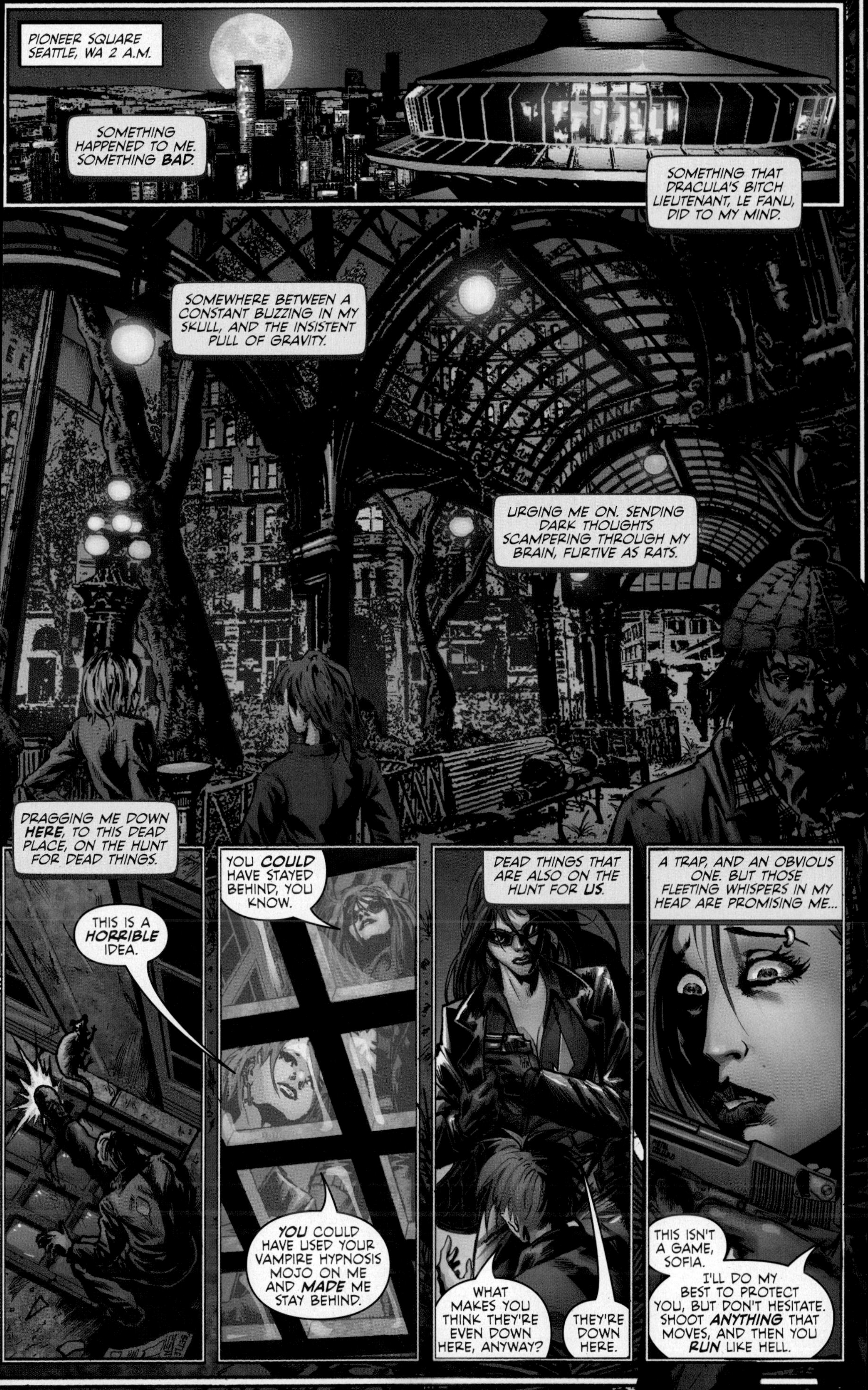
PIONEER SQUARE SEATTLE, WA 2 A.M.
SOMETHING HAPPENED TO ME. SOMETHING BAD.
SOMETHING THAT DRACULA'S BITCH LIEUTENANT, LE FANU, DID TO MY MIND.
SOMEWHERE BETWEEN A CONSTANT BUZZING IN MY SKULL, AND THE INSISTENT PULL OF GRAVITY.
URGING ME ON. SENDING DARK THOUGHTS SCAMPERING THROUGH MY BRAIN, FURTIVE AS RATS.
DRAGGING ME DOWN HERE, TO THIS DEAD PLACE, ON THE HUNT FOR DEAD THINGS.
THIS IS A HORRIBLE IDEA.
YOU COULD HAVE STAYED BEHIND, YOU KNOW.
YOU COULD HAVE USED YOUR VAMPIRE HYPNOSIS MOJO ON ME AND MADE ME STAY BEHIND.
DEAD THINGS THAT ARE ALSO ON THE HUNT FOR US.
WHAT MAKES YOU THINK THEY'RE EVEN DOWN HERE, ANYWAY?
THEY'RE DOWN HERE.
A TRAP, AND AN OBVIOUS ONE. BUT THOSE FLEETING WHISPERS IN MY HEAD ARE PROMISING ME...
THIS ISN'T A GAME, SOFIA.
I'LL DO MY BEST TO PROTECT YOU, BUT DON'T HESITATE. SHOOT ANYTHING THAT MOVES, AND THEN YOU RUN LIKE HELL.

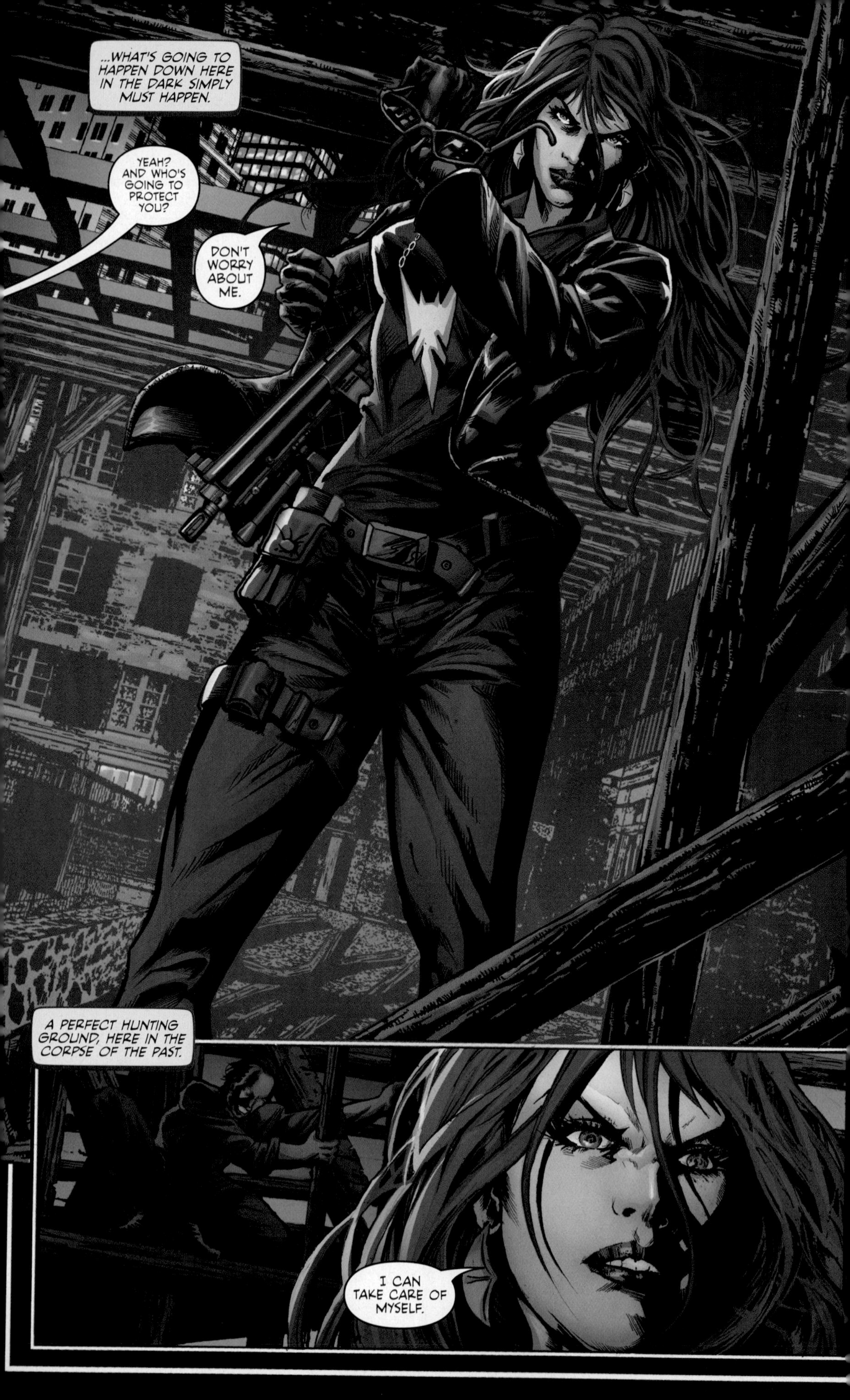
...WHAT'S GOING TO HAPPEN DOWN HERE IN THE DARK SIMPLY MUST HAPPEN.
YEAH? AND WHO'S GOING TO PROTECT YOU?
DON'T WORRY ABOUT ME.
A PERFECT HUNTING GROUND, HERE IN THE CORPSE OF THE PAST.
I CAN TAKE CARE OF MYSELF.

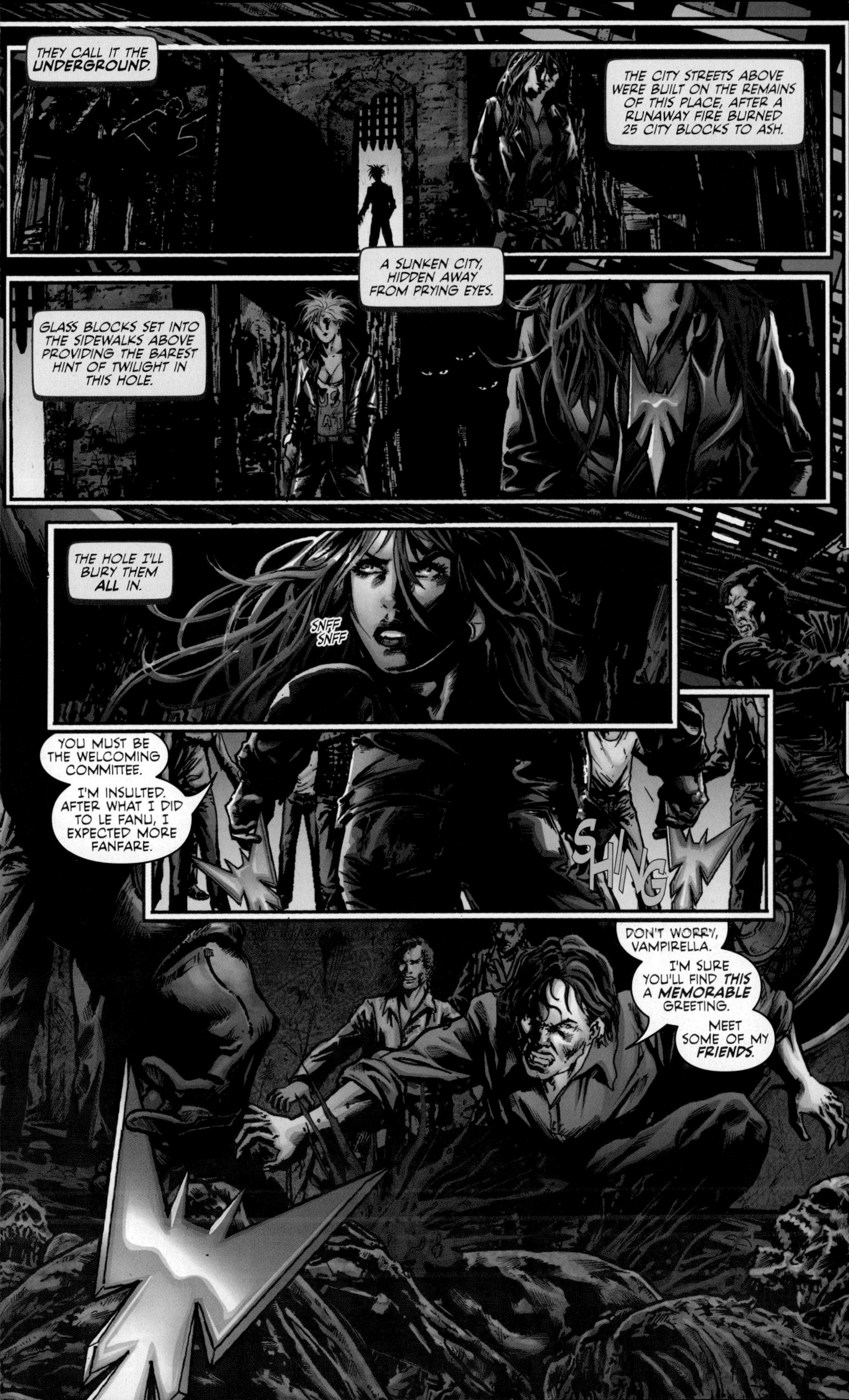
THEY CALL IT THE UNDERGROUND.
THE CITY STREETS ABOVE WERE BUILT ON THE REMAINS OF THIS PLACE, AFTER A RUNAWAY FIRE BURNED 25 CITY BLOCKS TO ASH.
A SUNKEN CITY, HIDDEN AWAY FROM PRYING EYES.
GLASS BLOCKS SET INTO THE SIDEWALKS ABOVE PROVIDING THE BAREST HINT OF TWILIGHT IN THIS HOLE.
THE HOLE I'LL BURY THEM ALL IN.
SNFF SNFF
YOU MUST BE THE WELCOMING COMMITTEE.
I'M INSULTED. AFTER WHAT I DID TO LE FANU, I EXPECTED MORE FANFARE.
SHING
DON'T WORRY, VAMPIRELLA.
I'M SURE YOU'LL FIND THIS A MEMORABLE GREETING.
MEET SOME OF MY FRIENDS.

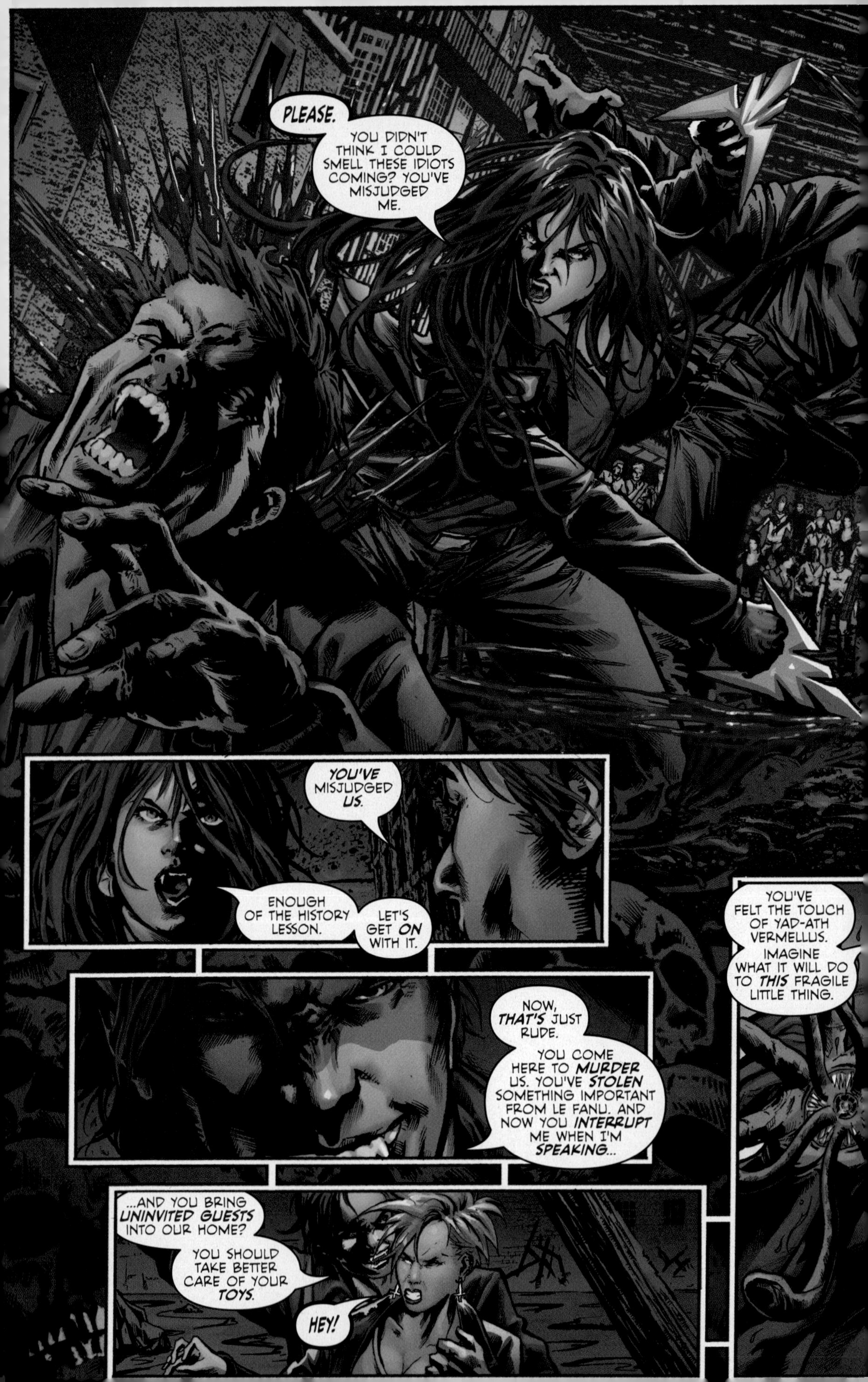
PLEASE.
YOU DIDN'T THINK I COULD SMELL THESE IDIOTS COMING? YOU'VE MISJUDGED ME.
YOU'VE MISJUDGED US.
ENOUGH OF THE HISTORY LESSON.
LET'S GET ON WITH IT.
NOW, THAT'S JUST RUDE.
YOU COME HERE TO MURDER US. YOU'VE STOLEN SOMETHING IMPORTANT FROM LE FANU. AND NOW YOU INTERRUPT ME WHEN I'M SPEAKING...
...AND YOU BRING UNINVITED GUESTS INTO OUR HOME?
YOU SHOULD TAKE BETTER CARE OF YOUR TOYS.
HEY!
YOU'VE FELT THE TOUCH OF YAD-ATH VERMELLUS. IMAGINE WHAT IT WILL DO TO THIS FRAGILE LITTLE THING.

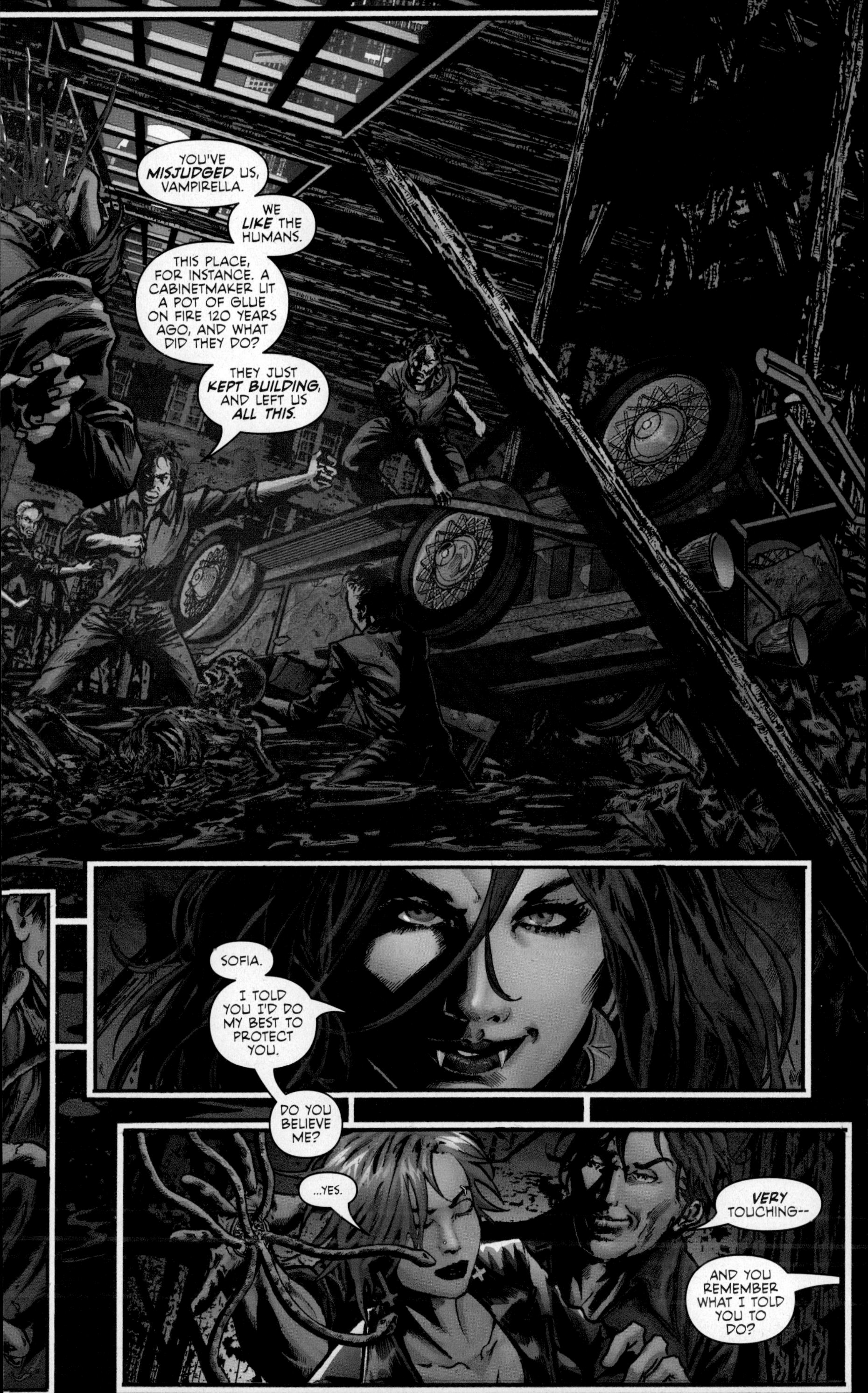
YOU'VE MISJUDGED US, VAMPIRELLA.
WE LIKE THE HUMANS.
THIS PLACE, FOR INSTANCE. A CABINETMAKER LIT A POT OF GLUE ON FIRE 120 YEARS AGO, AND WHAT DID THEY DO?
THEY JUST KEPT BUILDING, AND LEFT US ALL THIS.
SOFIA.
I TOLD YOU I'D DO MY BEST TO PROTECT YOU.
DO YOU BELIEVE ME?
...YES.
VERY TOUCHING--
AND YOU REMEMBER WHAT I TOLD YOU TO DO?

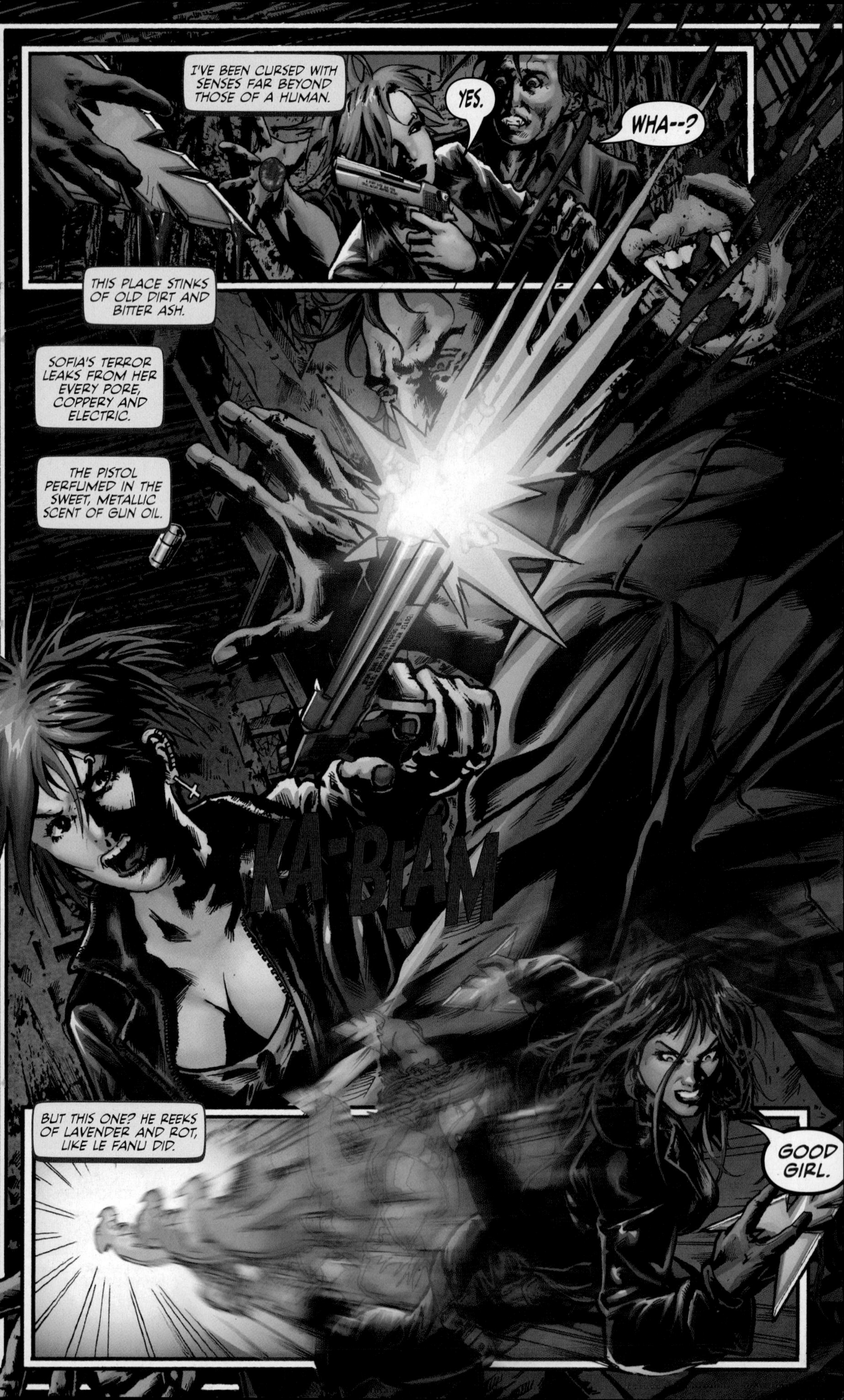

I'VE BEEN CURSED WITH SENSES FAR BEYOND THOSE OF A HUMAN.
YES.
WHA--?
THIS PLACE STINKS OF OLD DIRT AND BITTER ASH.
SOFIA'S TERROR LEAKS FROM HER EVERY PORE, COPPERY AND ELECTRIC.
THE PISTOL PERFUMED IN THE SWEET, METALLIC SCENT OF GUN OIL.
KA-BLAM
BUT THIS ONE? HE REEKS OF LAVENDER AND ROT, LIKE LE FANU DID.
GOOD GIRL.

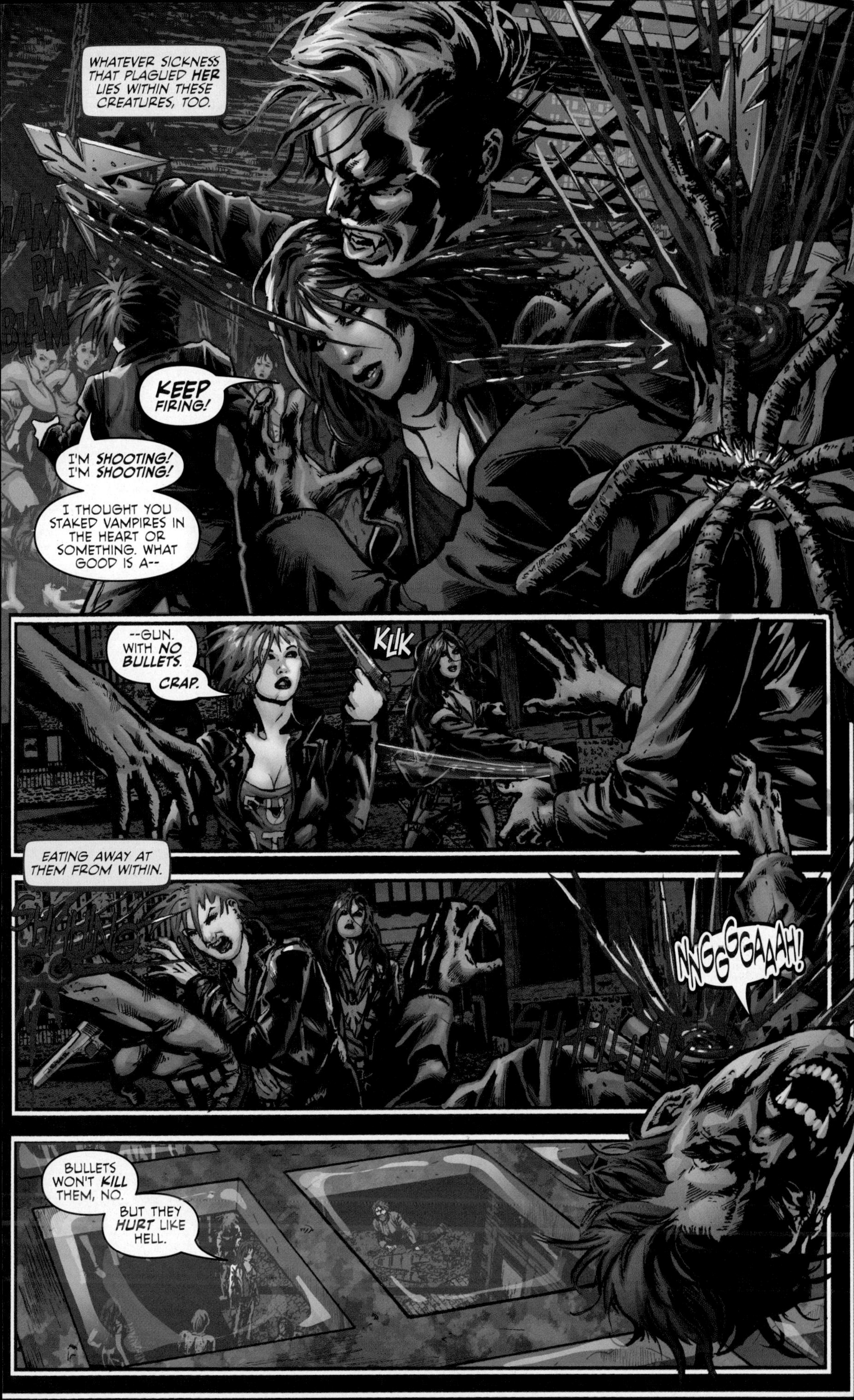
WHATEVER SICKNESS THAT PLAGUED HER LIES WITHIN THESE CREATURES, TOO.
BLAM BLAM BLAM
KEEP FIRING!
I'M SHOOTING! I'M SHOOTING!
I THOUGHT YOU STAKED VAMPIRES IN THE HEART OR SOMETHING. WHAT GOOD IS A--
--GUN. WITH NO BULLETS.
CRAP.
KLIK
EATING AWAY AT THEM FROM WITHIN.
NNGGGGAAAH!
SHHLUNK
BULLETS WON'T KILL THEM, NO.
BUT THEY HURT LIKE HELL.

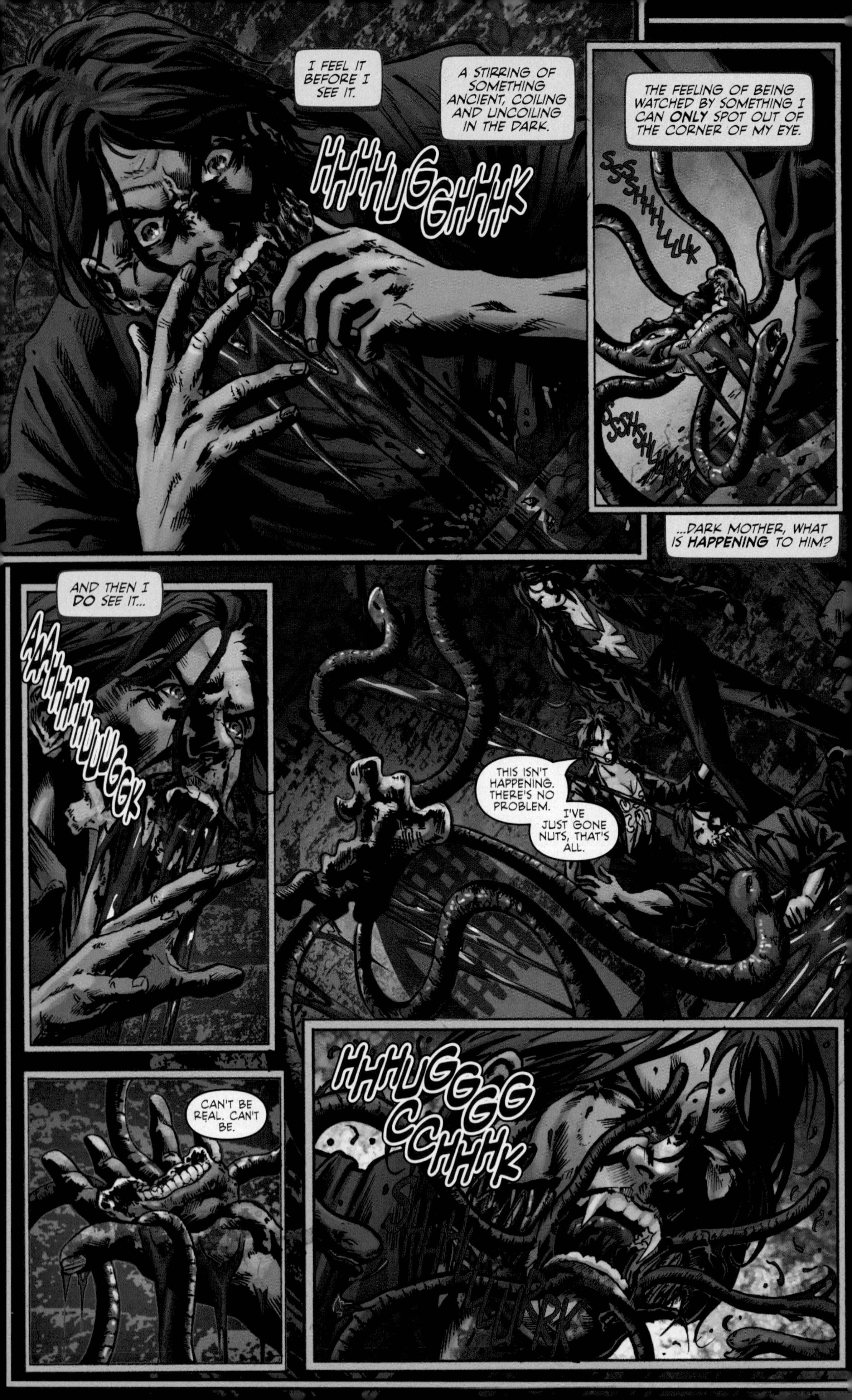

I FEEL IT BEFORE I SEE IT.
A STIRRING OF SOMETHING ANCIENT, COILING AND UNCOILING IN THE DARK.
HHHHUGGHHHK
THE FEELING OF BEING WATCHED BY SOMETHING I CAN ONLY SPOT OUT OF THE CORNER OF MY EYE.
SSSSHHHLLUUK
SSSSHSHLLKKRK
...DARK MOTHER, WHAT IS HAPPENING TO HIM?
AND THEN I DO SEE IT...
AAAHHHHUUUGGK
THIS ISN'T HAPPENING. THERE'S NO PROBLEM.
I'VE JUST GONE NUTS, THAT'S ALL.
CAN'T BE REAL. CAN'T BE.
HHHUGGGGG CCHHHK

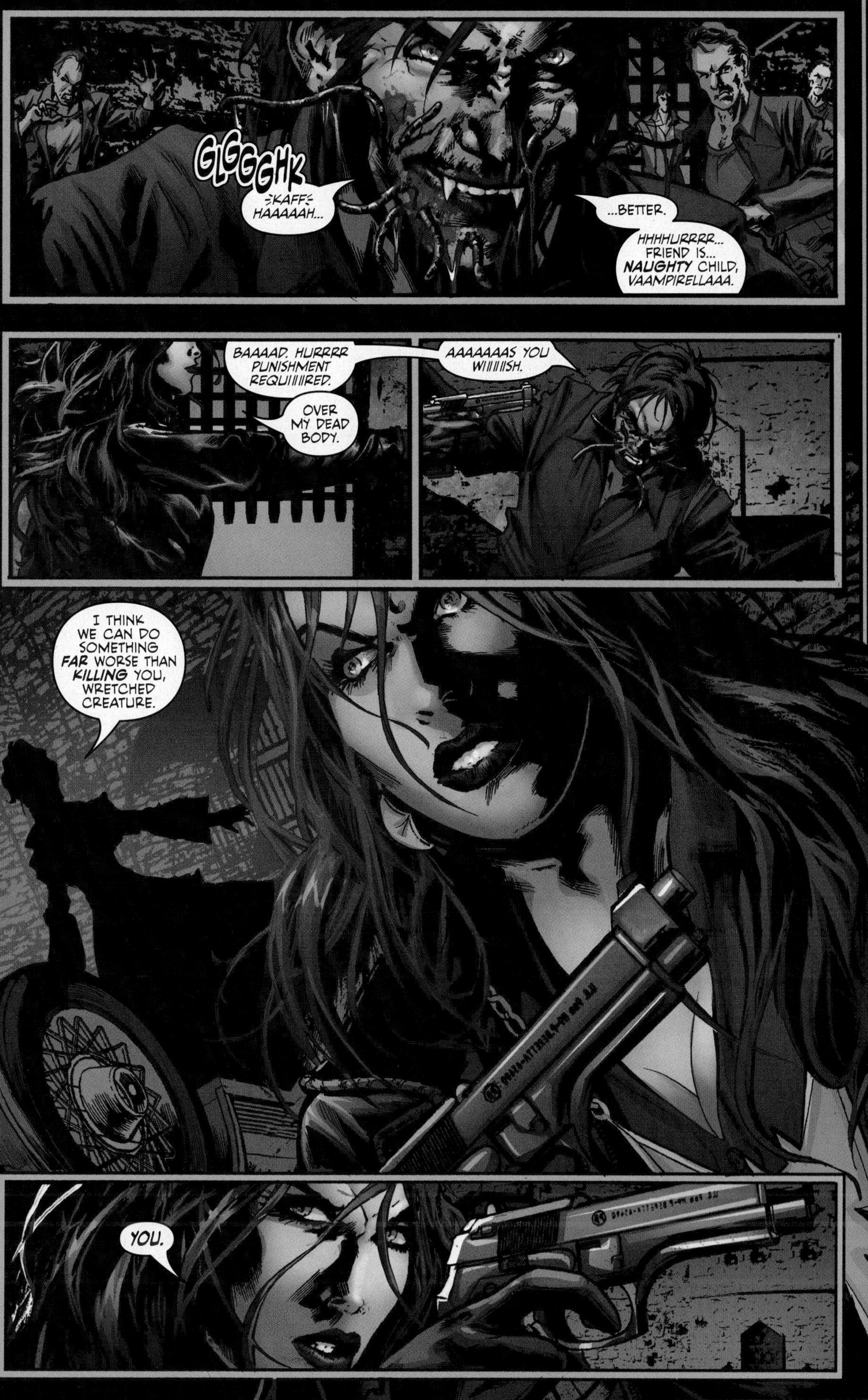
GLGGGHK
=KAFF= HAAAAAH...
...BETTER.
HHHHURRRR... FRIEND IS... NAUGHTY CHILD, VAAMPIRELLAAA.
BAAAAD. HURRRR PUNISHMENT REQUIIIIIRED.
OVER MY DEAD BODY.
AAAAAAAS YOU WIIIIIISH.
I THINK WE CAN DO SOMETHING FAR WORSE THAN KILLING YOU, WRETCHED CREATURE.
YOU.

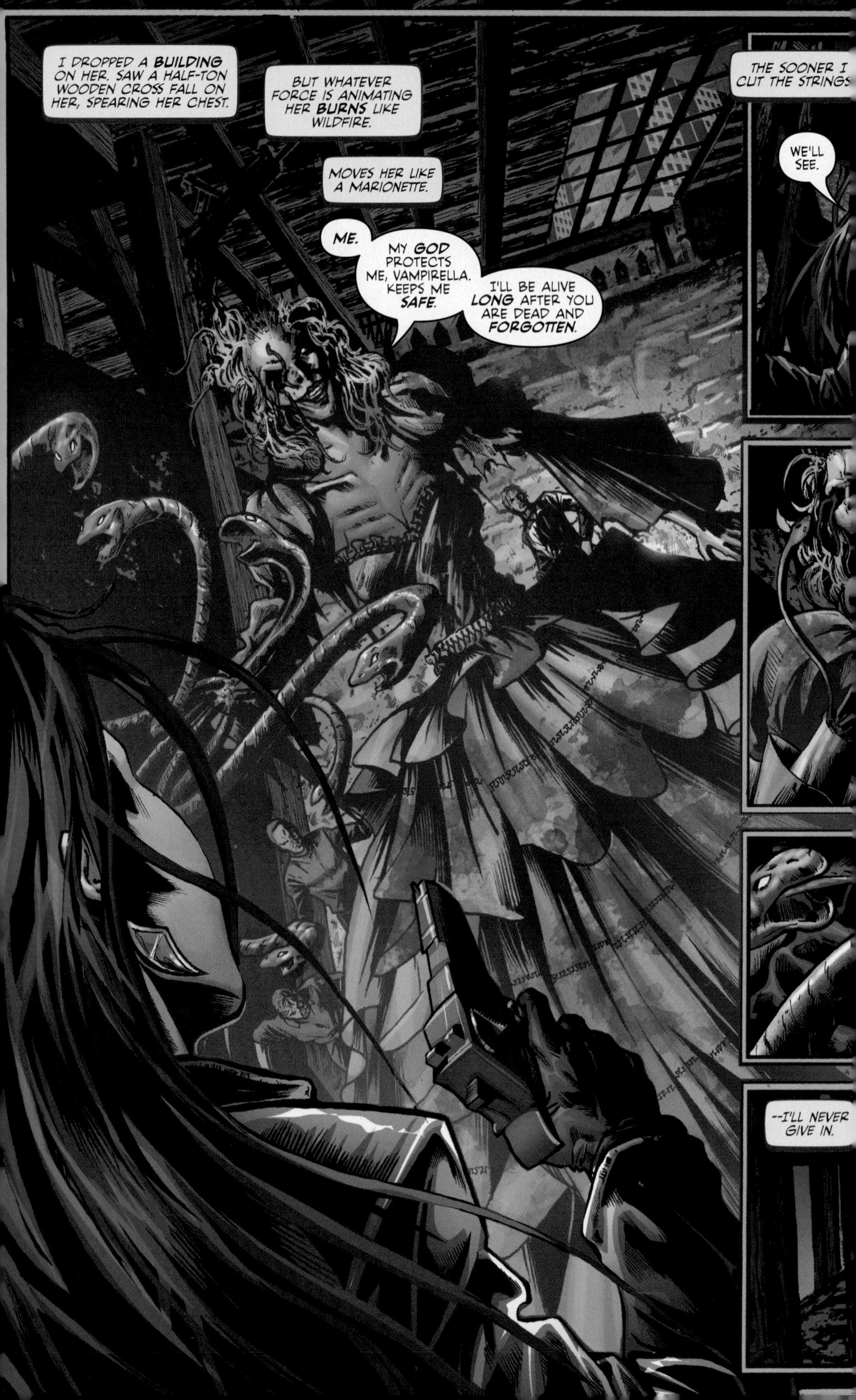
I DROPPED A BUILDING ON HER. SAW A HALF-TON WOODEN CROSS FALL ON HER, SPEARING HER CHEST.
BUT WHATEVER FORCE IS ANIMATING HER BURNS LIKE WILDFIRE.
MOVES HER LIKE A MARIONETTE.
ME.
MY GOD PROTECTS ME, VAMPIRELLA. KEEPS ME SAFE.
I'LL BE ALIVE LONG AFTER YOU ARE DEAD AND FORGOTTEN.
THE SOONER I CUT THE STRINGS
WE'LL SEE.
--I'LL NEVER GIVE IN.

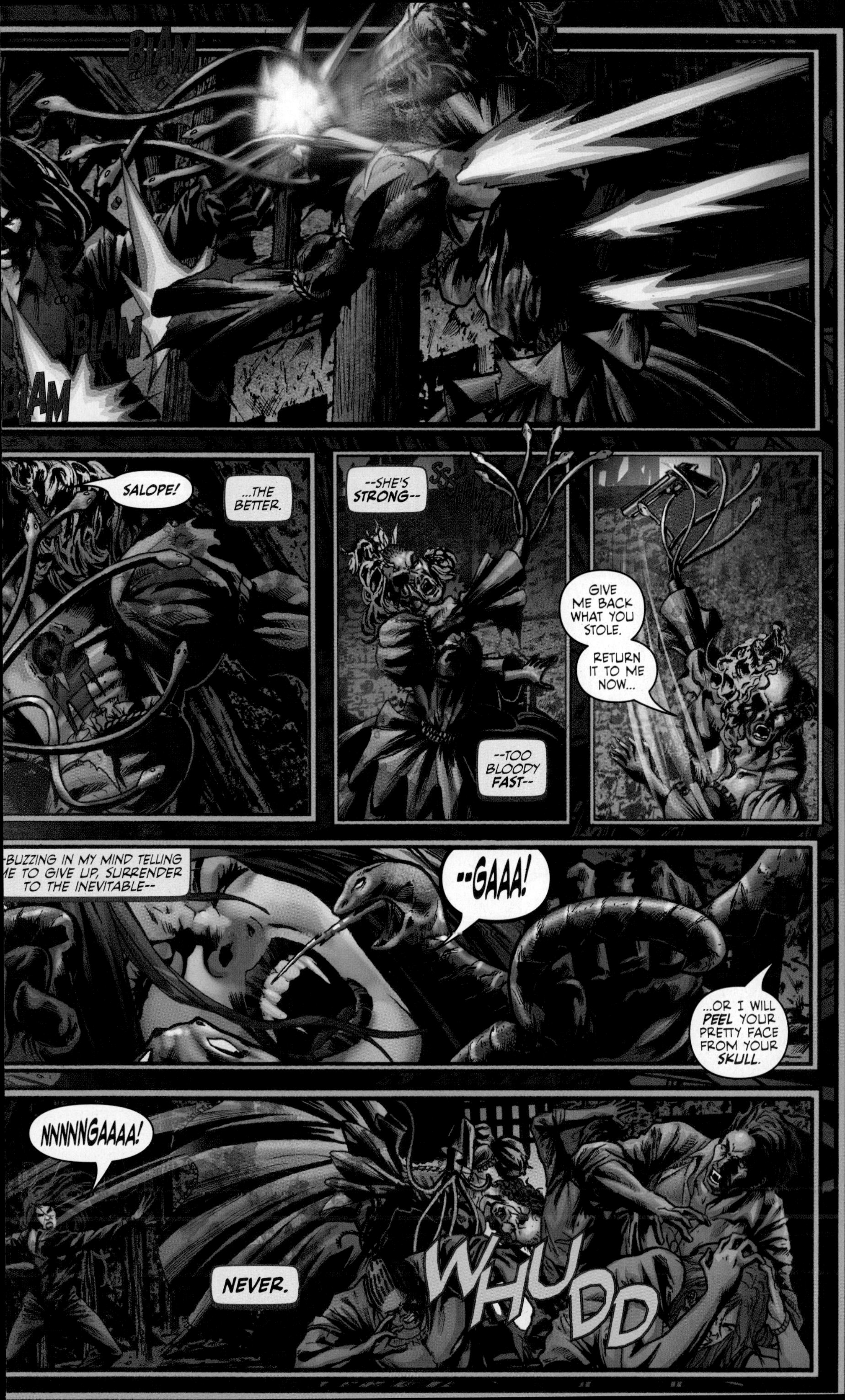
BLAM
BLAM
BLAM
SALOPE!
...THE BETTER.
--SHE'S STRONG--
--TOO BLOODY FAST--
GIVE ME BACK WHAT YOU STOLE.
RETURN IT TO ME NOW...
-BUZZING IN MY MIND TELLING ME TO GIVE UP, SURRENDER TO THE INEVITABLE--
--GAAA!
...OR I WILL PEEL YOUR PRETTY FACE FROM YOUR SKULL.
NNNNNGAAAA!
NEVER.
WHUDD

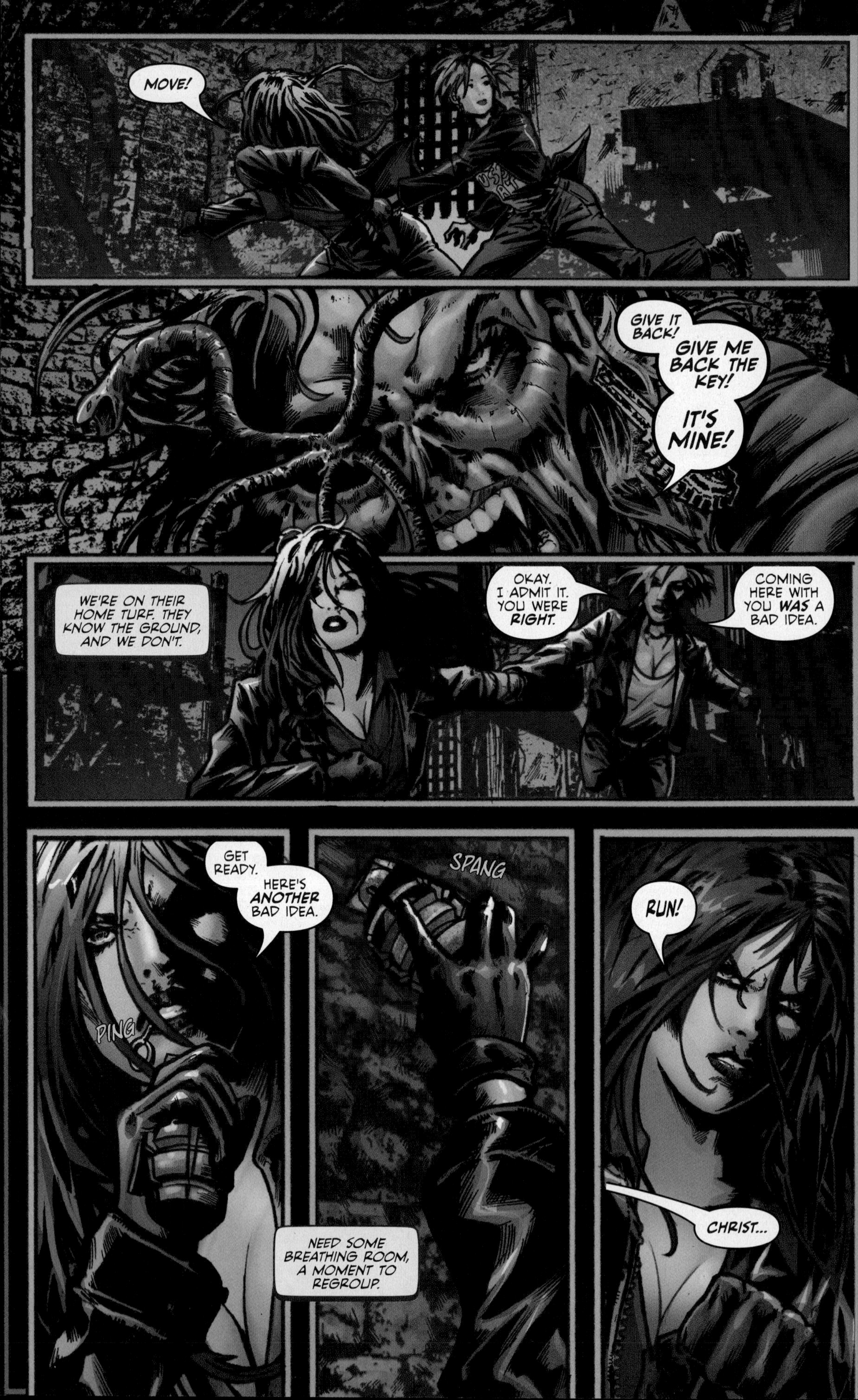
MOVE!
GIVE IT BACK!
GIVE ME BACK THE KEY!
IT'S MINE!
WE'RE ON THEIR HOME TURF. THEY KNOW THE GROUND, AND WE DON'T.
OKAY. I ADMIT IT. YOU WERE RIGHT.
COMING HERE WITH YOU WAS A BAD IDEA.
GET READY.
HERE'S ANOTHER BAD IDEA.
PING
SPANG
NEED SOME BREATHING ROOM, A MOMENT TO REGROUP.
RUN!
CHRIST...

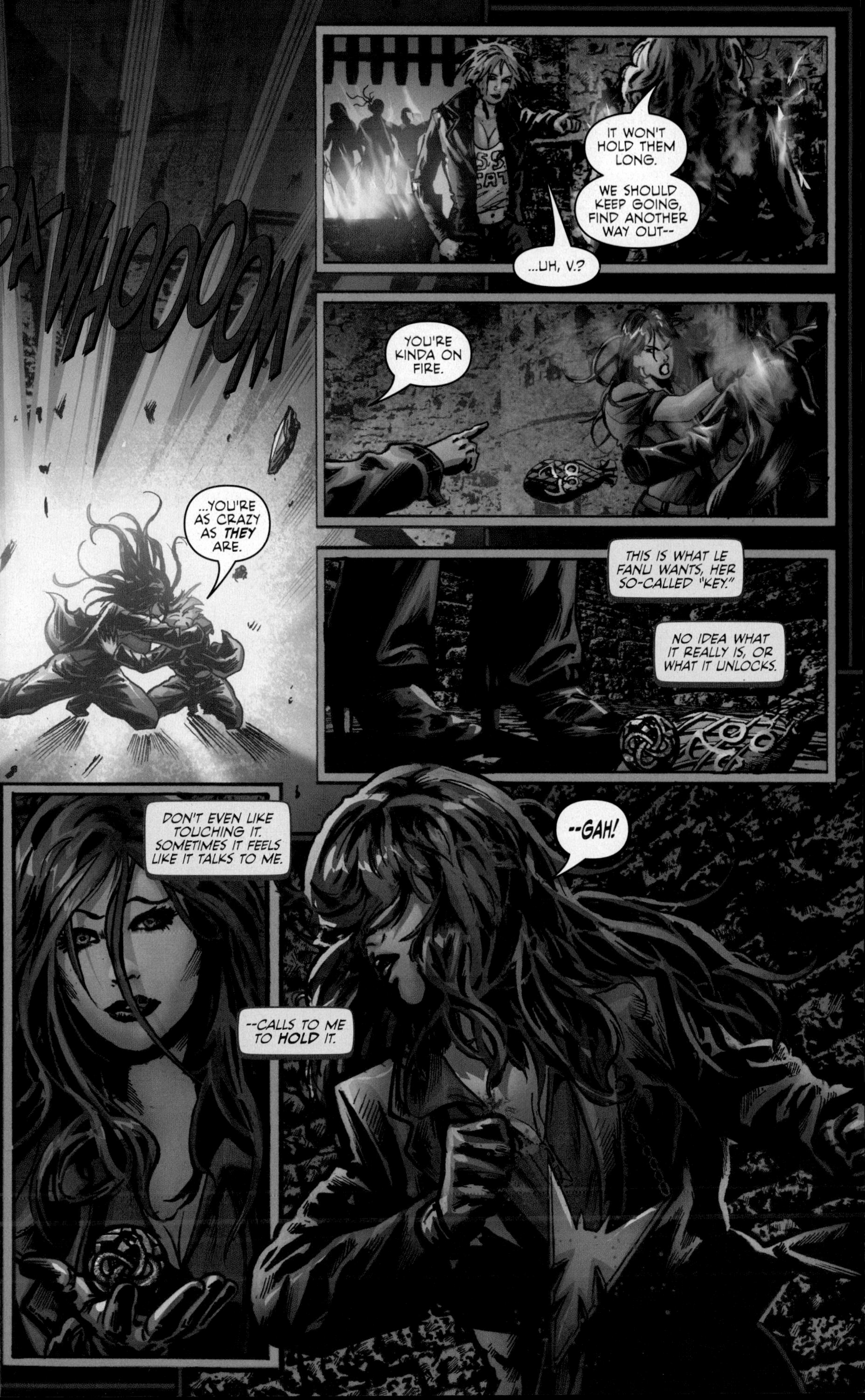
BA-WHOOOOM
IT WON'T HOLD THEM LONG.
WE SHOULD KEEP GOING, FIND ANOTHER WAY OUT--
...UH, V.?
YOU'RE KINDA ON FIRE.
...YOU'RE AS CRAZY AS THEY ARE.
THIS IS WHAT LE FANU WANTS, HER SO-CALLED "KEY."
NO IDEA WHAT IT REALLY IS, OR WHAT IT UNLOCKS.
DON'T EVEN LIKE TOUCHING IT. SOMETIMES IT FEELS LIKE IT TALKS TO ME.
--CALLS TO ME TO HOLD IT.
--GAH!

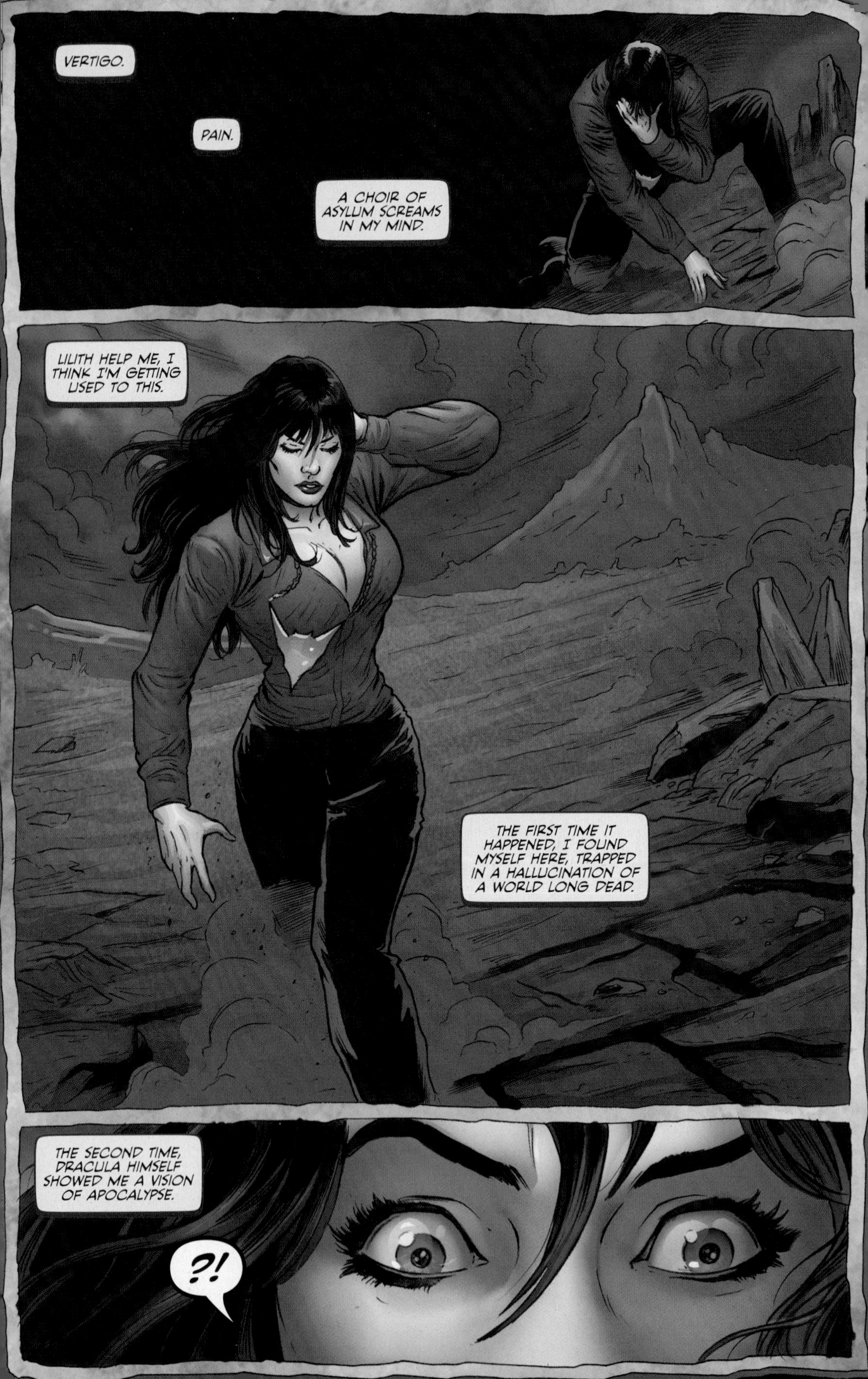
VERTIGO.
PAIN.
A CHOIR OF ASYLUM SCREAMS IN MY MIND.
LILITH HELP ME, I THINK I'M GETTING USED TO THIS.
THE FIRST TIME IT HAPPENED, I FOUND MYSELF HERE, TRAPPED IN A HALLUCINATION OF A WORLD LONG DEAD.
THE SECOND TIME, DRACULA HIMSELF SHOWED ME A VISION OF APOCALYPSE.
?!

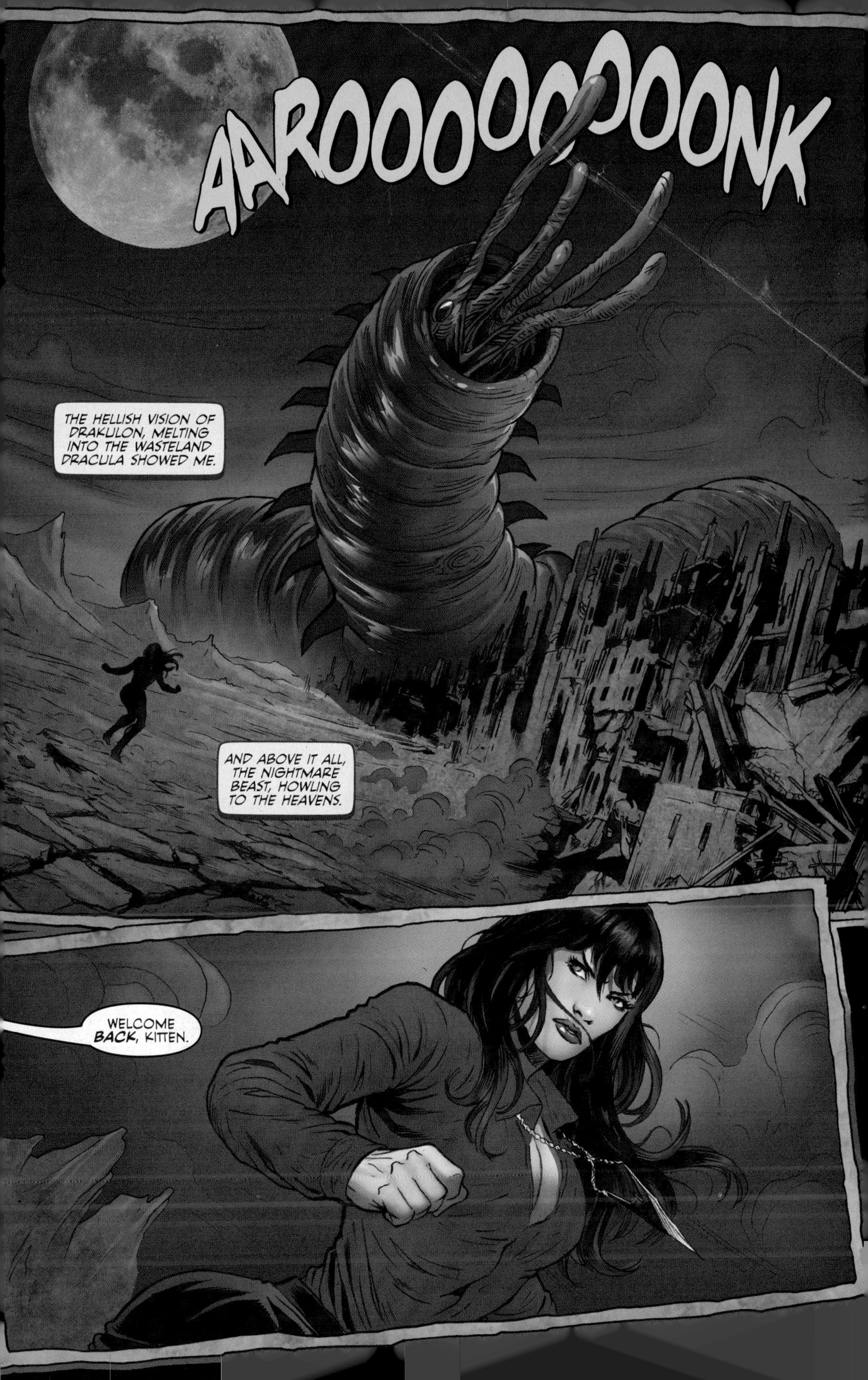
AAROOOOOOOONK
THE HELLISH VISION OF DRAKULON, MELTING INTO THE WASTELAND DRACULA SHOWED ME.
AND ABOVE IT ALL, THE NIGHTMARE BEAST, HOWLING TO THE HEAVENS.
WELCOME BACK, KITTEN.

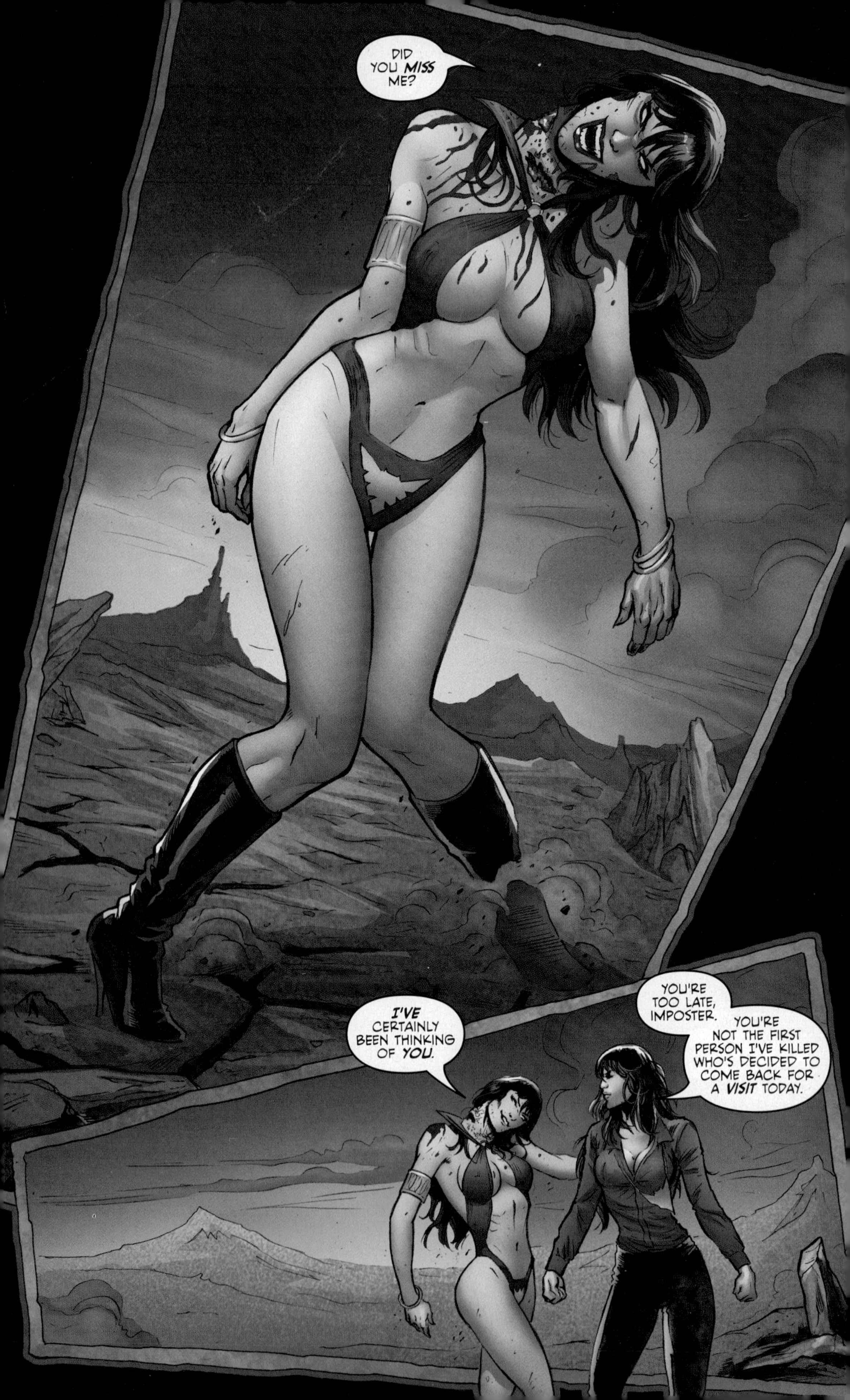
DID YOU MISS ME?
I'VE CERTAINLY BEEN THINKING OF YOU.
YOU'RE TOO LATE, IMPOSTER.
YOU'RE NOT THE FIRST PERSON I'VE KILLED WHO'S DECIDED TO COME BACK FOR A VISIT TODAY.

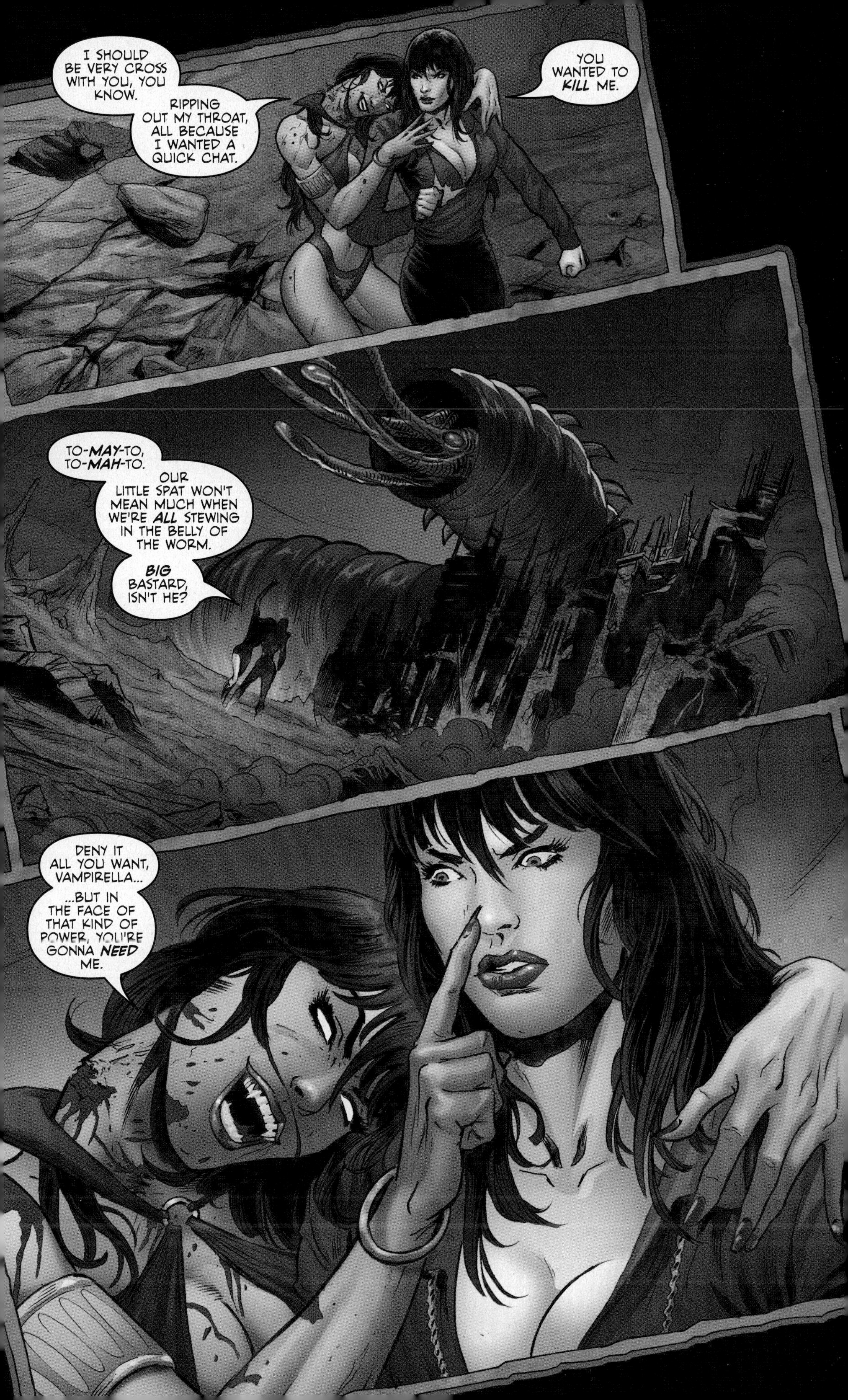
I SHOULD BE VERY CROSS WITH YOU, YOU KNOW.
RIPPING OUT MY THROAT, ALL BECAUSE I WANTED A QUICK CHAT.
YOU WANTED TO KILL ME.
TO-MAY-TO, TO-MAH-TO.
OUR LITTLE SPAT WON'T MEAN MUCH WHEN WE'RE ALL STEWING IN THE BELLY OF THE WORM.
BIG BASTARD, ISN'T HE?
DENY IT ALL YOU WANT, VAMPIRELLA...
...BUT IN THE FACE OF THAT KIND OF POWER, YOU'RE GONNA NEED ME.

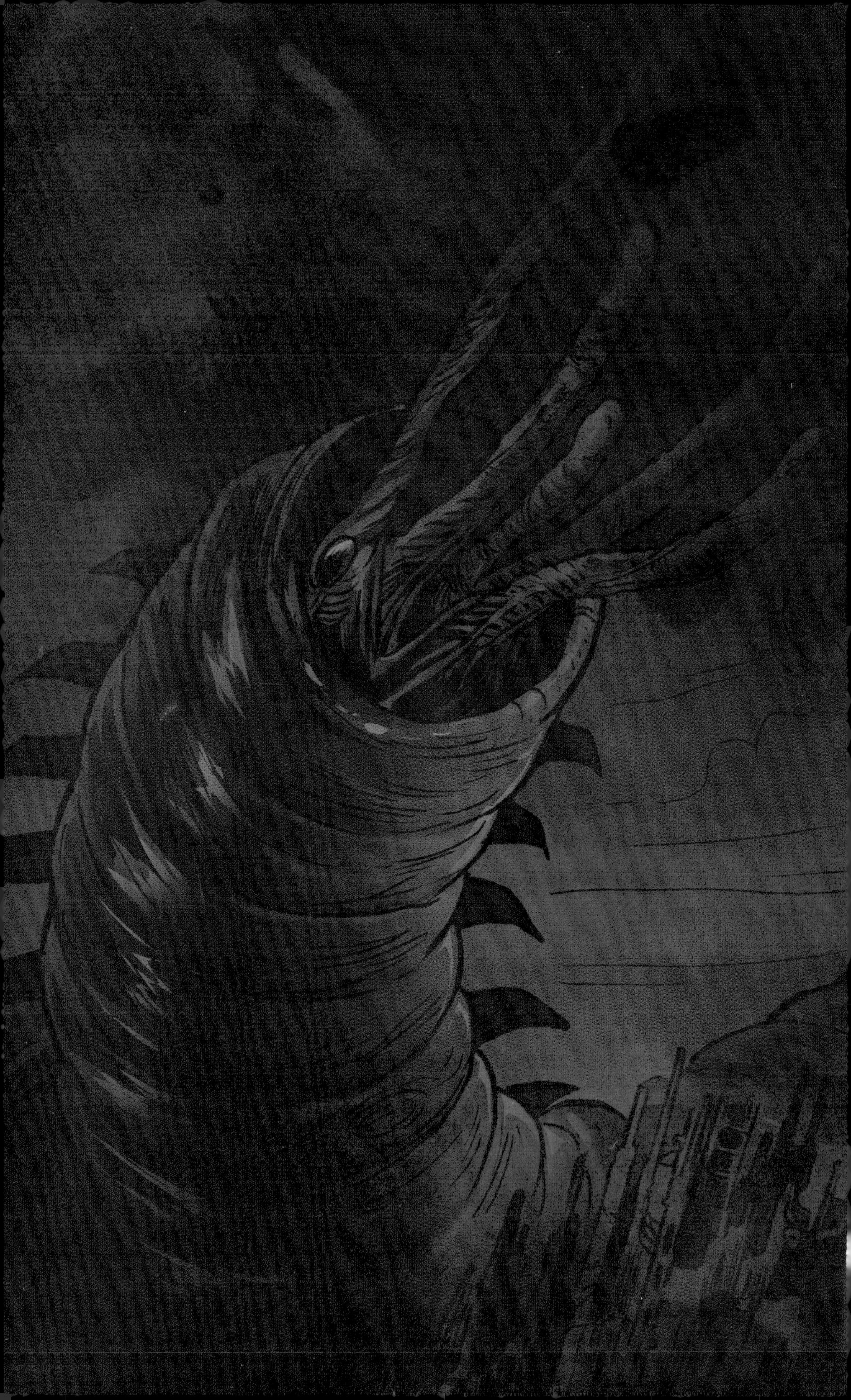

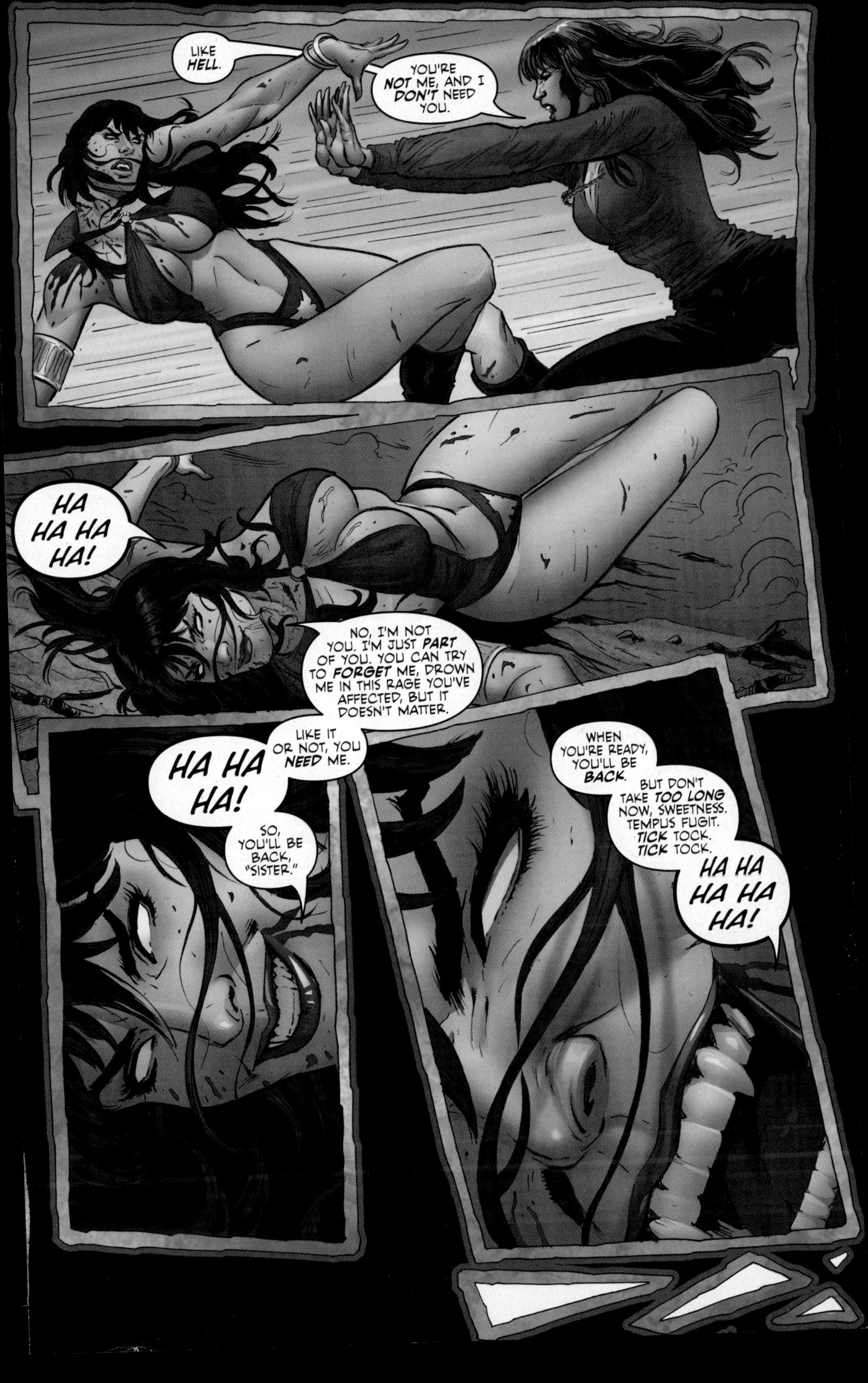
LIKE HELL.
YOU'RE NOT ME, AND I DON'T NEED YOU.
HA HA HA HA!
NO, I'M NOT YOU. I'M JUST PART OF YOU. YOU CAN TRY TO FORGET ME, DROWN ME IN THIS RAGE YOU'VE AFFECTED, BUT IT DOESN'T MATTER.
LIKE IT OR NOT, YOU NEED ME.
HA HA HA!
SO, YOU'LL BE BACK, "SISTER."
WHEN YOU'RE READY, YOU'LL BE BACK.
BUT DON'T TAKE TOO LONG NOW, SWEETNESS. TEMPUS FUGIT. TICK TOCK. TICK TOCK.
HA HA HA HA HA!

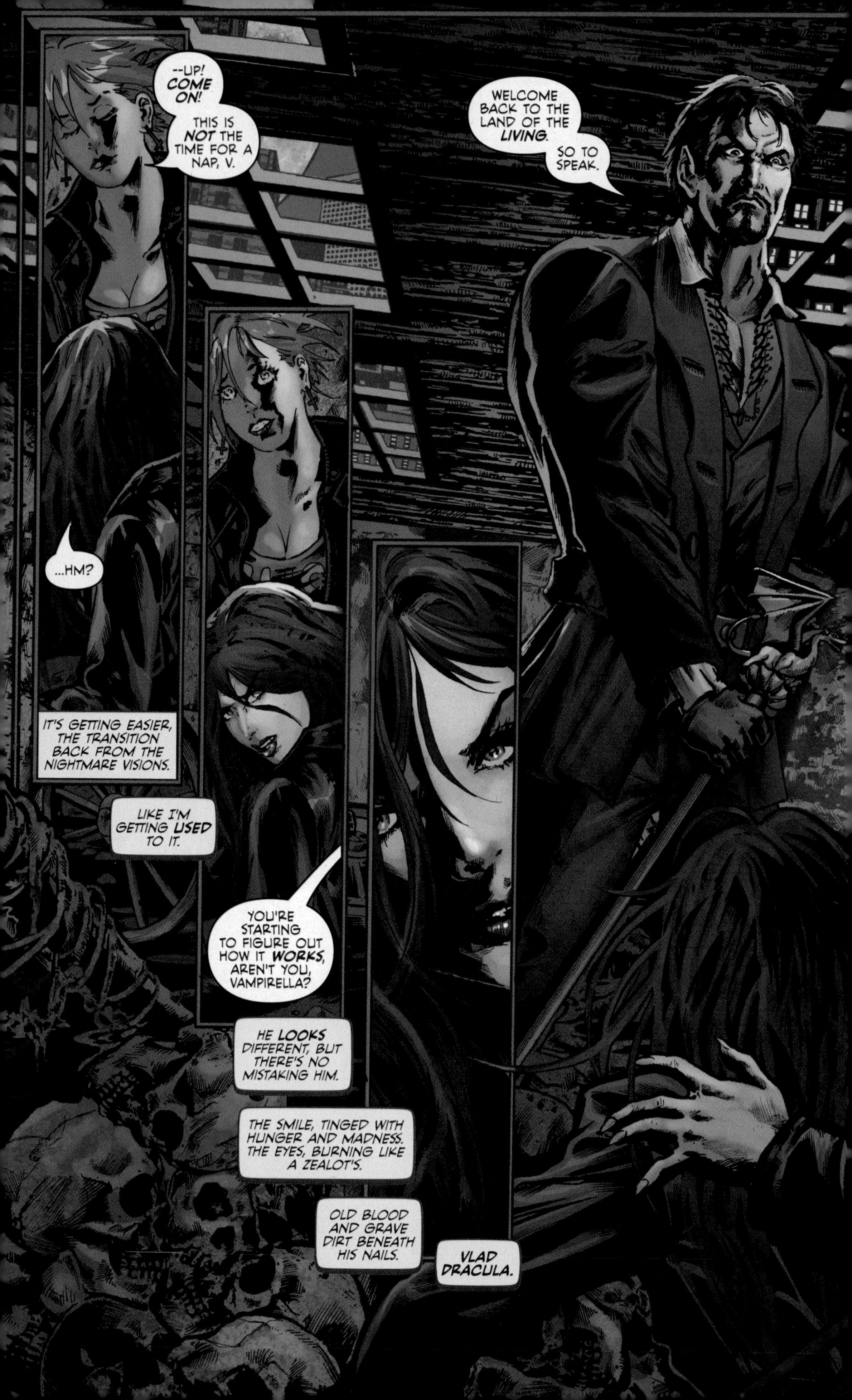
--UP! COME ON!
THIS IS NOT THE TIME FOR A NAP, V.
...HM?
IT'S GETTING EASIER, THE TRANSITION BACK FROM THE NIGHTMARE VISIONS.
LIKE I'M GETTING USED TO IT.
WELCOME BACK TO THE LAND OF THE LIVING.
SO TO SPEAK.
YOU'RE STARTING TO FIGURE OUT HOW IT WORKS, AREN'T YOU, VAMPIRELLA?
HE LOOKS DIFFERENT, BUT THERE'S NO MISTAKING HIM.
THE SMILE, TINGED WITH HUNGER AND MADNESS. THE EYES, BURNING LIKE A ZEALOT'S.
OLD BLOOD AND GRAVE DIRT BENEATH HIS NAILS.
VLAD DRACULA.

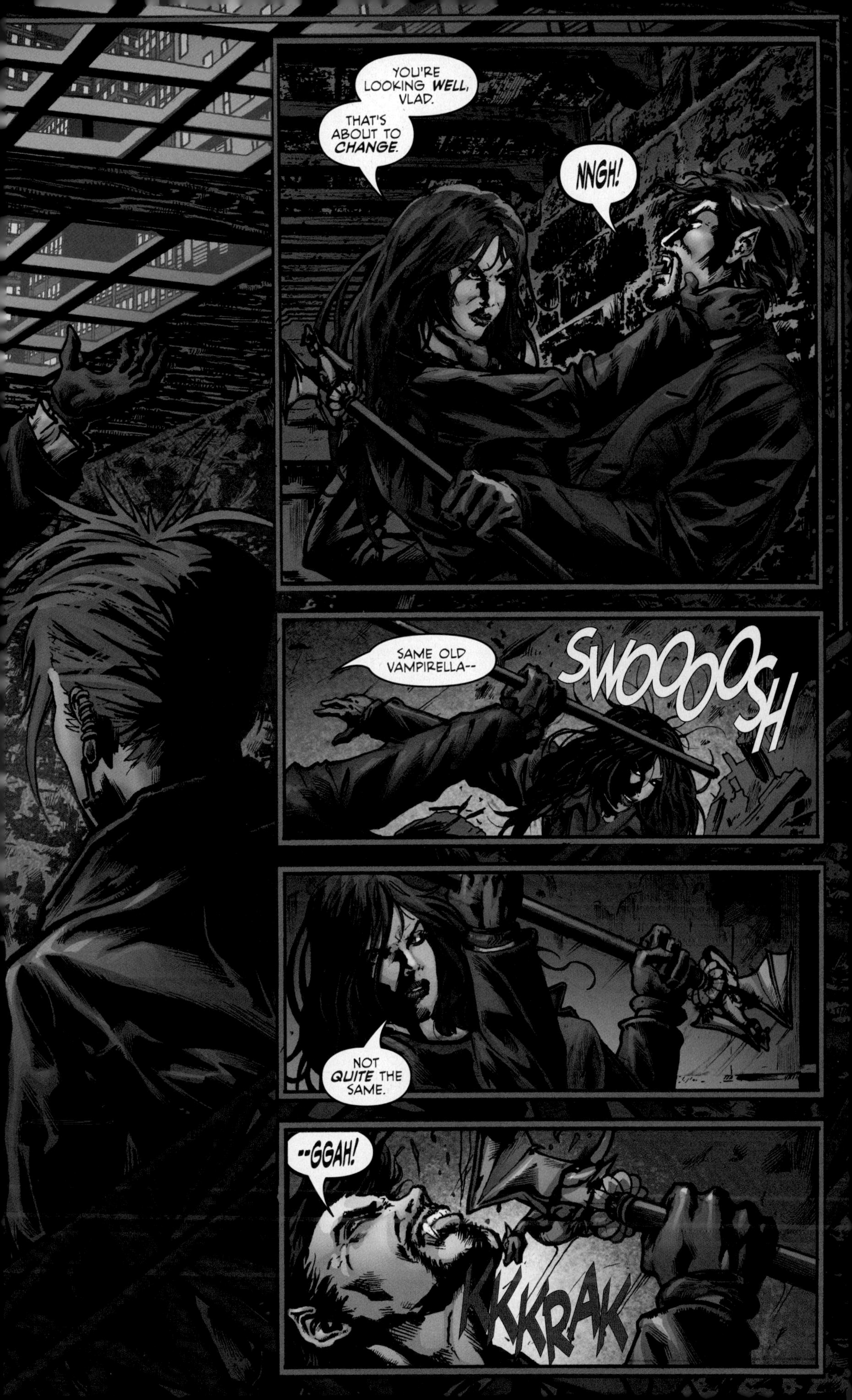

YOU'RE LOOKING WELL, VLAD.
THAT'S ABOUT TO CHANGE.
NNGH!
SAME OLD VAMPIRELLA--
SWOOOOSH
NOT QUITE THE SAME.
--GGAH!
KKKRAK

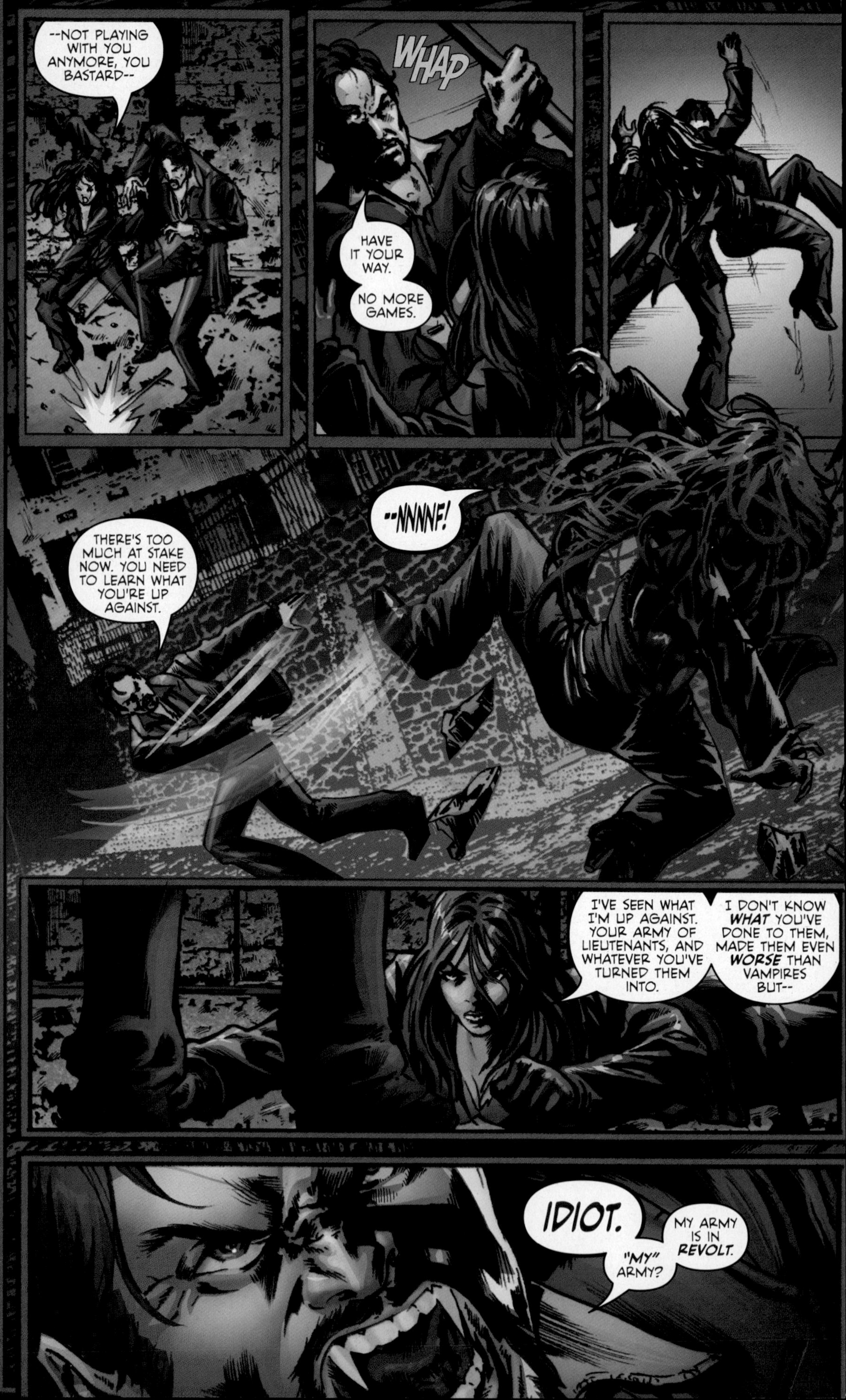
--NOT PLAYING WITH YOU ANYMORE, YOU BASTARD--
WHAP
HAVE IT YOUR WAY.
NO MORE GAMES.
--NNNNF!
THERE'S TOO MUCH AT STAKE NOW. YOU NEED TO LEARN WHAT YOU'RE UP AGAINST.
I'VE SEEN WHAT I'M UP AGAINST. YOUR ARMY OF LIEUTENANTS, AND WHATEVER YOU'VE TURNED THEM INTO.
I DON'T KNOW *WHAT* YOU'VE DONE TO THEM, MADE THEM EVEN *WORSE* THAN VAMPIRES BUT--
IDIOT.
"MY" ARMY?
MY ARMY IS IN *REVOLT*.

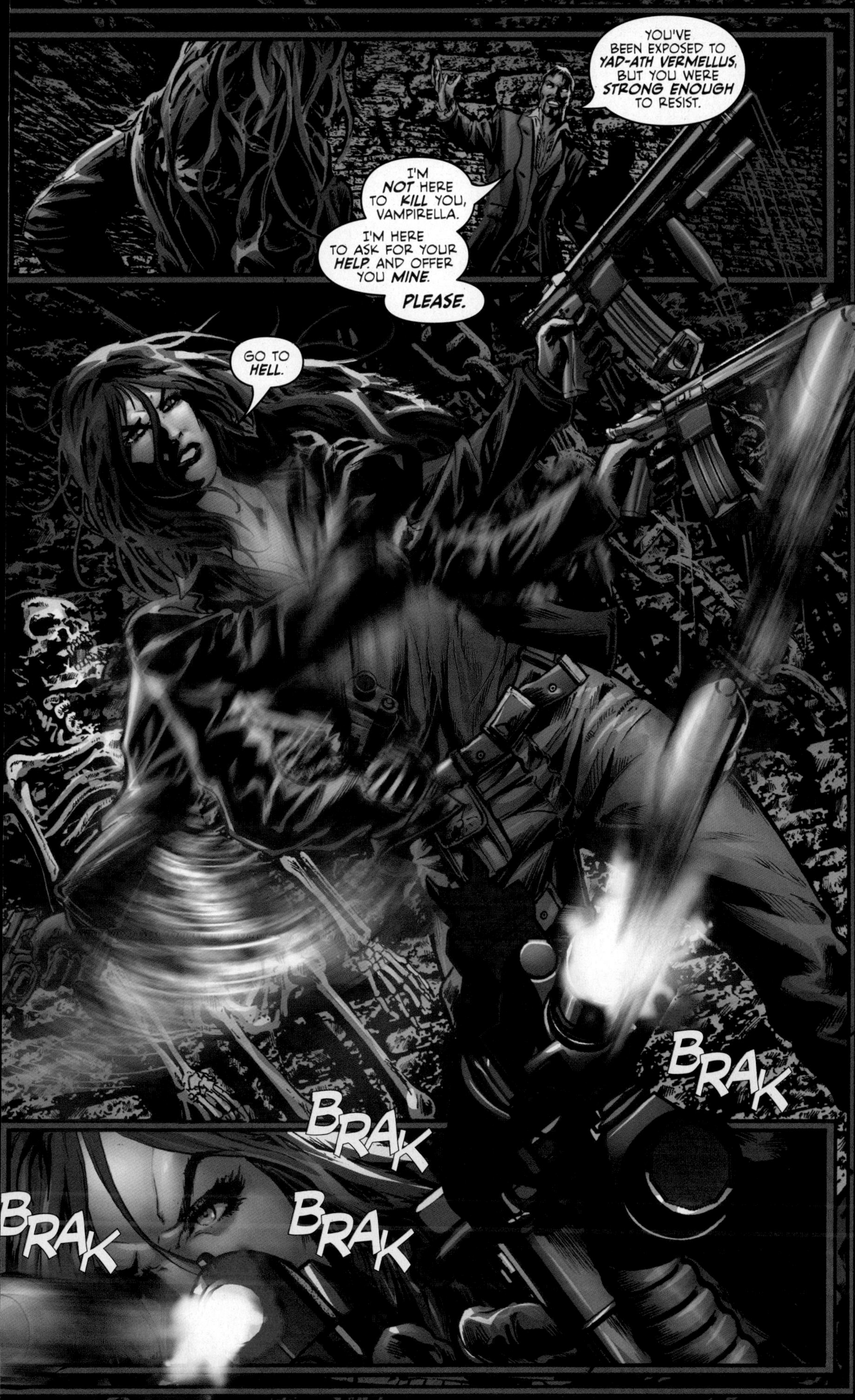
YOU'VE BEEN EXPOSED TO YAD-ATH VERMELLUS, BUT YOU WERE STRONG ENOUGH TO RESIST.
I'M NOT HERE TO KILL YOU, VAMPIRELLA.
I'M HERE TO ASK FOR YOUR HELP. AND OFFER YOU MINE.
PLEASE.
GO TO HELL.
BRAK
BRAK
BRAK
BRAK

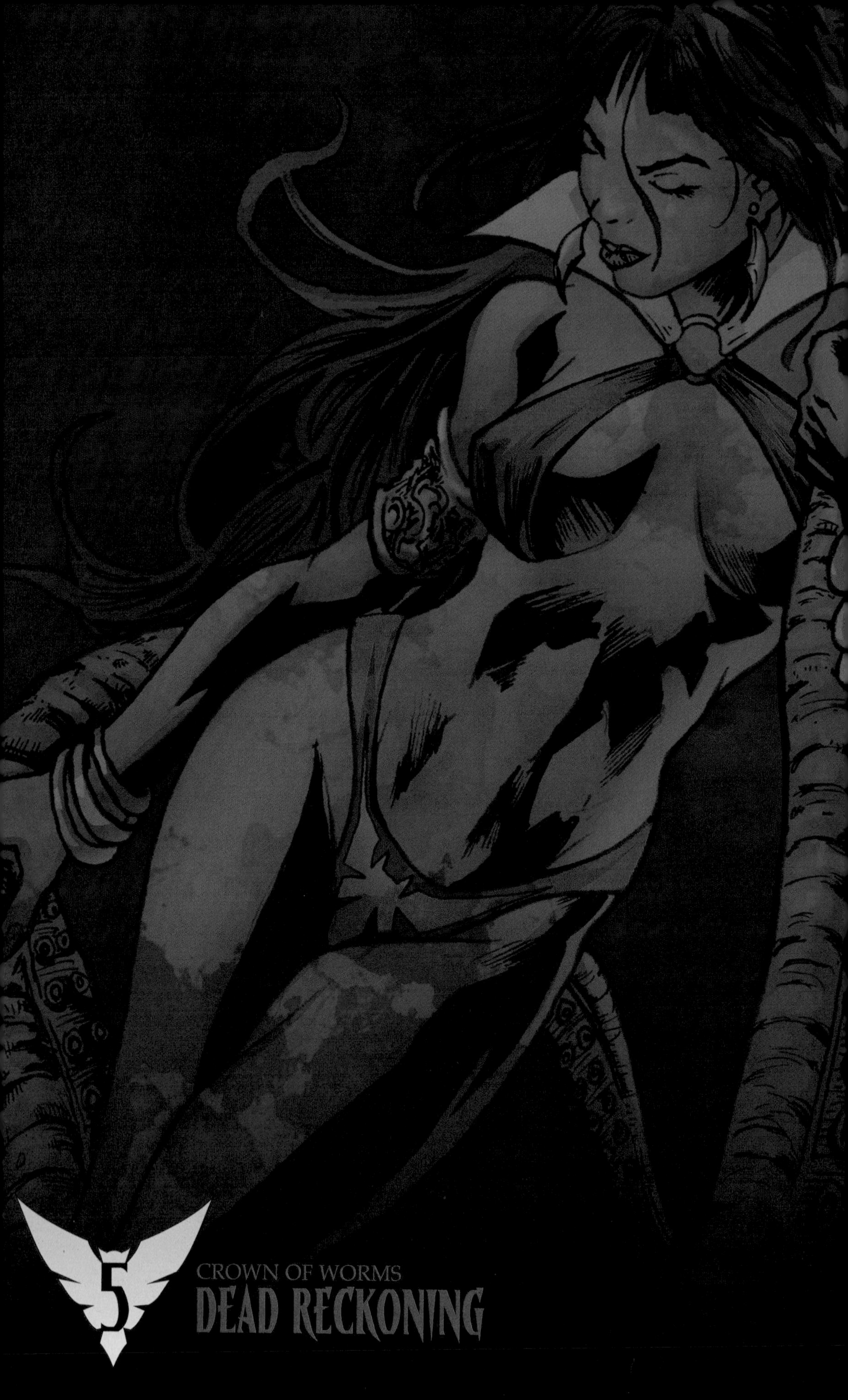

5

CROWN OF WORMS

DEAD RECKONING

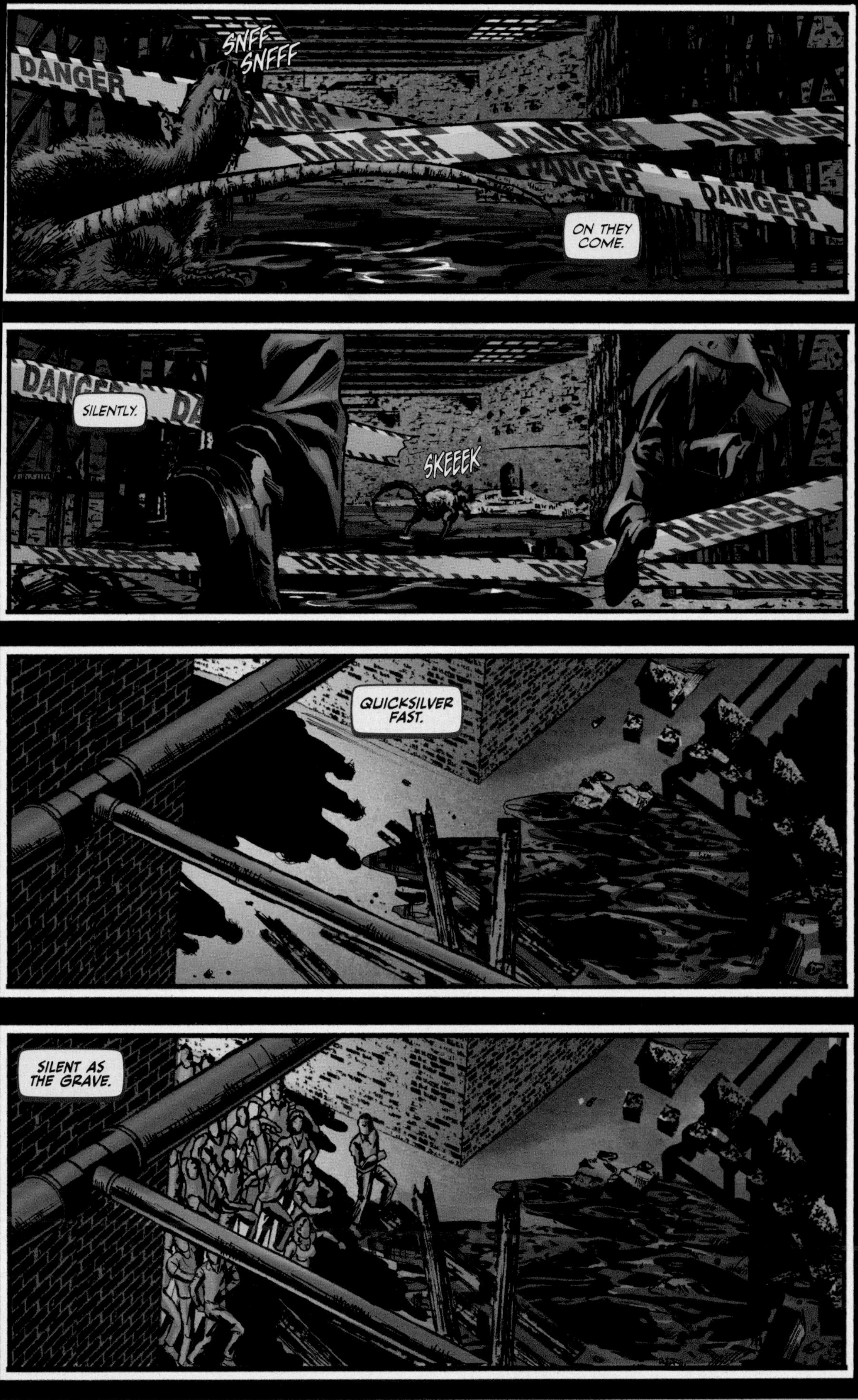
SNFF SNFFF
DANGER
ON THEY COME.
SILENTLY.
SKEEEK
QUICKSILVER FAST.
SILENT AS THE GRAVE.

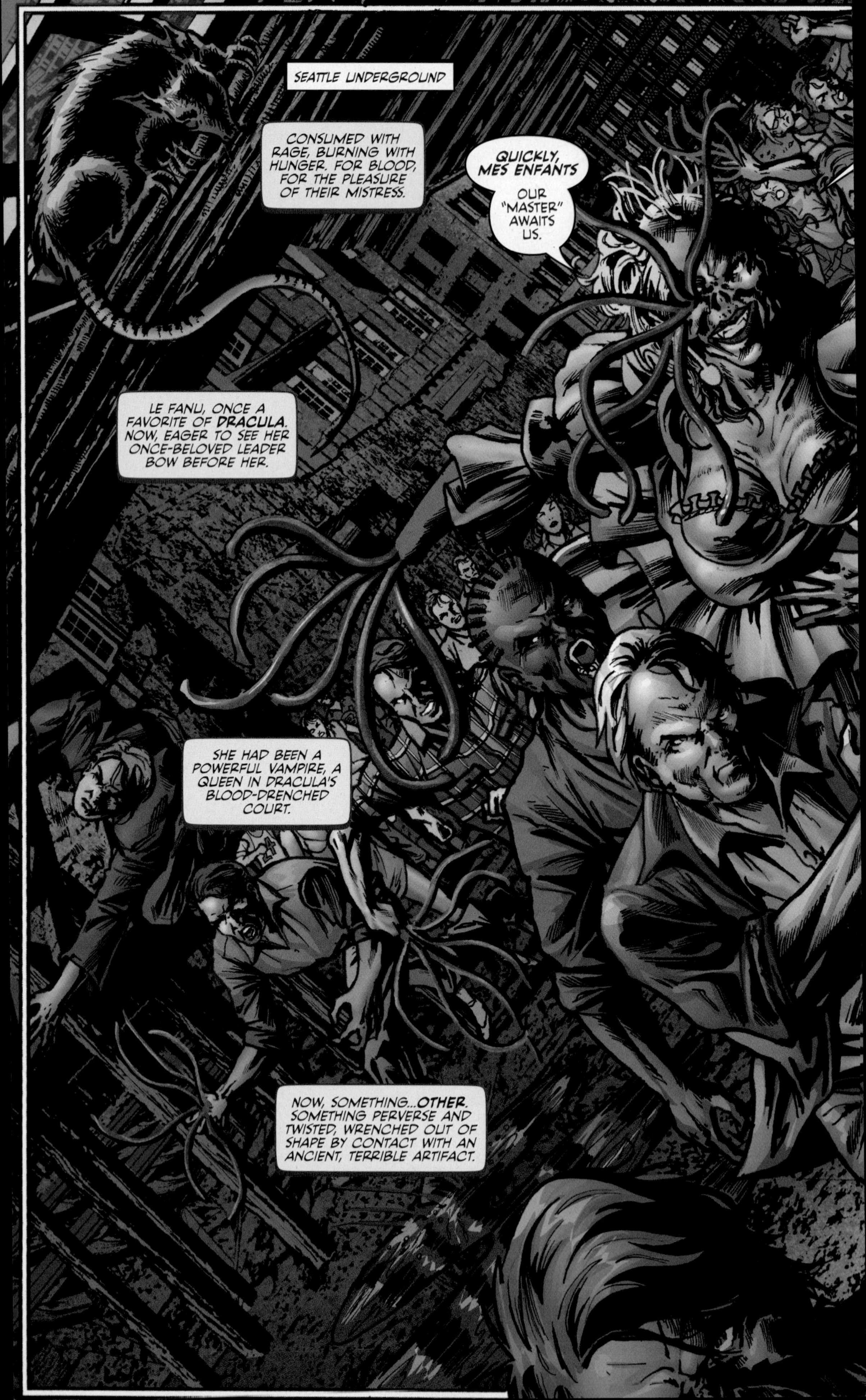
SEATTLE UNDERGROUND
CONSUMED WITH RAGE, BURNING WITH HUNGER. FOR BLOOD, FOR THE PLEASURE OF THEIR MISTRESS.
QUICKLY, MES ENFANTS OUR "MASTER" AWAITS US.
LE FANU, ONCE A FAVORITE OF DRACULA. NOW, EAGER TO SEE HER ONCE-BELOVED LEADER BOW BEFORE HER.
SHE HAD BEEN A POWERFUL VAMPIRE, A QUEEN IN DRACULA'S BLOOD-DRENCHED COURT.
NOW, SOMETHING...OTHER. SOMETHING PERVERSE AND TWISTED, WRENCHED OUT OF SHAPE BY CONTACT WITH AN ANCIENT, TERRIBLE ARTIFACT.

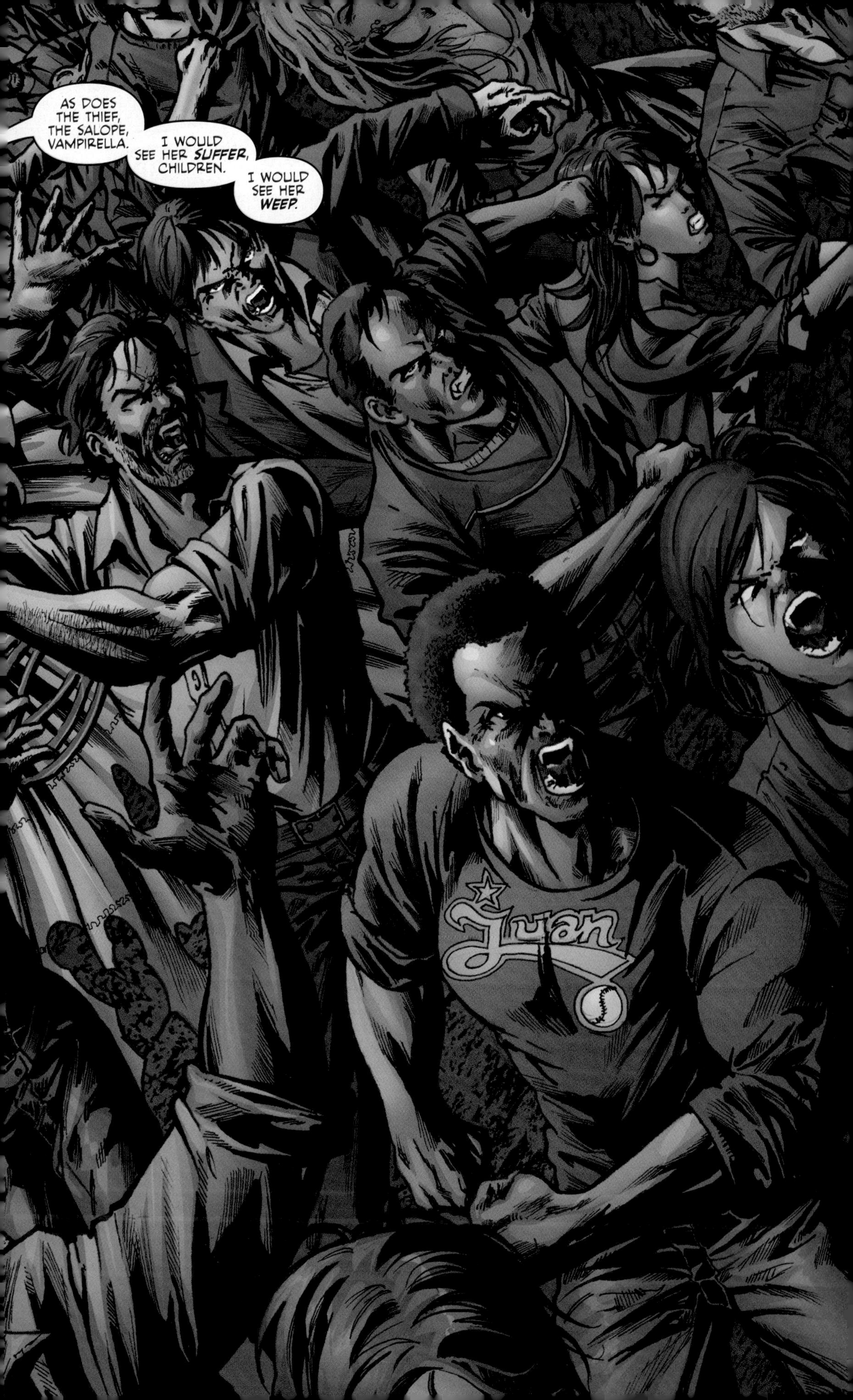
AS DOES THE THIEF, THE SALOPE, VAMPIRELLA.
I WOULD SEE HER *SUFFER*, CHILDREN.
I WOULD SEE HER *WEEP*.
JUAN

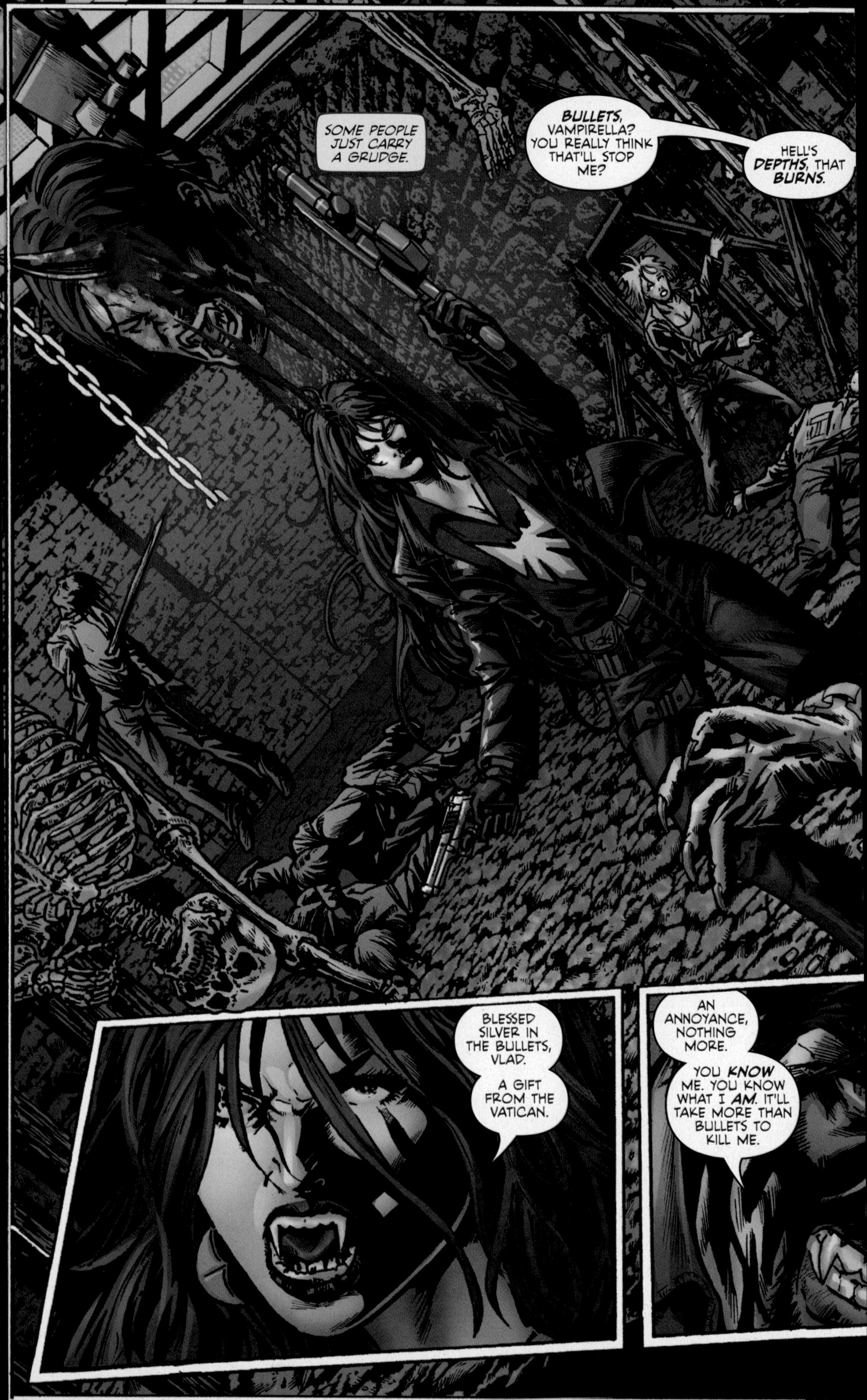
SOME PEOPLE JUST CARRY A GRUDGE.
BULLETS, VAMPIRELLA? YOU REALLY THINK THAT'LL STOP ME?
HELL'S DEPTHS, THAT BURNS.
BLESSED SILVER IN THE BULLETS, VLAD.
A GIFT FROM THE VATICAN.
AN ANNOYANCE, NOTHING MORE.
YOU KNOW ME. YOU KNOW WHAT I AM. IT'LL TAKE MORE THAN BULLETS TO KILL ME.

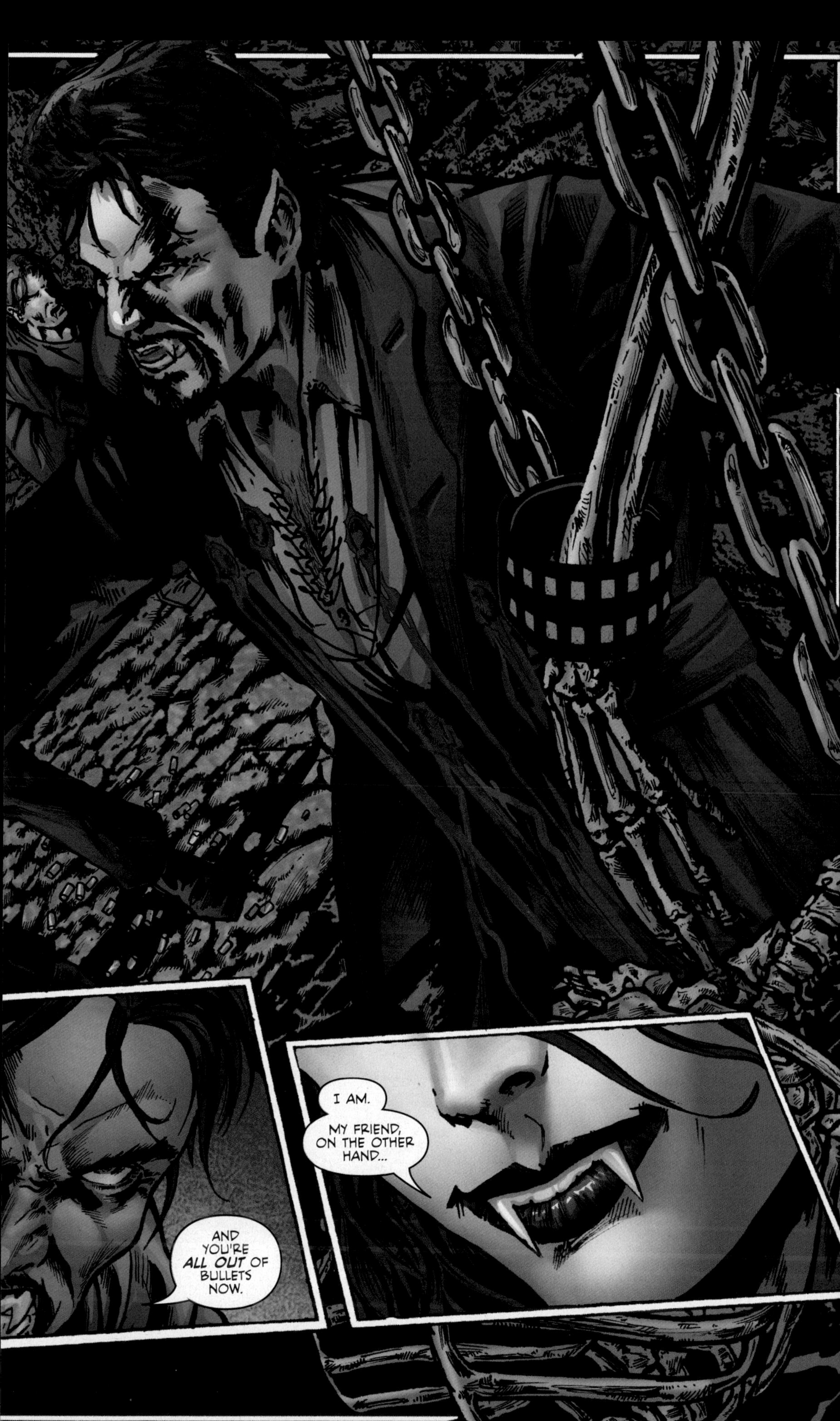
AND YOU'RE ALL OUT OF BULLETS NOW.
I AM.
MY FRIEND, ON THE OTHER HAND...

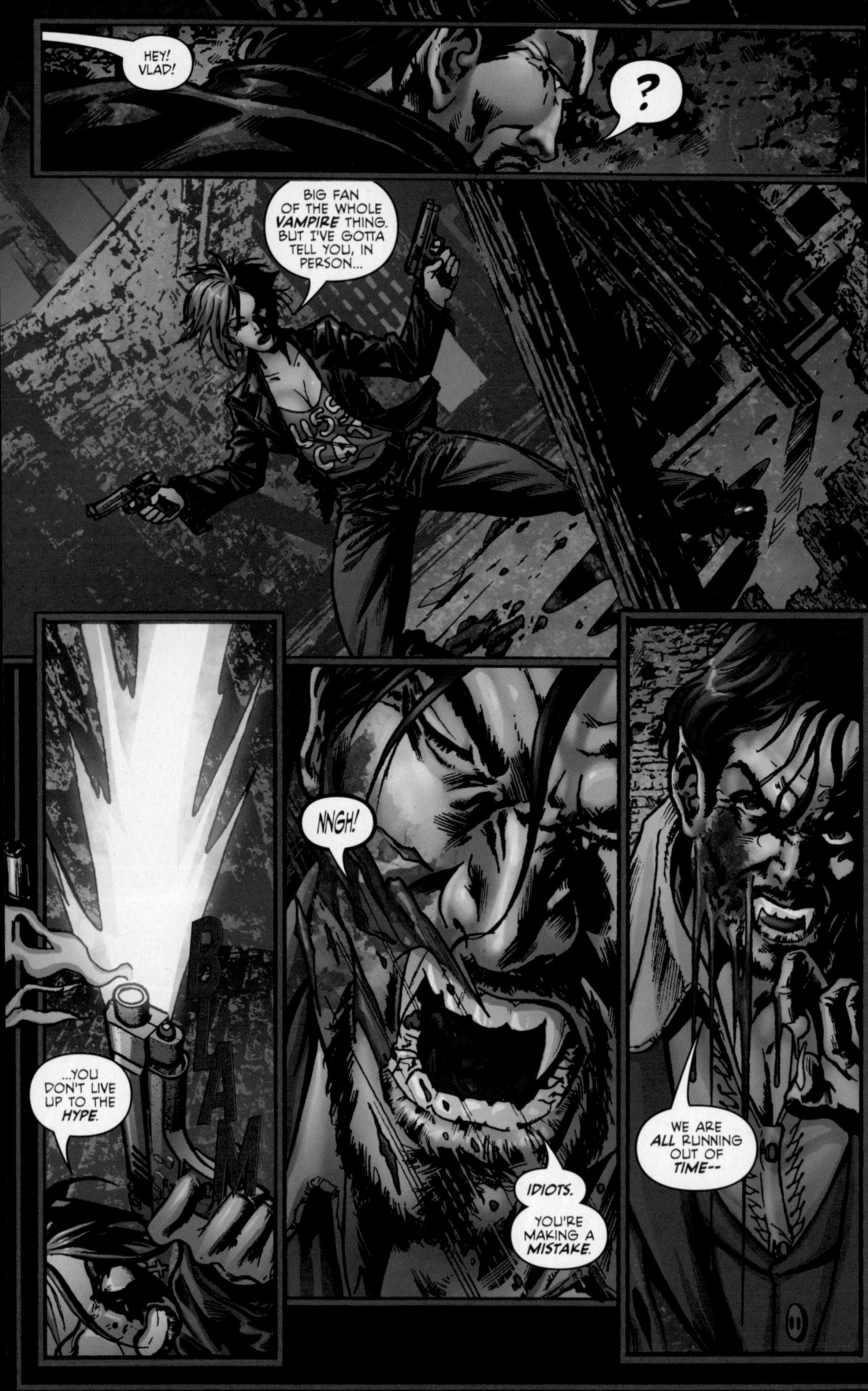
HEY! VLAD!
?
BIG FAN OF THE WHOLE *VAMPIRE* THING. BUT I'VE GOTTA TELL YOU, IN PERSON...
...YOU DON'T LIVE UP TO THE *HYPE*.
BLAM
NNGH!
IDIOTS.
YOU'RE MAKING A *MISTAKE*.
WE ARE *ALL* RUNNING OUT OF *TIME*--

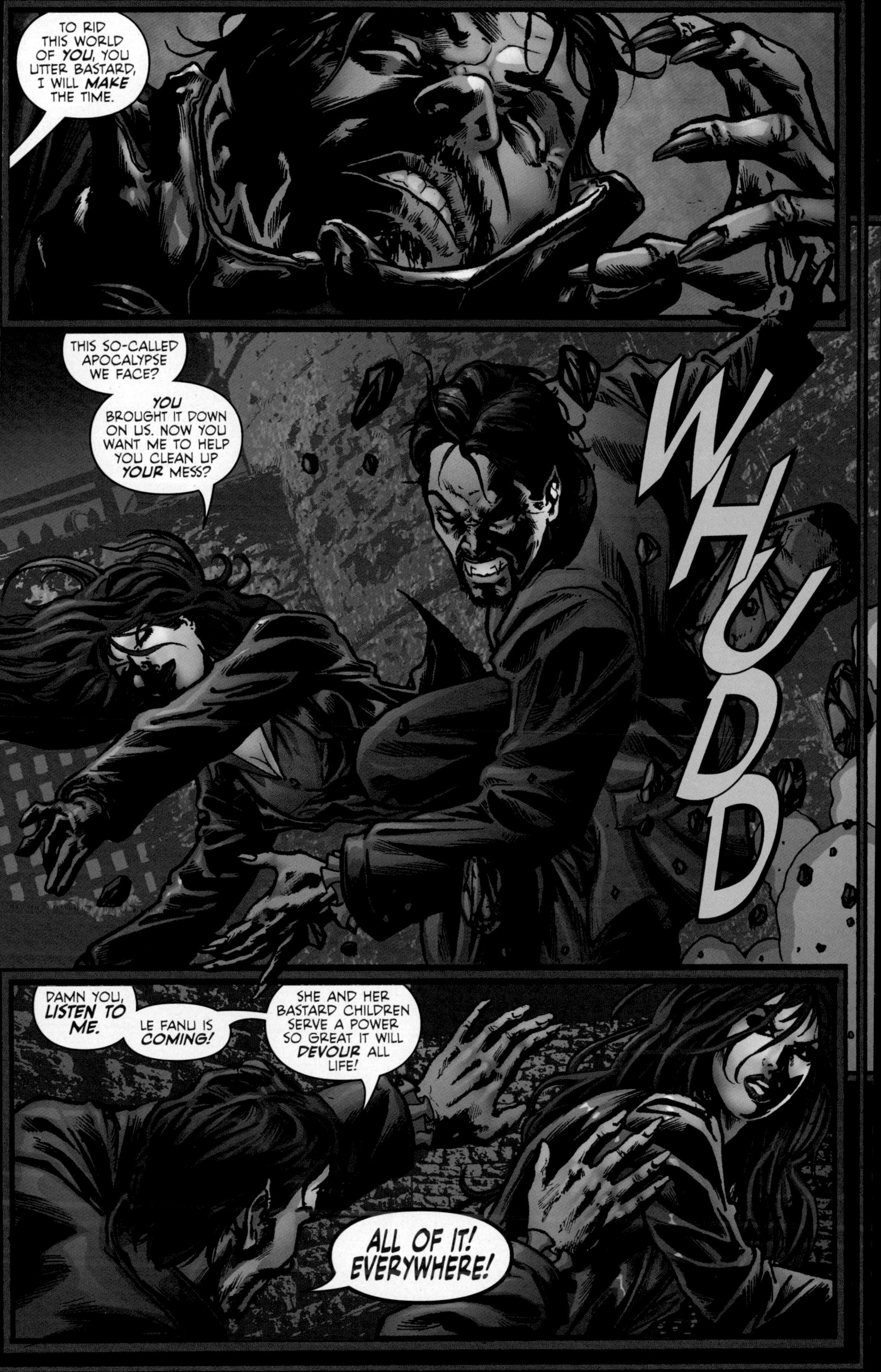
TO RID THIS WORLD OF YOU, YOU UTTER BASTARD, I WILL MAKE THE TIME.
THIS SO-CALLED APOCALYPSE WE FACE?
YOU BROUGHT IT DOWN ON US. NOW YOU WANT ME TO HELP YOU CLEAN UP YOUR MESS?
WHUDD
DAMN YOU, LISTEN TO ME.
LE FANU IS COMING!
SHE AND HER BASTARD CHILDREN SERVE A POWER SO GREAT IT WILL DEVOUR ALL LIFE!
ALL OF IT! EVERYWHERE!

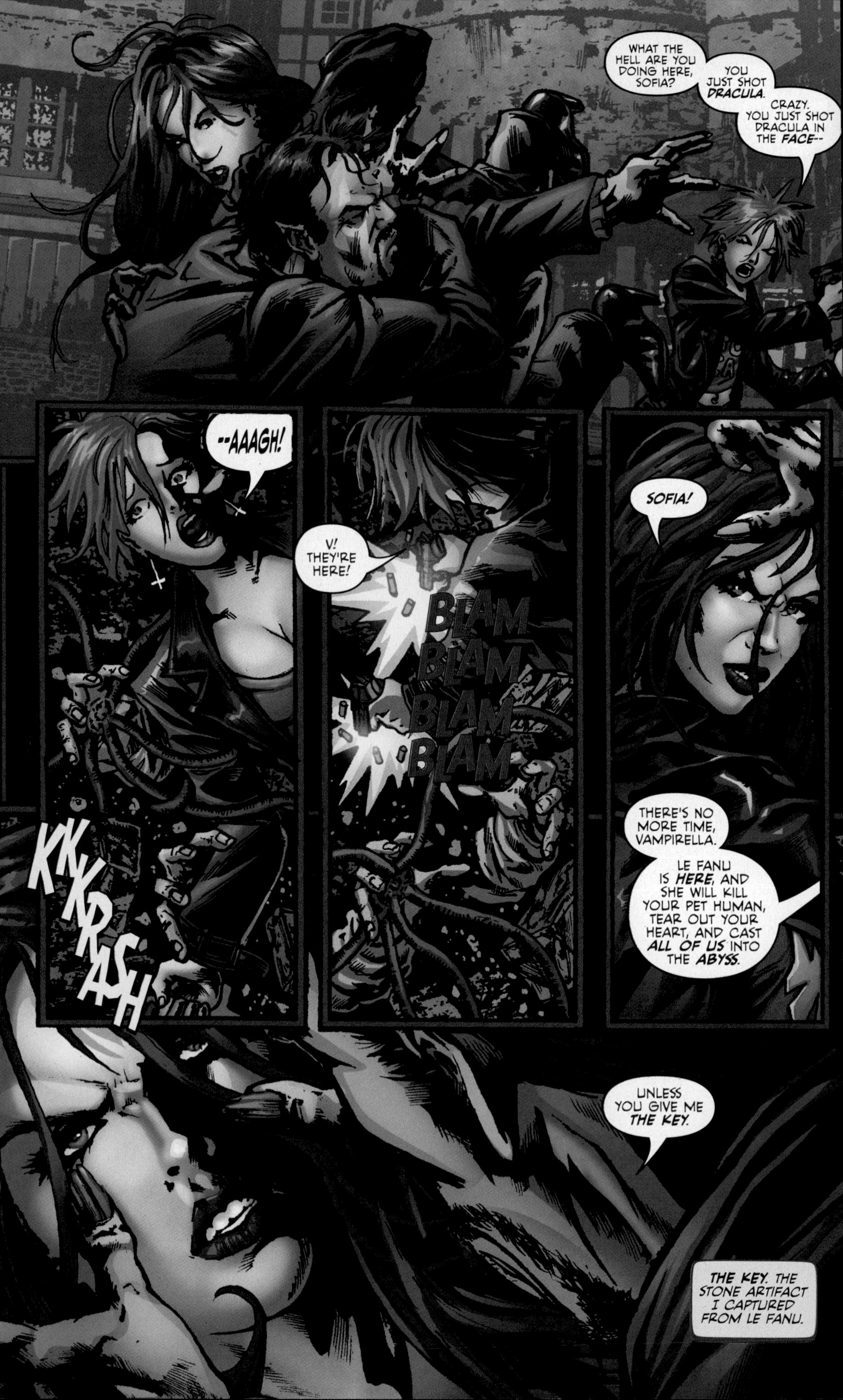
WHAT THE HELL ARE YOU DOING HERE, SOFIA?
YOU JUST SHOT DRACULA.
CRAZY. YOU JUST SHOT DRACULA IN THE FACE--
--AAAGH!
V! THEY'RE HERE!
BLAM BLAM BLAM BLAM
KKKRASH
SOFIA!
THERE'S NO MORE TIME, VAMPIRELLA.
LE FANU IS HERE, AND SHE WILL KILL YOUR PET HUMAN, TEAR OUT YOUR HEART, AND CAST ALL OF US INTO THE ABYSS.
UNLESS YOU GIVE ME THE KEY.
THE KEY. THE STONE ARTIFACT I CAPTURED FROM LE FANU.

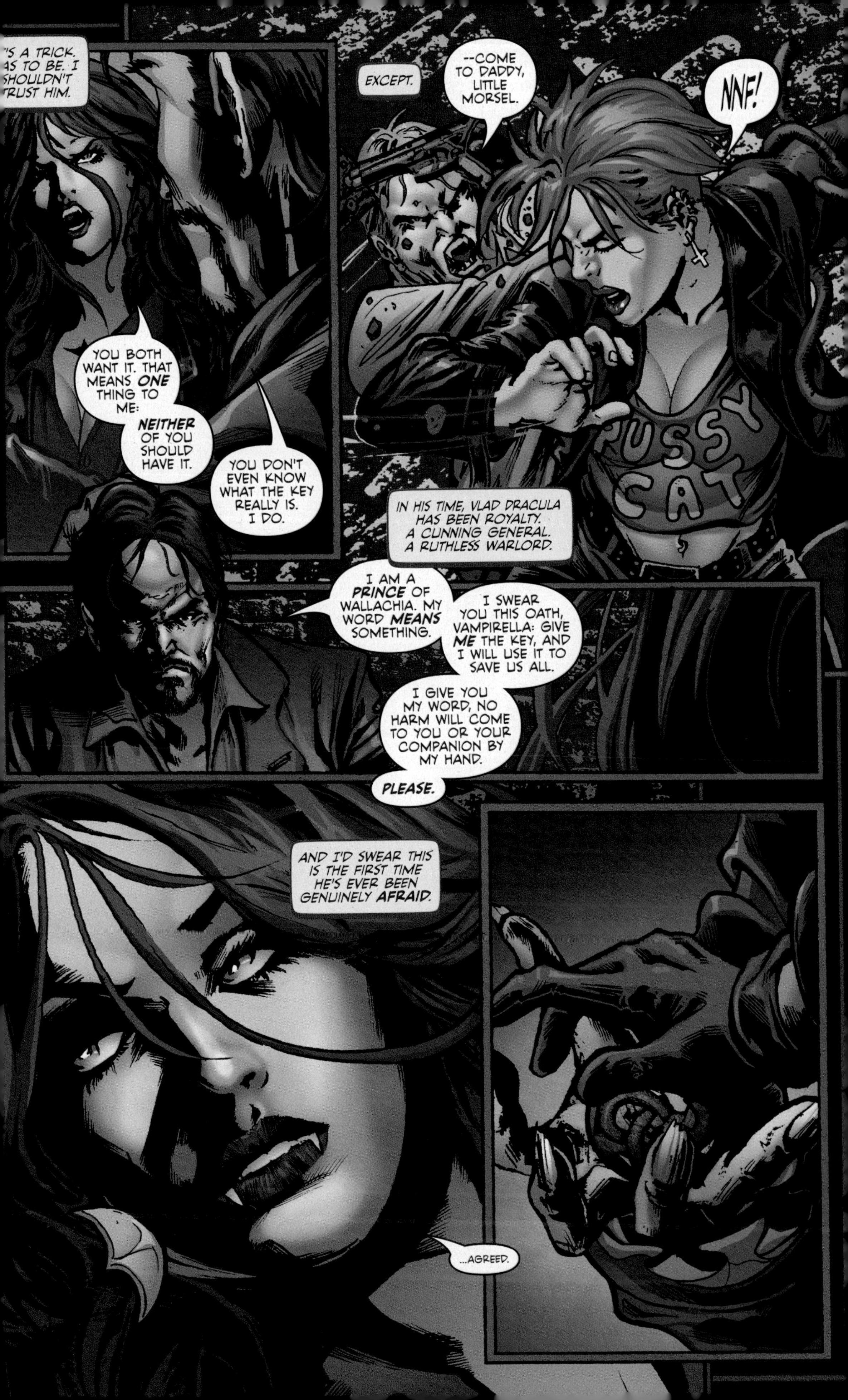

'S A TRICK. AS TO BE. I SHOULDN'T TRUST HIM.
YOU BOTH WANT IT. THAT MEANS ONE THING TO ME: NEITHER OF YOU SHOULD HAVE IT.
YOU DON'T EVEN KNOW WHAT THE KEY REALLY IS. I DO.
EXCEPT.
--COME TO DADDY, LITTLE MORSEL.
NNF!
IN HIS TIME, VLAD DRACULA HAS BEEN ROYALTY. A CUNNING GENERAL. A RUTHLESS WARLORD.
I AM A PRINCE OF WALLACHIA. MY WORD MEANS SOMETHING.
I SWEAR YOU THIS OATH, VAMPIRELLA: GIVE ME THE KEY, AND I WILL USE IT TO SAVE US ALL.
I GIVE YOU MY WORD, NO HARM WILL COME TO YOU OR YOUR COMPANION BY MY HAND.
PLEASE.
AND I'D SWEAR THIS IS THE FIRST TIME HE'S EVER BEEN GENUINELY AFRAID.
...AGREED.

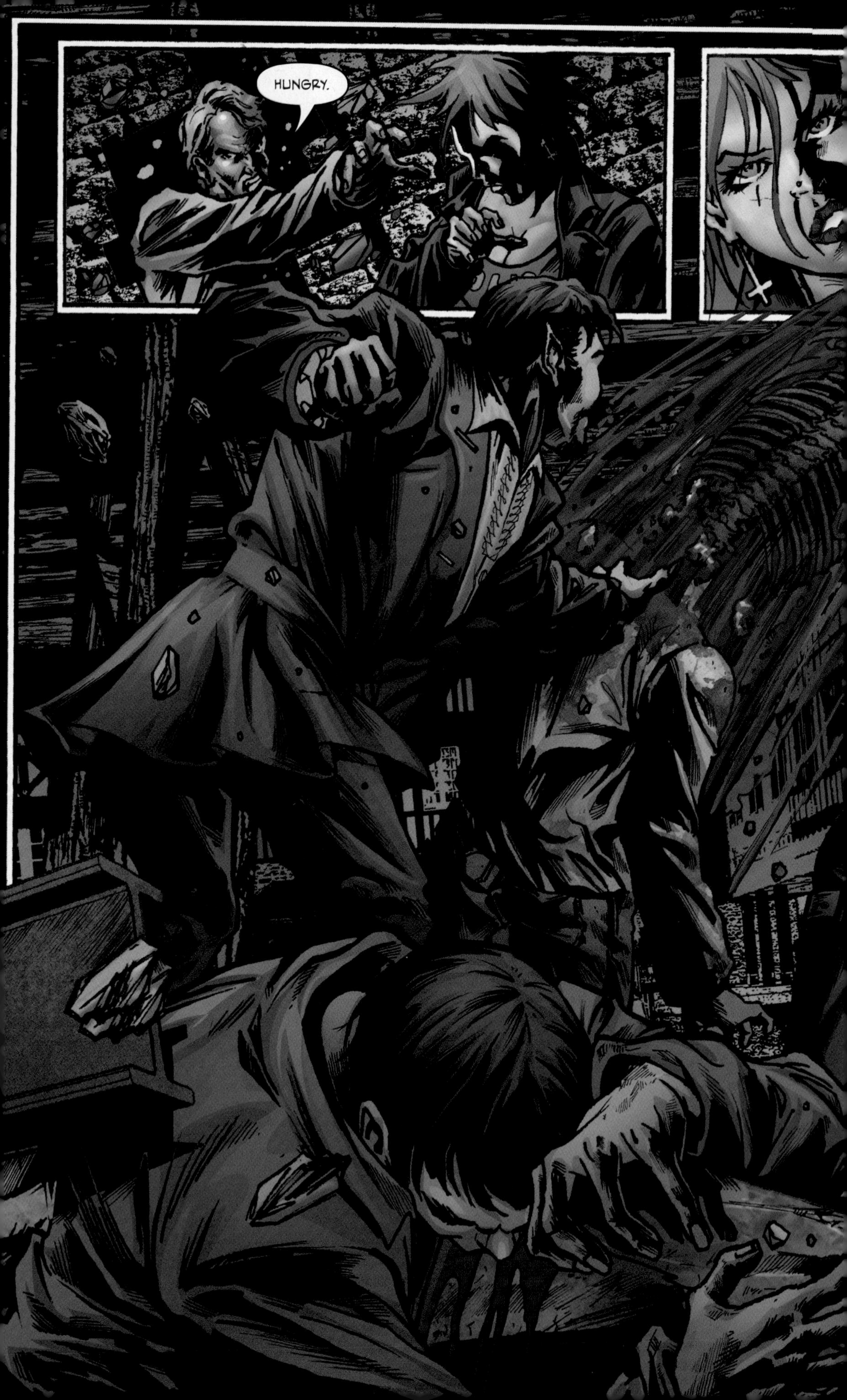
HUNGRY.

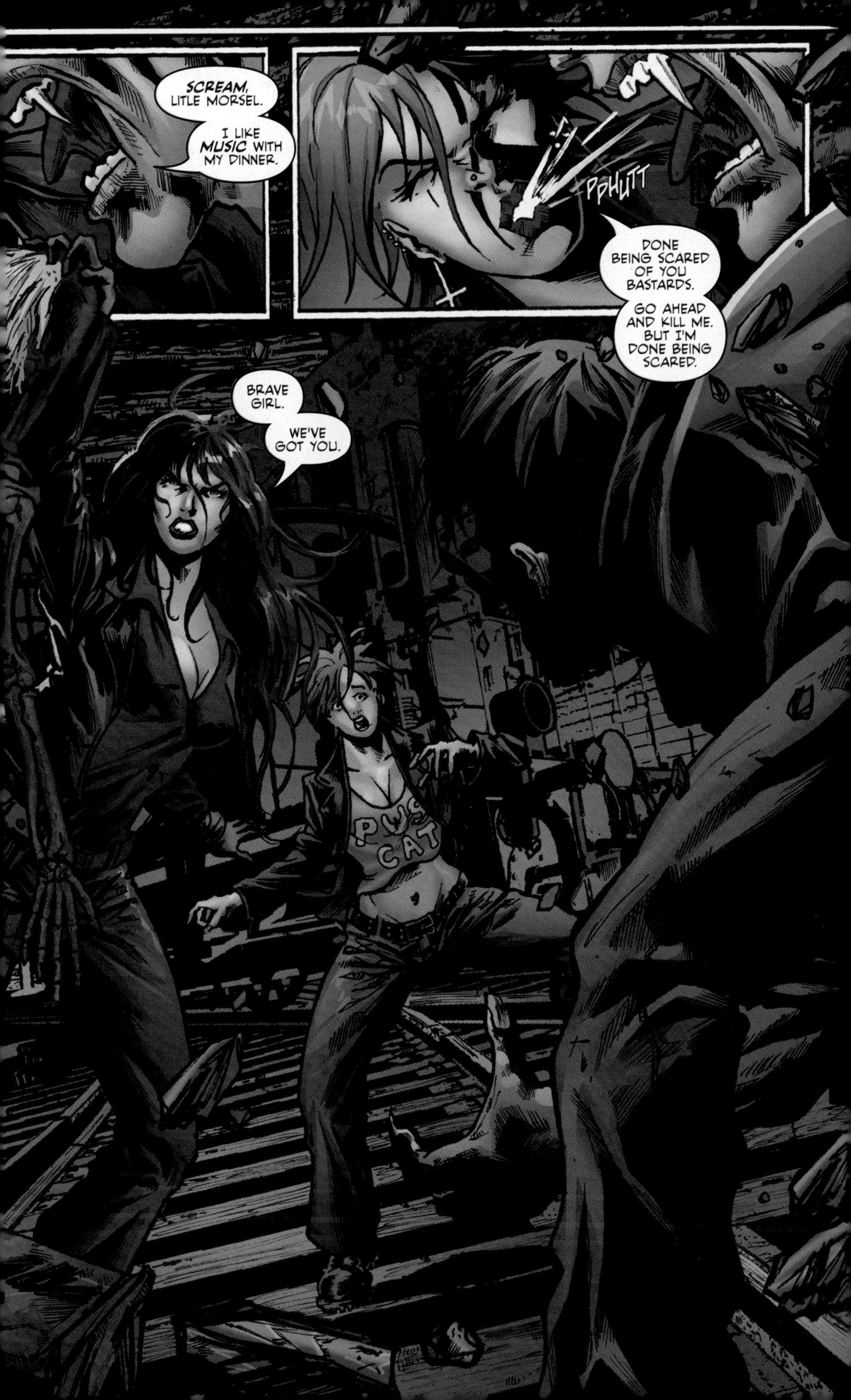
SCREAM, LITLE MORSEL.
I LIKE MUSIC WITH MY DINNER.
PPHUTT
DONE BEING SCARED OF YOU BASTARDS.
GO AHEAD AND KILL ME. BUT I'M DONE BEING SCARED.
BRAVE GIRL.
WE'VE GOT YOU.
PUSS CAT

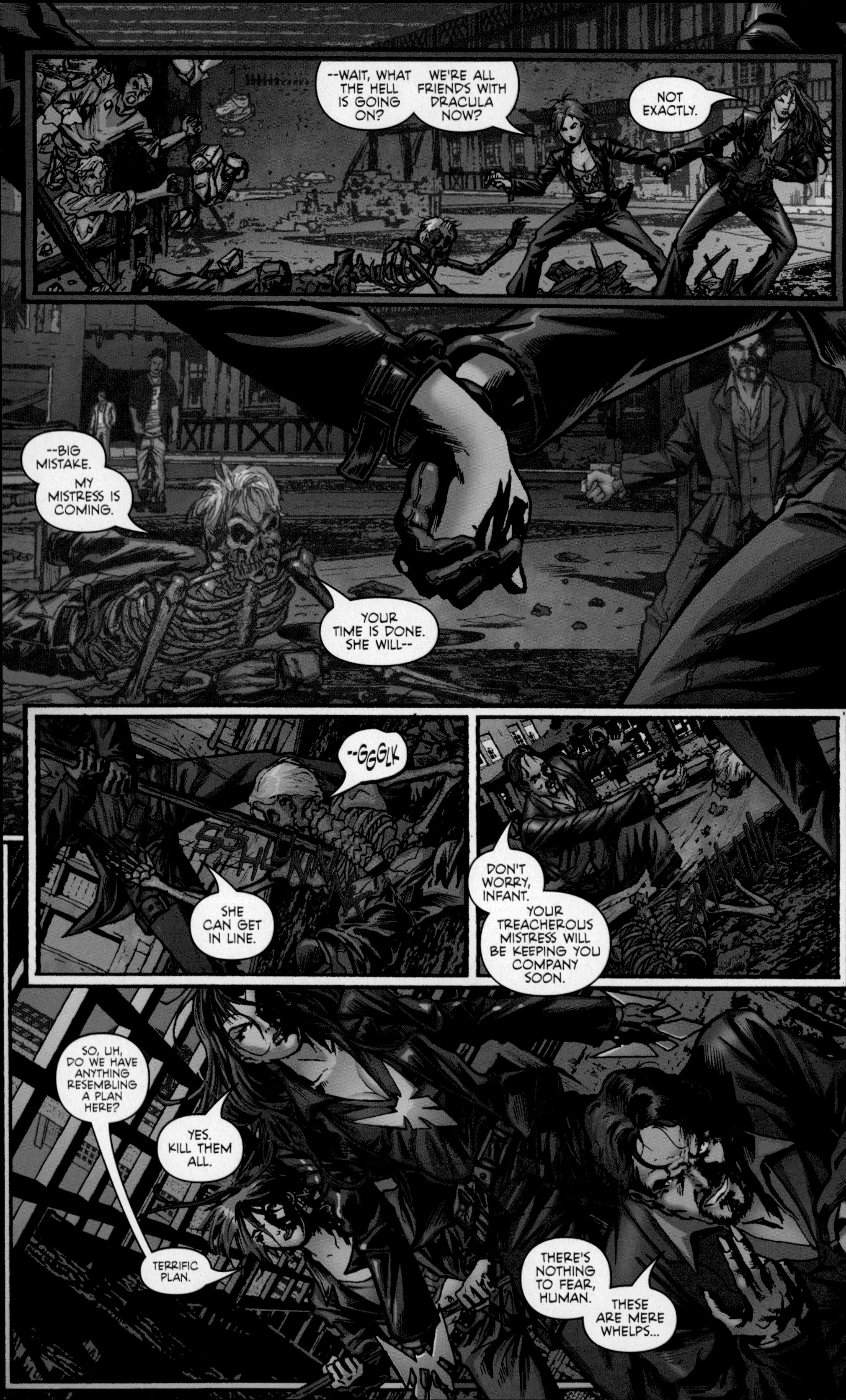
--WAIT, WHAT THE HELL IS GOING ON?
WE'RE ALL FRIENDS WITH DRACULA NOW?
NOT EXACTLY.
--BIG MISTAKE.
MY MISTRESS IS COMING.
YOUR TIME IS DONE. SHE WILL--
--GGGLK
SSHUNNNK
SHE CAN GET IN LINE.
DON'T WORRY, INFANT.
YOUR TREACHEROUS MISTRESS WILL BE KEEPING YOU COMPANY SOON.
SO, UH, DO WE HAVE ANYTHING RESEMBLING A PLAN HERE?
YES. KILL THEM ALL.
TERRIFIC PLAN.
THERE'S NOTHING TO FEAR, HUMAN.
THESE ARE MERE WHELPS...

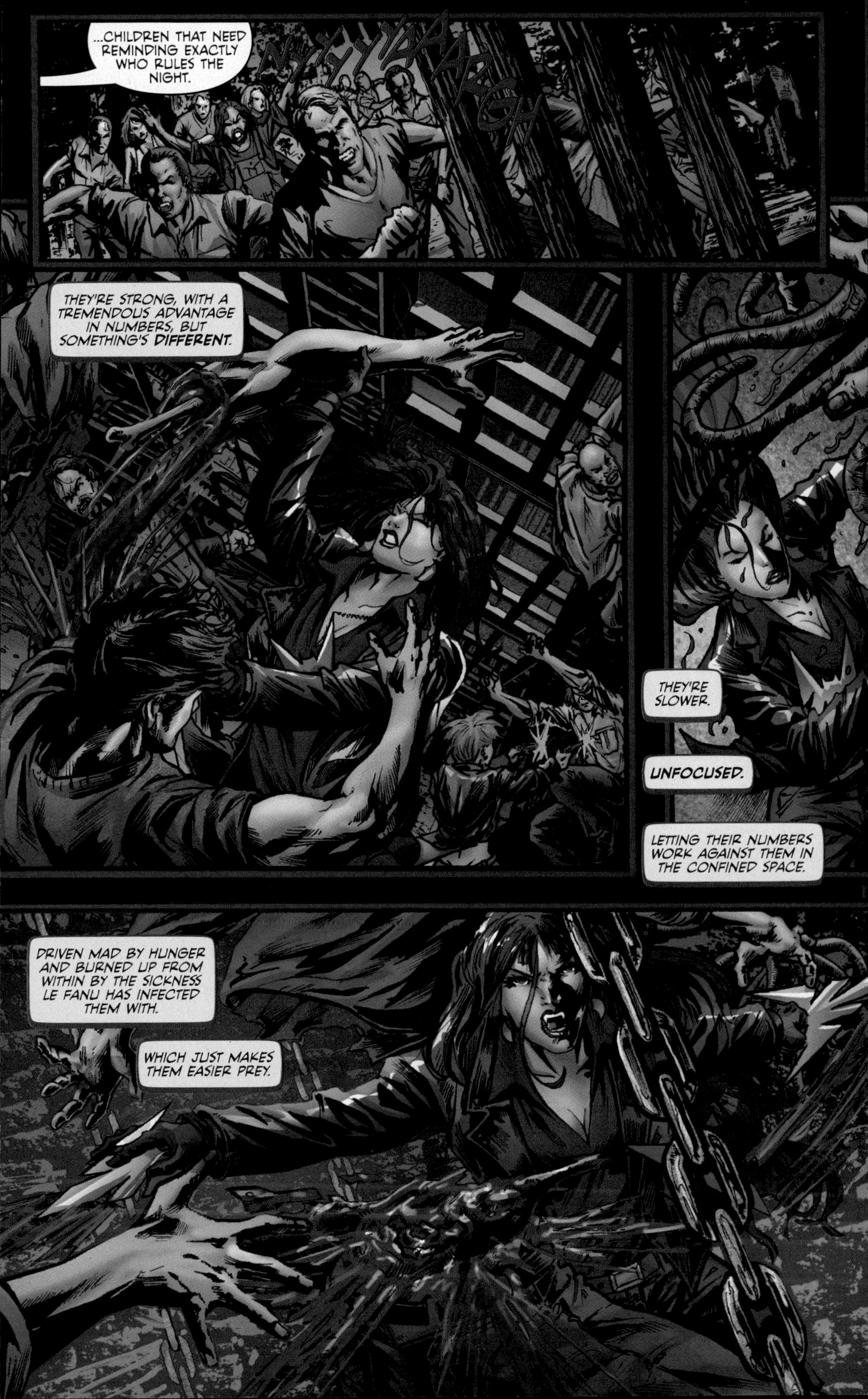
...CHILDREN THAT NEED REMINDING EXACTLY WHO RULES THE NIGHT.
NYYYYAAARGH
THEY'RE STRONG, WITH A TREMENDOUS ADVANTAGE IN NUMBERS, BUT SOMETHING'S DIFFERENT.
THEY'RE SLOWER.
UNFOCUSED.
LETTING THEIR NUMBERS WORK AGAINST THEM IN THE CONFINED SPACE.
DRIVEN MAD BY HUNGER AND BURNED UP FROM WITHIN BY THE SICKNESS LE FANU HAS INFECTED THEM WITH.
WHICH JUST MAKES THEM EASIER PREY.

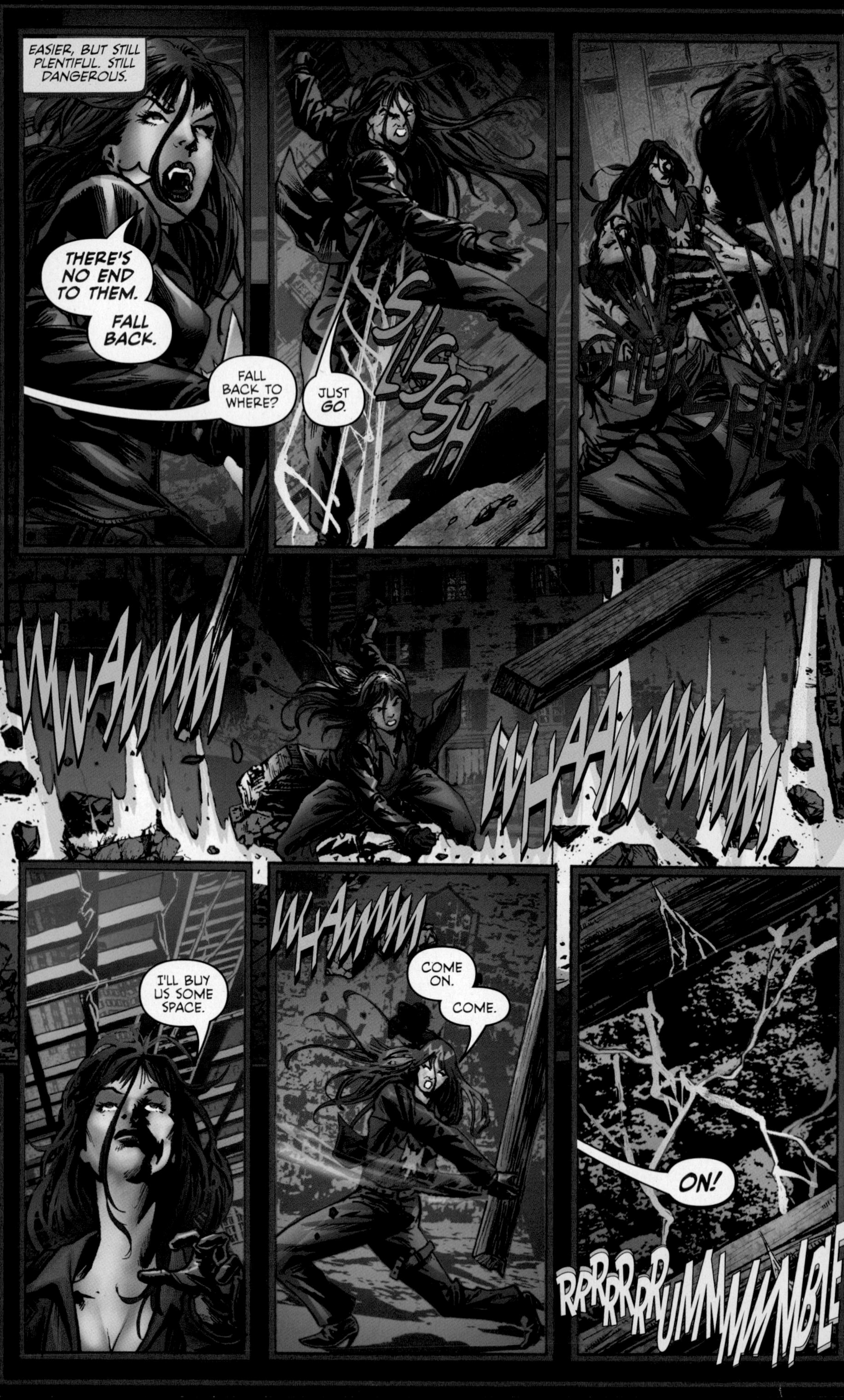
EASIER, BUT STILL PLENTIFUL. STILL DANGEROUS.
THERE'S NO END TO THEM.
FALL BACK.
FALL BACK TO WHERE?
JUST GO.
SSLISSH
SHLUK SHLUK SHLUK
WHAMM
WHAAMMMM
I'LL BUY US SOME SPACE.
WHAMM
COME ON.
COME.
ON!
RRRRRRRRUMMMMMBLE

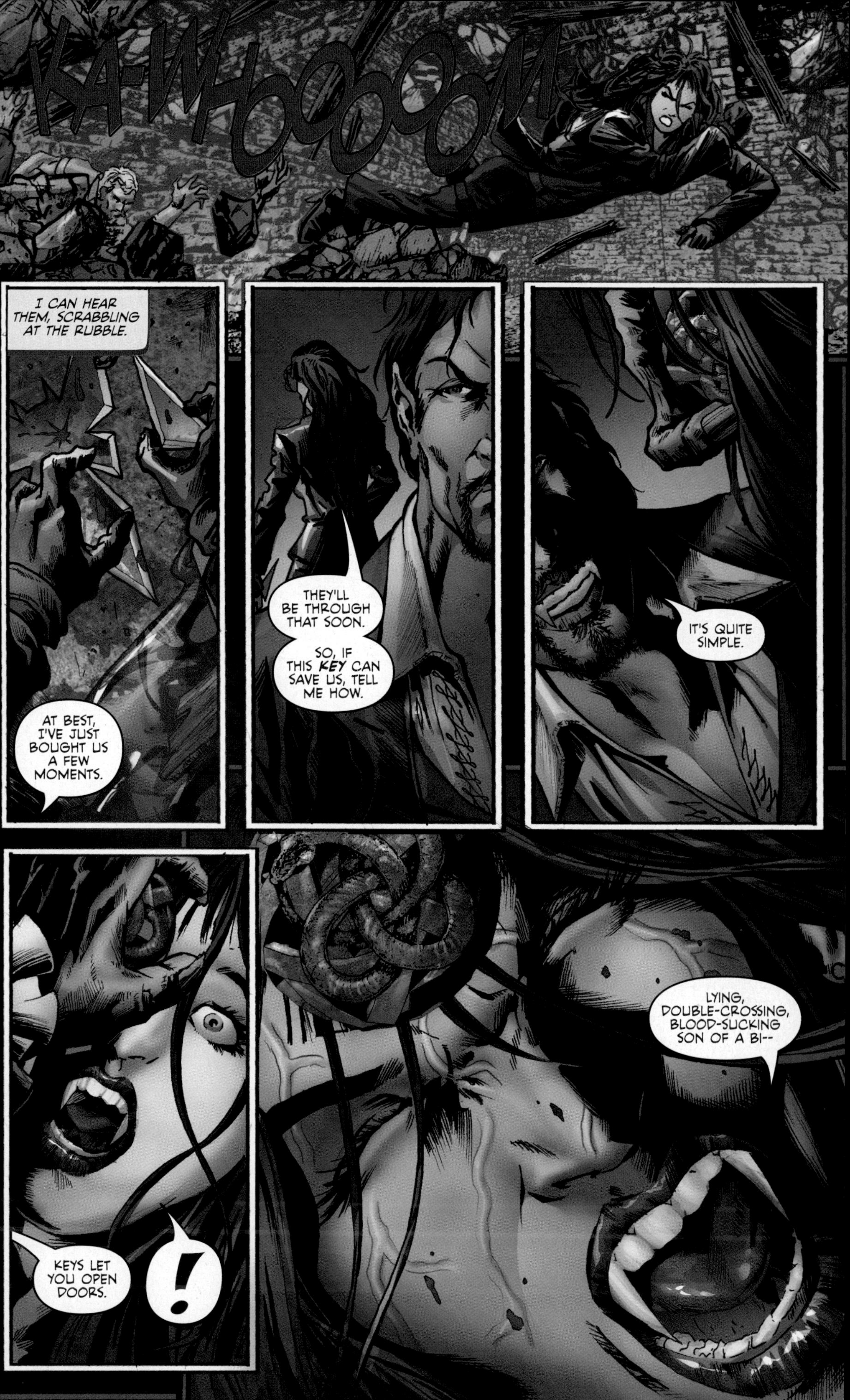
KA-WHOOOOOM
I CAN HEAR THEM, SCRABBLING AT THE RUBBLE.
AT BEST, I'VE JUST BOUGHT US A FEW MOMENTS.
THEY'LL BE THROUGH THAT SOON.
SO, IF THIS KEY CAN SAVE US, TELL ME HOW.
IT'S QUITE SIMPLE.
KEYS LET YOU OPEN DOORS.
!
LYING, DOUBLE-CROSSING, BLOOD-SUCKING SON OF A BI--

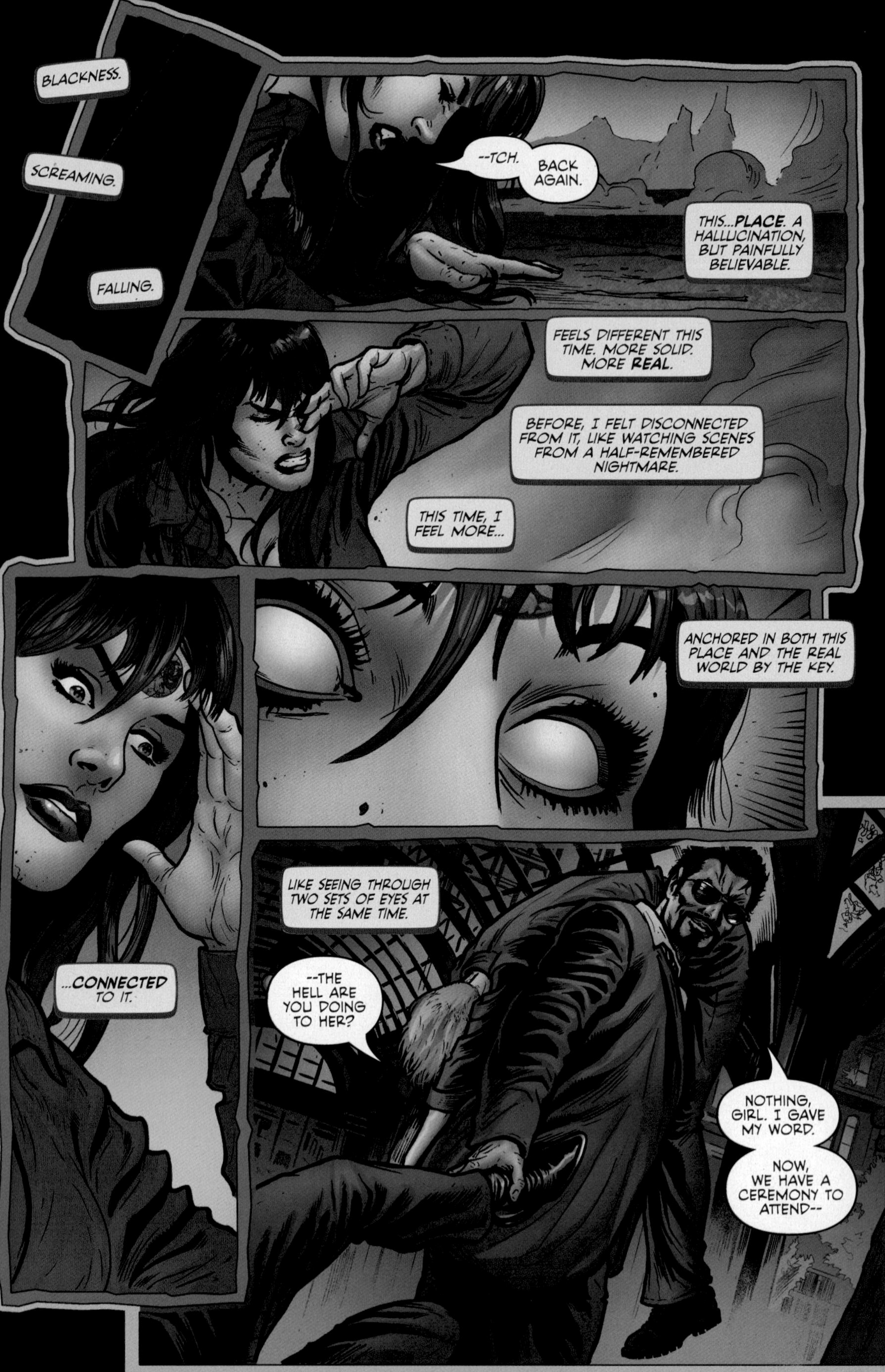
BLACKNESS.
SCREAMING.
FALLING.
--TCH.
BACK AGAIN.
THIS...PLACE. A HALLUCINATION, BUT PAINFULLY BELIEVABLE.
FEELS DIFFERENT THIS TIME. MORE SOLID. MORE REAL.
BEFORE, I FELT DISCONNECTED FROM IT, LIKE WATCHING SCENES FROM A HALF-REMEMBERED NIGHTMARE.
THIS TIME, I FEEL MORE...
...CONNECTED TO IT.
ANCHORED IN BOTH THIS PLACE AND THE REAL WORLD BY THE KEY.
LIKE SEEING THROUGH TWO SETS OF EYES AT THE SAME TIME.
--THE HELL ARE YOU DOING TO HER?
NOTHING, GIRL. I GAVE MY WORD.
NOW, WE HAVE A CEREMONY TO ATTEND--

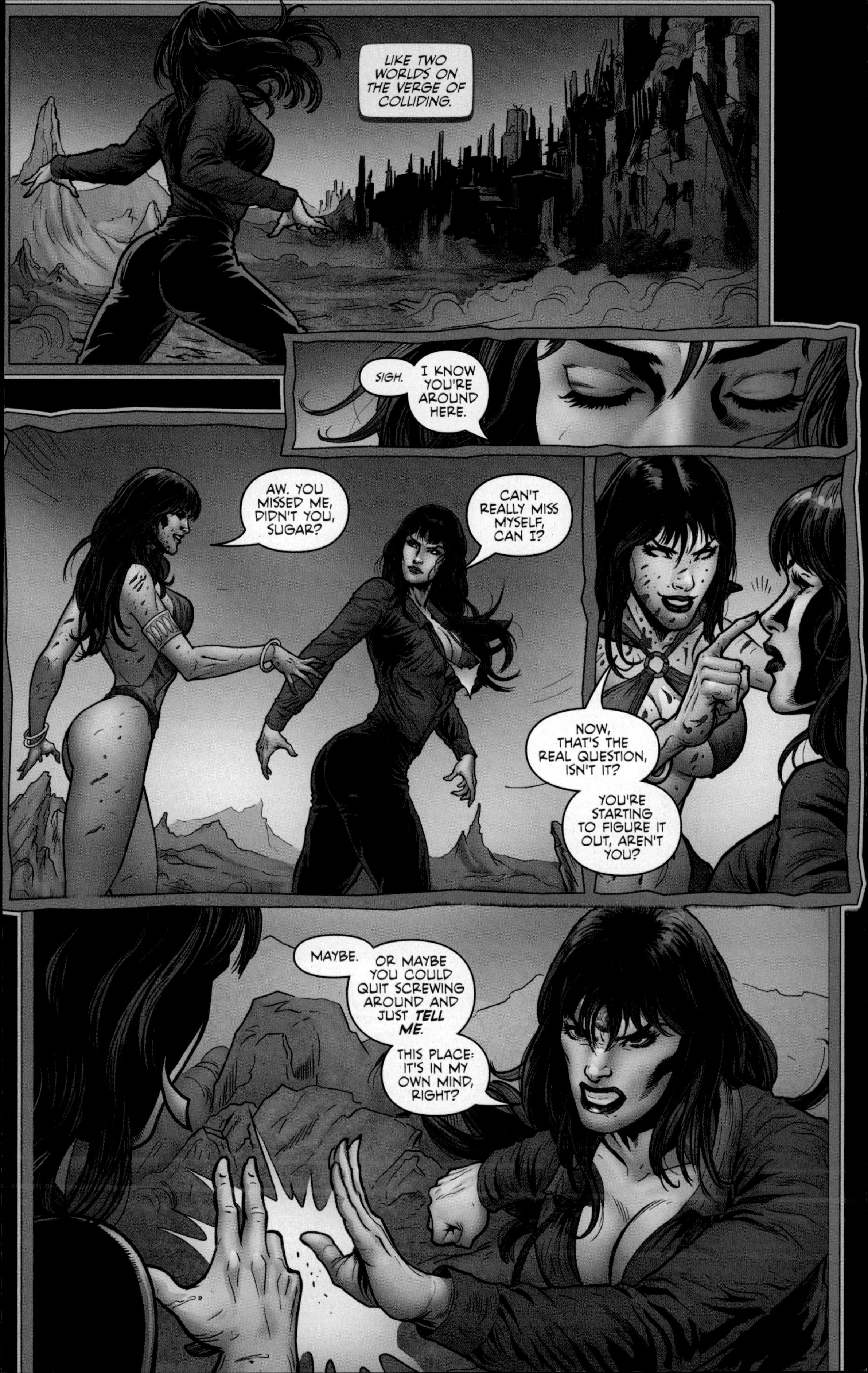
LIKE TWO WORLDS ON THE VERGE OF COLLIDING.
SIGH.
I KNOW YOU'RE AROUND HERE.
AW. YOU MISSED ME, DIDN'T YOU, SUGAR?
CAN'T REALLY MISS MYSELF, CAN I?
NOW, THAT'S THE REAL QUESTION, ISN'T IT?
YOU'RE STARTING TO FIGURE IT OUT, AREN'T YOU?
MAYBE.
OR MAYBE YOU COULD QUIT SCREWING AROUND AND JUST **TELL ME**.
THIS PLACE: IT'S IN MY OWN MIND, RIGHT?

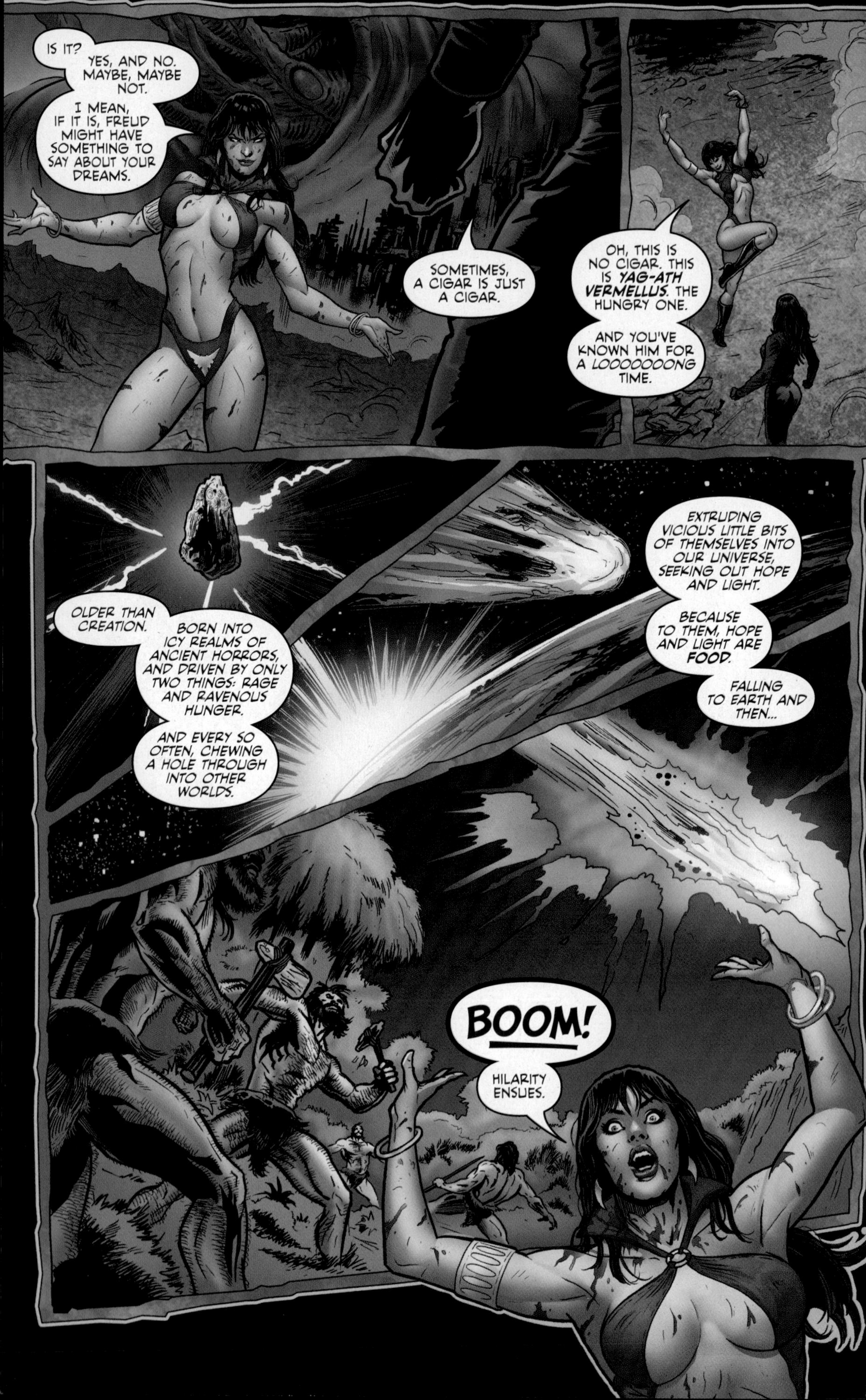
IS IT?
YES, AND NO. MAYBE, MAYBE NOT.
I MEAN, IF IT IS, FREUD MIGHT HAVE SOMETHING TO SAY ABOUT YOUR DREAMS.
SOMETIMES, A CIGAR IS JUST A CIGAR.
OH, THIS IS NO CIGAR. THIS IS YAG-ATH VERMELLUS. THE HUNGRY ONE.
AND YOU'VE KNOWN HIM FOR A LOOOOOOONG TIME.
OLDER THAN CREATION.
BORN INTO ICY REALMS OF ANCIENT HORRORS, AND DRIVEN BY ONLY TWO THINGS: RAGE AND RAVENOUS HUNGER.
AND EVERY SO OFTEN, CHEWING A HOLE THROUGH INTO OTHER WORLDS.
EXTRUDING VICIOUS LITTLE BITS OF THEMSELVES INTO OUR UNIVERSE, SEEKING OUT HOPE AND LIGHT.
BECAUSE TO THEM, HOPE AND LIGHT ARE FOOD.
FALLING TO EARTH AND THEN...
BOOM!
HILARITY ENSUES.

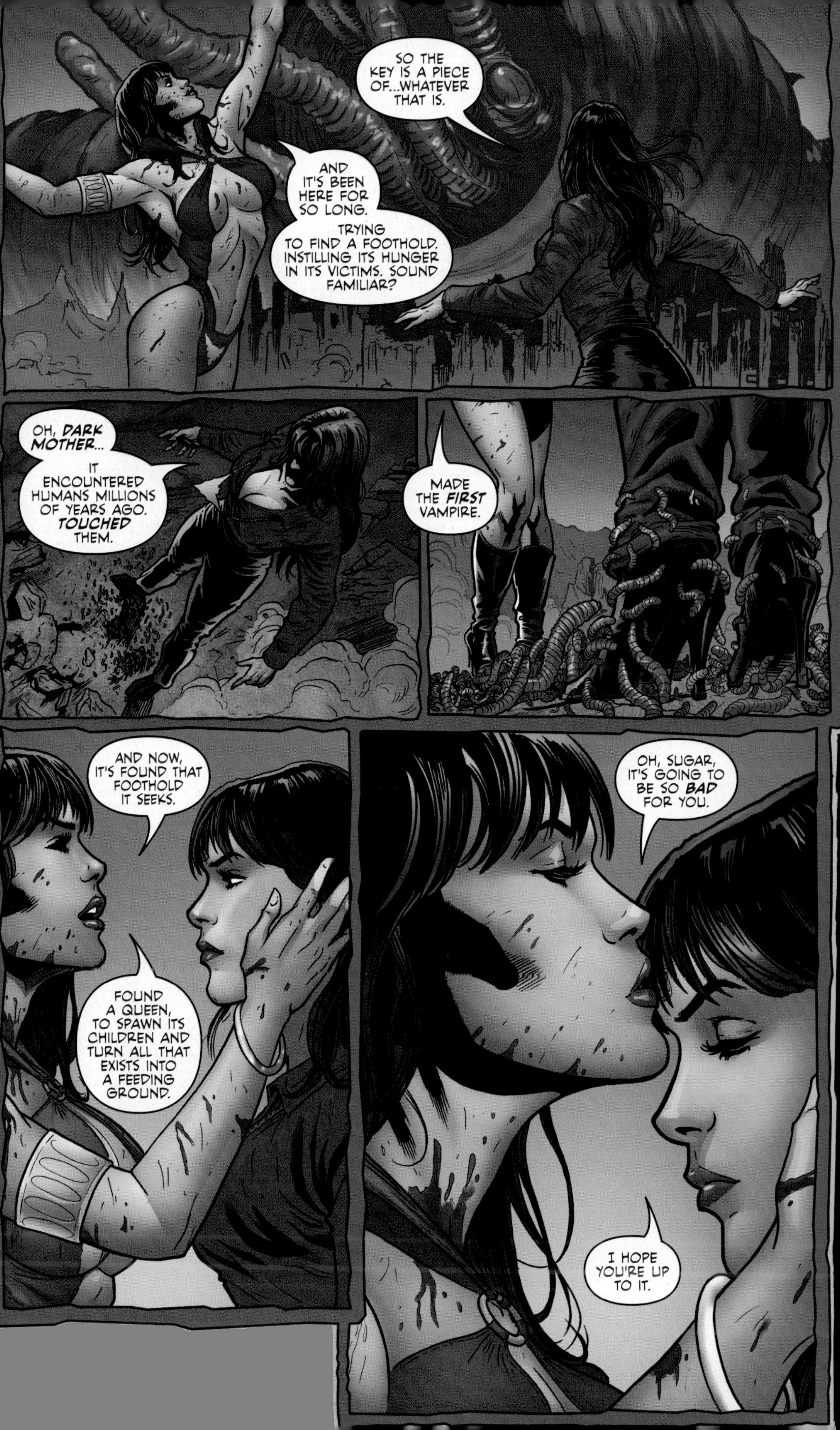
SO THE KEY IS A PIECE OF...WHATEVER THAT IS.
AND IT'S BEEN HERE FOR SO LONG.
TRYING TO FIND A FOOTHOLD. INSTILLING ITS HUNGER IN ITS VICTIMS. SOUND FAMILIAR?
OH, *DARK MOTHER*...
IT ENCOUNTERED HUMANS MILLIONS OF YEARS AGO. *TOUCHED* THEM.
MADE THE *FIRST* VAMPIRE.
AND NOW, IT'S FOUND THAT FOOTHOLD IT SEEKS.
FOUND A QUEEN, TO SPAWN ITS CHILDREN AND TURN ALL THAT EXISTS INTO A FEEDING GROUND.
OH, SUGAR, IT'S GOING TO BE SO *BAD* FOR YOU.
I HOPE YOU'RE UP TO IT.

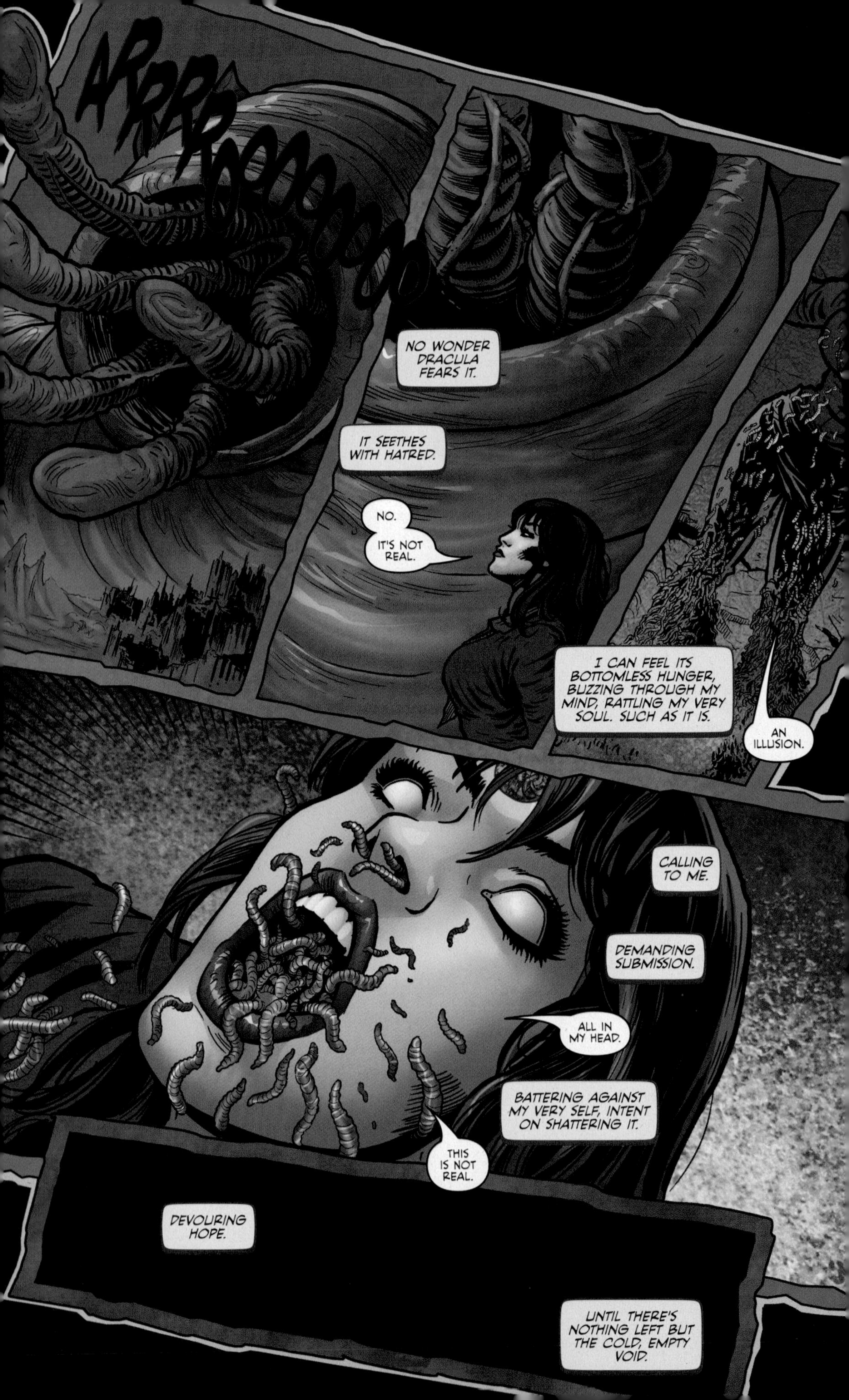
ARRRROOOOOOOO
NO WONDER DRACULA FEARS IT.
IT SEETHES WITH HATRED.
NO.
IT'S NOT REAL.
I CAN FEEL ITS BOTTOMLESS HUNGER, BUZZING THROUGH MY MIND, RATTLING MY VERY SOUL. SUCH AS IT IS.
AN ILLUSION.
CALLING TO ME.
DEMANDING SUBMISSION.
ALL IN MY HEAD.
BATTERING AGAINST MY VERY SELF, INTENT ON SHATTERING IT.
THIS IS NOT REAL.
DEVOURING HOPE.
UNTIL THERE'S NOTHING LEFT BUT THE COLD, EMPTY VOID.

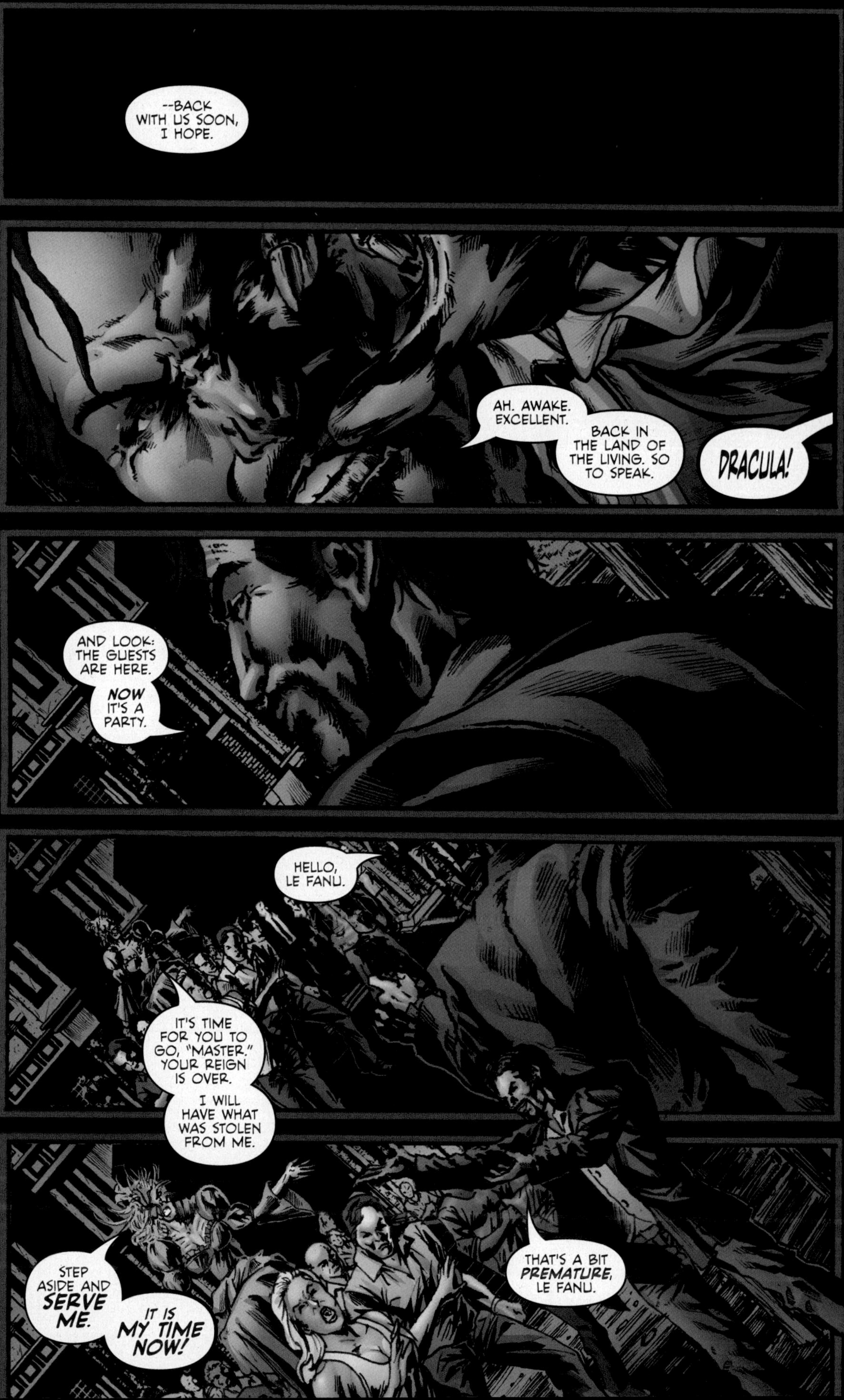
--BACK WITH US SOON, I HOPE.
AH. AWAKE. EXCELLENT.
BACK IN THE LAND OF THE LIVING. SO TO SPEAK.
DRACULA!
AND LOOK: THE GUESTS ARE HERE.
NOW IT'S A PARTY.
HELLO, LE FANU.
IT'S TIME FOR YOU TO GO, "MASTER." YOUR REIGN IS OVER.
I WILL HAVE WHAT WAS STOLEN FROM ME.
THAT'S A BIT PREMATURE, LE FANU.
STEP ASIDE AND SERVE ME.
IT IS MY TIME NOW!

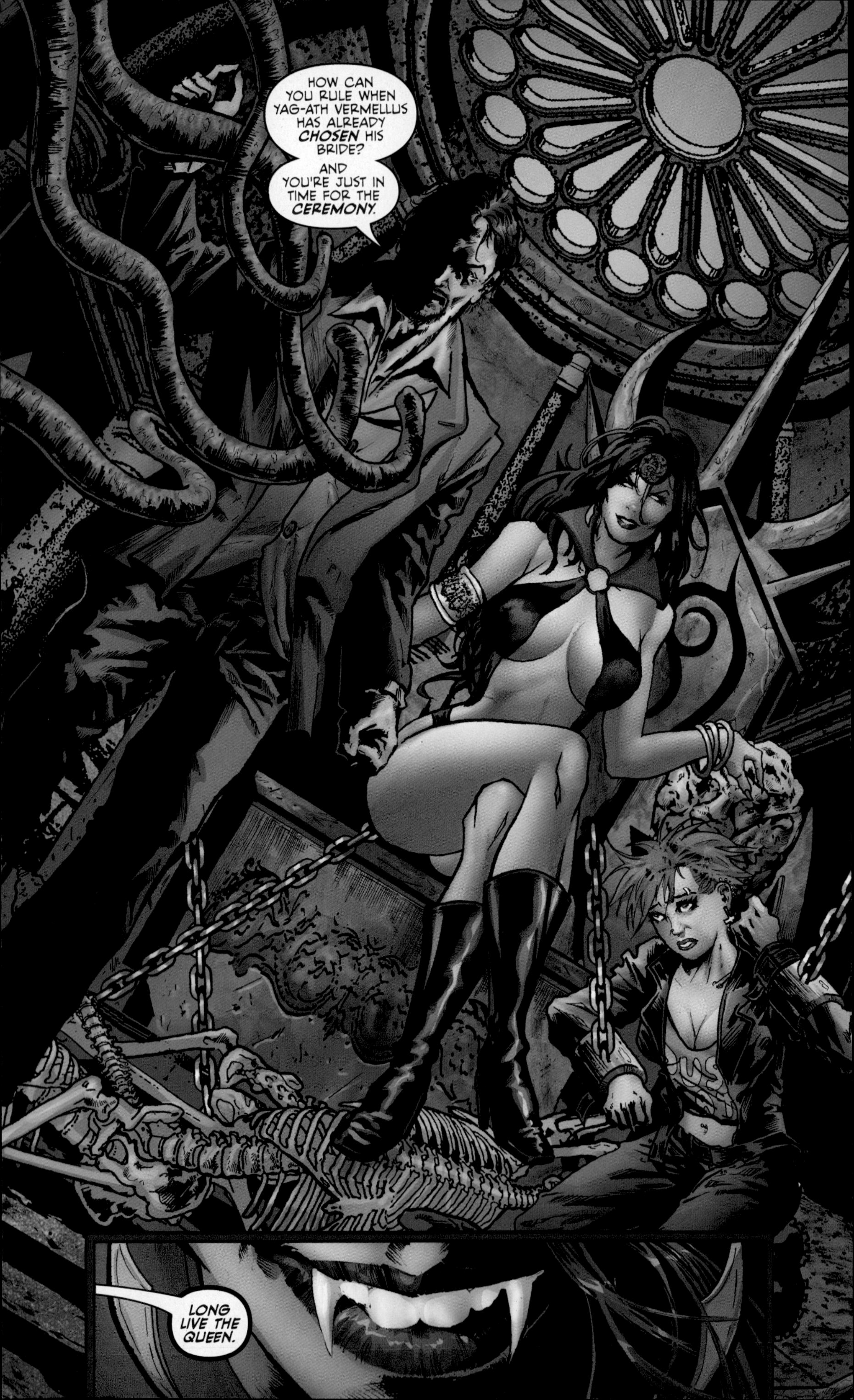
HOW CAN YOU RULE WHEN YAG-ATH VERMELLUS HAS ALREADY CHOSEN HIS BRIDE?
AND YOU'RE JUST IN TIME FOR THE CEREMONY.
LONG LIVE THE QUEEN.

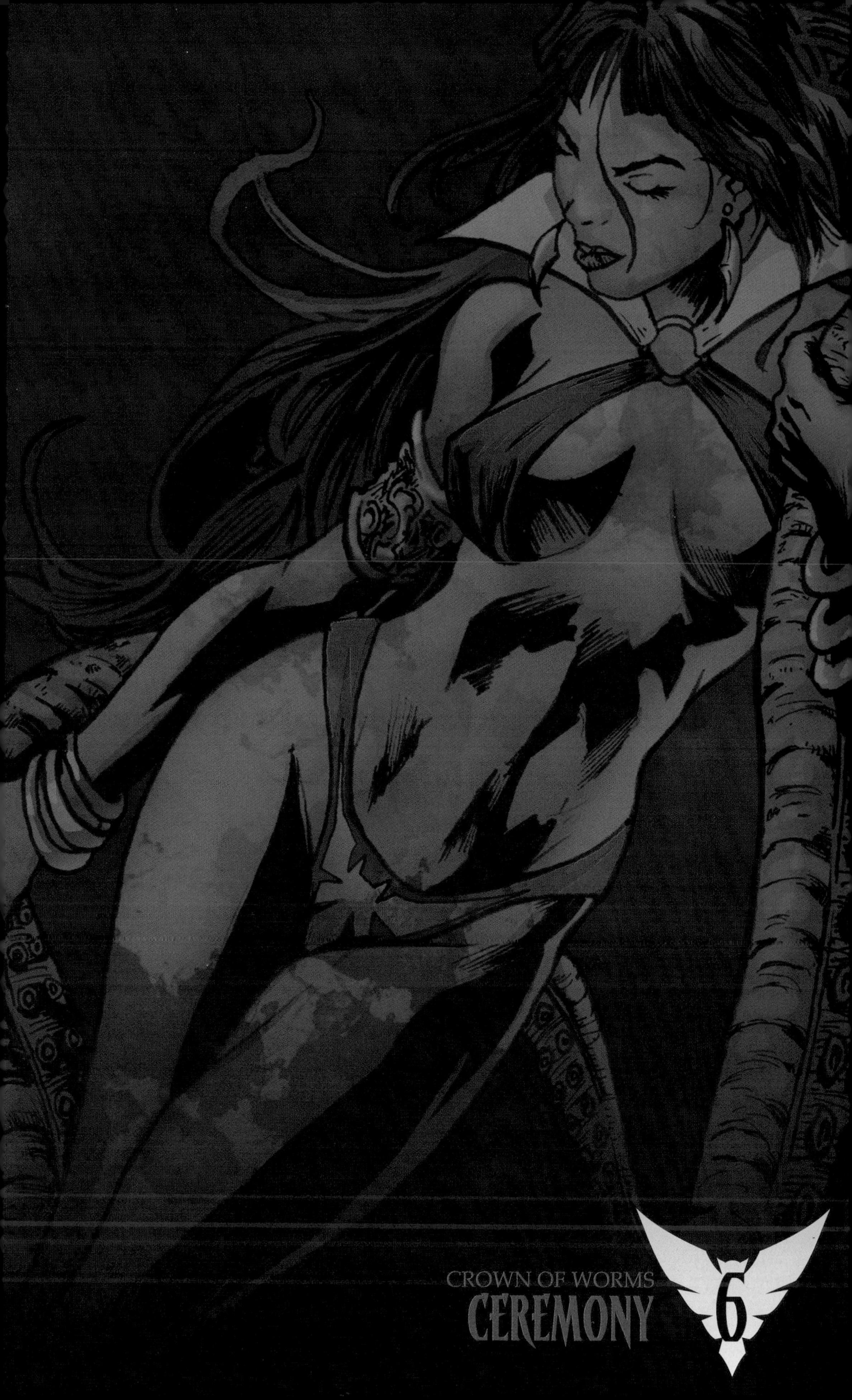
CROWN OF WORMS
CEREMONY
6

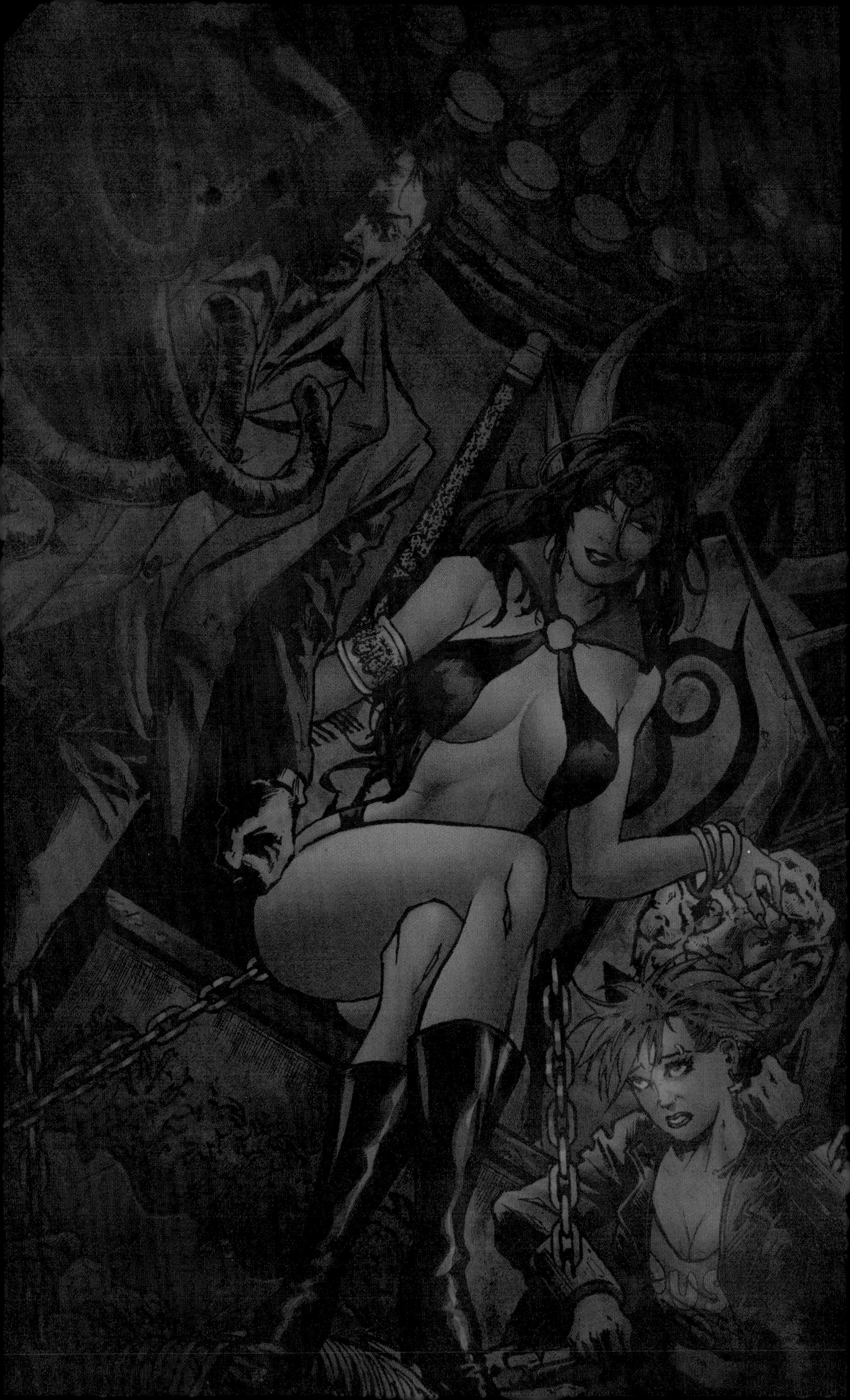

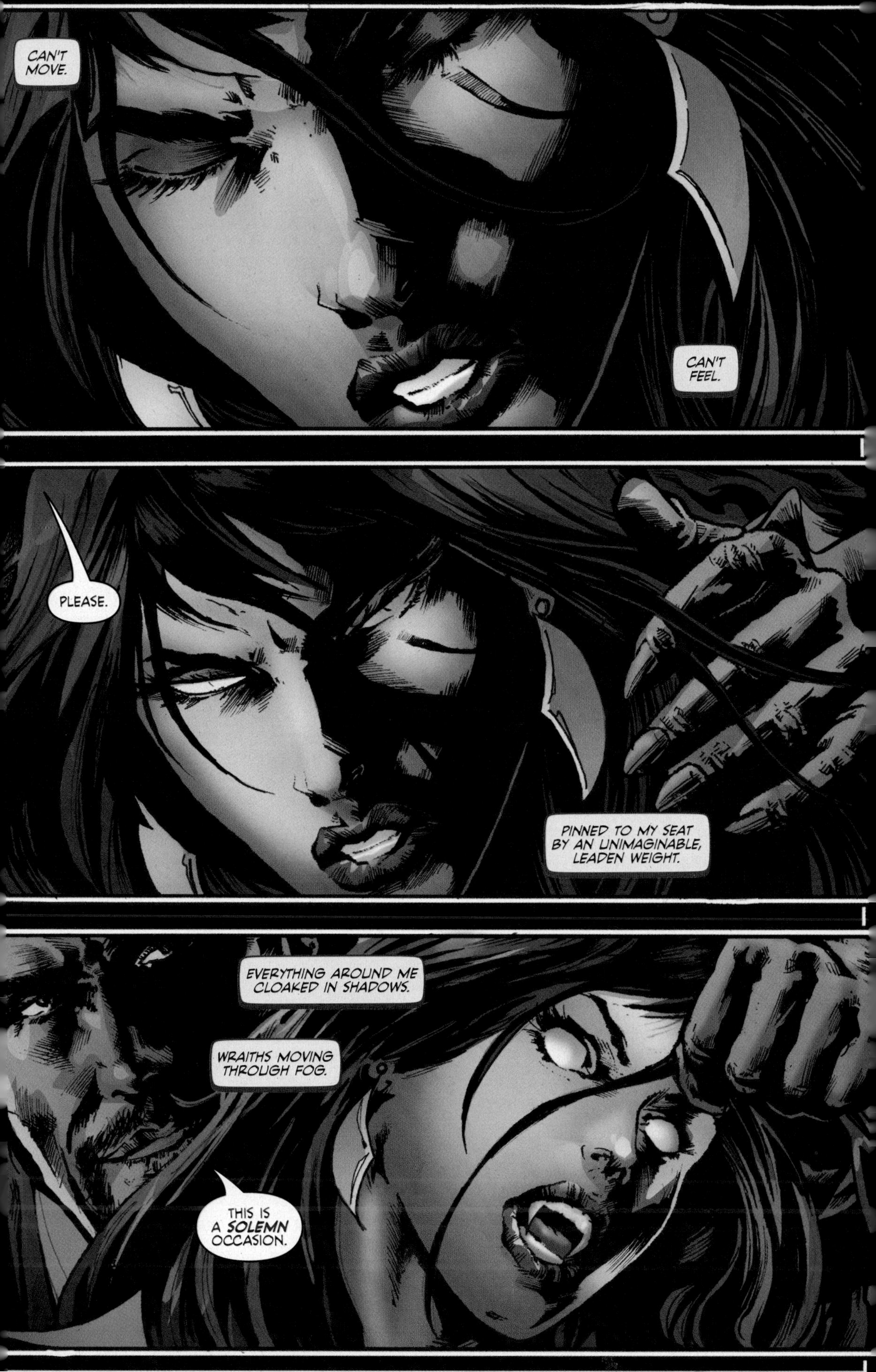
CAN'T MOVE.
CAN'T FEEL.
PLEASE.
PINNED TO MY SEAT BY AN UNIMAGINABLE, LEADEN WEIGHT.
EVERYTHING AROUND ME CLOAKED IN SHADOWS.
WRAITHS MOVING THROUGH FOG.
THIS IS A SOLEMN OCCASION.

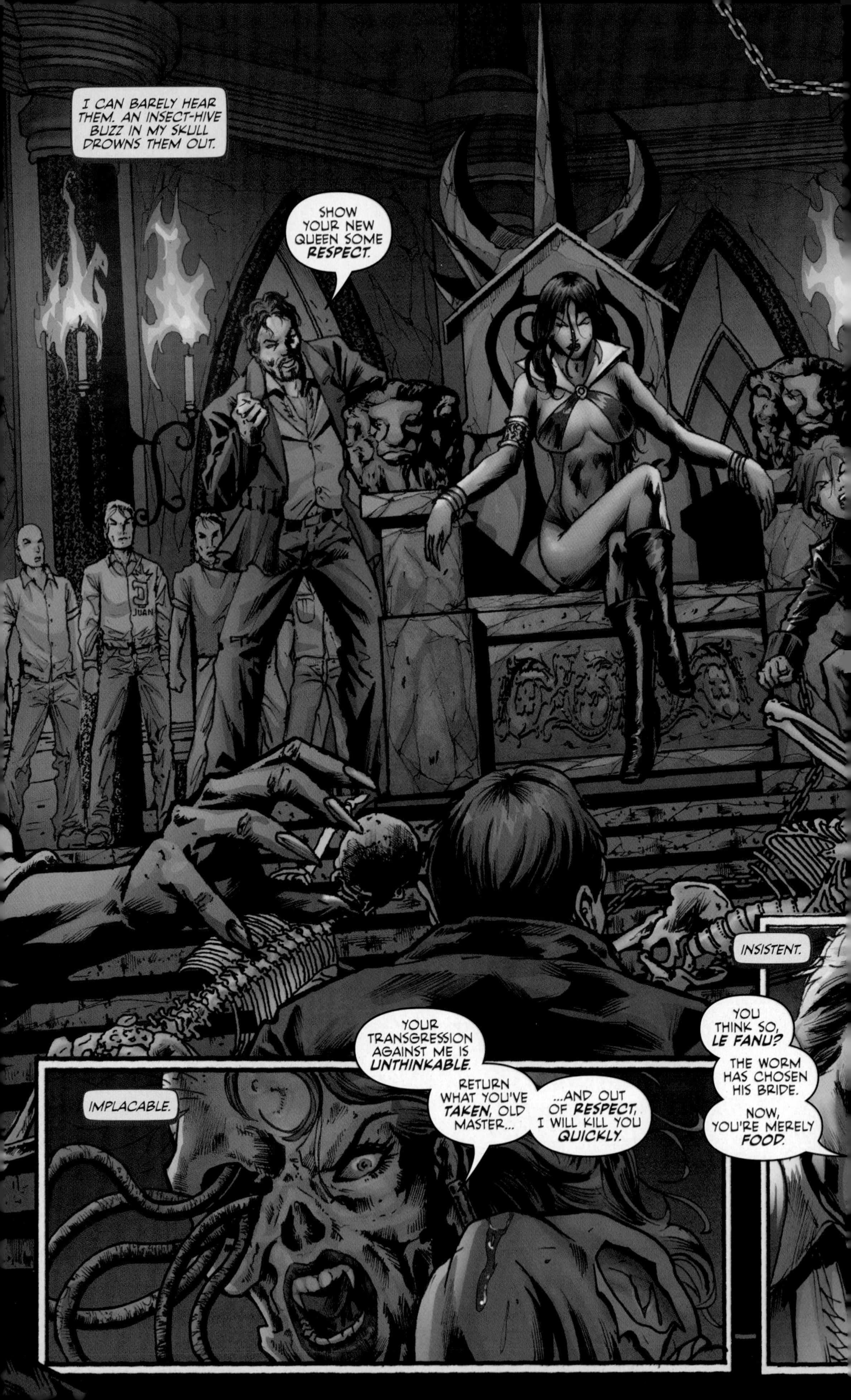
I CAN BARELY HEAR THEM. AN INSECT-HIVE BUZZ IN MY SKULL DROWNS THEM OUT.
SHOW YOUR NEW QUEEN SOME RESPECT.
JUAN
INSISTENT.
IMPLACABLE.
YOUR TRANSGRESSION AGAINST ME IS UNTHINKABLE.
RETURN WHAT YOU'VE TAKEN, OLD MASTER...
...AND OUT OF RESPECT, I WILL KILL YOU QUICKLY.
YOU THINK SO, LE FANU?
THE WORM HAS CHOSEN HIS BRIDE.
NOW, YOU'RE MERELY FOOD.

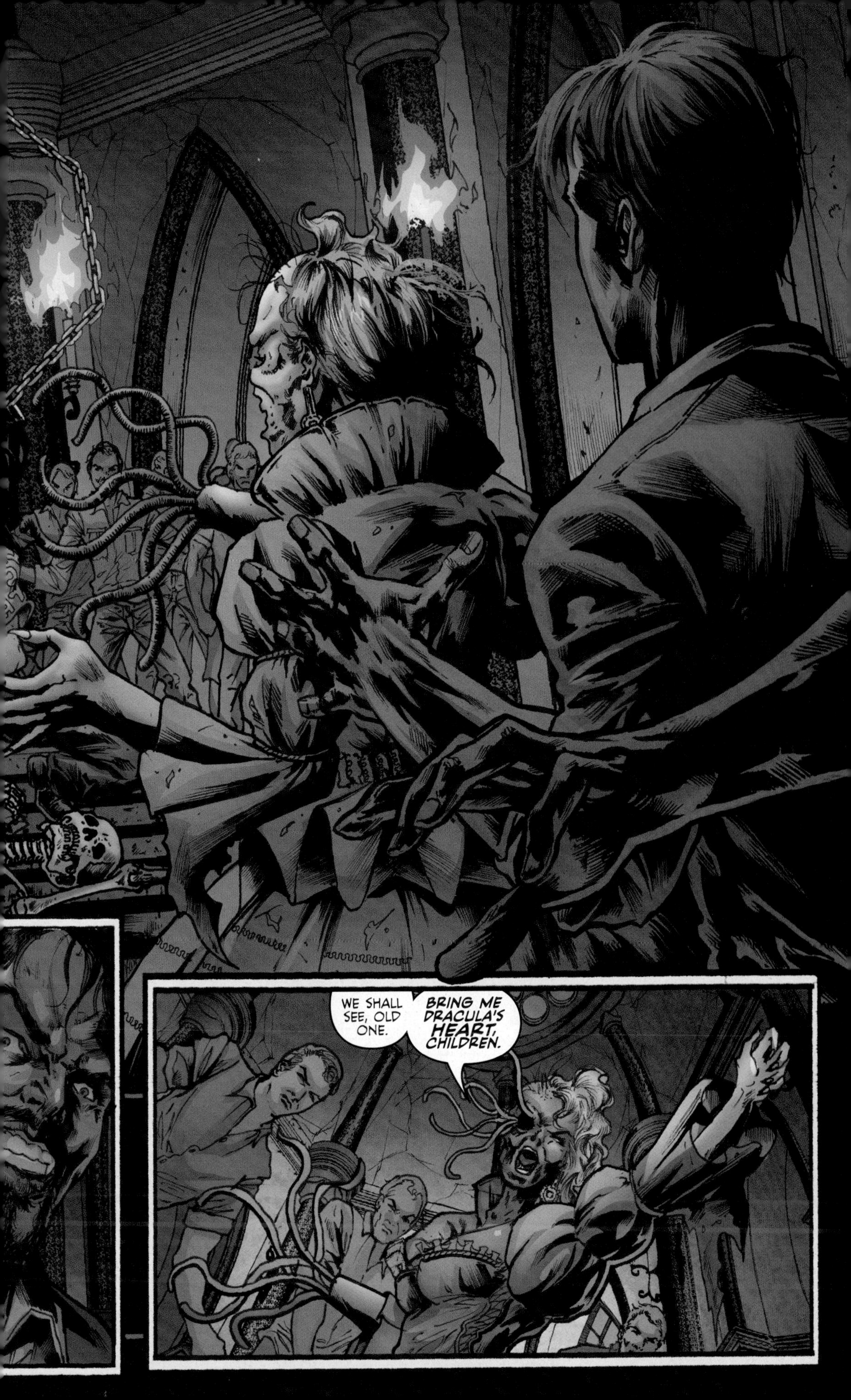
WE SHALL SEE, OLD ONE.
BRING ME DRACULA'S HEART, CHILDREN.

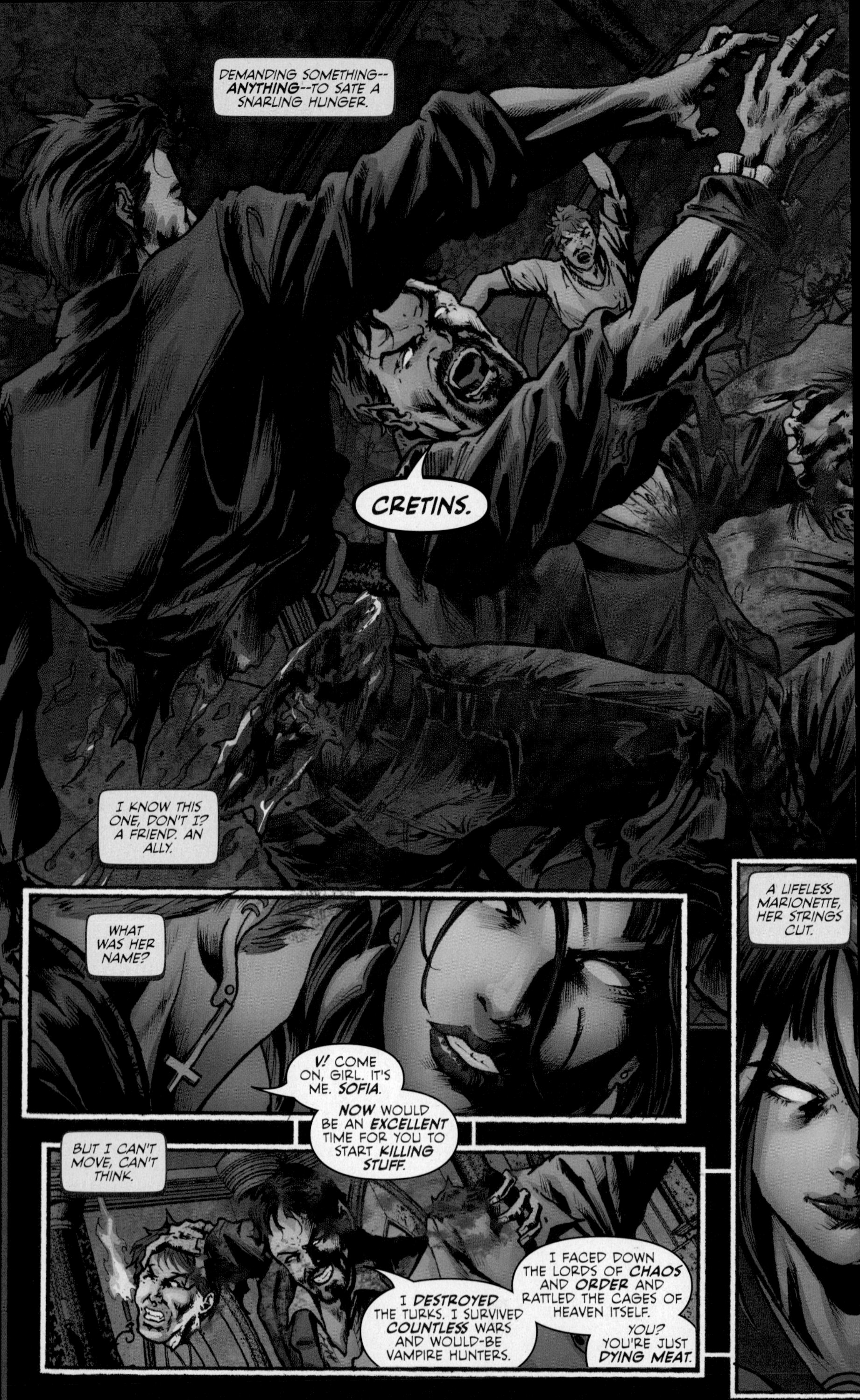
DEMANDING SOMETHING--ANYTHING--TO SATE A SNARLING HUNGER.
CRETINS.
I KNOW THIS ONE, DON'T I? A FRIEND. AN ALLY.
WHAT WAS HER NAME?
V! COME ON, GIRL. IT'S ME. SOFIA.
NOW WOULD BE AN EXCELLENT TIME FOR YOU TO START KILLING STUFF.
A LIFELESS MARIONETTE, HER STRINGS CUT.
BUT I CAN'T MOVE, CAN'T THINK.
I DESTROYED THE TURKS. I SURVIVED COUNTLESS WARS AND WOULD-BE VAMPIRE HUNTERS.
I FACED DOWN THE LORDS OF CHAOS AND ORDER AND RATTLED THE CAGES OF HEAVEN ITSELF.
YOU? YOU'RE JUST DYING MEAT.

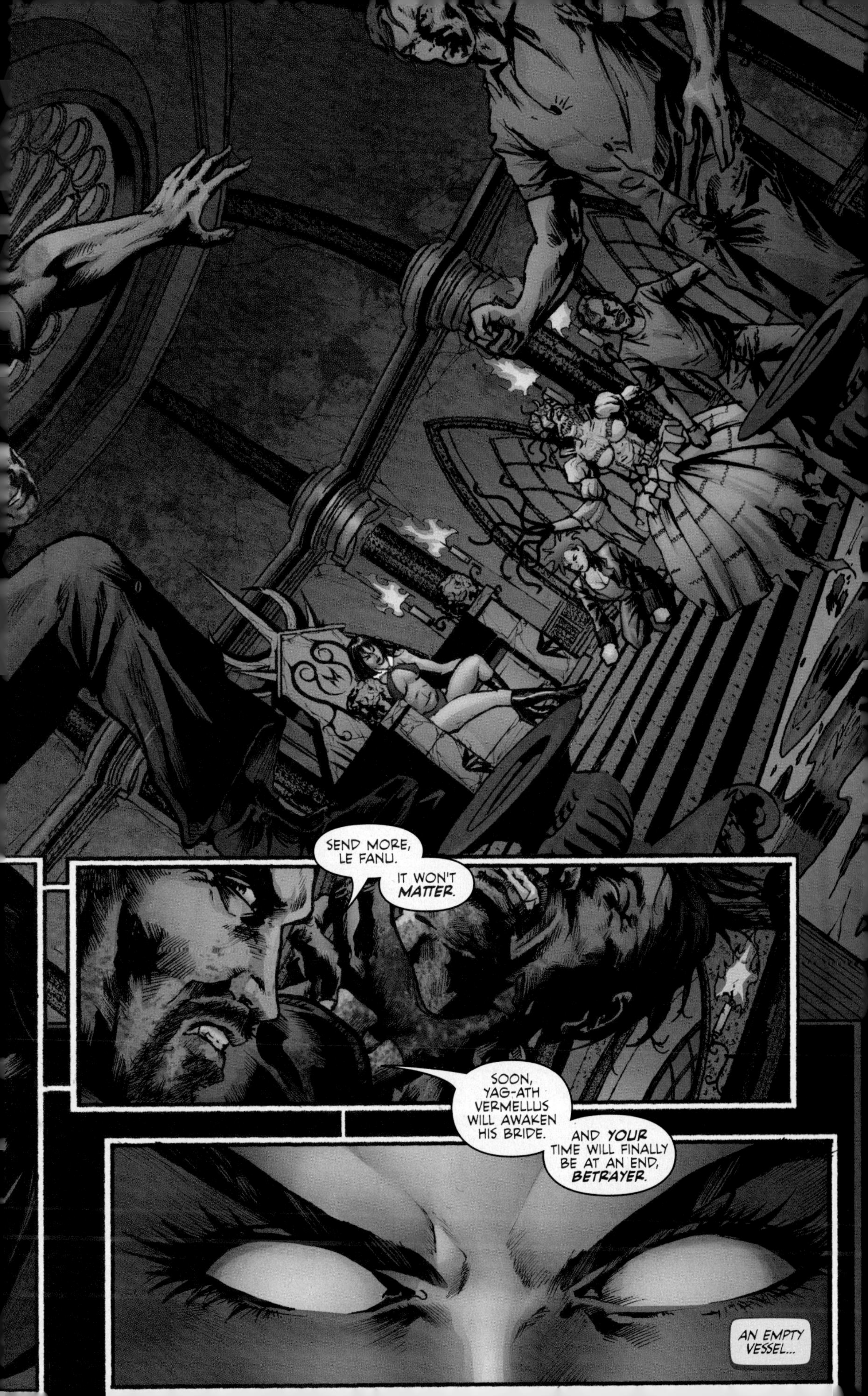
SEND MORE, LE FANU.
IT WON'T MATTER.
SOON, YAG-ATH VERMELLUS WILL AWAKEN HIS BRIDE.
AND YOUR TIME WILL FINALLY BE AT AN END, BETRAYER.
AN EMPTY VESSEL...

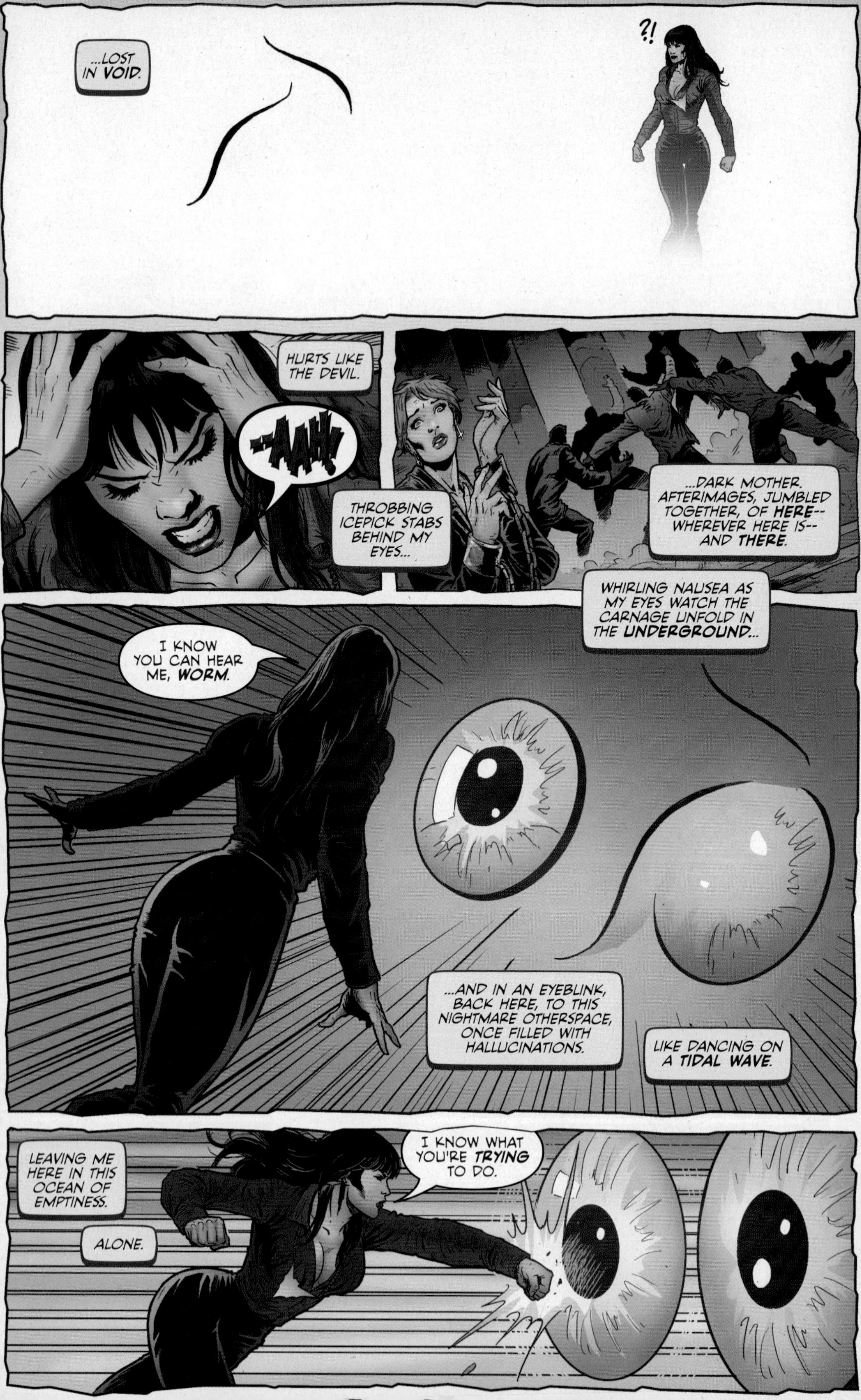

...LOST IN VOID.
?!
HURTS LIKE THE DEVIL.
--AAH!
THROBBING ICEPICK STABS BEHIND MY EYES...
...DARK MOTHER. AFTERIMAGES, JUMBLED TOGETHER, OF HERE-- WHEREVER HERE IS-- AND THERE.
WHIRLING NAUSEA AS MY EYES WATCH THE CARNAGE UNFOLD IN THE UNDERGROUND...
I KNOW YOU CAN HEAR ME, WORM.
...AND IN AN EYEBLINK, BACK HERE, TO THIS NIGHTMARE OTHERSPACE, ONCE FILLED WITH HALLUCINATIONS.
LIKE DANCING ON A TIDAL WAVE.
LEAVING ME HERE IN THIS OCEAN OF EMPTINESS.
ALONE.
I KNOW WHAT YOU'RE TRYING TO DO.

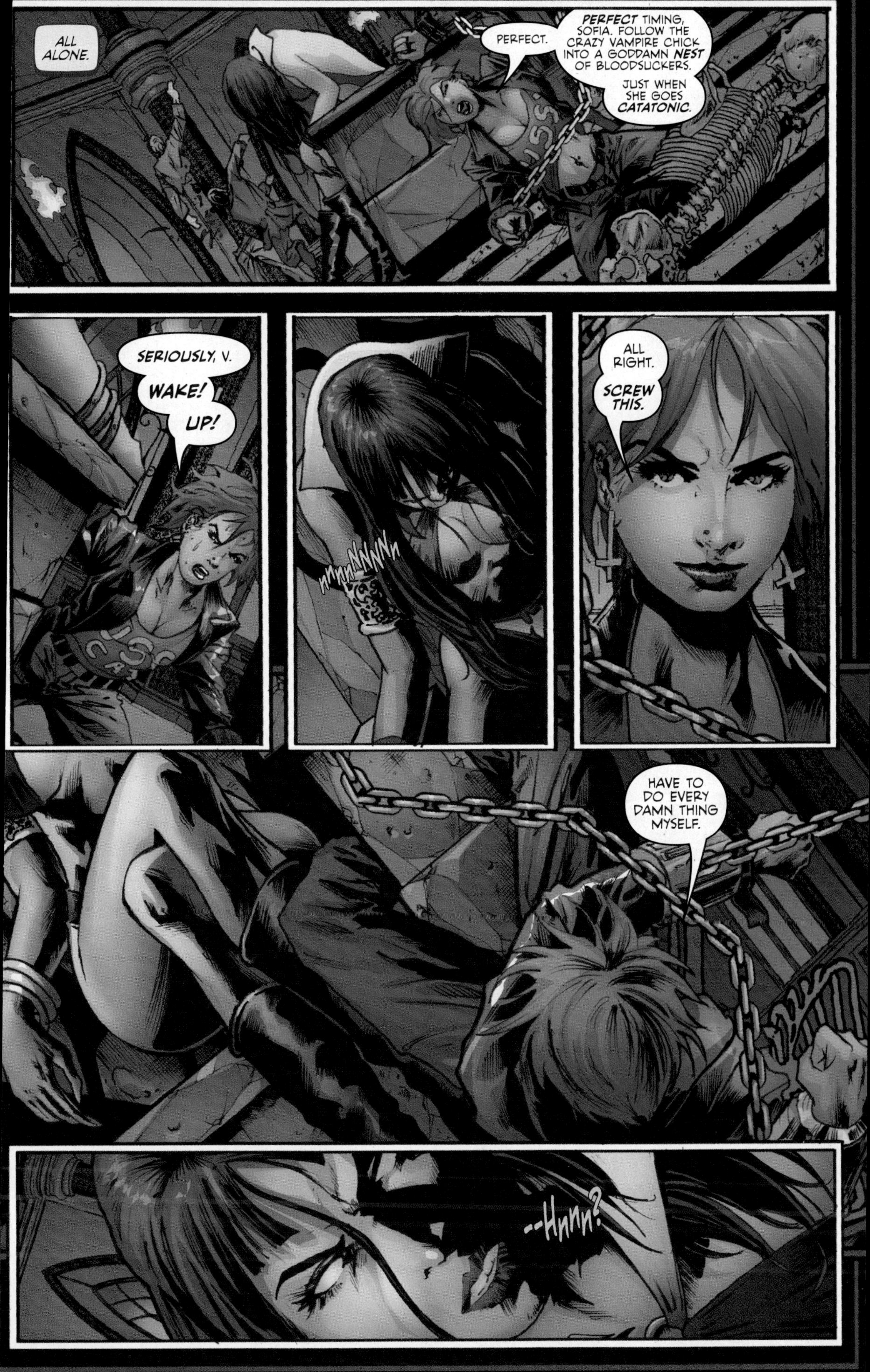
ALL ALONE.
PERFECT.
PERFECT TIMING, SOFIA. FOLLOW THE CRAZY VAMPIRE CHICK INTO A GODDAMN NEST OF BLOODSUCKERS.
JUST WHEN SHE GOES CATATONIC.
SERIOUSLY, V.
WAKE!
UP!
nnnnNNNNn
ALL RIGHT.
SCREW THIS.
HAVE TO DO EVERY DAMN THING MYSELF.
--Hnnn?

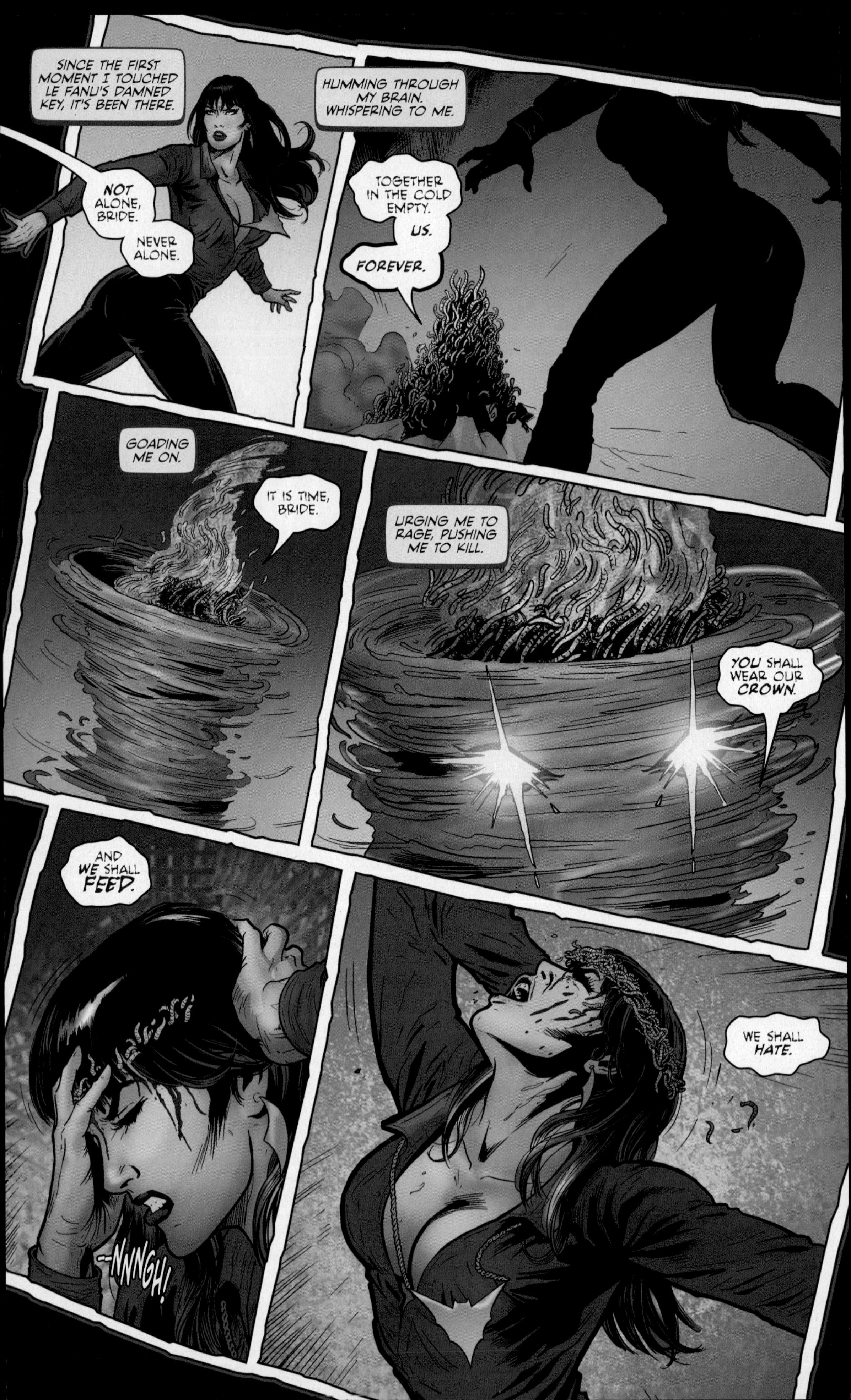
SINCE THE FIRST MOMENT I TOUCHED LE FANU'S DAMNED KEY, IT'S BEEN THERE.
NOT ALONE, BRIDE.
NEVER ALONE.
HUMMING THROUGH MY BRAIN. WHISPERING TO ME.
TOGETHER IN THE COLD EMPTY.
US.
FOREVER.
GOADING ME ON.
IT IS TIME, BRIDE.
URGING ME TO RAGE, PUSHING ME TO KILL.
YOU SHALL WEAR OUR CROWN.
AND WE SHALL FEED.
WE SHALL HATE.
-NNNGH!

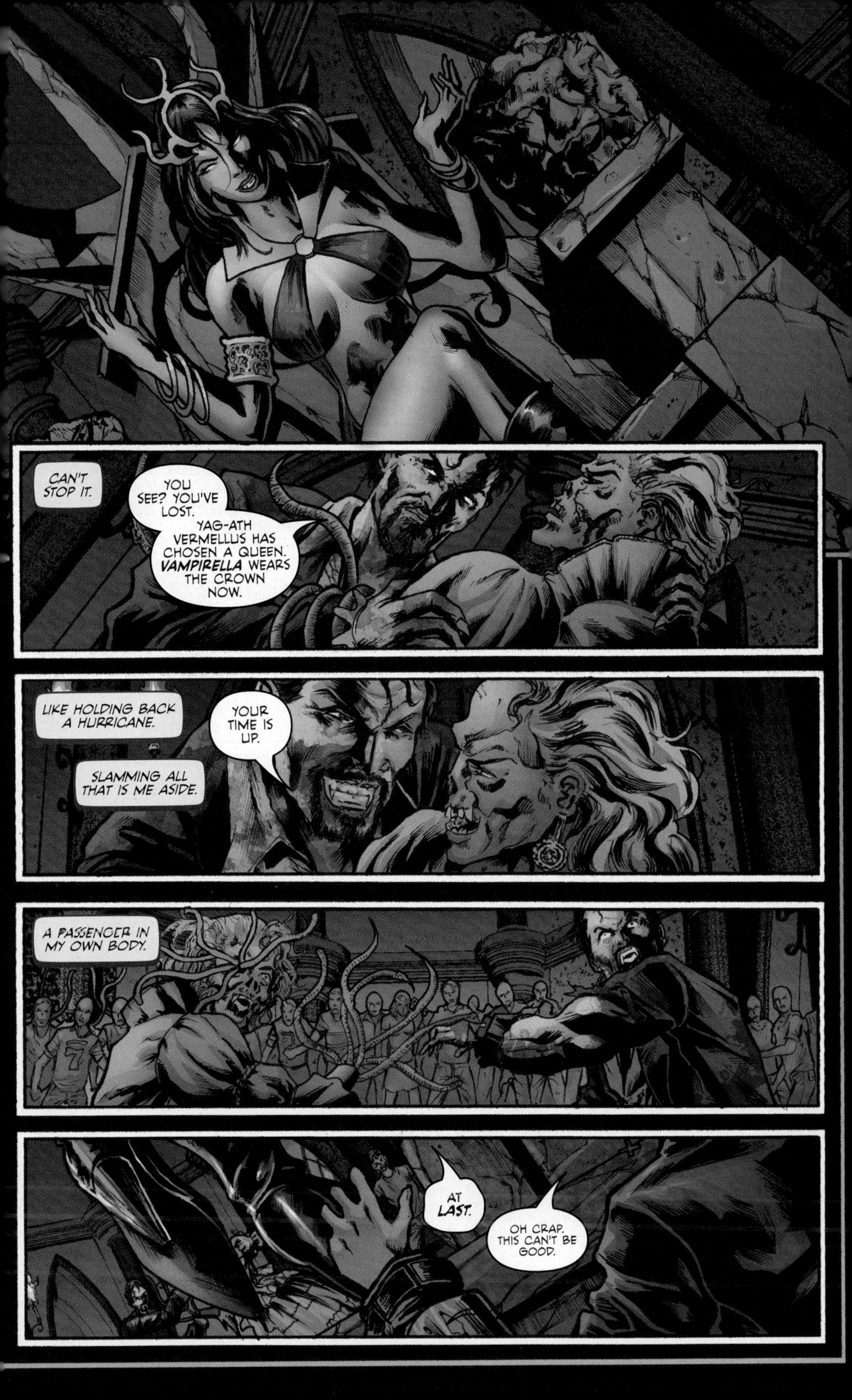
CAN'T STOP IT.
YOU SEE? YOU'VE LOST.
YAG-ATH VERMELLUS HAS CHOSEN A QUEEN. VAMPIRELLA WEARS THE CROWN NOW.
LIKE HOLDING BACK A HURRICANE.
YOUR TIME IS UP.
SLAMMING ALL THAT IS ME ASIDE.
A PASSENGER IN MY OWN BODY.
AT LAST.
OH CRAP. THIS CAN'T BE GOOD.

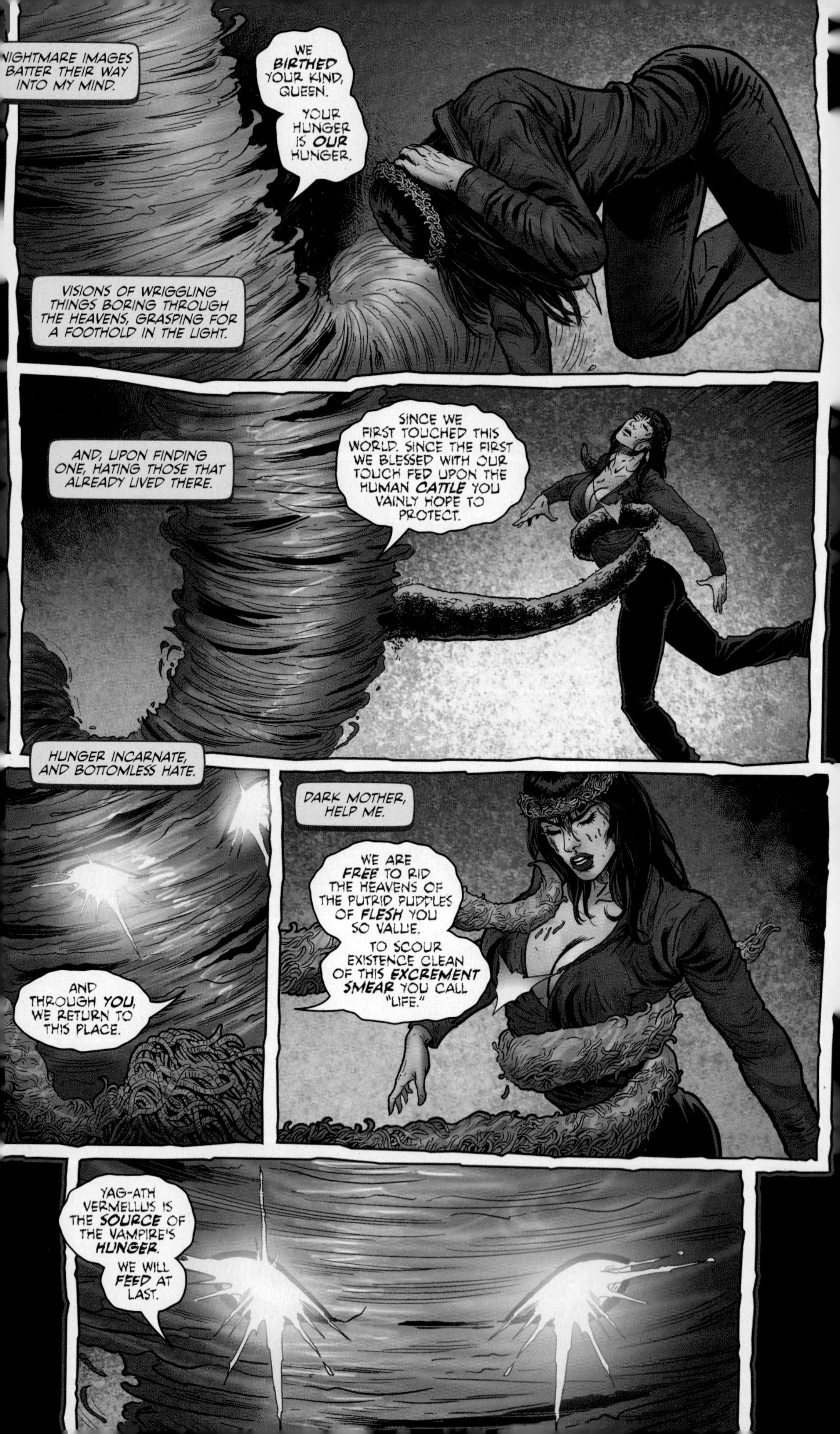
NIGHTMARE IMAGES BATTER THEIR WAY INTO MY MIND.
WE BIRTHED YOUR KIND, QUEEN.
YOUR HUNGER IS OUR HUNGER.
VISIONS OF WRIGGLING THINGS BORING THROUGH THE HEAVENS, GRASPING FOR A FOOTHOLD IN THE LIGHT.
AND, UPON FINDING ONE, HATING THOSE THAT ALREADY LIVED THERE.
SINCE WE FIRST TOUCHED THIS WORLD. SINCE THE FIRST WE BLESSED WITH OUR TOUCH FED UPON THE HUMAN CATTLE YOU VAINLY HOPE TO PROTECT.
HUNGER INCARNATE, AND BOTTOMLESS HATE.
AND THROUGH YOU, WE RETURN TO THIS PLACE.
DARK MOTHER, HELP ME.
WE ARE FREE TO RID THE HEAVENS OF THE PUTRID PUDDLES OF FLESH YOU SO VALUE.
TO SCOUR EXISTENCE CLEAN OF THIS EXCREMENT SMEAR YOU CALL "LIFE."
YAG-ATH VERMELLUS IS THE SOURCE OF THE VAMPIRE'S HUNGER.
WE WILL FEED AT LAST.

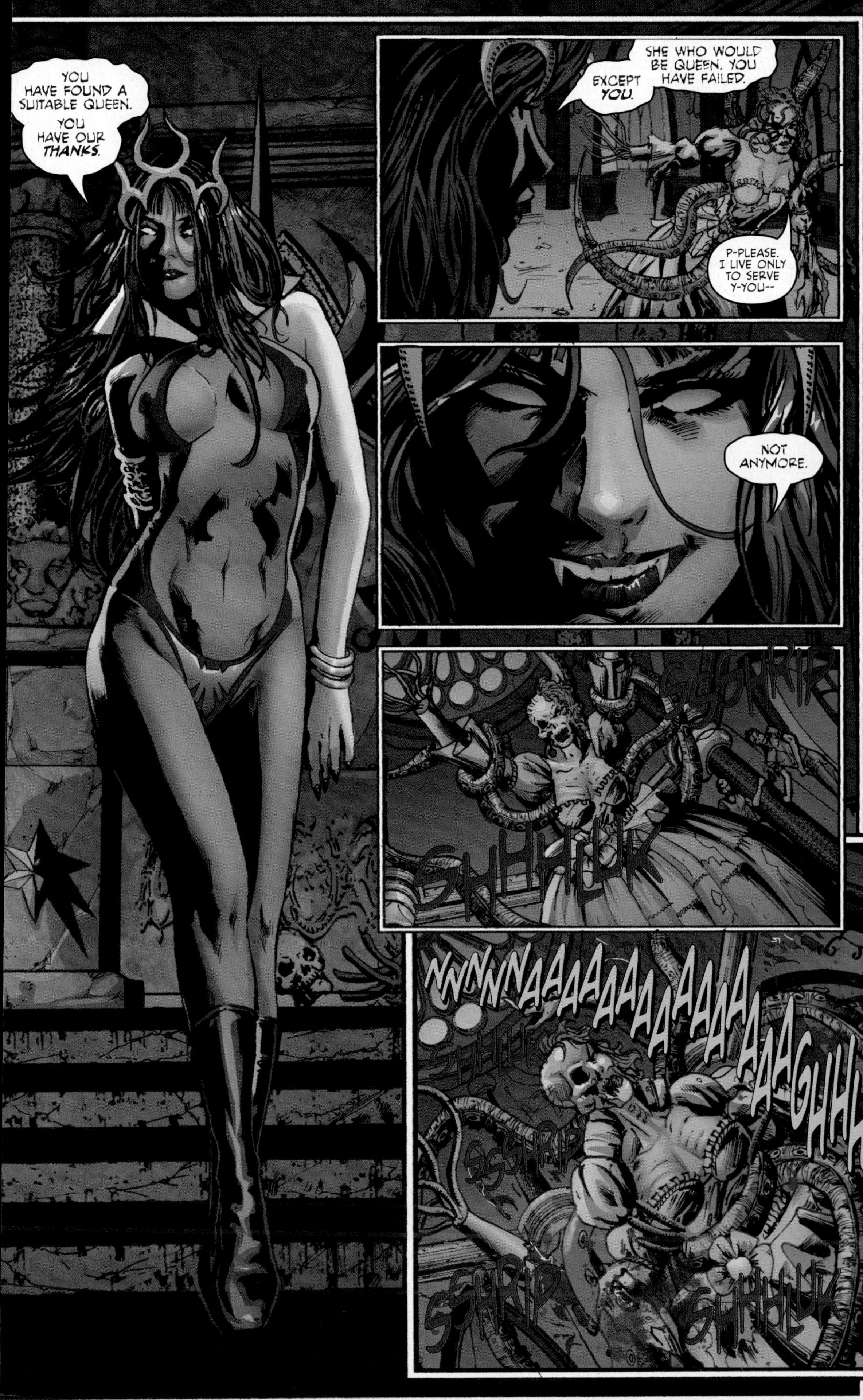
YOU HAVE FOUND A SUITABLE QUEEN.
YOU HAVE OUR *THANKS*.
EXCEPT *YOU*.
SHE WHO WOULD BE QUEEN. YOU HAVE FAILED.
P-PLEASE. I LIVE ONLY TO SERVE Y-YOU--
NOT ANYMORE.
SSSHRIP
SHHHLUK
NNNNAAAAAAAAAAAAAAGHHH
SHHLUK
SSSHRIP
SSHRIP
SHHLUK

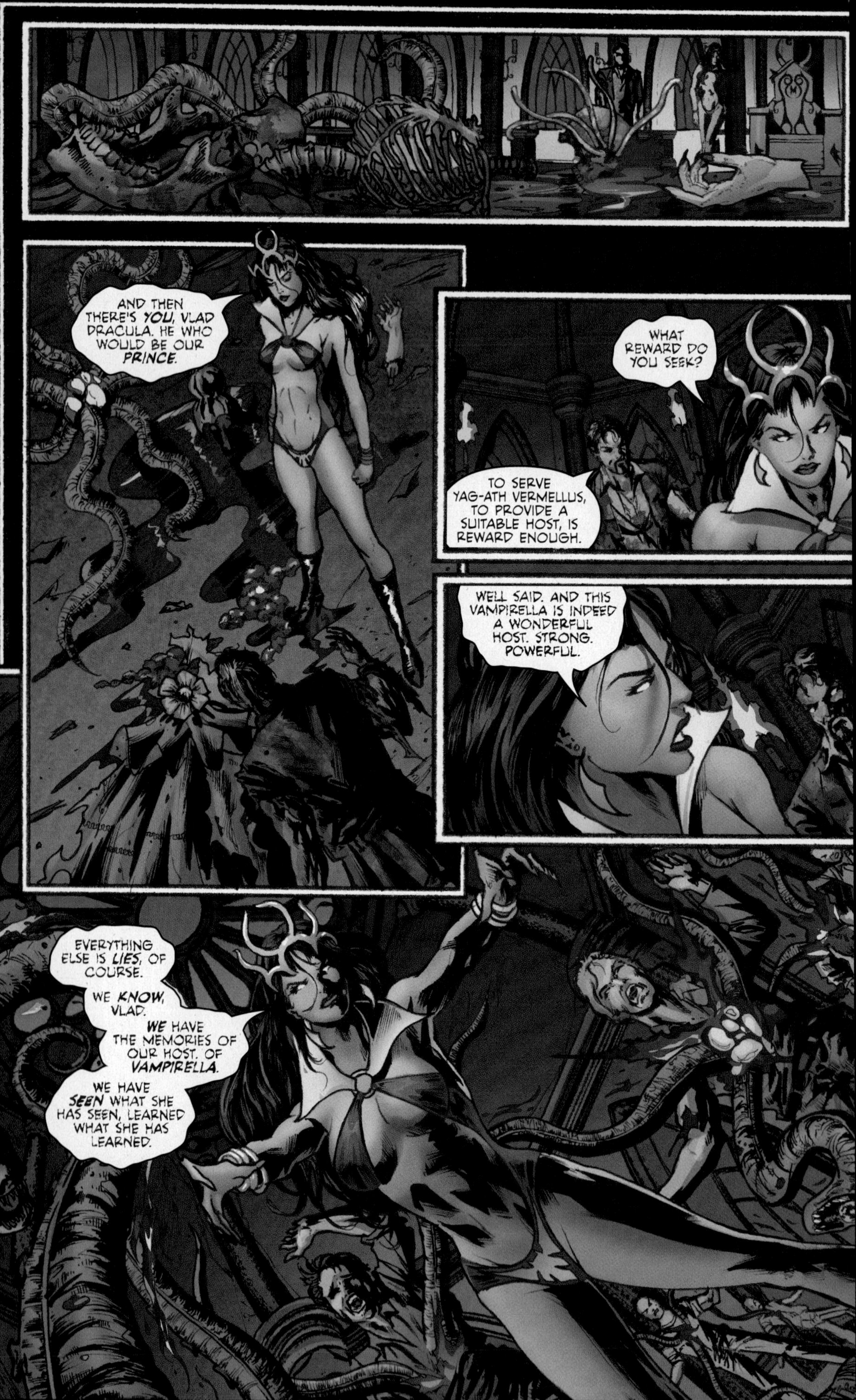
AND THEN THERE'S YOU, VLAD DRACULA. HE WHO WOULD BE OUR PRINCE.
WHAT REWARD DO YOU SEEK?
TO SERVE YAG-ATH VERMELLUS, TO PROVIDE A SUITABLE HOST, IS REWARD ENOUGH.
WELL SAID. AND THIS VAMPIRELLA IS INDEED A WONDERFUL HOST. STRONG. POWERFUL.
EVERYTHING ELSE IS LIES, OF COURSE.
WE KNOW, VLAD.
WE HAVE THE MEMORIES OF OUR HOST. OF VAMPIRELLA.
WE HAVE SEEN WHAT SHE HAS SEEN, LEARNED WHAT SHE HAS LEARNED.

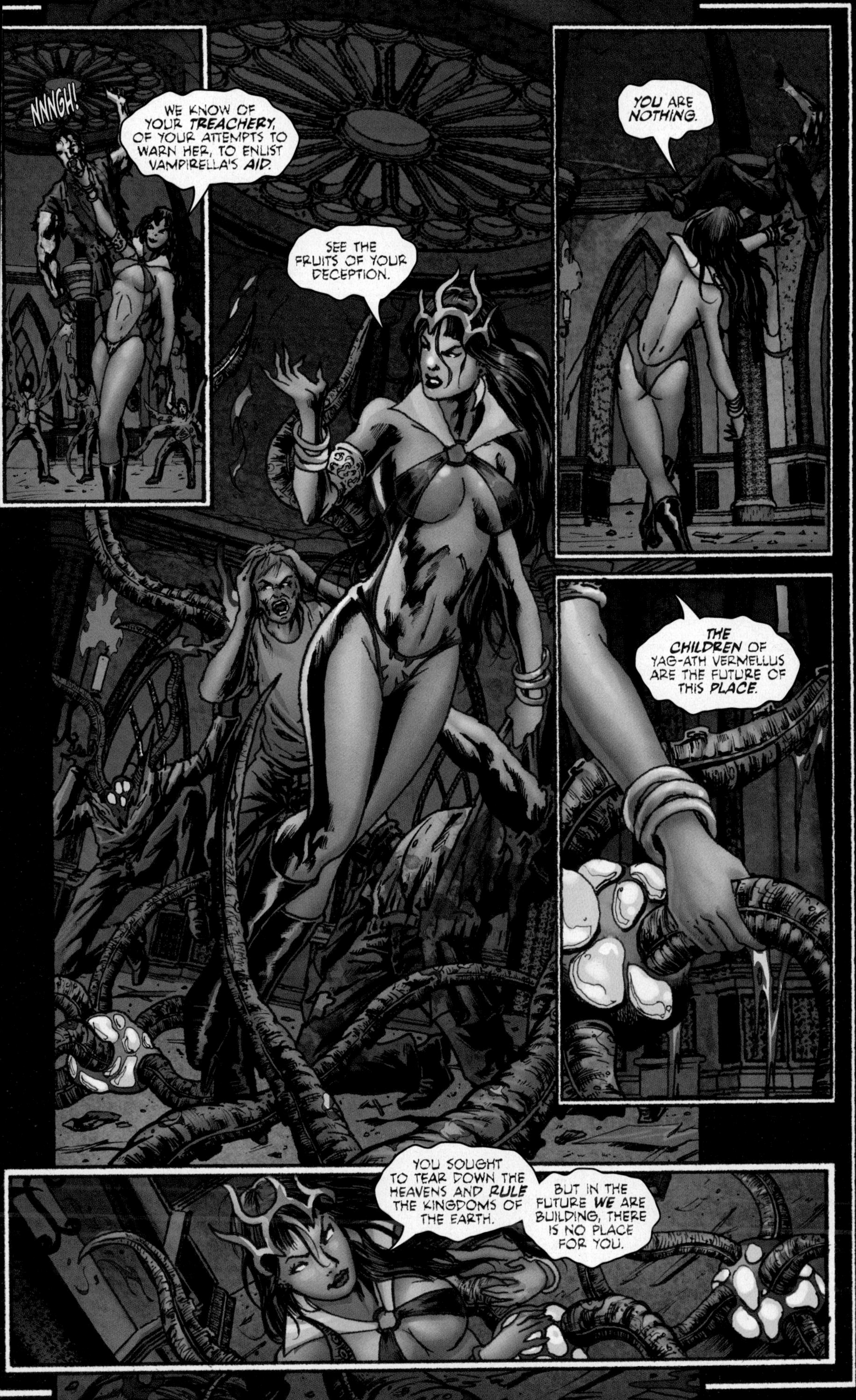
NNNGH!
WE KNOW OF YOUR TREACHERY, OF YOUR ATTEMPTS TO WARN HER, TO ENLIST VAMPIRELLA'S AID.
YOU ARE NOTHING.
SEE THE FRUITS OF YOUR DECEPTION.
THE CHILDREN OF YAG-ATH VERMELLUS ARE THE FUTURE OF THIS PLACE.
YOU SOUGHT TO TEAR DOWN THE HEAVENS AND RULE THE KINGDOMS OF THE EARTH.
BUT IN THE FUTURE WE ARE BUILDING, THERE IS NO PLACE FOR YOU.

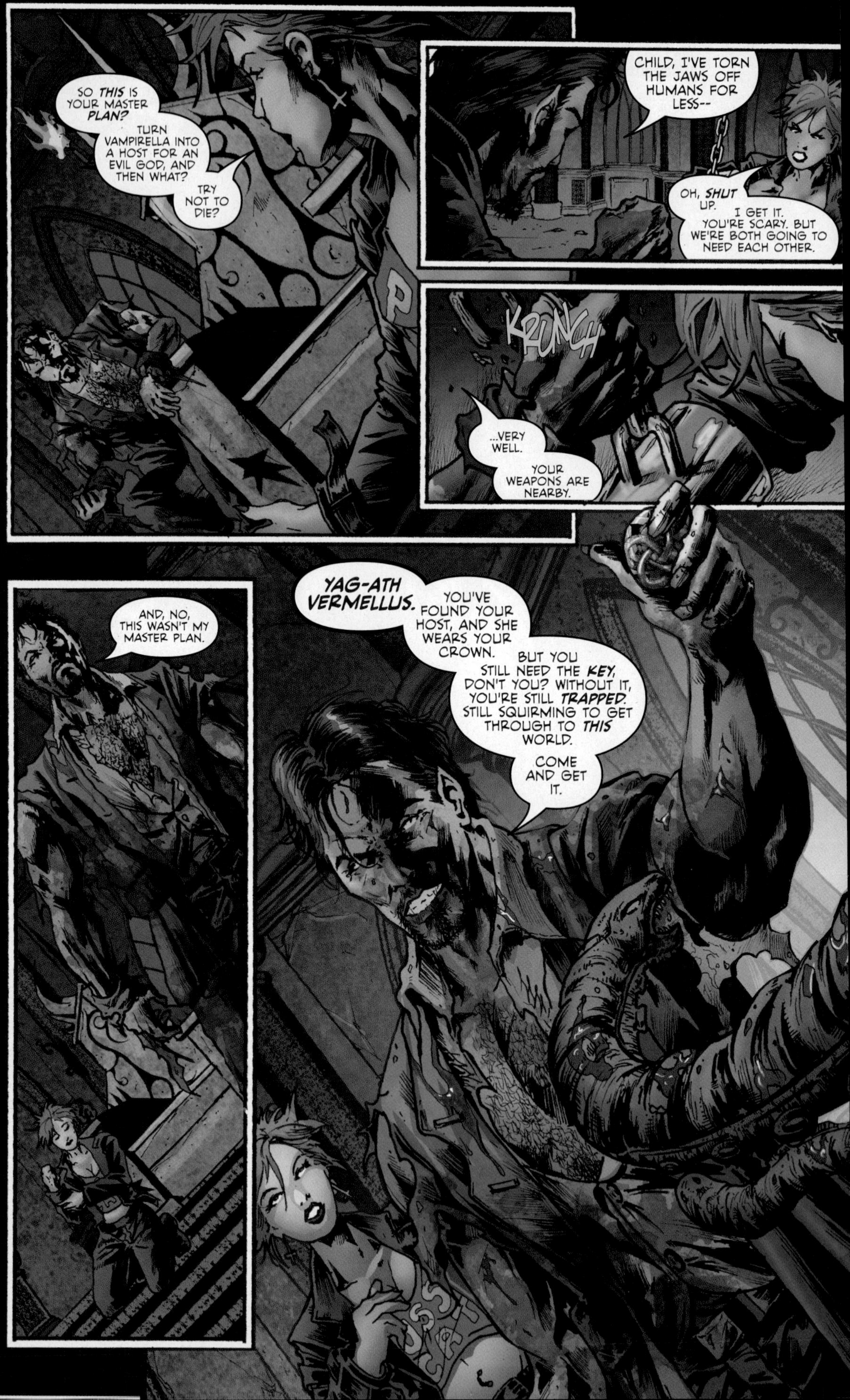
SO THIS IS YOUR MASTER PLAN?
TURN VAMPIRELLA INTO A HOST FOR AN EVIL GOD, AND THEN WHAT?
TRY NOT TO DIE?
CHILD, I'VE TORN THE JAWS OFF HUMANS FOR LESS--
OH, SHUT UP.
I GET IT. YOU'RE SCARY. BUT WE'RE BOTH GOING TO NEED EACH OTHER.
KRUNCH
...VERY WELL.
YOUR WEAPONS ARE NEARBY.
AND, NO, THIS WASN'T MY MASTER PLAN.
YAG-ATH VERMELLUS.
YOU'VE FOUND YOUR HOST, AND SHE WEARS YOUR CROWN.
BUT YOU STILL NEED THE KEY, DON'T YOU? WITHOUT IT, YOU'RE STILL TRAPPED. STILL SQUIRMING TO GET THROUGH TO THIS WORLD.
COME AND GET IT.

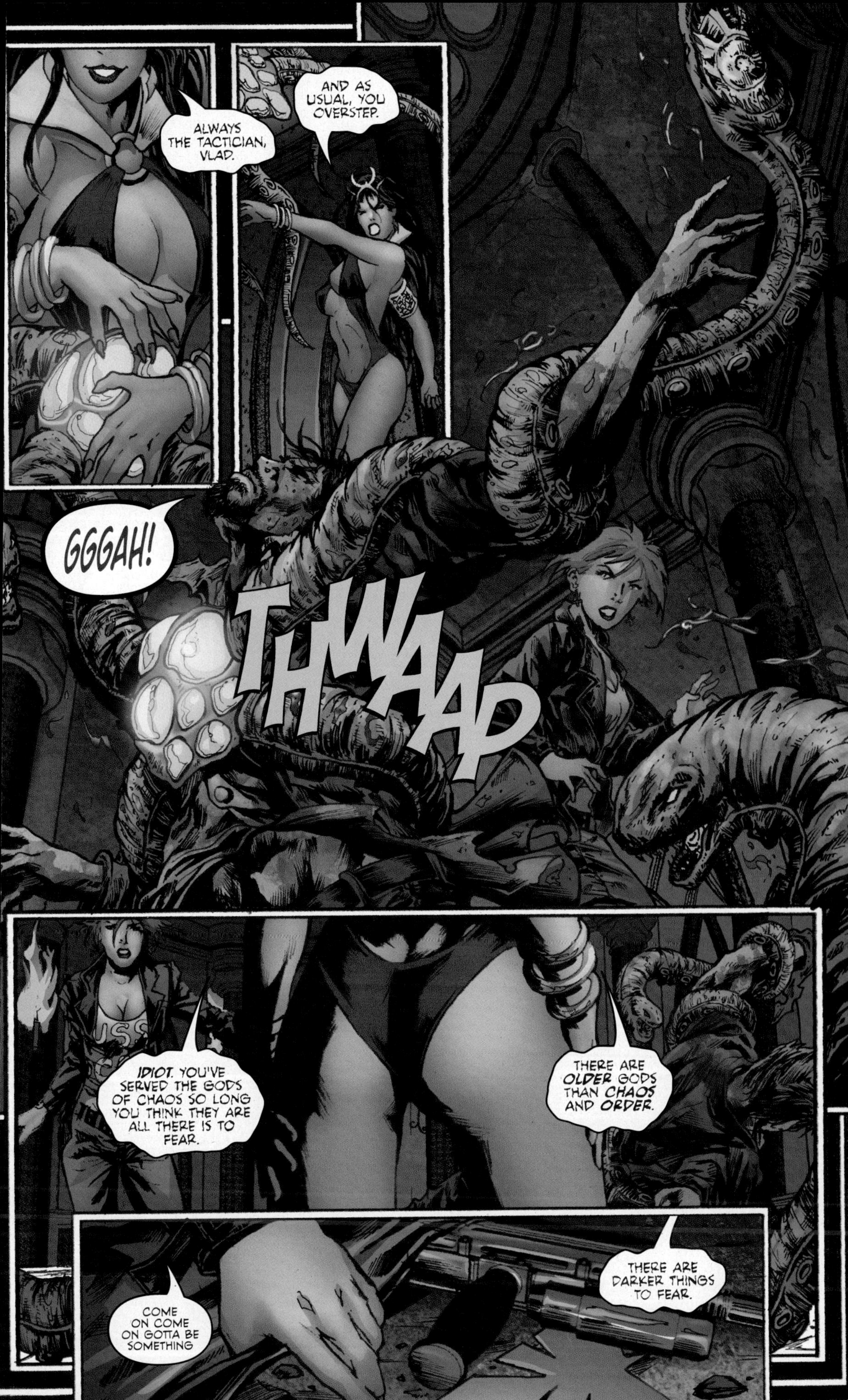
ALWAYS THE TACTICIAN, VLAD.
AND AS USUAL, YOU OVERSTEP.
GGGAH!
THWAAP
IDIOT. YOU'VE SERVED THE GODS OF CHAOS SO LONG YOU THINK THEY ARE ALL THERE IS TO FEAR.
THERE ARE OLDER GODS THAN CHAOS AND ORDER.
COME ON COME ON GOTTA BE SOMETHING
THERE ARE DARKER THINGS TO FEAR.

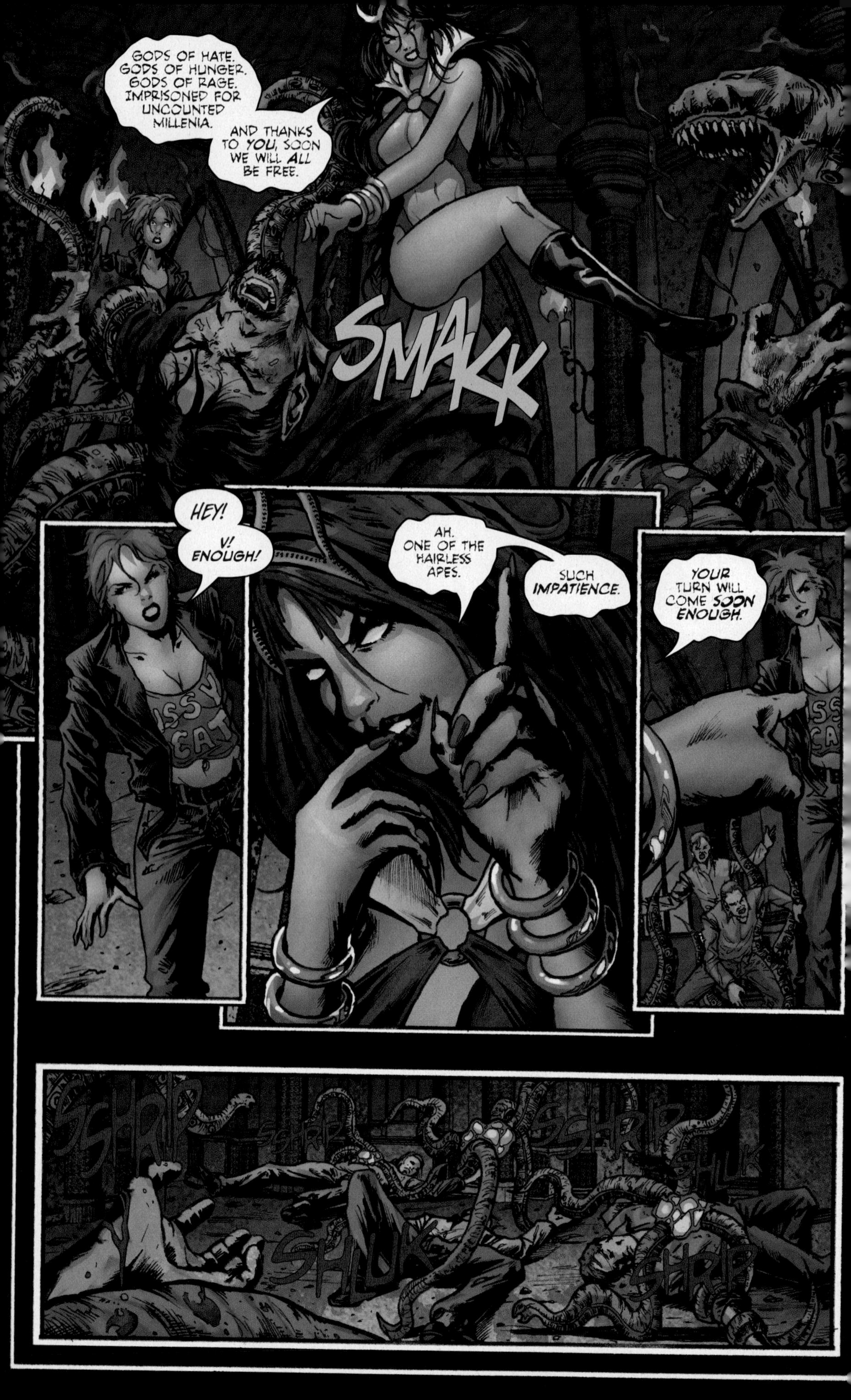
GODS OF HATE. GODS OF HUNGER. GODS OF RAGE. IMPRISONED FOR UNCOUNTED MILLENIA.
AND THANKS TO YOU, SOON WE WILL ALL BE FREE.
SMAKK
HEY!
V! ENOUGH!
AH. ONE OF THE HAIRLESS APES.
SUCH IMPATIENCE.
YOUR TURN WILL COME SOON ENOUGH.
SHLUK

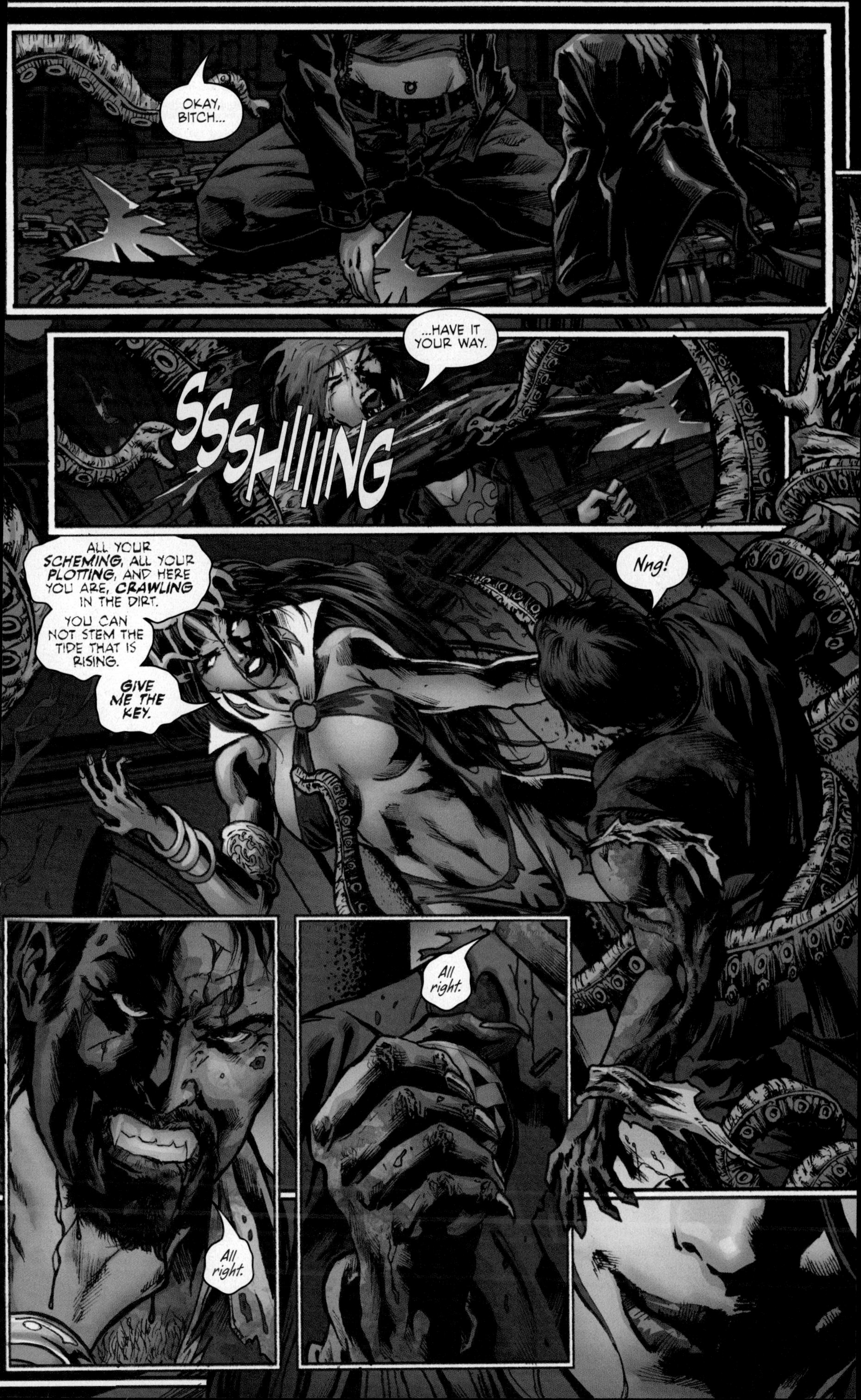
OKAY, BITCH...
...HAVE IT YOUR WAY.
SSSHIIIIING
ALL YOUR SCHEMING, ALL YOUR PLOTTING, AND HERE YOU ARE, CRAWLING IN THE DIRT.
YOU CAN NOT STEM THE TIDE THAT IS RISING.
GIVE ME THE KEY.
Nng!
All right.
All right.

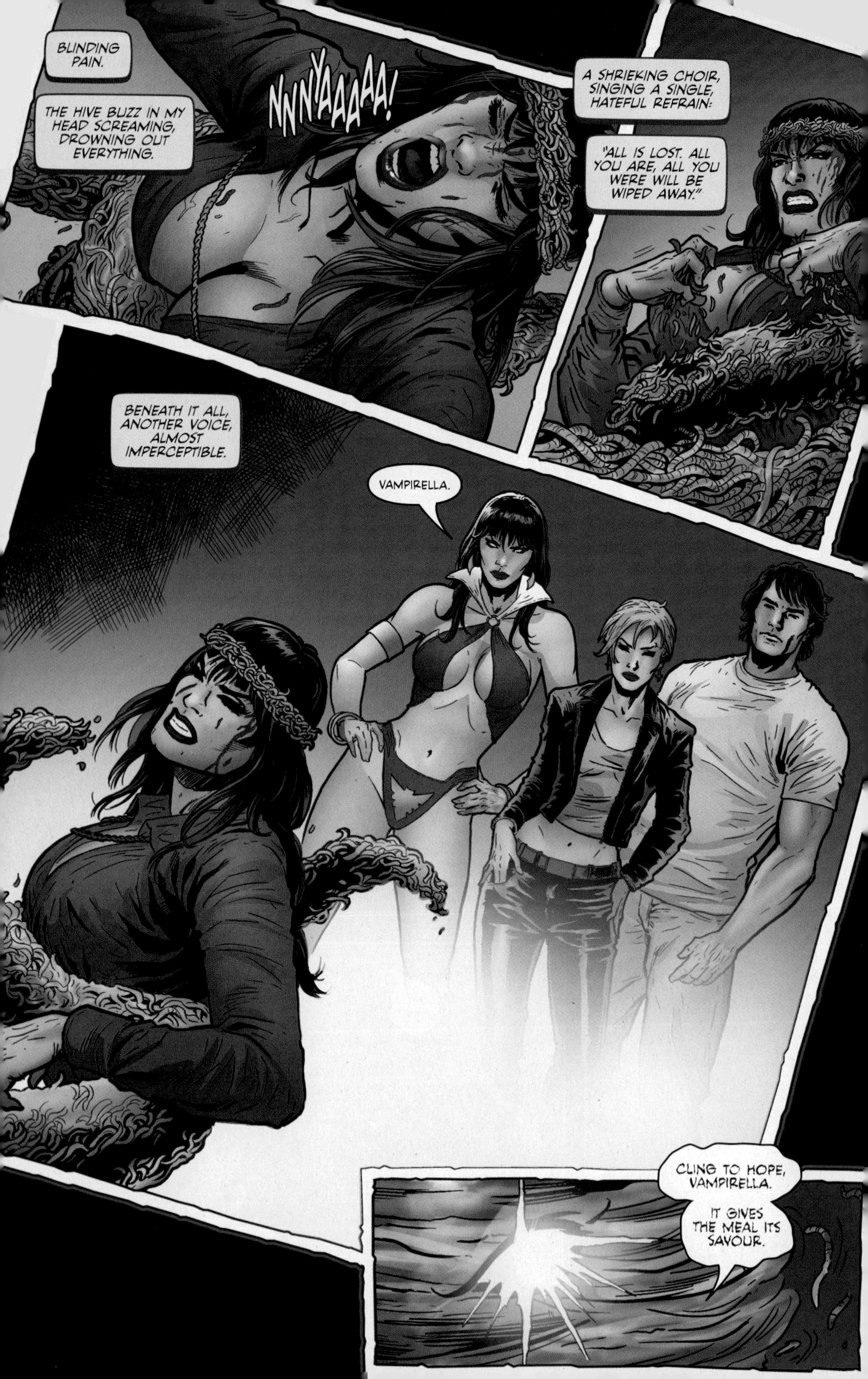
BLINDING PAIN.
THE HIVE BUZZ IN MY HEAD SCREAMING, DROWNING OUT EVERYTHING.
NNNYAAAAA!
A SHRIEKING CHOIR, SINGING A SINGLE, HATEFUL REFRAIN:
"ALL IS LOST. ALL YOU ARE, ALL YOU WERE WILL BE WIPED AWAY."
BENEATH IT ALL, ANOTHER VOICE, ALMOST IMPERCEPTIBLE.
VAMPIRELLA.
CLING TO HOPE, VAMPIRELLA.
IT GIVES THE MEAL ITS SAVOUR.

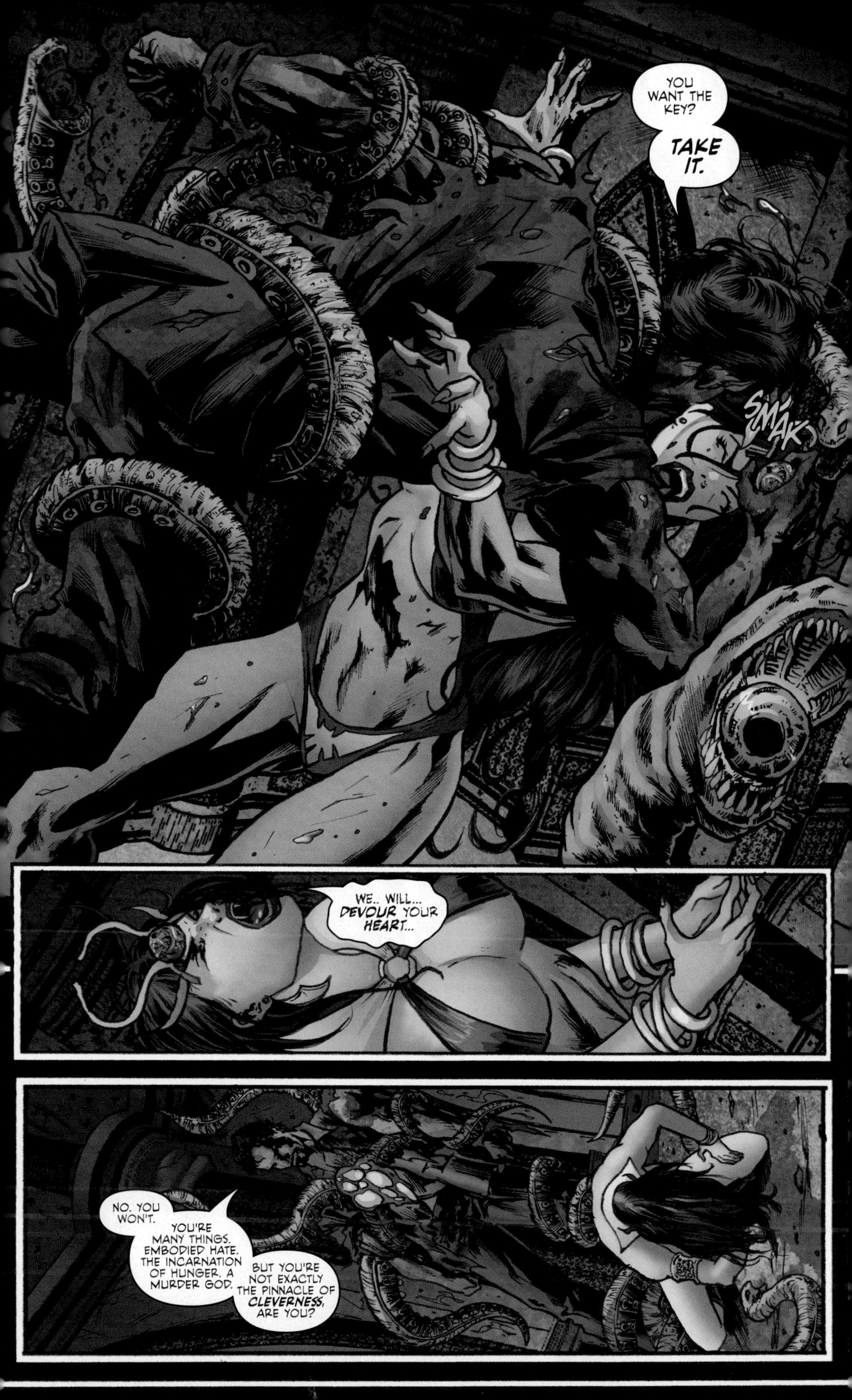
YOU WANT THE KEY?
TAKE IT.
SMAK
WE.. WILL... DEVOUR YOUR HEART...
NO. YOU WON'T.
YOU'RE MANY THINGS. EMBODIED HATE. THE INCARNATION OF HUNGER. A MURDER GOD.
BUT YOU'RE NOT EXACTLY THE PINNACLE OF CLEVERNESS, ARE YOU?

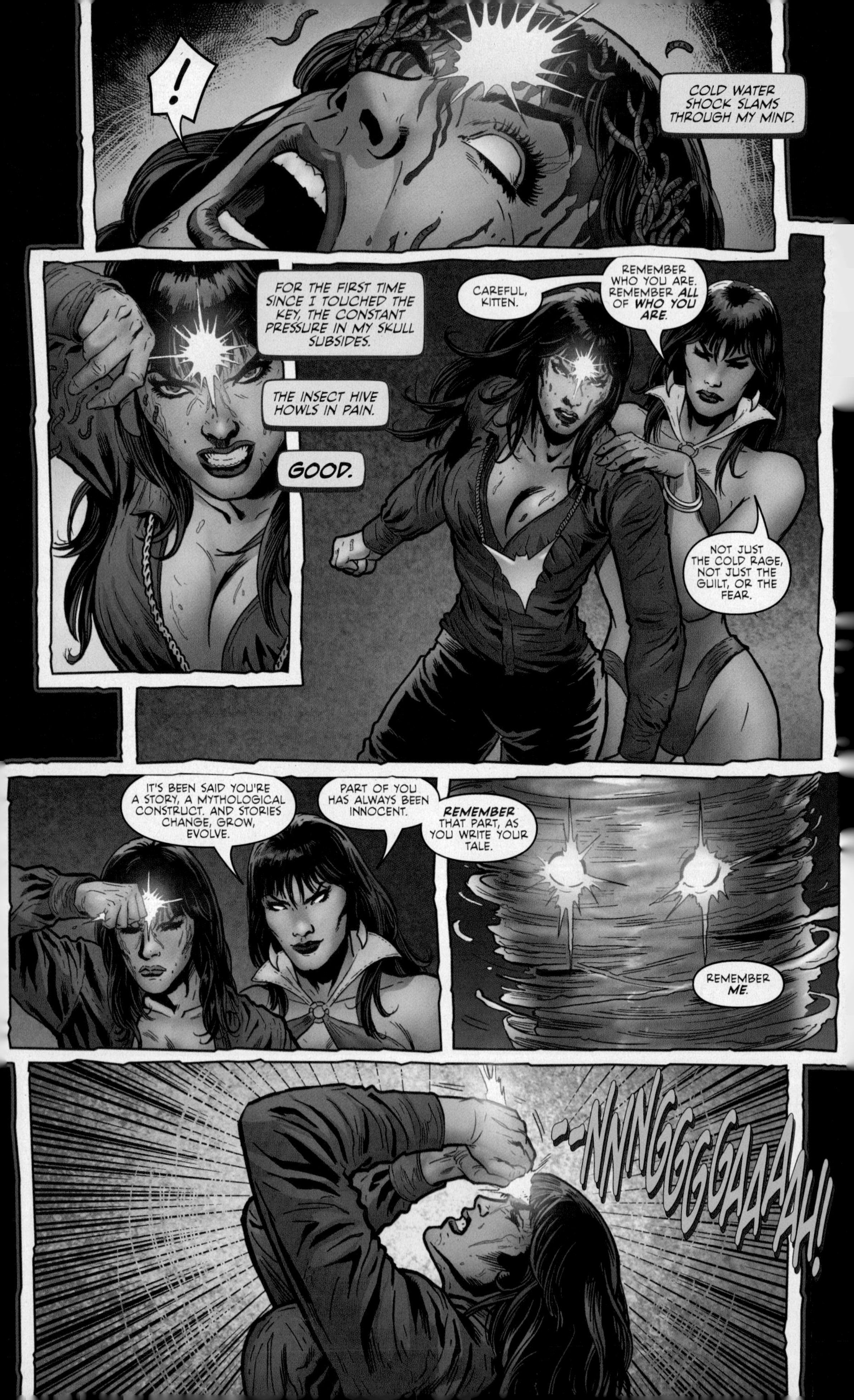
!
COLD WATER SHOCK SLAMS THROUGH MY MIND.
FOR THE FIRST TIME SINCE I TOUCHED THE KEY, THE CONSTANT PRESSURE IN MY SKULL SUBSIDES.
THE INSECT HIVE HOWLS IN PAIN.
GOOD.
CAREFUL, KITTEN.
REMEMBER WHO YOU ARE. REMEMBER ALL OF WHO YOU ARE.
NOT JUST THE COLD RAGE, NOT JUST THE GUILT, OR THE FEAR.
IT'S BEEN SAID YOU'RE A STORY, A MYTHOLOGICAL CONSTRUCT. AND STORIES CHANGE, GROW, EVOLVE.
PART OF YOU HAS ALWAYS BEEN INNOCENT.
REMEMBER THAT PART, AS YOU WRITE YOUR TALE.
REMEMBER ME.
--NNNGGGGAAAAH!

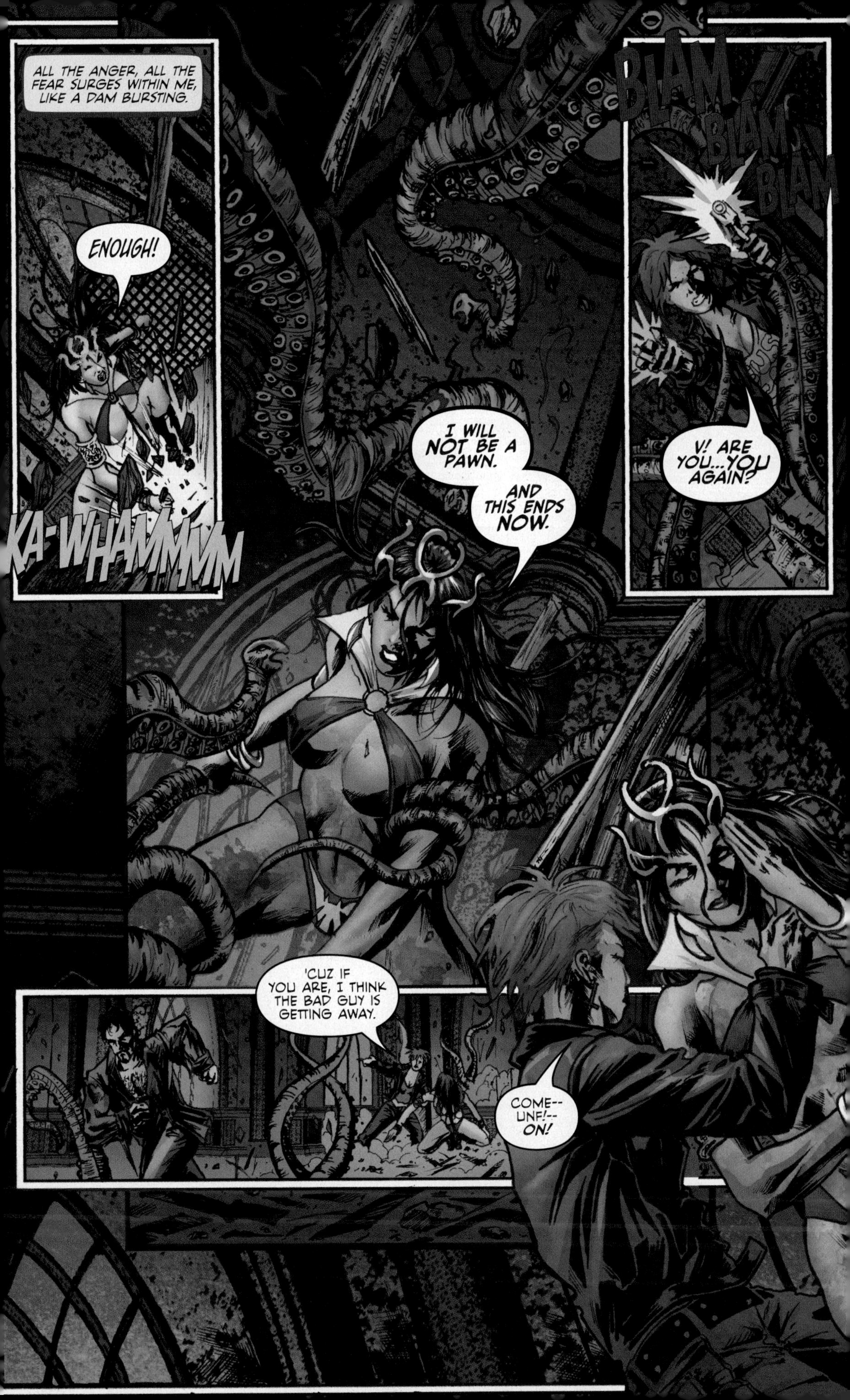
ALL THE ANGER, ALL THE FEAR SURGES WITHIN ME, LIKE A DAM BURSTING.
ENOUGH!
KA-WHAMMMM
I WILL NOT BE A PAWN.
AND THIS ENDS NOW.
BLAM BLAM BLAM
V! ARE YOU...YOU AGAIN?
'CUZ IF YOU ARE, I THINK THE BAD GUY IS GETTING AWAY.
COME-- UNF!-- ON!

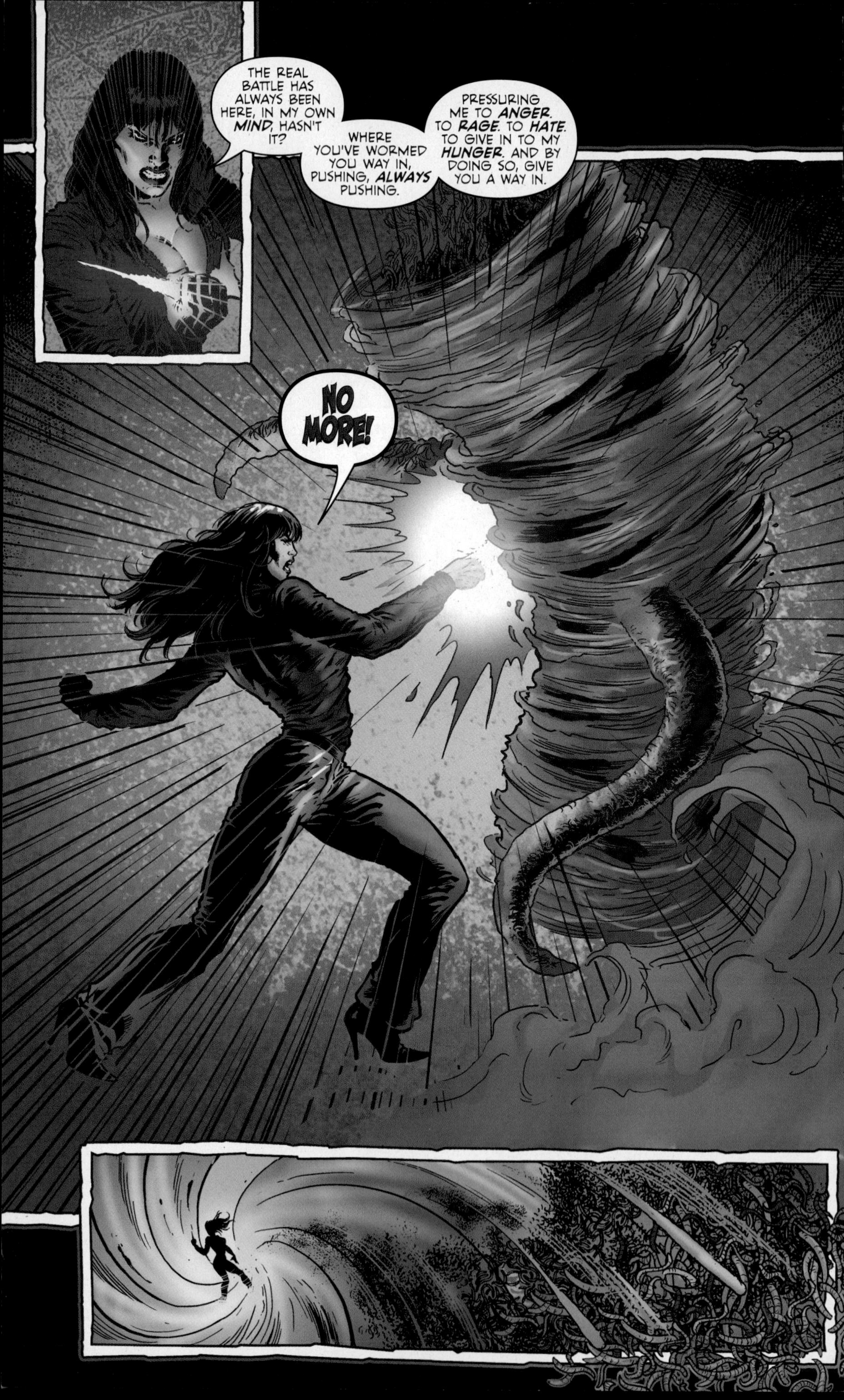
THE REAL BATTLE HAS ALWAYS BEEN HERE, IN MY OWN MIND, HASN'T IT?
WHERE YOU'VE WORMED YOU WAY IN, PUSHING, ALWAYS PUSHING.
PRESSURING ME TO ANGER. TO RAGE. TO HATE. TO GIVE IN TO MY HUNGER. AND BY DOING SO, GIVE YOU A WAY IN.
NO MORE!

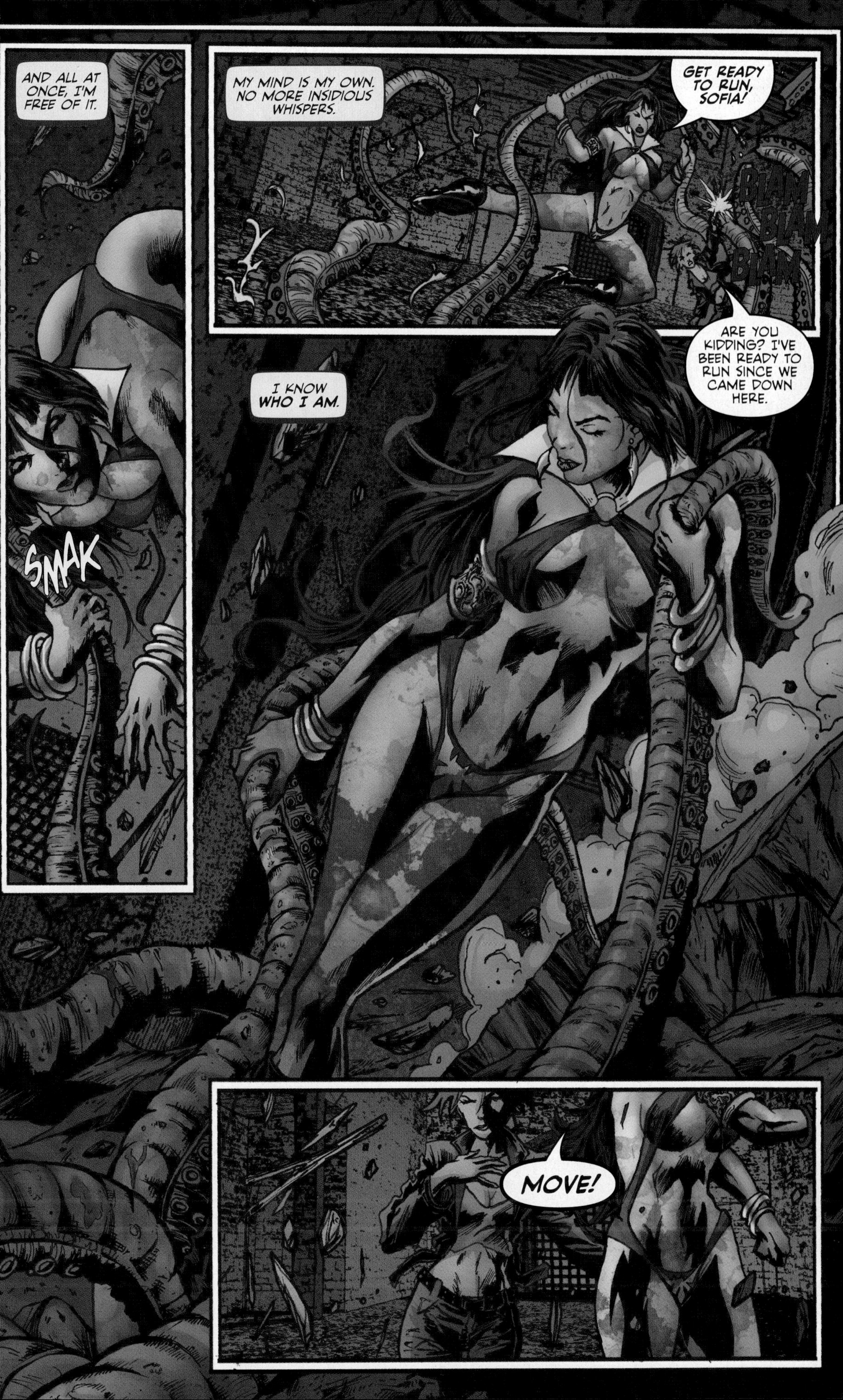
AND ALL AT ONCE, I'M FREE OF IT.
SMAK
MY MIND IS MY OWN. NO MORE INSIDIOUS WHISPERS.
GET READY TO RUN, SOFIA!
BLAM BLAM BLAM
ARE YOU KIDDING? I'VE BEEN READY TO RUN SINCE WE CAME DOWN HERE.
I KNOW WHO I AM.
MOVE!

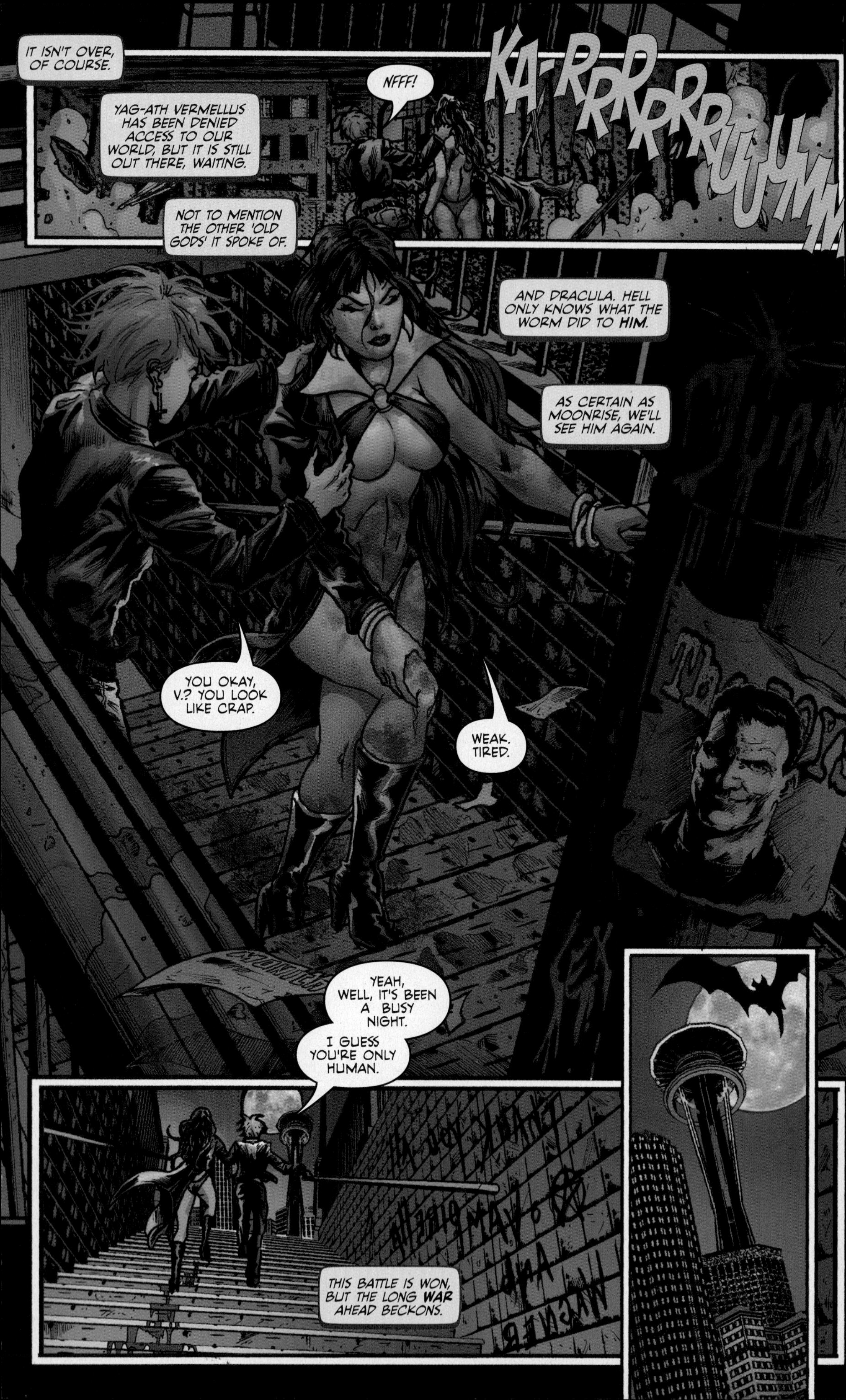
IT ISN'T OVER, OF COURSE.
YAG-ATH VERMELLUS HAS BEEN DENIED ACCESS TO OUR WORLD, BUT IT IS STILL OUT THERE, WAITING.
NFFF!
KA-RRRRRRUUUMM
NOT TO MENTION THE OTHER 'OLD GODS' IT SPOKE OF.
AND DRACULA. HELL ONLY KNOWS WHAT THE WORM DID TO **HIM**.
AS CERTAIN AS MOONRISE, WE'LL SEE HIM AGAIN.
YOU OKAY, V.? YOU LOOK LIKE CRAP.
WEAK. TIRED.
YEAH, WELL, IT'S BEEN A BUSY NIGHT.
I GUESS YOU'RE ONLY HUMAN.
THIS BATTLE IS WON, BUT THE LONG **WAR** AHEAD BECKONS.

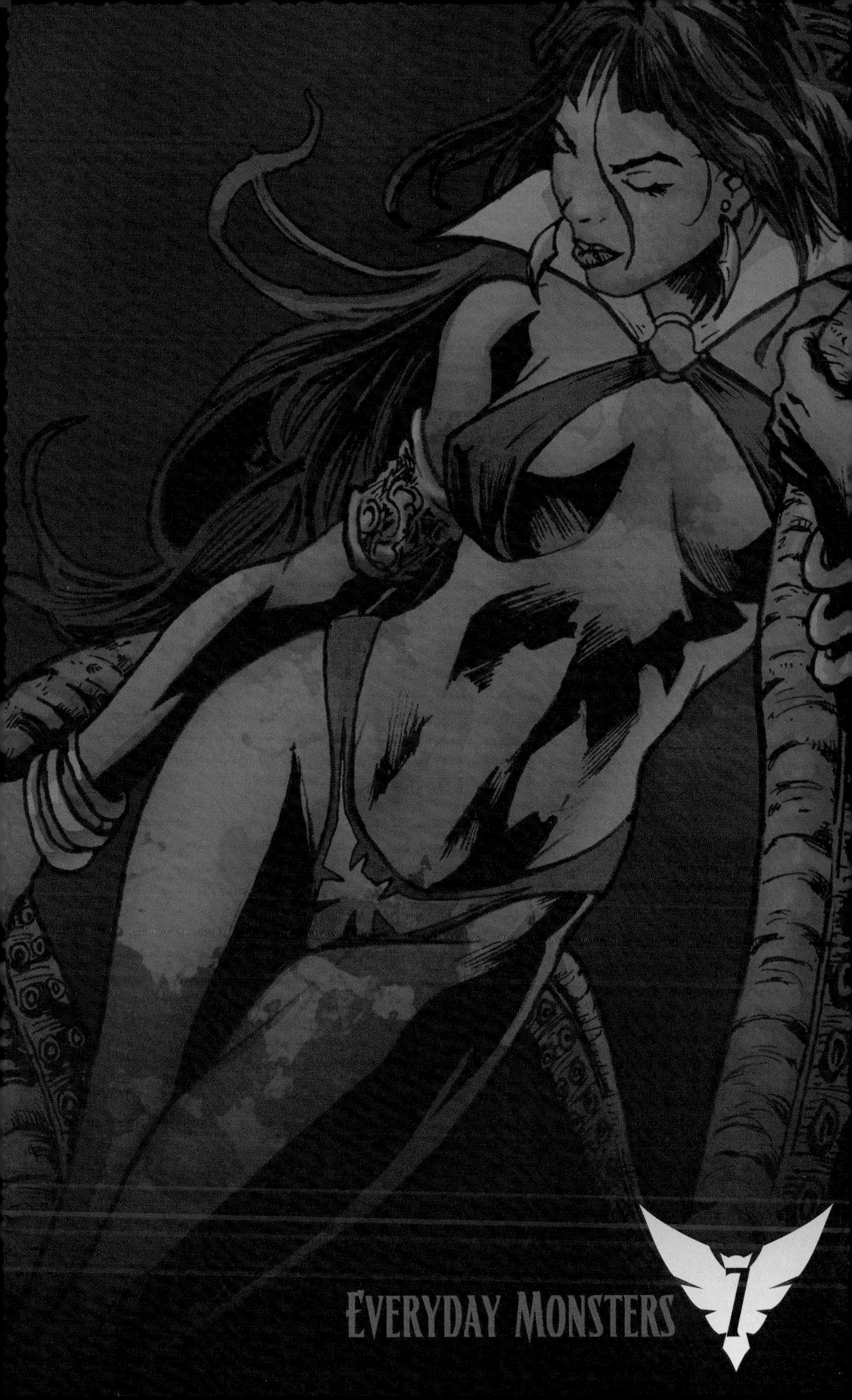
Everyday Monsters

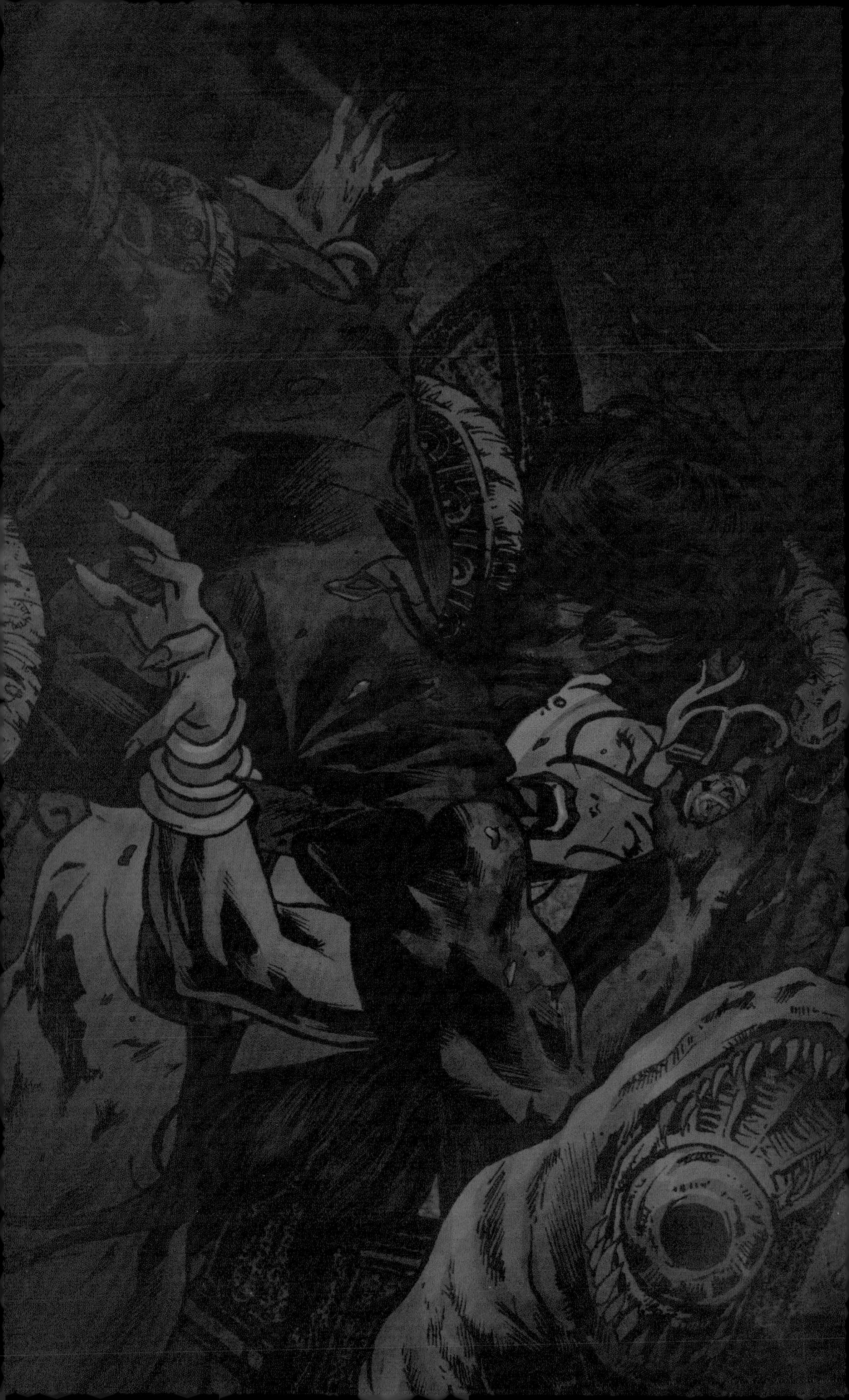

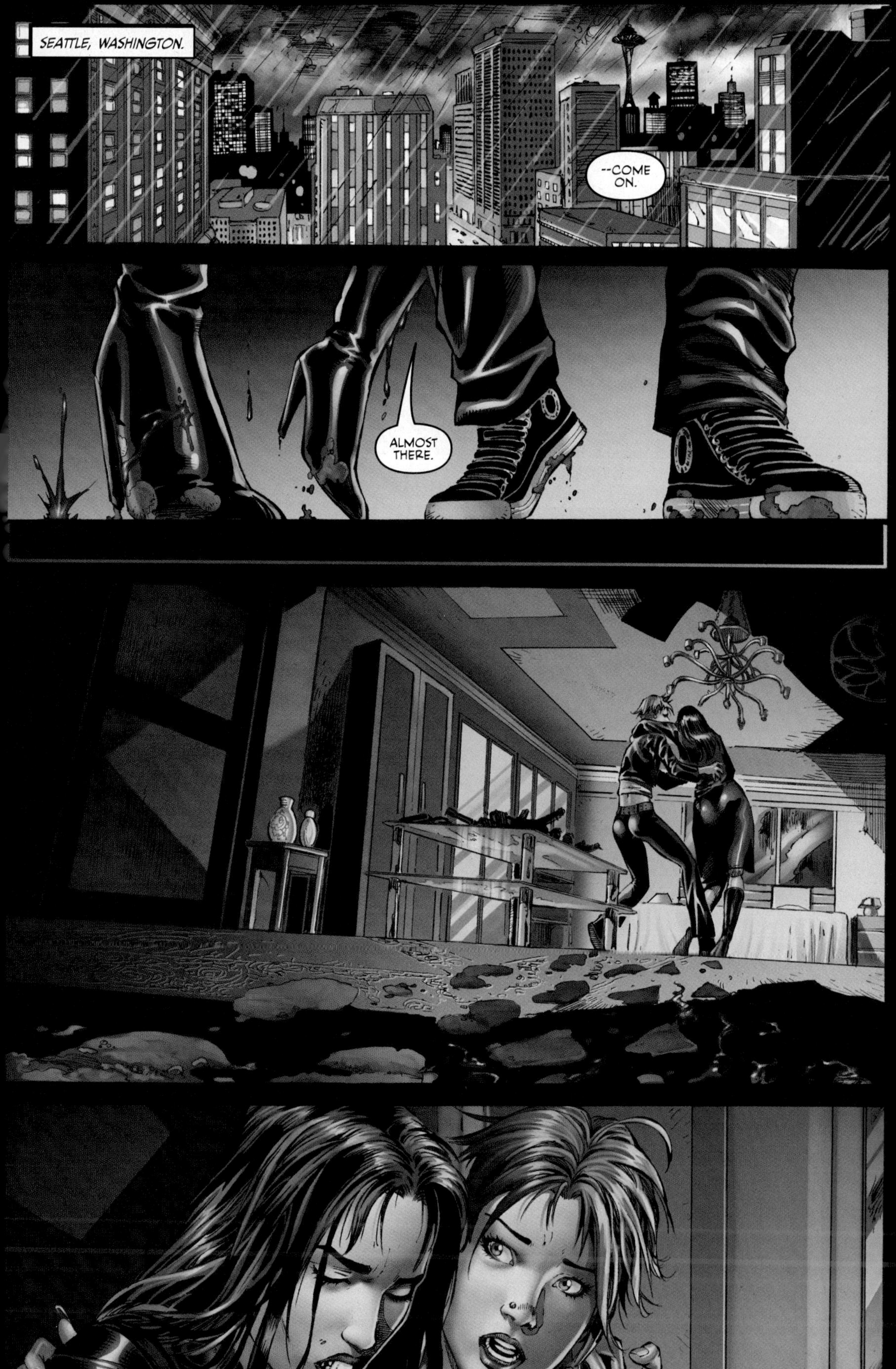
SEATTLE, WASHINGTON.
--COME ON.
ALMOST THERE.

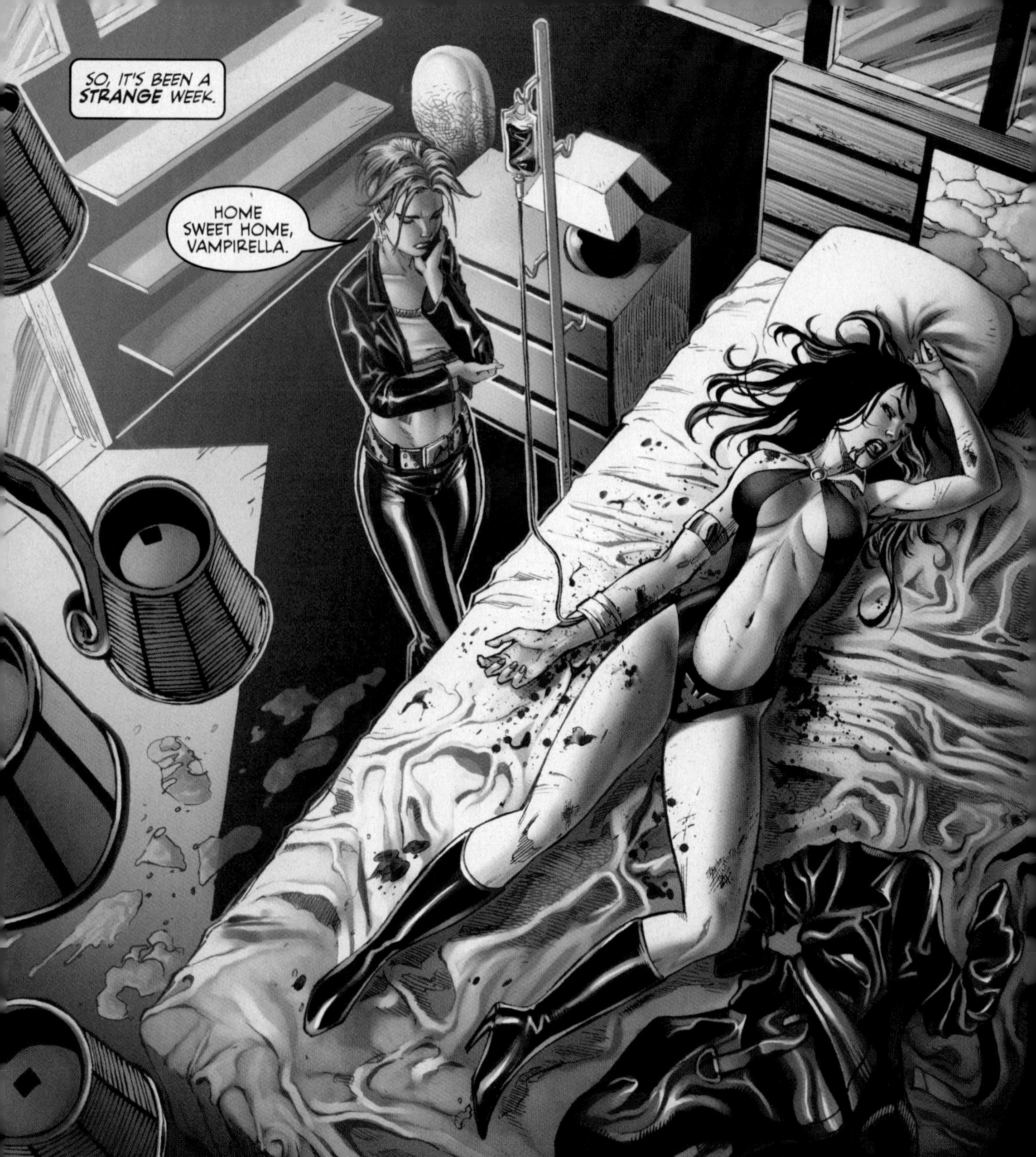
SO, IT'S BEEN A STRANGE WEEK.
HOME SWEET HOME, VAMPIRELLA.

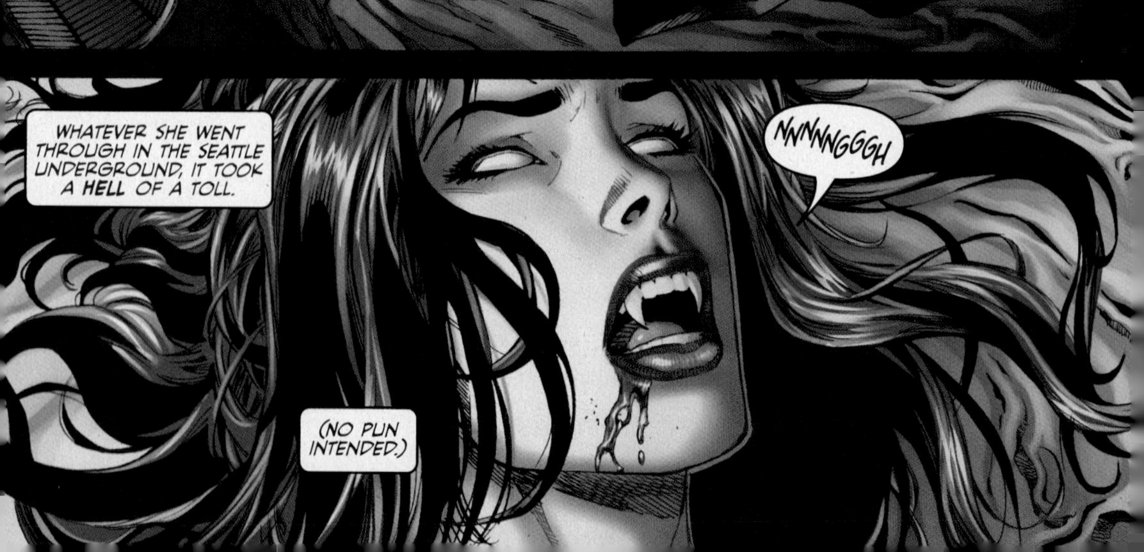
WHATEVER SHE WENT THROUGH IN THE SEATTLE UNDERGROUND, IT TOOK A HELL OF A TOLL.
NNNNNGGGH
(NO PUN INTENDED.)

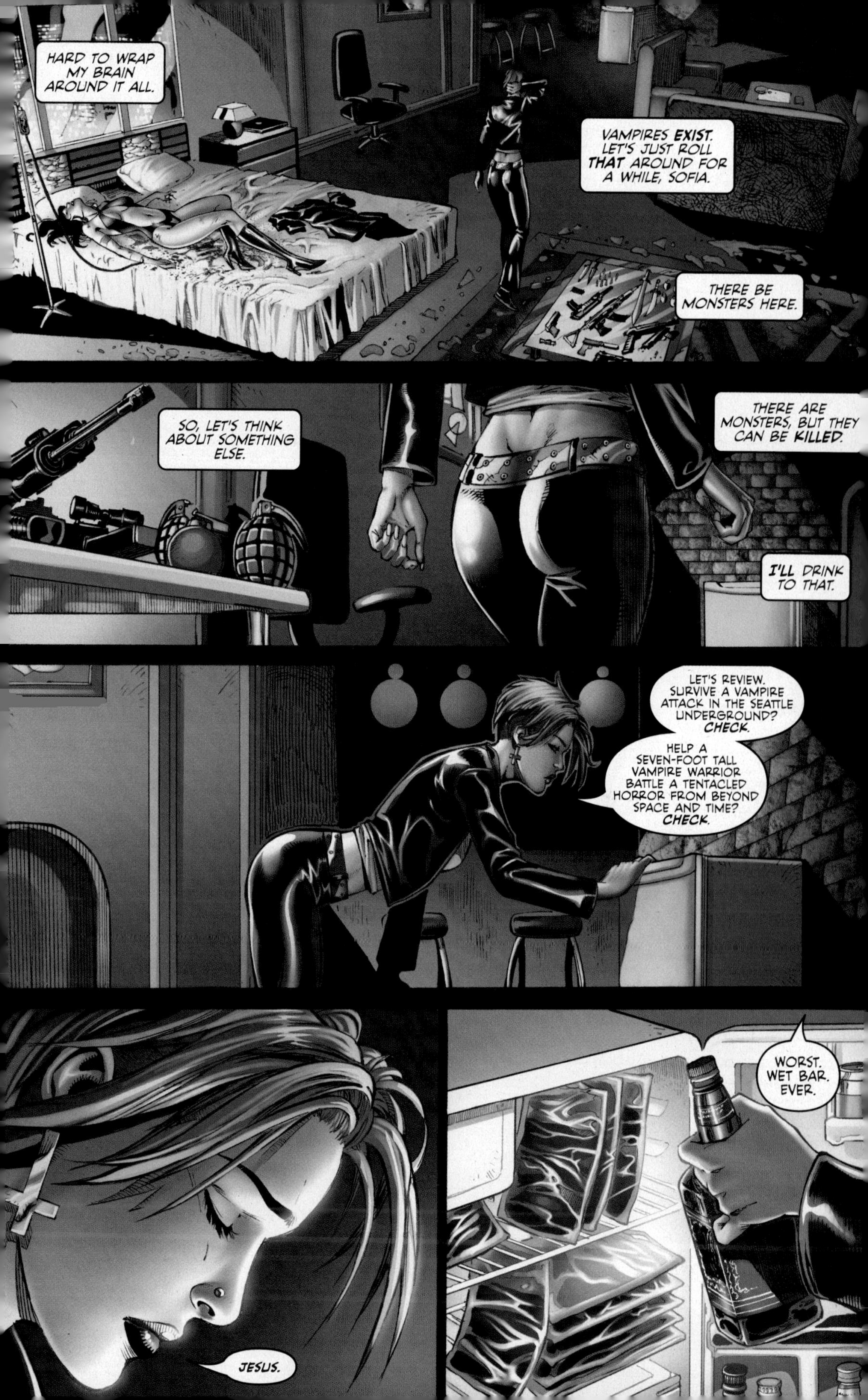

HARD TO WRAP MY BRAIN AROUND IT ALL.
VAMPIRES EXIST. LET'S JUST ROLL THAT AROUND FOR A WHILE, SOFIA.
THERE BE MONSTERS HERE.
SO, LET'S THINK ABOUT SOMETHING ELSE.
THERE ARE MONSTERS, BUT THEY CAN BE KILLED.
I'LL DRINK TO THAT.
LET'S REVIEW. SURVIVE A VAMPIRE ATTACK IN THE SEATTLE UNDERGROUND? CHECK.
HELP A SEVEN-FOOT TALL VAMPIRE WARRIOR BATTLE A TENTACLED HORROR FROM BEYOND SPACE AND TIME? CHECK.
JESUS.
WORST. WET BAR. EVER.

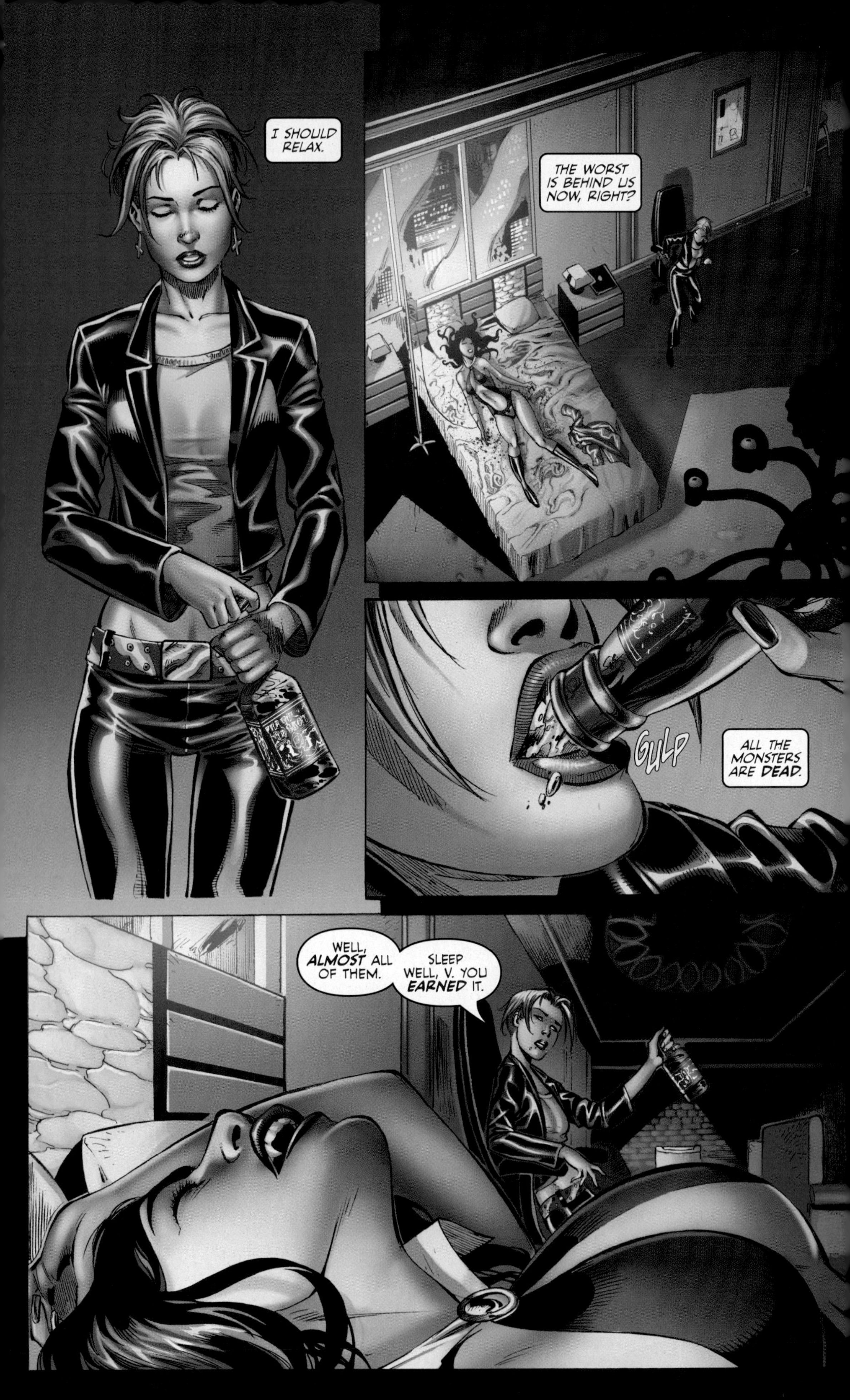
I SHOULD RELAX.
THE WORST IS BEHIND US NOW, RIGHT?
GULP
ALL THE MONSTERS ARE DEAD.
WELL, ALMOST ALL OF THEM.
SLEEP WELL, V. YOU EARNED IT.

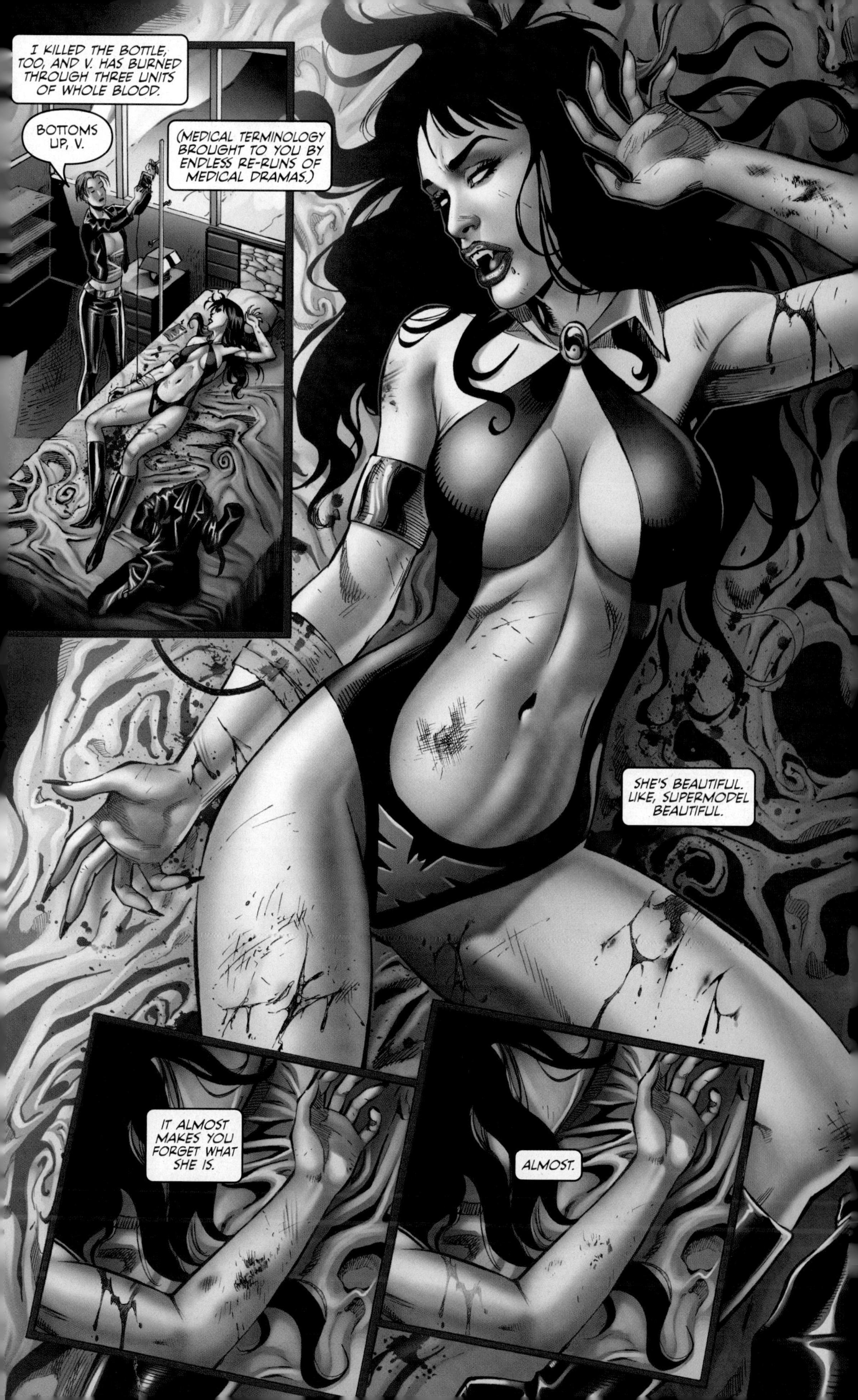
I KILLED THE BOTTLE, TOO, AND V. HAS BURNED THROUGH THREE UNITS OF WHOLE BLOOD.
BOTTOMS UP, V.
(MEDICAL TERMINOLOGY BROUGHT TO YOU BY ENDLESS RE-RUNS OF MEDICAL DRAMAS.)
SHE'S BEAUTIFUL. LIKE, SUPERMODEL BEAUTIFUL.
IT ALMOST MAKES YOU FORGET WHAT SHE IS.
ALMOST.

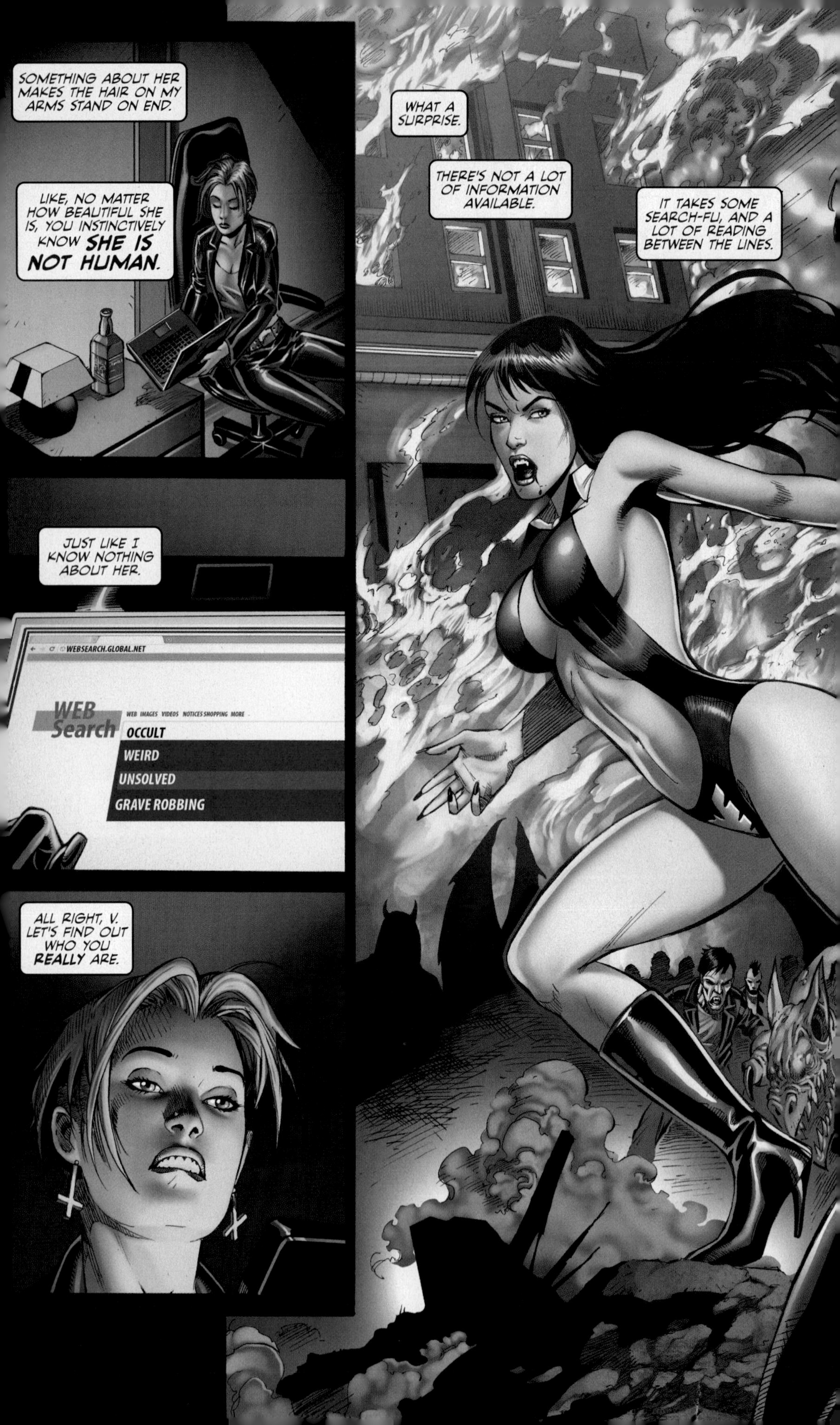
SOMETHING ABOUT HER MAKES THE HAIR ON MY ARMS STAND ON END.
LIKE, NO MATTER HOW BEAUTIFUL SHE IS, YOU INSTINCTIVELY KNOW **SHE IS NOT HUMAN.**
JUST LIKE I KNOW NOTHING ABOUT HER.
WEBSEARCH.GLOBAL.NET
WEB Search
WEB IMAGES VIDEOS NOTICES SHOPPING MORE
OCCULT
WEIRD
UNSOLVED
GRAVE ROBBING
ALL RIGHT, V. LET'S FIND OUT WHO YOU **REALLY** ARE.
WHAT A SURPRISE.
THERE'S NOT A LOT OF INFORMATION AVAILABLE.
IT TAKES SOME SEARCH-FU, AND A LOT OF READING BETWEEN THE LINES.

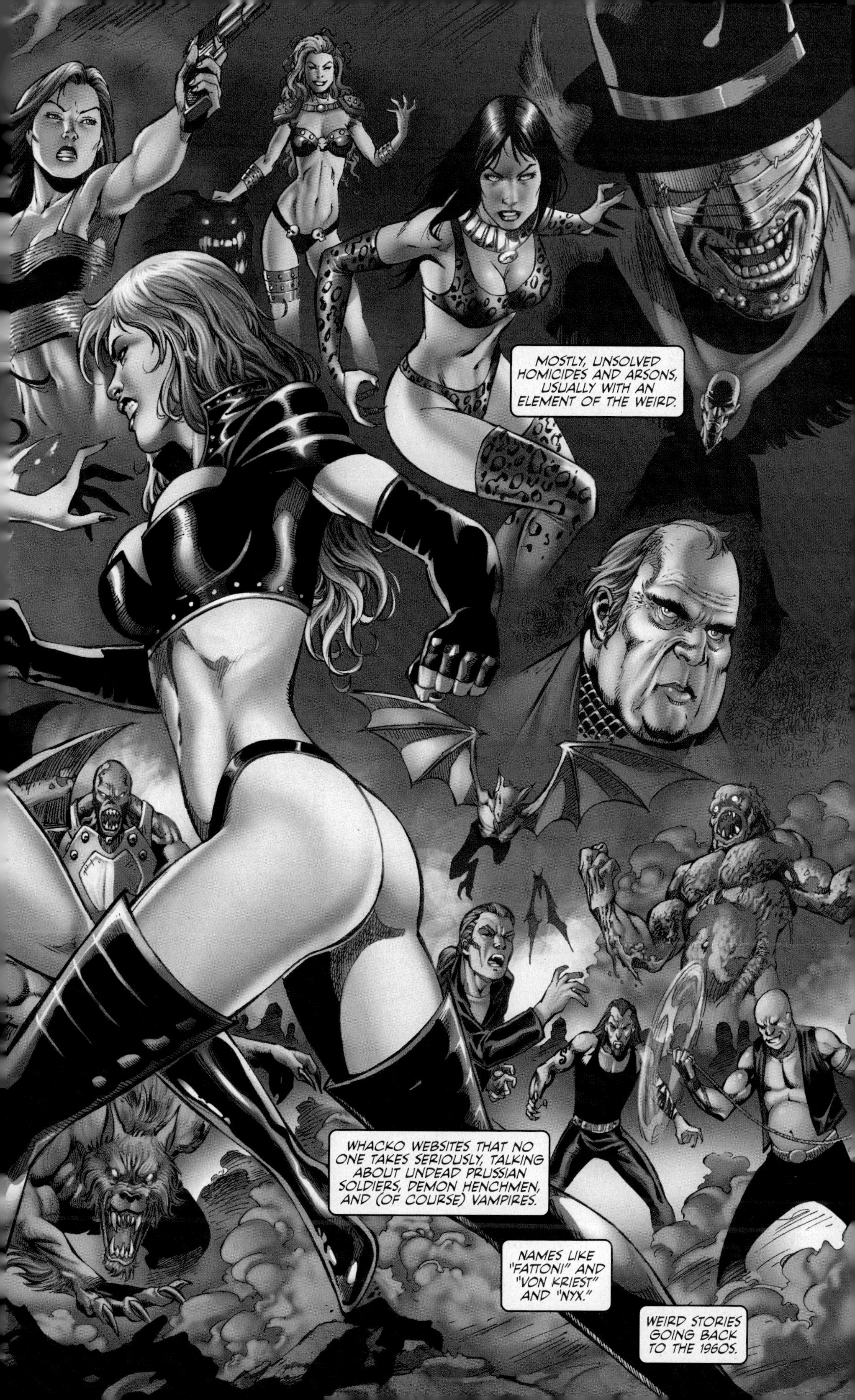
MOSTLY, UNSOLVED HOMICIDES AND ARSONS, USUALLY WITH AN ELEMENT OF THE WEIRD.
WHACKO WEBSITES THAT NO ONE TAKES SERIOUSLY, TALKING ABOUT UNDEAD PRUSSIAN SOLDIERS, DEMON HENCHMEN, AND (OF COURSE) VAMPIRES.
NAMES LIKE "FATTONI" AND "VON KRIEST" AND "NYX."
WEIRD STORIES GOING BACK TO THE 1960S.

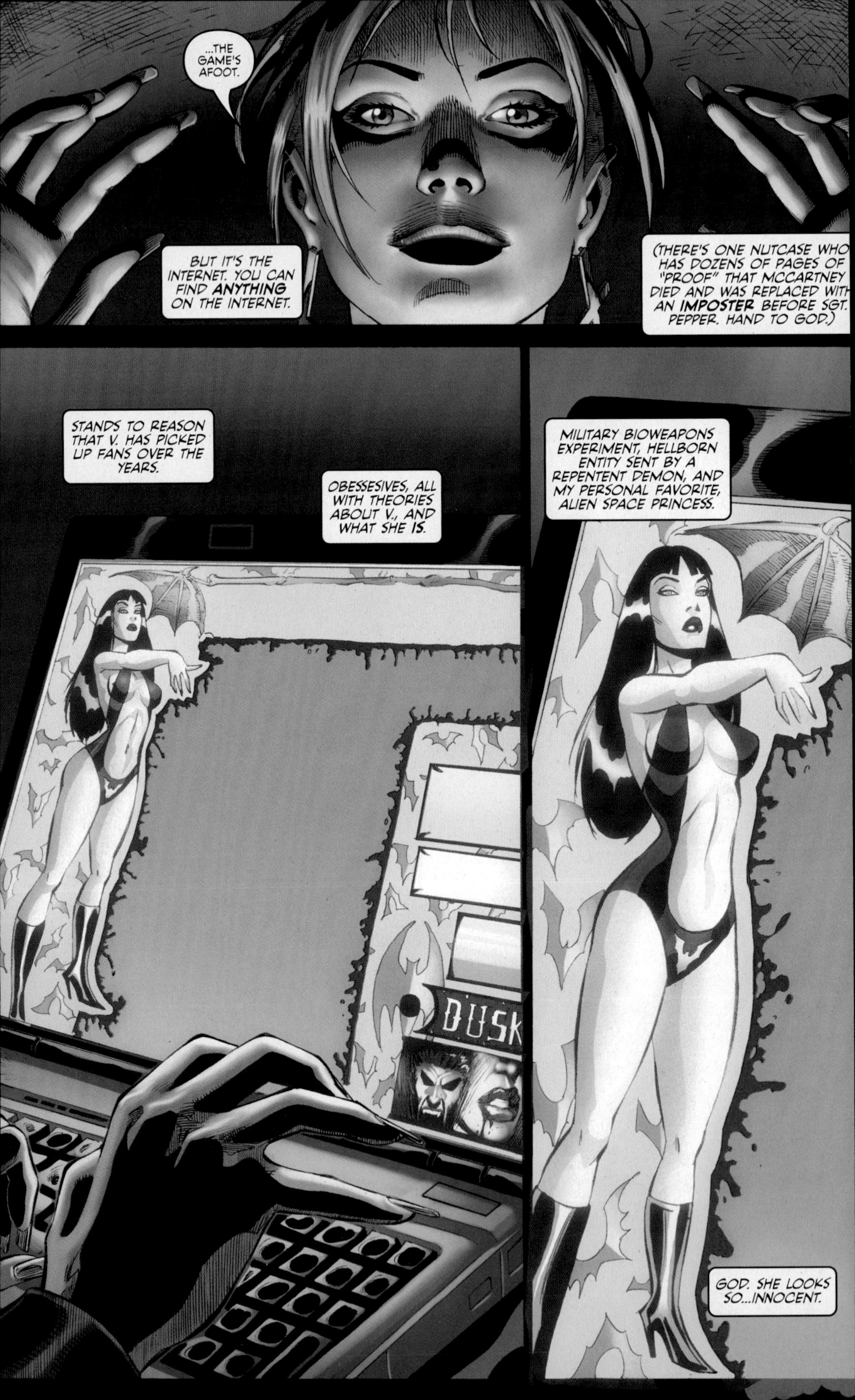
...THE GAME'S AFOOT.
BUT IT'S THE INTERNET. YOU CAN FIND **ANYTHING** ON THE INTERNET.
(THERE'S ONE NUTCASE WHO HAS DOZENS OF PAGES OF "PROOF" THAT MCCARTNEY DIED AND WAS REPLACED WITH AN **IMPOSTER** BEFORE SGT. PEPPER. HAND TO GOD.)
STANDS TO REASON THAT V. HAS PICKED UP FANS OVER THE YEARS.
OBESSESIVES, ALL WITH THEORIES ABOUT V., AND WHAT SHE **IS**.
DUSK
MILITARY BIOWEAPONS EXPERIMENT, HELLBORN ENTITY SENT BY A REPENTENT DEMON, AND MY PERSONAL FAVORITE, ALIEN SPACE PRINCESS.
GOD. SHE LOOKS SO...INNOCENT.

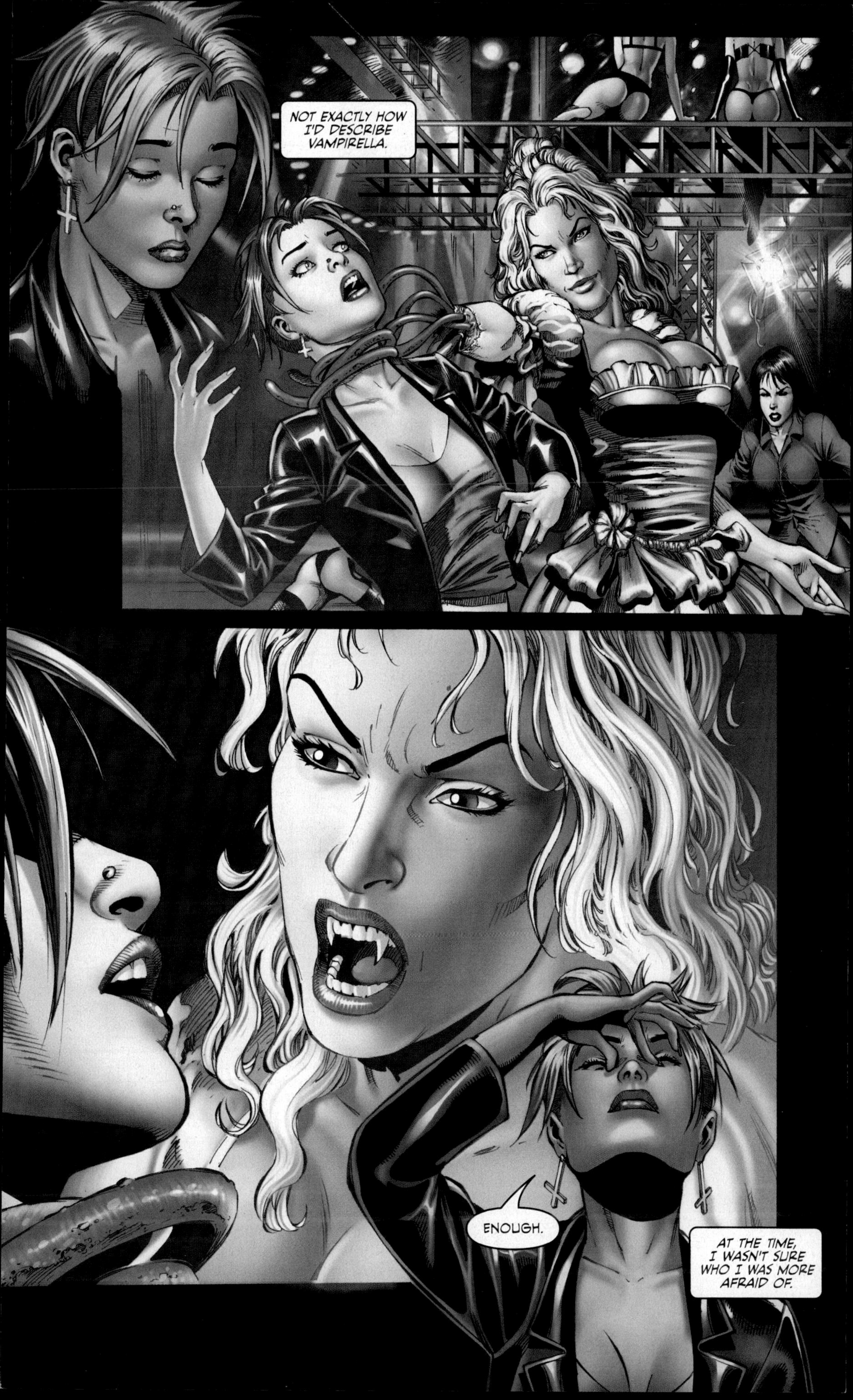

NOT EXACTLY HOW I'D DESCRIBE VAMPIRELLA.
ENOUGH.
AT THE TIME, I WASN'T SURE WHO I WAS MORE AFRAID OF.

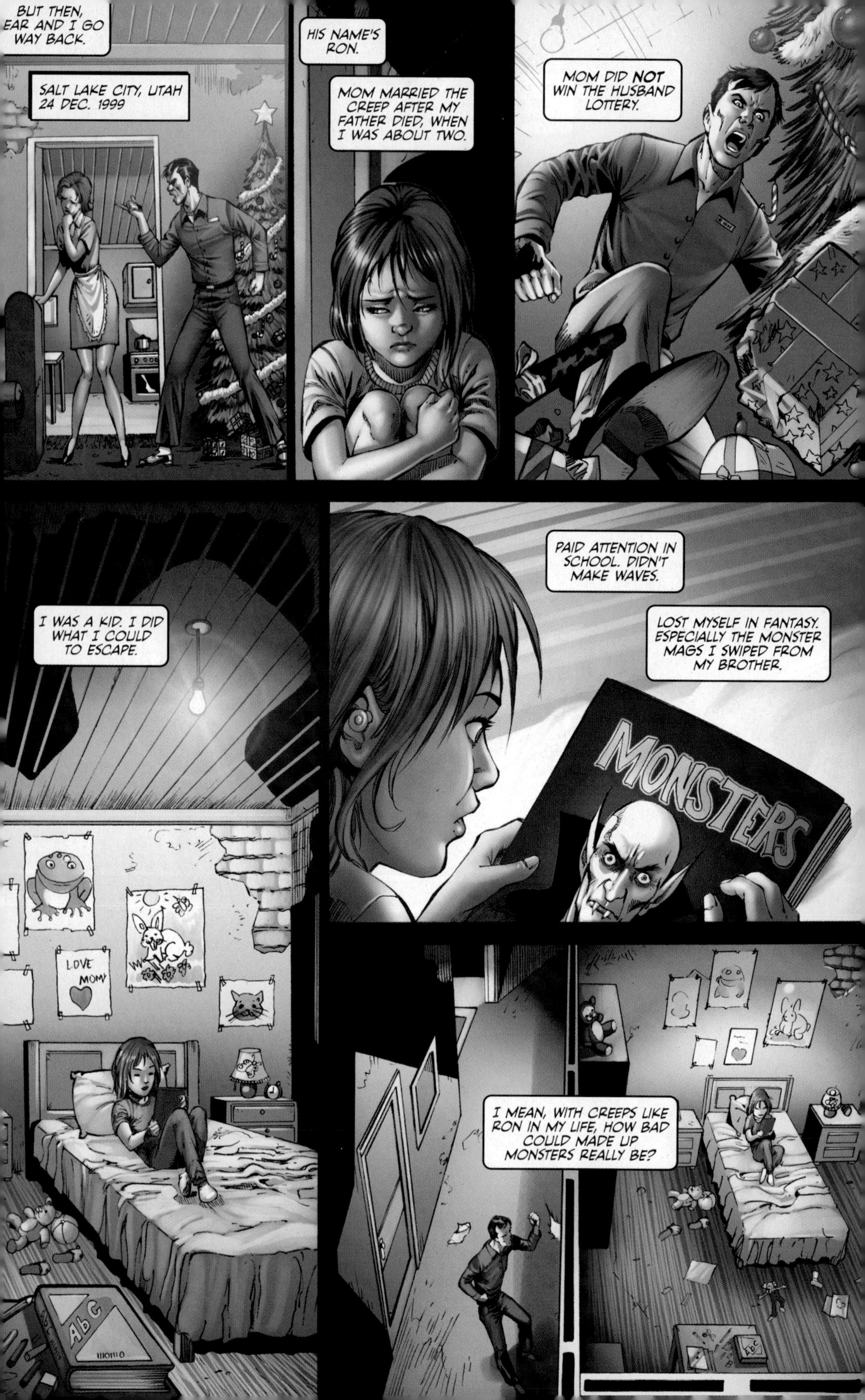
BUT THEN, EAR AND I GO WAY BACK.
SALT LAKE CITY, UTAH 24 DEC. 1999
HIS NAME'S RON.
MOM MARRIED THE CREEP AFTER MY FATHER DIED, WHEN I WAS ABOUT TWO.
MOM DID **NOT** WIN THE HUSBAND LOTTERY.
I WAS A KID. I DID WHAT I COULD TO ESCAPE.
LOVE MOMY
PAID ATTENTION IN SCHOOL. DIDN'T MAKE WAVES.
LOST MYSELF IN FANTASY. ESPECIALLY THE MONSTER MAGS I SWIPED FROM MY BROTHER.
MONSTERS
I MEAN, WITH CREEPS LIKE RON IN MY LIFE, HOW BAD COULD MADE UP MONSTERS REALLY BE?

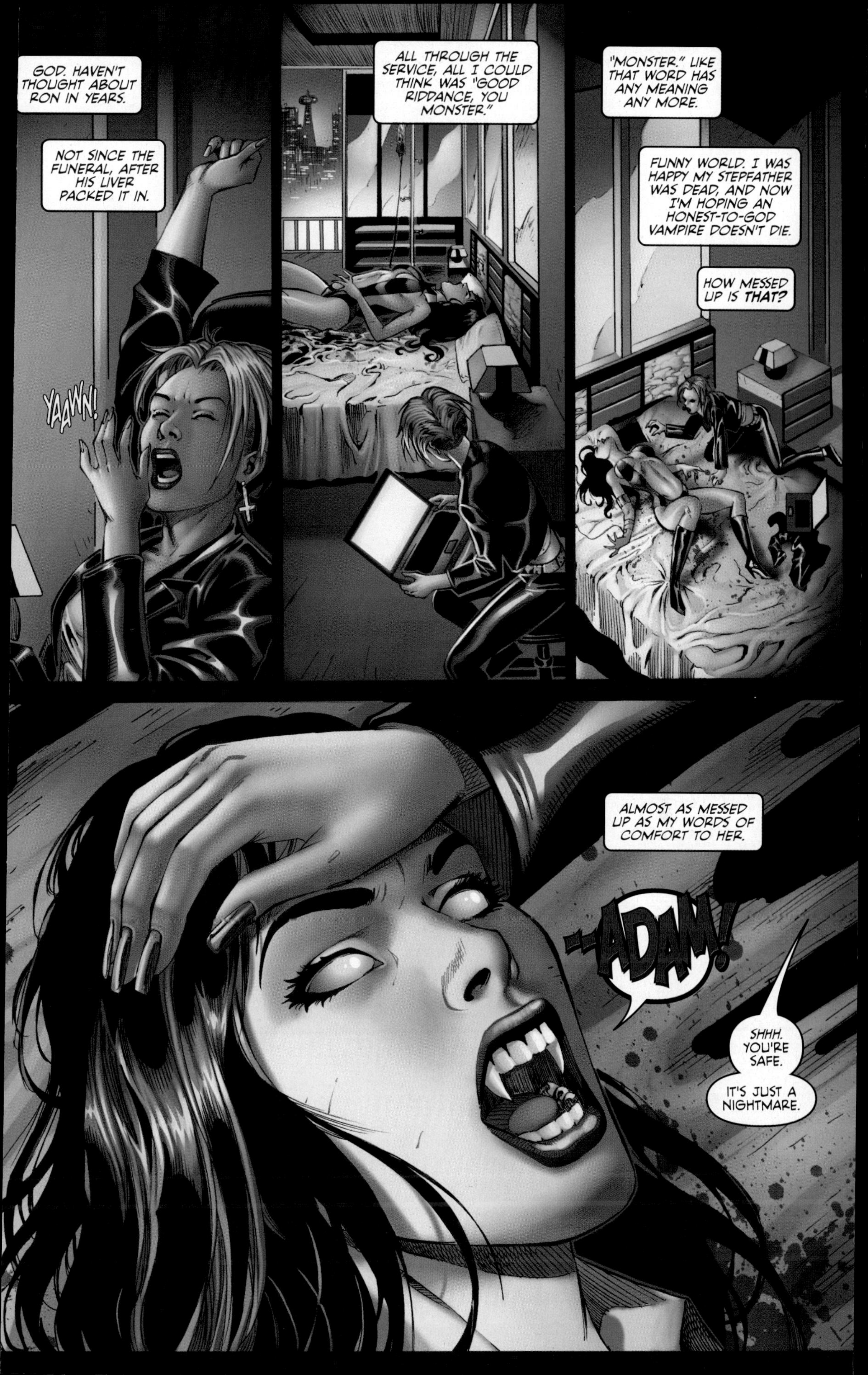
GOD. HAVEN'T THOUGHT ABOUT RON IN YEARS.
NOT SINCE THE FUNERAL, AFTER HIS LIVER PACKED IT IN.
YAAWN!
ALL THROUGH THE SERVICE, ALL I COULD THINK WAS "GOOD RIDDANCE, YOU MONSTER."
"MONSTER." LIKE THAT WORD HAS ANY MEANING ANY MORE.
FUNNY WORLD. I WAS HAPPY MY STEPFATHER WAS DEAD, AND NOW I'M HOPING AN HONEST-TO-GOD VAMPIRE DOESN'T DIE.
HOW MESSED UP IS THAT?
ALMOST AS MESSED UP AS MY WORDS OF COMFORT TO HER.
--ADAM!
SHHH. YOU'RE SAFE.
IT'S JUST A NIGHTMARE.

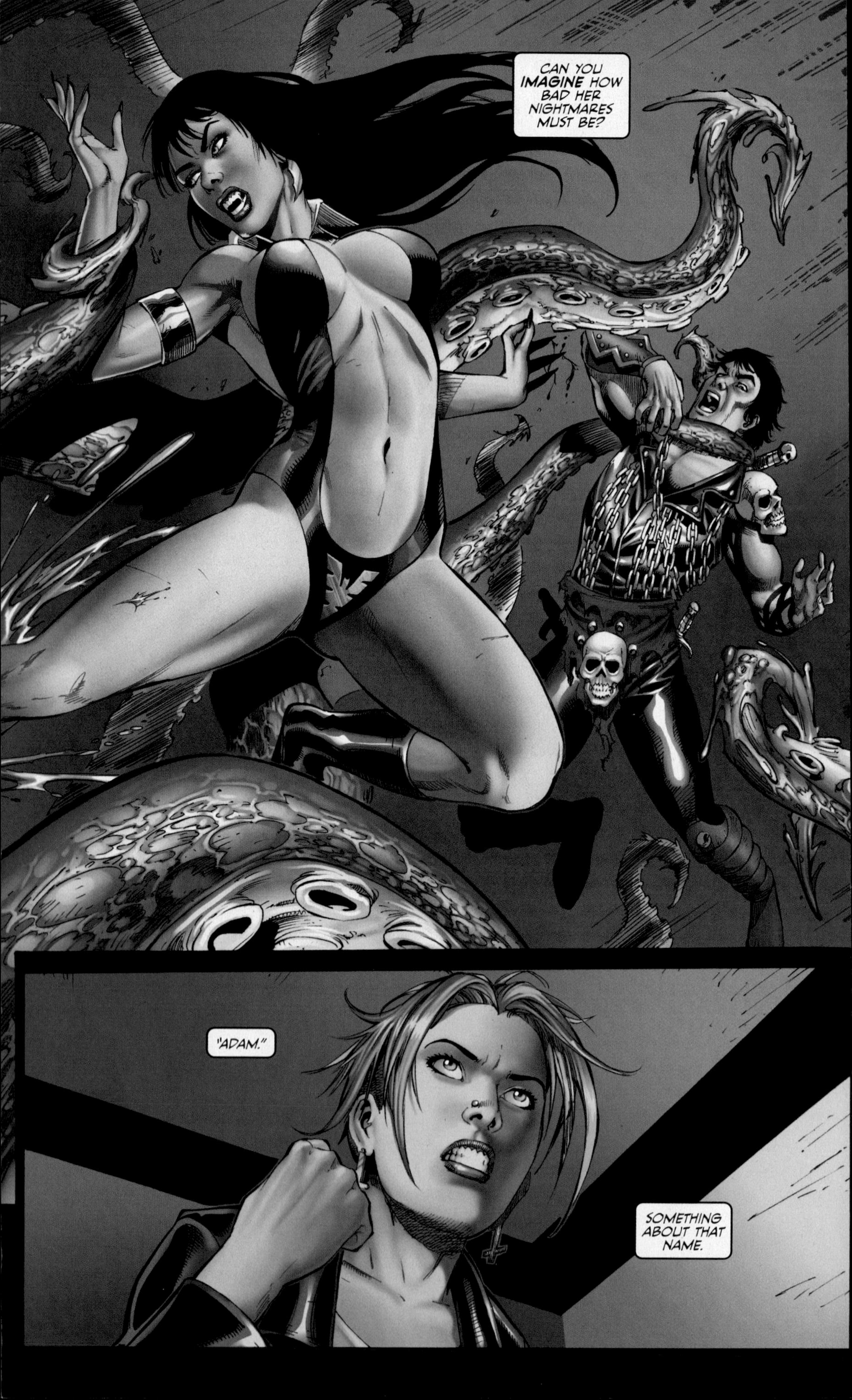
CAN YOU **IMAGINE** HOW BAD HER NIGHTMARES MUST BE?
"ADAM."
SOMETHING ABOUT THAT NAME.

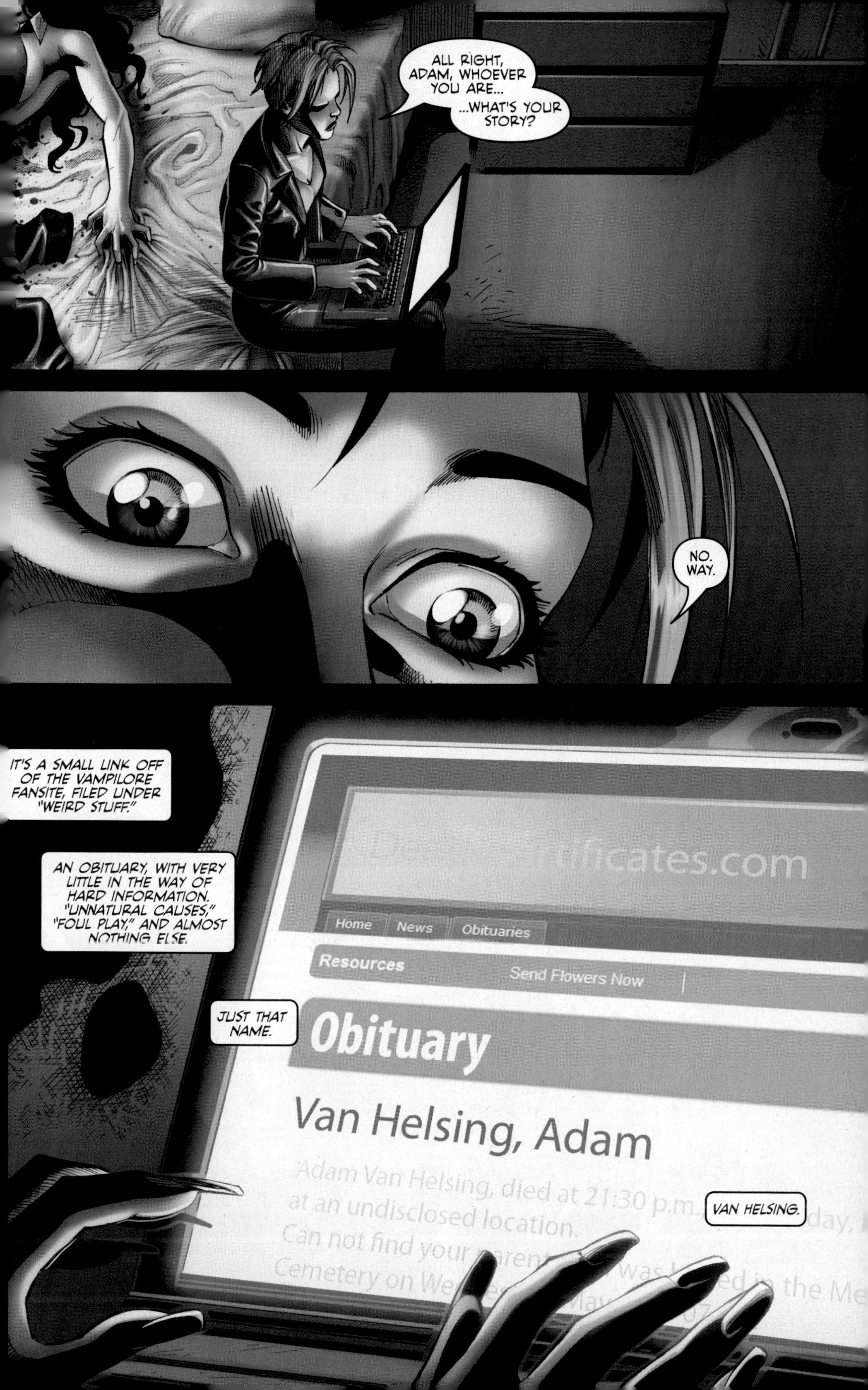

ALL RIGHT, ADAM, WHOEVER YOU ARE...
...WHAT'S YOUR STORY?
NO. WAY.
IT'S A SMALL LINK OFF OF THE VAMPILORE FANSITE, FILED UNDER "WEIRD STUFF."
AN OBITUARY, WITH VERY LITTLE IN THE WAY OF HARD INFORMATION. "UNNATURAL CAUSES," "FOUL PLAY," AND ALMOST NOTHING ELSE.
Home
News
Obituaries
Resources
Send Flowers Now
JUST THAT NAME.
Obituary
Van Helsing, Adam
at an undisclosed location.
VAN HELSING.

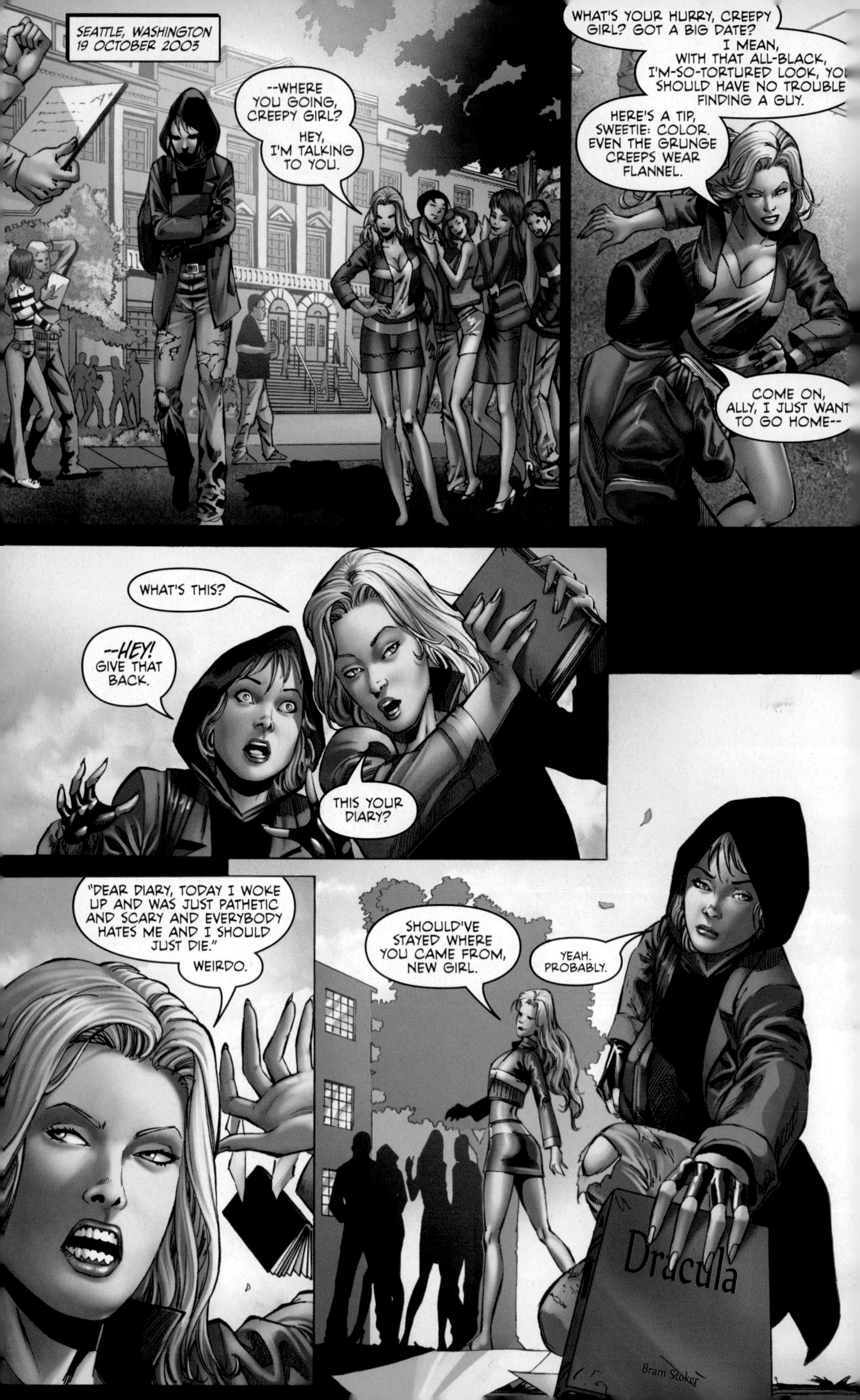
SEATTLE, WASHINGTON
19 OCTOBER 2003
--WHERE YOU GOING, CREEPY GIRL?
HEY, I'M TALKING TO YOU.
WHAT'S YOUR HURRY, CREEPY GIRL? GOT A BIG DATE?
I MEAN, WITH THAT ALL-BLACK, I'M-SO-TORTURED LOOK, YOU SHOULD HAVE NO TROUBLE FINDING A GUY.
HERE'S A TIP, SWEETIE: COLOR. EVEN THE GRUNGE CREEPS WEAR FLANNEL.
COME ON, ALLY, I JUST WANT TO GO HOME--
WHAT'S THIS?
--HEY! GIVE THAT BACK.
THIS YOUR DIARY?
"DEAR DIARY, TODAY I WOKE UP AND WAS JUST PATHETIC AND SCARY AND EVERYBODY HATES ME AND I SHOULD JUST DIE."
WEIRDO.
SHOULD'VE STAYED WHERE YOU CAME FROM, NEW GIRL.
YEAH. PROBABLY.
Dracula
Bram Stoker

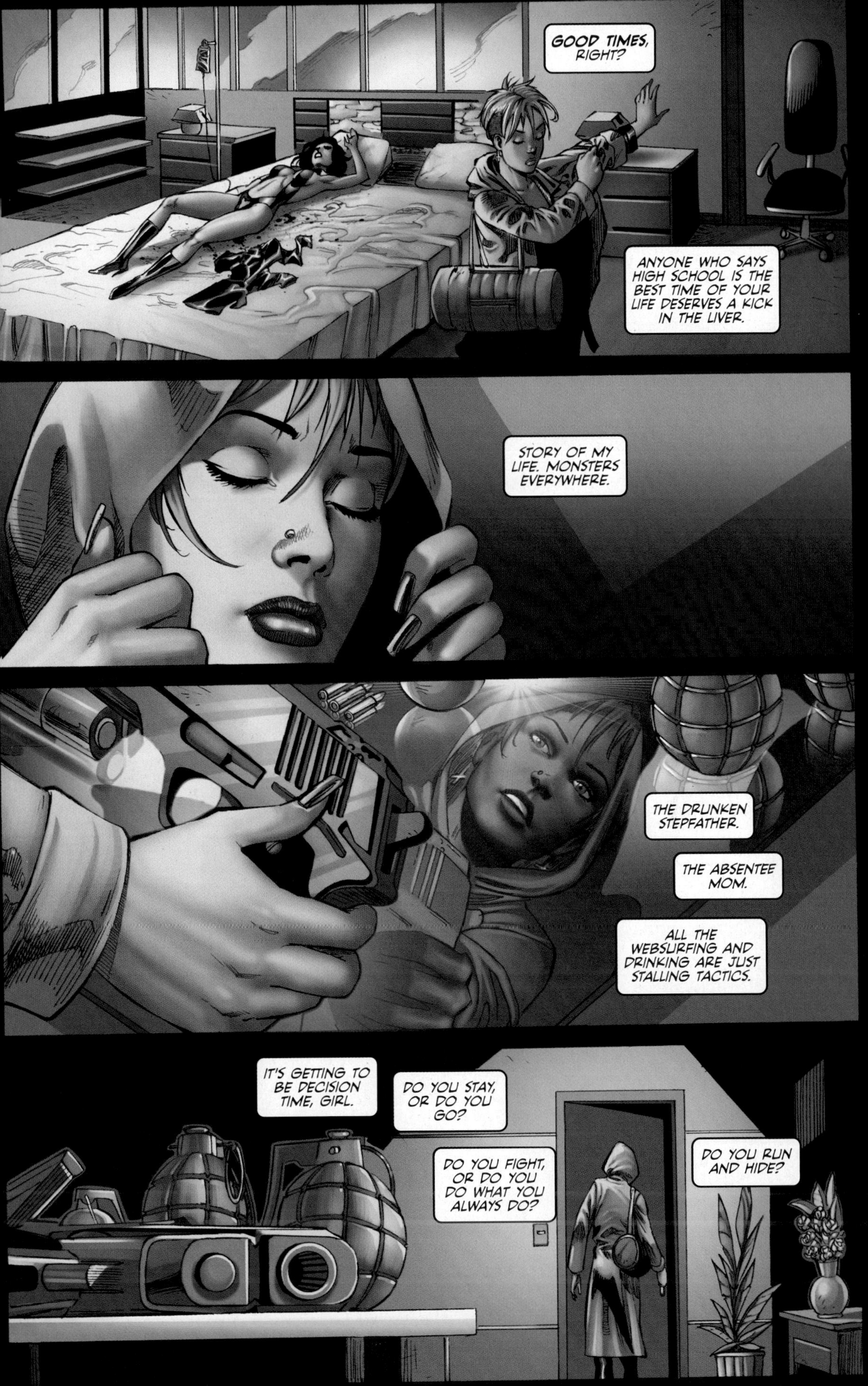
GOOD TIMES, RIGHT?
ANYONE WHO SAYS HIGH SCHOOL IS THE BEST TIME OF YOUR LIFE DESERVES A KICK IN THE LIVER.
STORY OF MY LIFE. MONSTERS EVERYWHERE.
THE DRUNKEN STEPFATHER.
THE ABSENTEE MOM.
ALL THE WEBSURFING AND DRINKING ARE JUST STALLING TACTICS.
IT'S GETTING TO BE DECISION TIME, GIRL.
DO YOU STAY, OR DO YOU GO?
DO YOU FIGHT, OR DO YOU DO WHAT YOU ALWAYS DO?
DO YOU RUN AND HIDE?

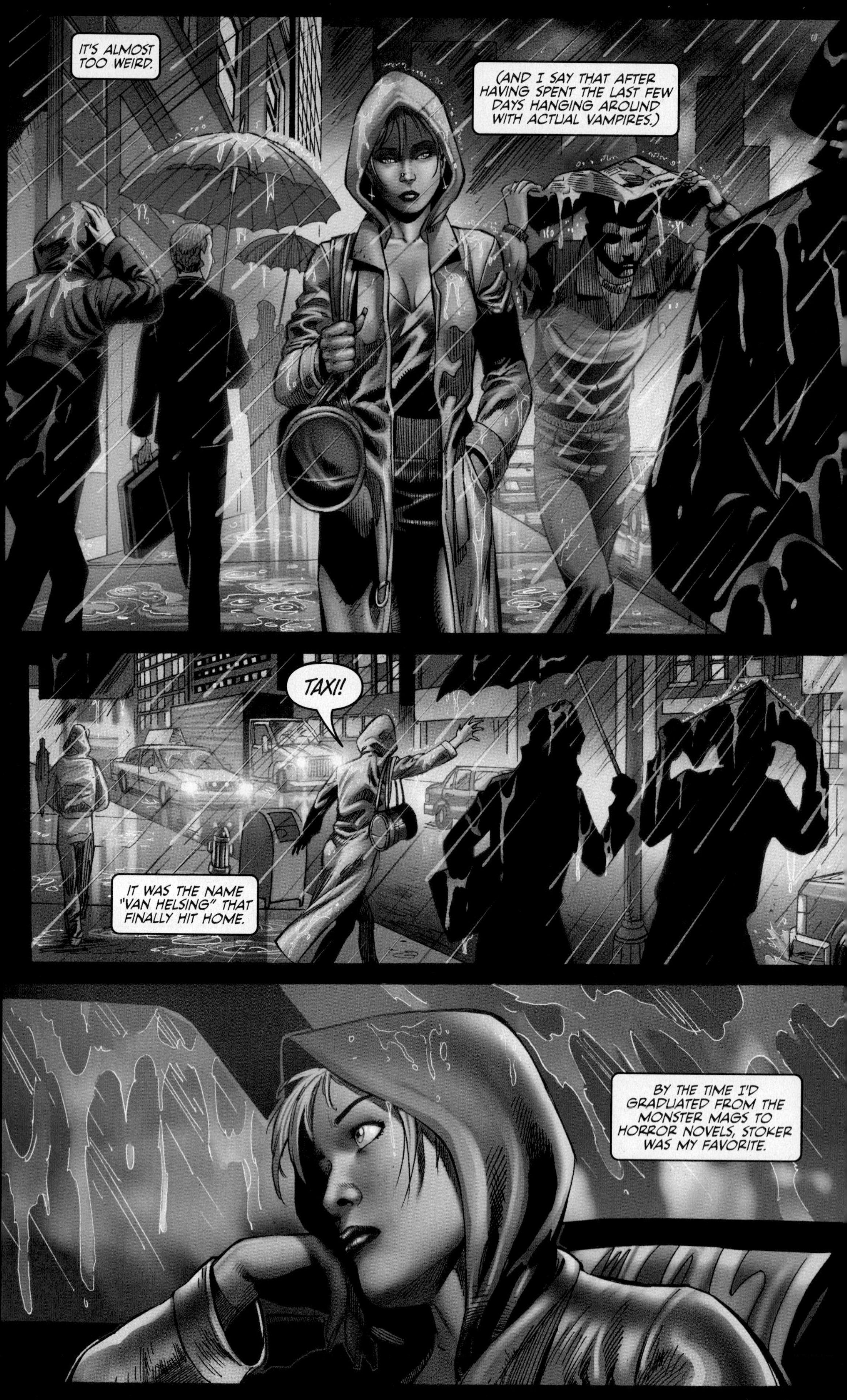
IT'S ALMOST TOO WEIRD.
(AND I SAY THAT AFTER HAVING SPENT THE LAST FEW DAYS HANGING AROUND WITH ACTUAL VAMPIRES.)
TAXI!
IT WAS THE NAME "VAN HELSING" THAT FINALLY HIT HOME.
BY THE TIME I'D GRADUATED FROM THE MONSTER MAGS TO HORROR NOVELS, STOKER WAS MY FAVORITE.

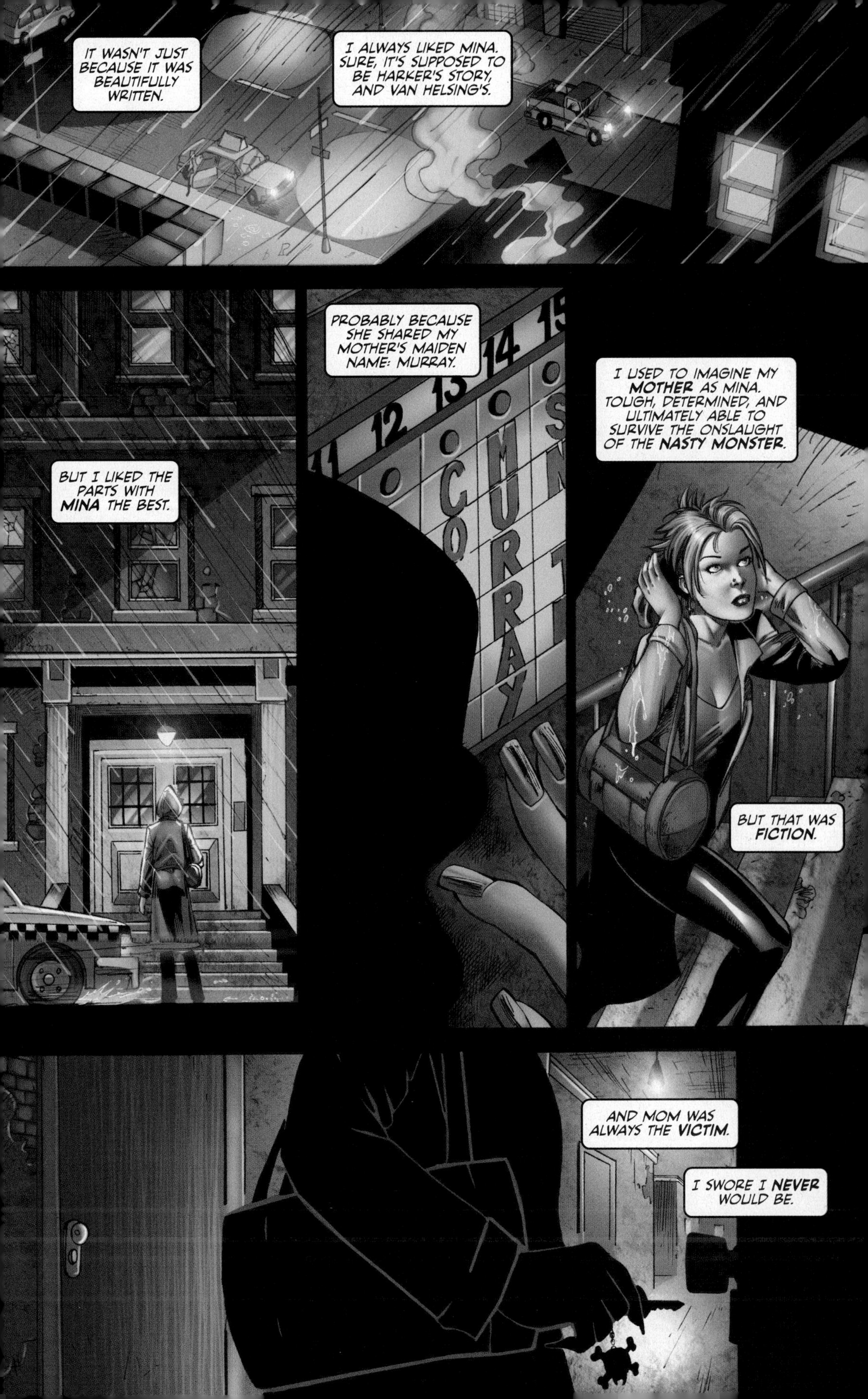
IT WASN'T JUST BECAUSE IT WAS BEAUTIFULLY WRITTEN.
I ALWAYS LIKED MINA. SURE, IT'S SUPPOSED TO BE HARKER'S STORY, AND VAN HELSING'S.
BUT I LIKED THE PARTS WITH MINA THE BEST.
PROBABLY BECAUSE SHE SHARED MY MOTHER'S MAIDEN NAME: MURRAY.
11 12 13 14 15
MURRAY
I USED TO IMAGINE MY MOTHER AS MINA. TOUGH, DETERMINED, AND ULTIMATELY ABLE TO SURVIVE THE ONSLAUGHT OF THE NASTY MONSTER.
BUT THAT WAS FICTION.
AND MOM WAS ALWAYS THE VICTIM.
I SWORE I NEVER WOULD BE.

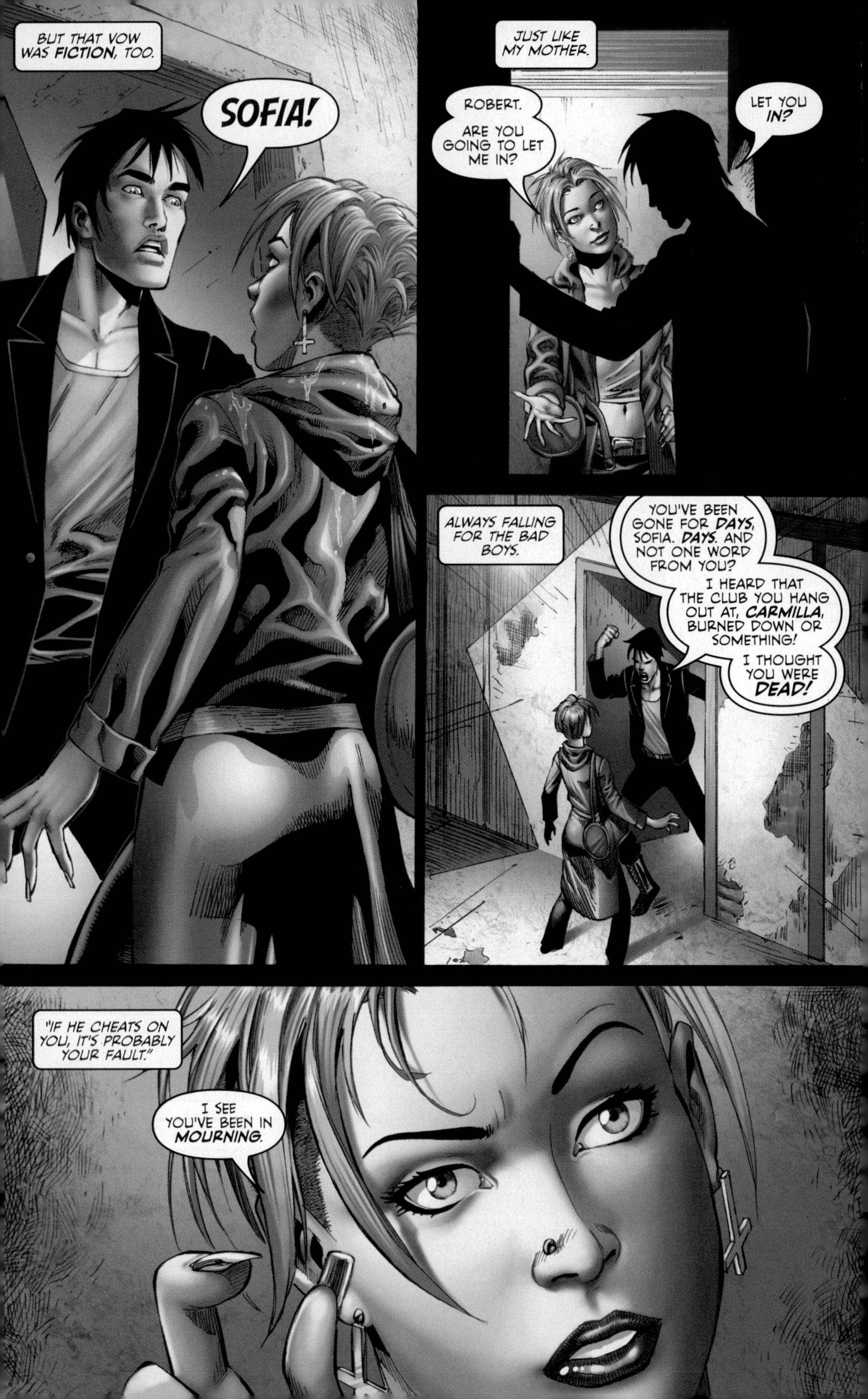
BUT THAT VOW WAS FICTION, TOO.
SOFIA!
JUST LIKE MY MOTHER.
ROBERT.
ARE YOU GOING TO LET ME IN?
LET YOU IN?
ALWAYS FALLING FOR THE BAD BOYS.
YOU'VE BEEN GONE FOR DAYS, SOFIA. DAYS. AND NOT ONE WORD FROM YOU?
I HEARD THAT THE CLUB YOU HANG OUT AT, CARMILLA, BURNED DOWN OR SOMETHING!
I THOUGHT YOU WERE DEAD!
"IF HE CHEATS ON YOU, IT'S PROBABLY YOUR FAULT."
I SEE YOU'VE BEEN IN MOURNING.

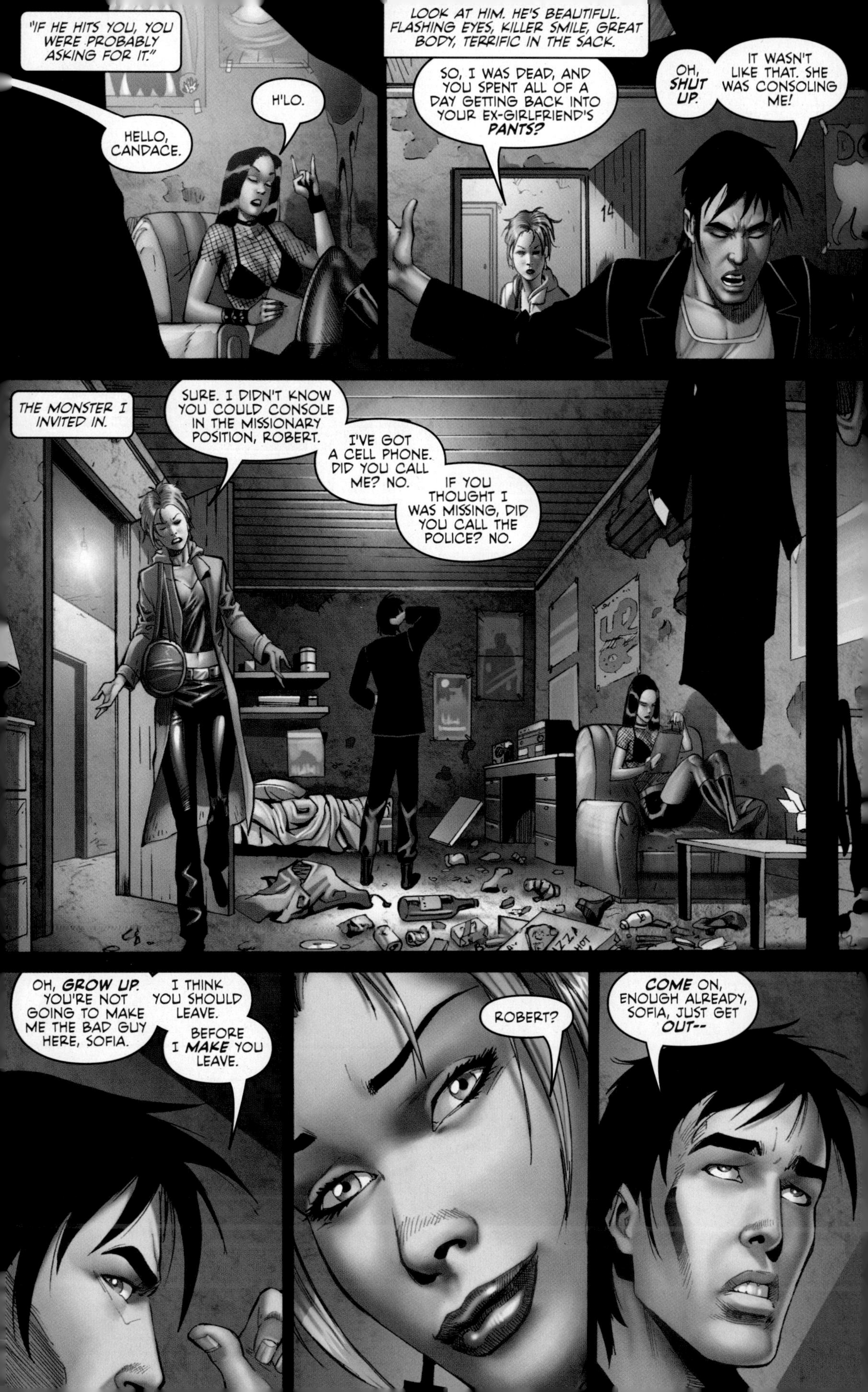
"IF HE HITS YOU, YOU WERE PROBABLY ASKING FOR IT."
HELLO, CANDACE.
H'LO.
LOOK AT HIM. HE'S BEAUTIFUL. FLASHING EYES, KILLER SMILE, GREAT BODY, TERRIFIC IN THE SACK.
SO, I WAS DEAD, AND YOU SPENT ALL OF A DAY GETTING BACK INTO YOUR EX-GIRLFRIEND'S PANTS?
OH, SHUT UP.
IT WASN'T LIKE THAT. SHE WAS CONSOLING ME!
THE MONSTER I INVITED IN.
SURE. I DIDN'T KNOW YOU COULD CONSOLE IN THE MISSIONARY POSITION, ROBERT.
I'VE GOT A CELL PHONE. DID YOU CALL ME? NO.
IF YOU THOUGHT I WAS MISSING, DID YOU CALL THE POLICE? NO.
OH, GROW UP. YOU'RE NOT GOING TO MAKE ME THE BAD GUY HERE, SOFIA.
I THINK YOU SHOULD LEAVE.
BEFORE I MAKE YOU LEAVE.
ROBERT?
COME ON, ENOUGH ALREADY, SOFIA, JUST GET OUT--

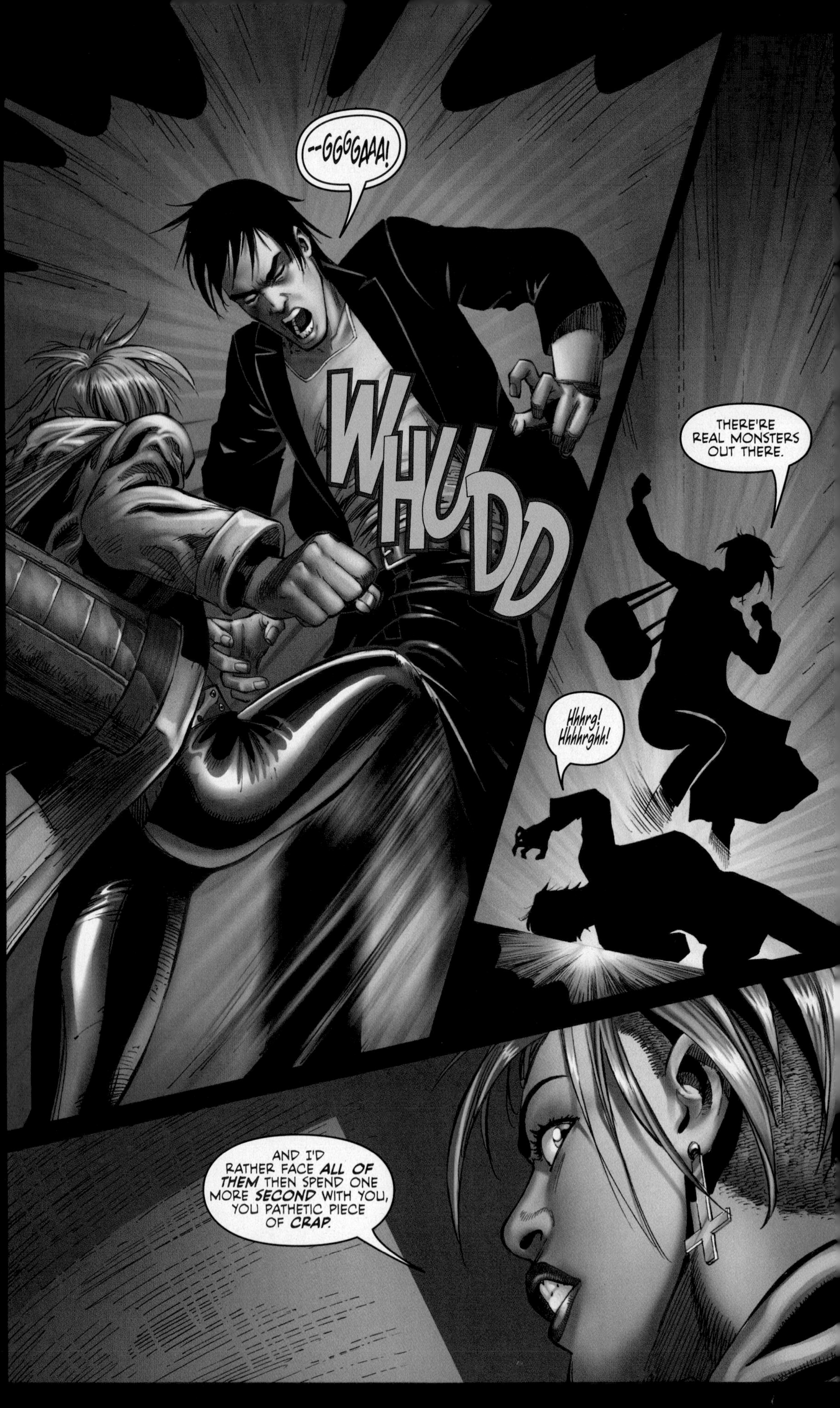
--GGGGAAA!
WHUDD
THERE'RE REAL MONSTERS OUT THERE.
Hhhrg! Hhhhrghh!
AND I'D RATHER FACE ALL OF THEM THEN SPEND ONE MORE SECOND WITH YOU, YOU PATHETIC PIECE OF CRAP.

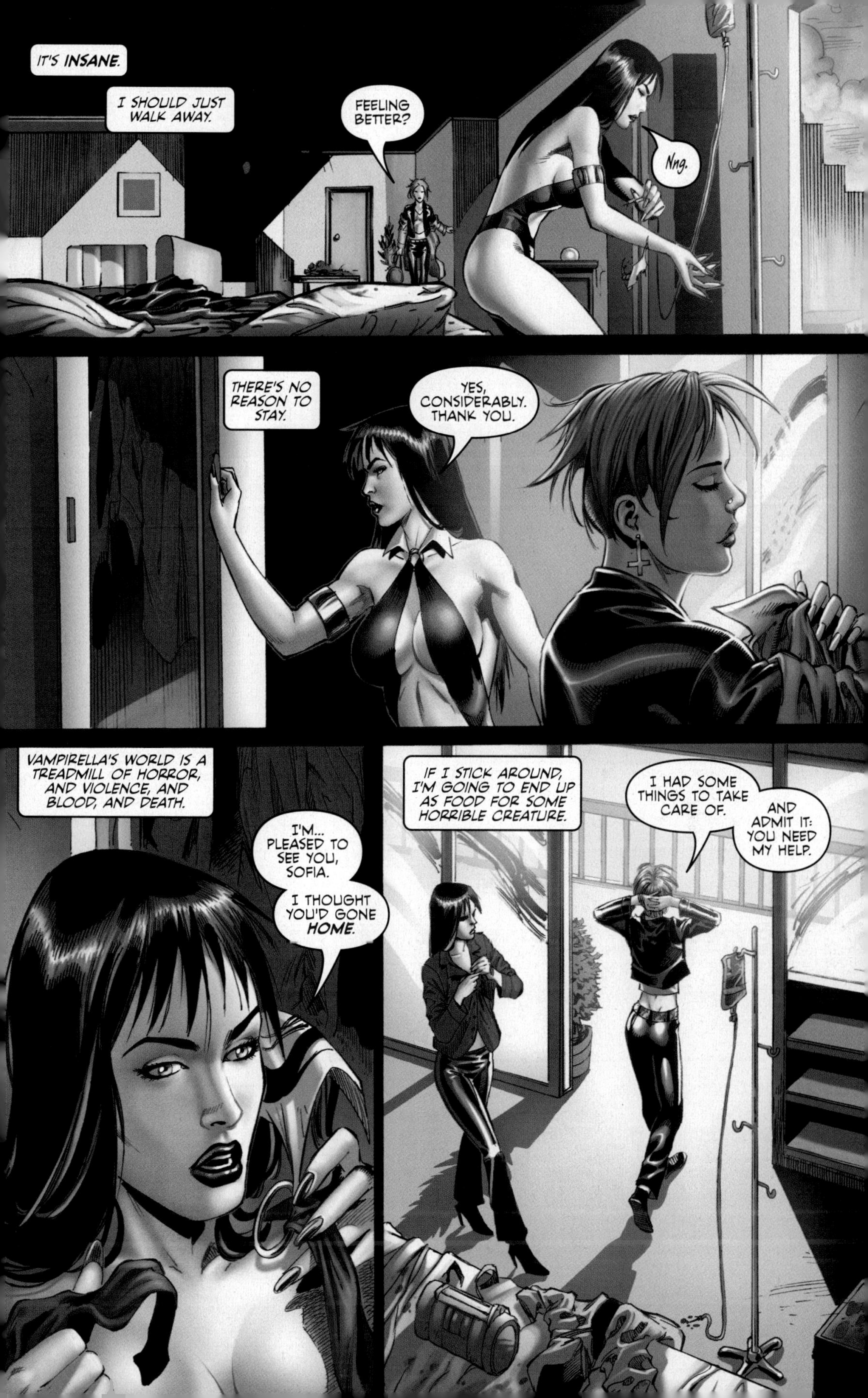

IT'S INSANE.
I SHOULD JUST WALK AWAY.
FEELING BETTER?
Nng.
THERE'S NO REASON TO STAY.
YES, CONSIDERABLY. THANK YOU.
VAMPIRELLA'S WORLD IS A TREADMILL OF HORROR, AND VIOLENCE, AND BLOOD, AND DEATH.
I'M... PLEASED TO SEE YOU, SOFIA.
I THOUGHT YOU'D GONE HOME.
IF I STICK AROUND, I'M GOING TO END UP AS FOOD FOR SOME HORRIBLE CREATURE.
I HAD SOME THINGS TO TAKE CARE OF.
AND ADMIT IT: YOU NEED MY HELP.

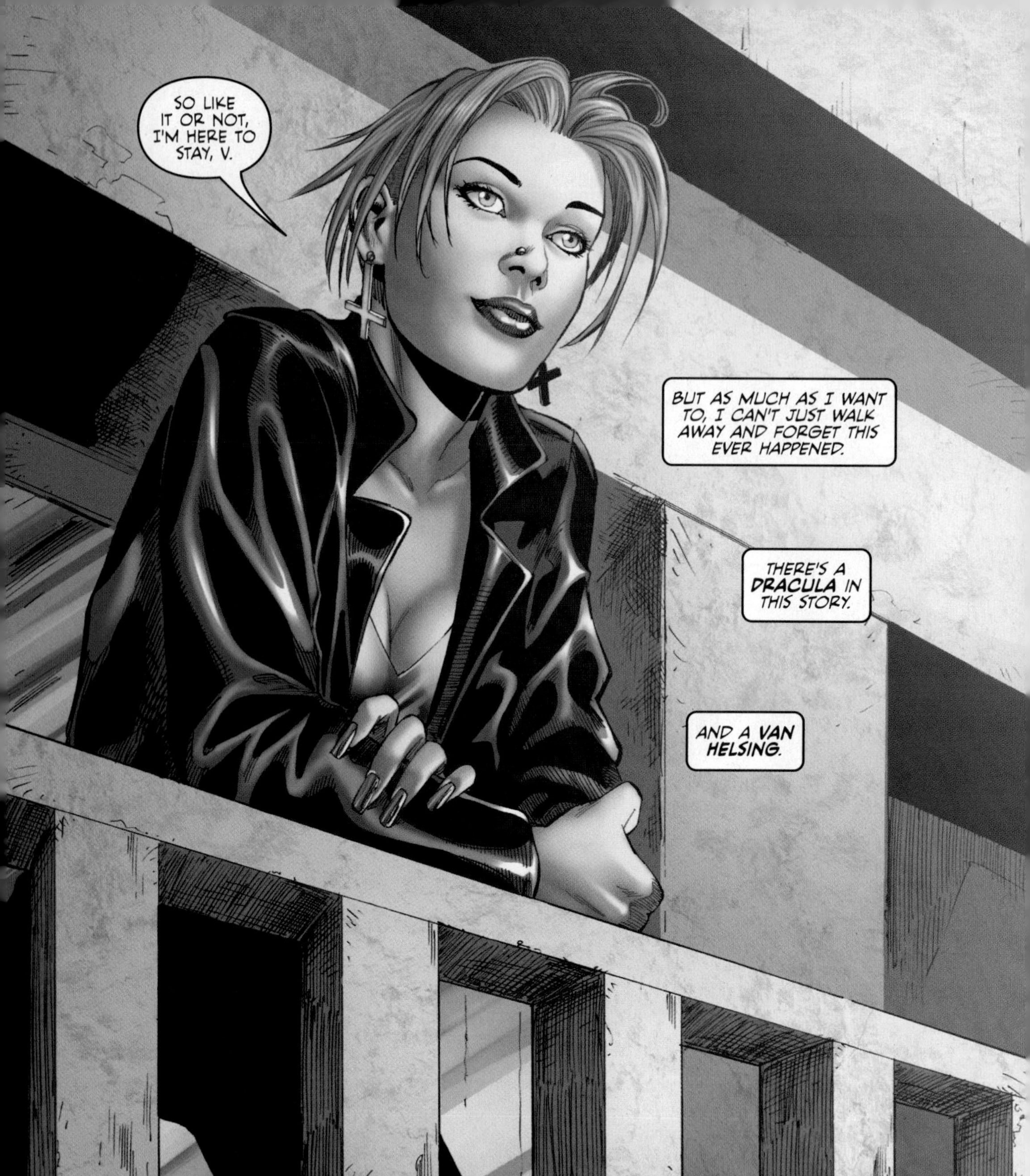
SO LIKE IT OR NOT, I'M HERE TO STAY, V.
BUT AS MUCH AS I WANT TO, I CAN'T JUST WALK AWAY AND FORGET THIS EVER HAPPENED.
THERE'S A DRACULA IN THIS STORY.
AND A VAN HELSING.

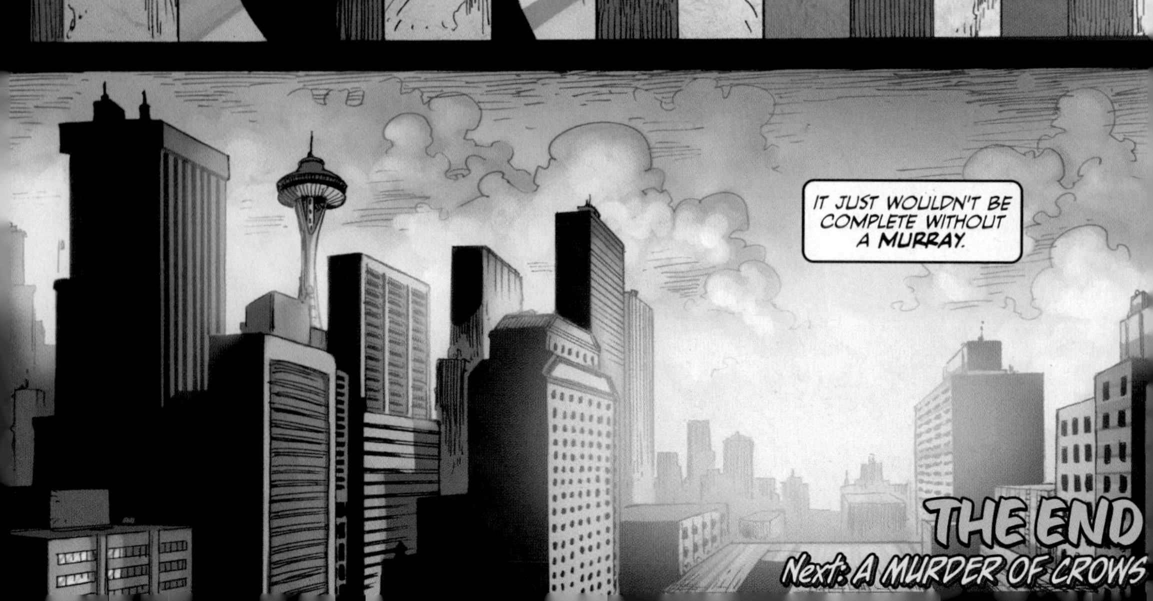
IT JUST WOULDN'T BE COMPLETE WITHOUT A MURRAY.
THE END
Next: A MURDER OF CROWS

COVER GALLERY

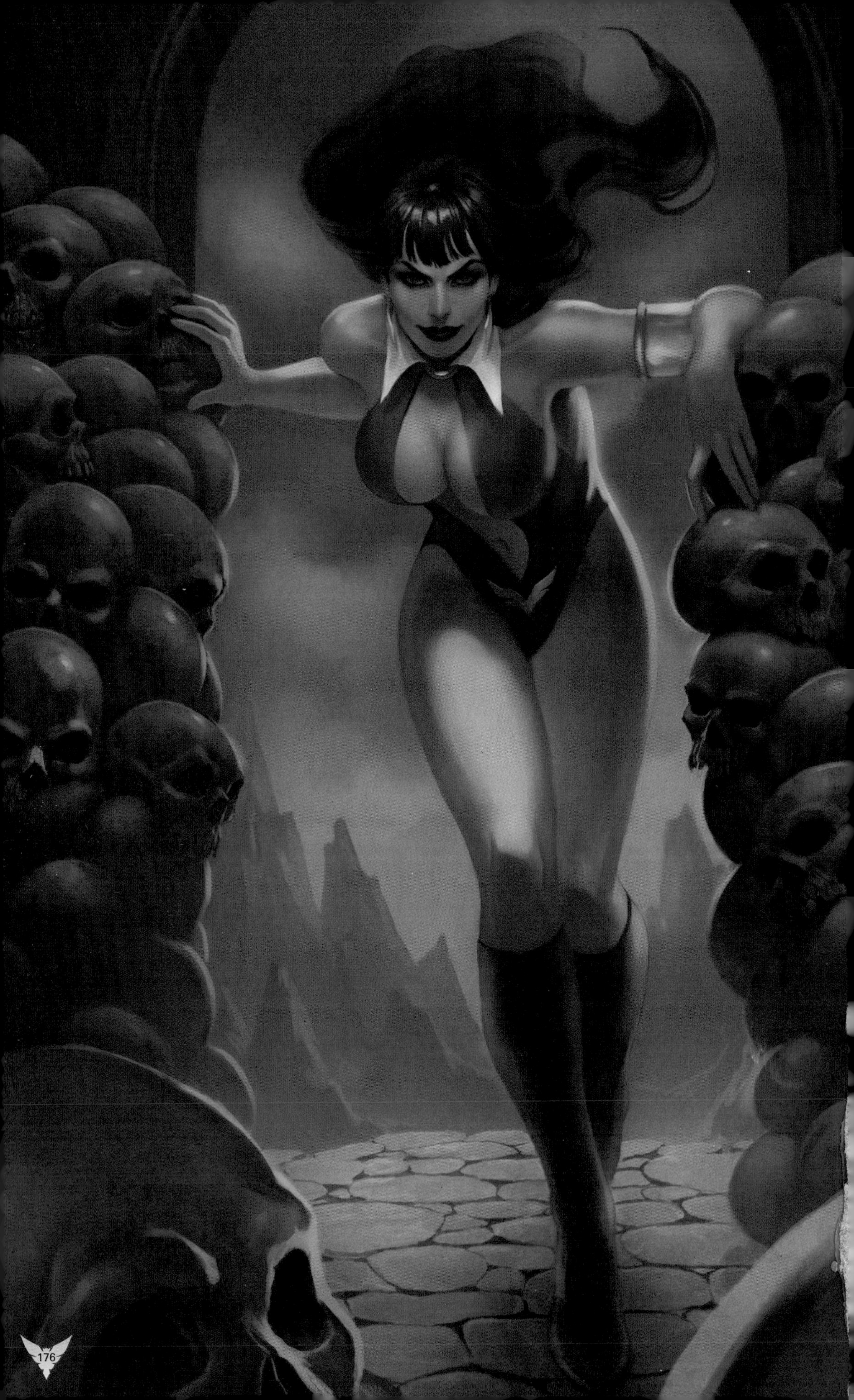

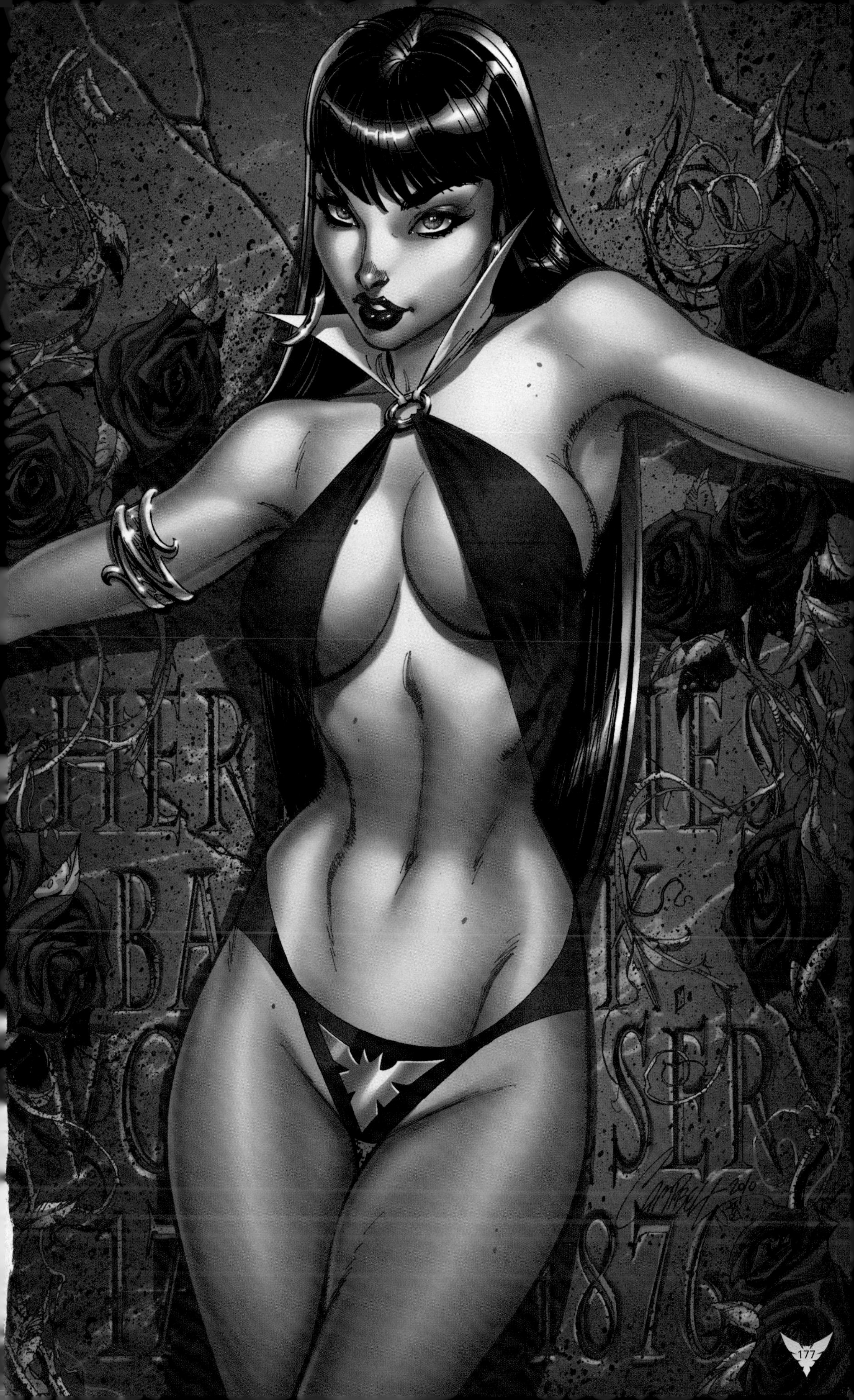

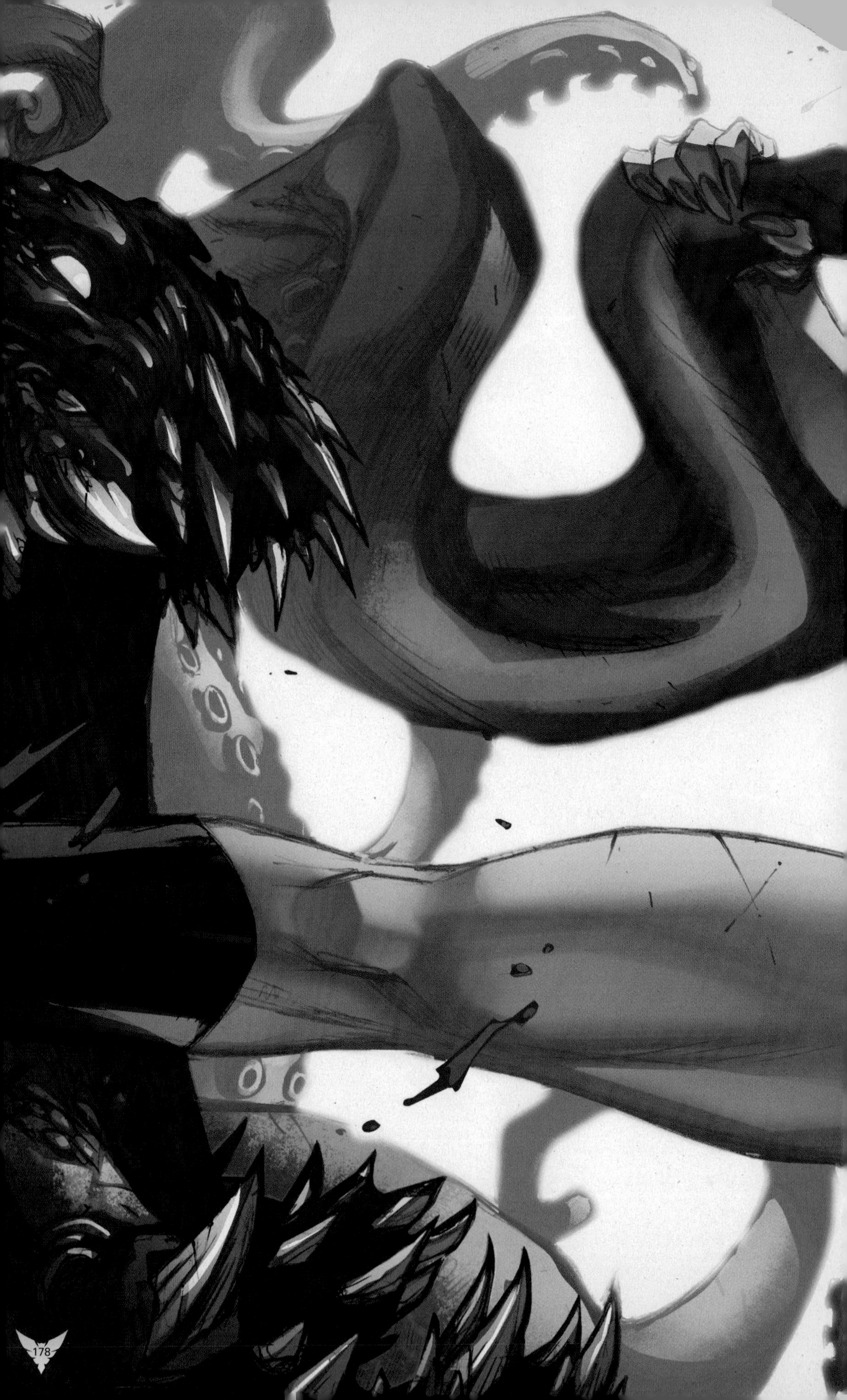

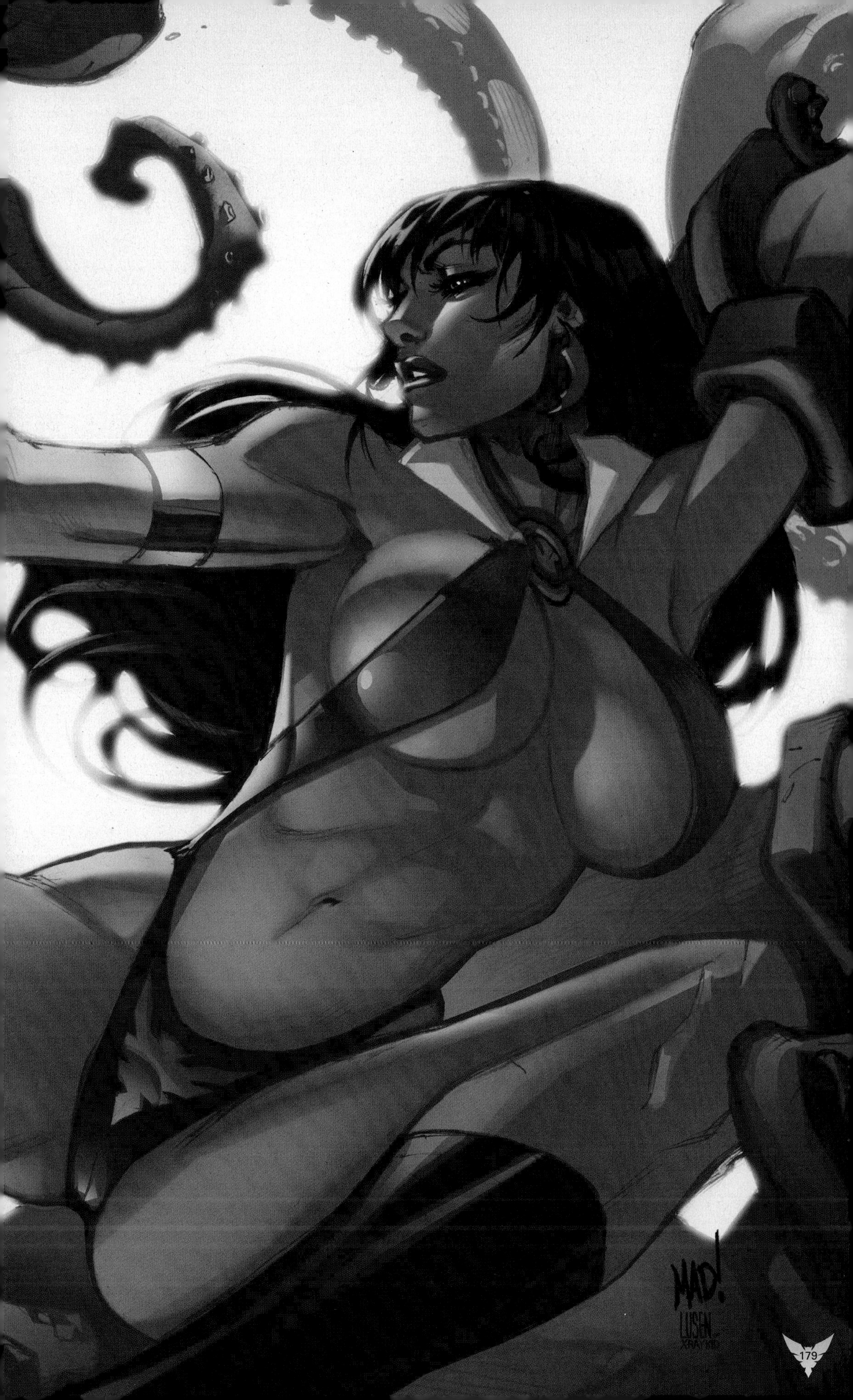
MAD!
LUSEN

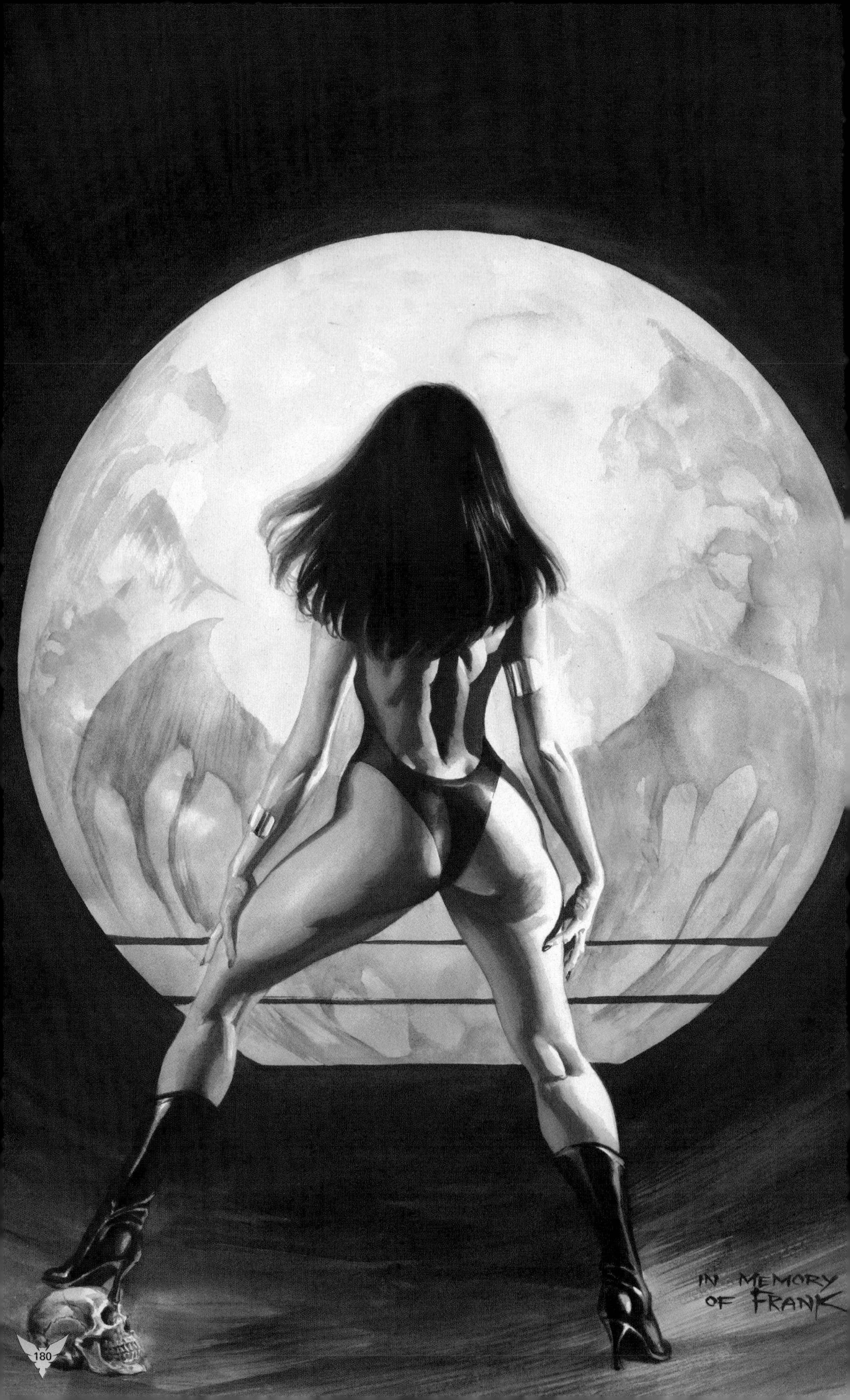
IN MEMORY
OF FRANK

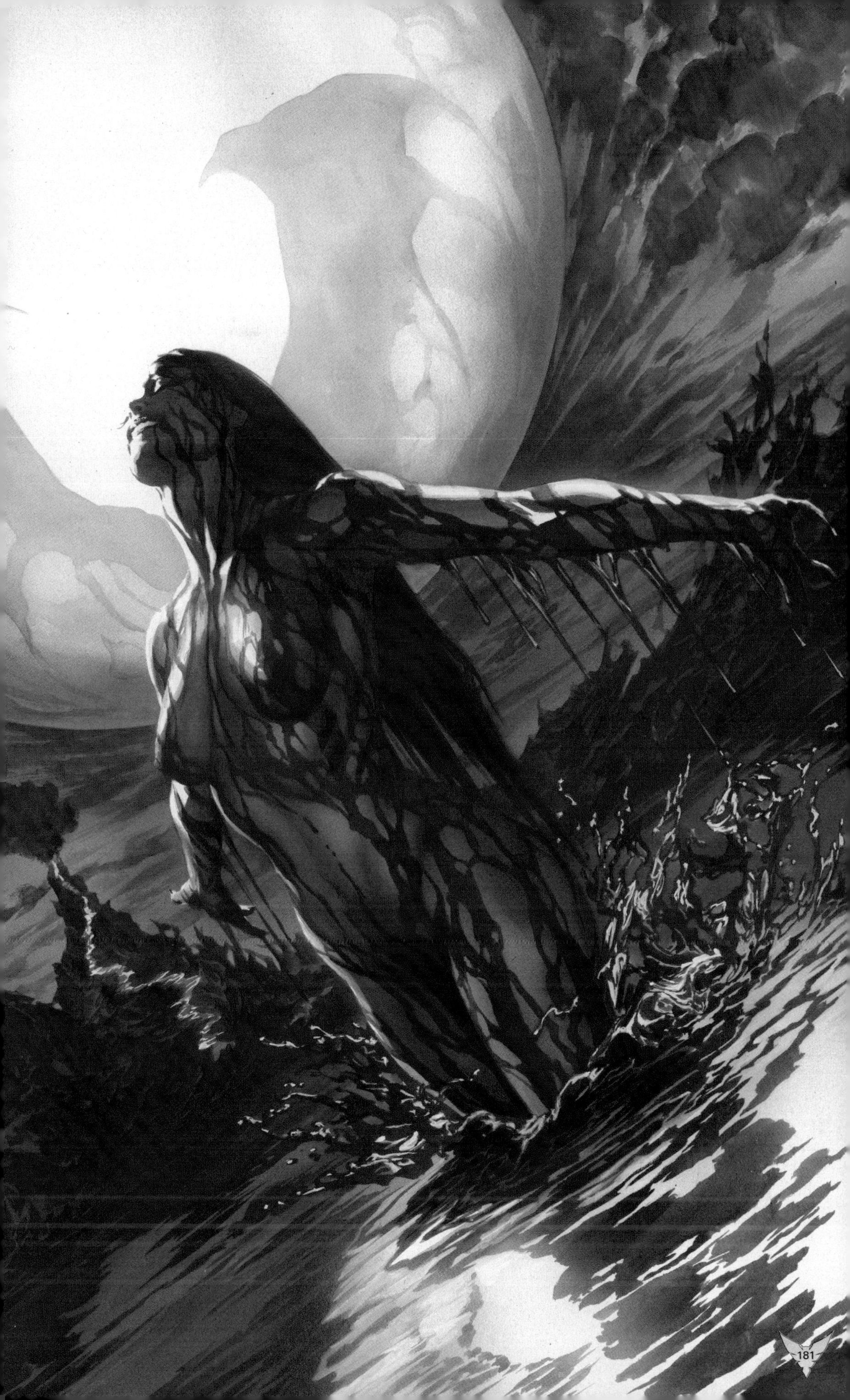

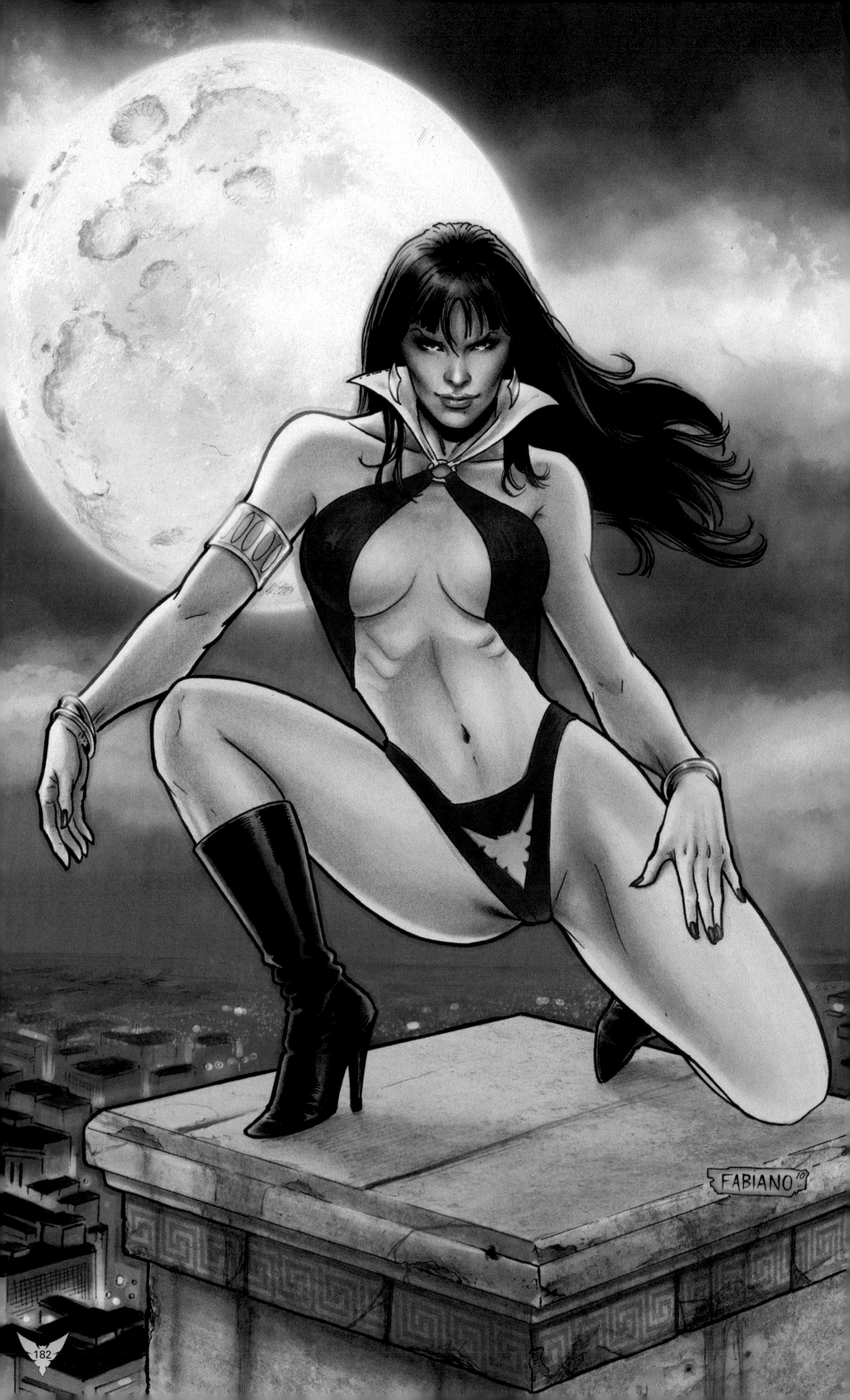
FABIANO '10

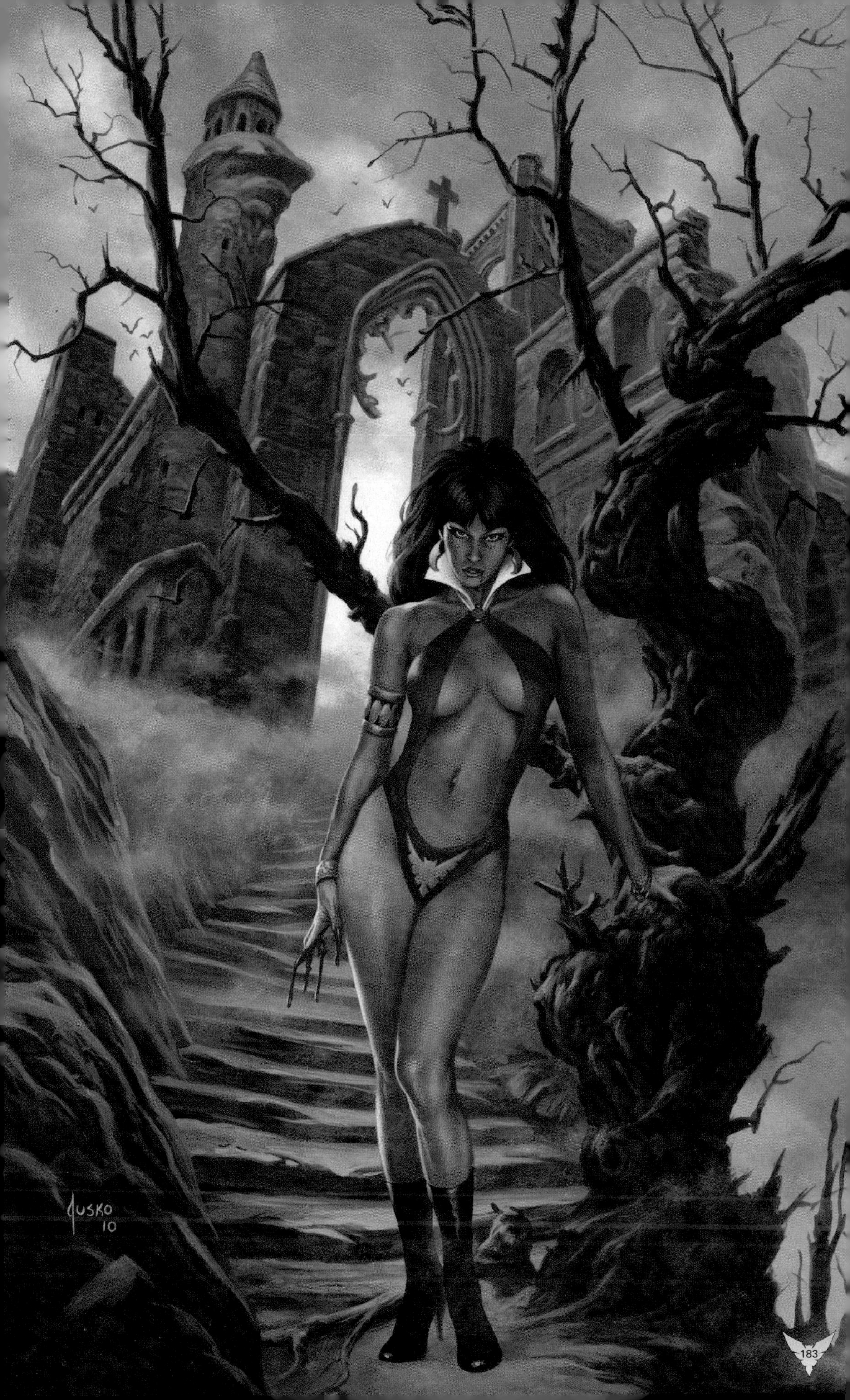
JUSKO
10

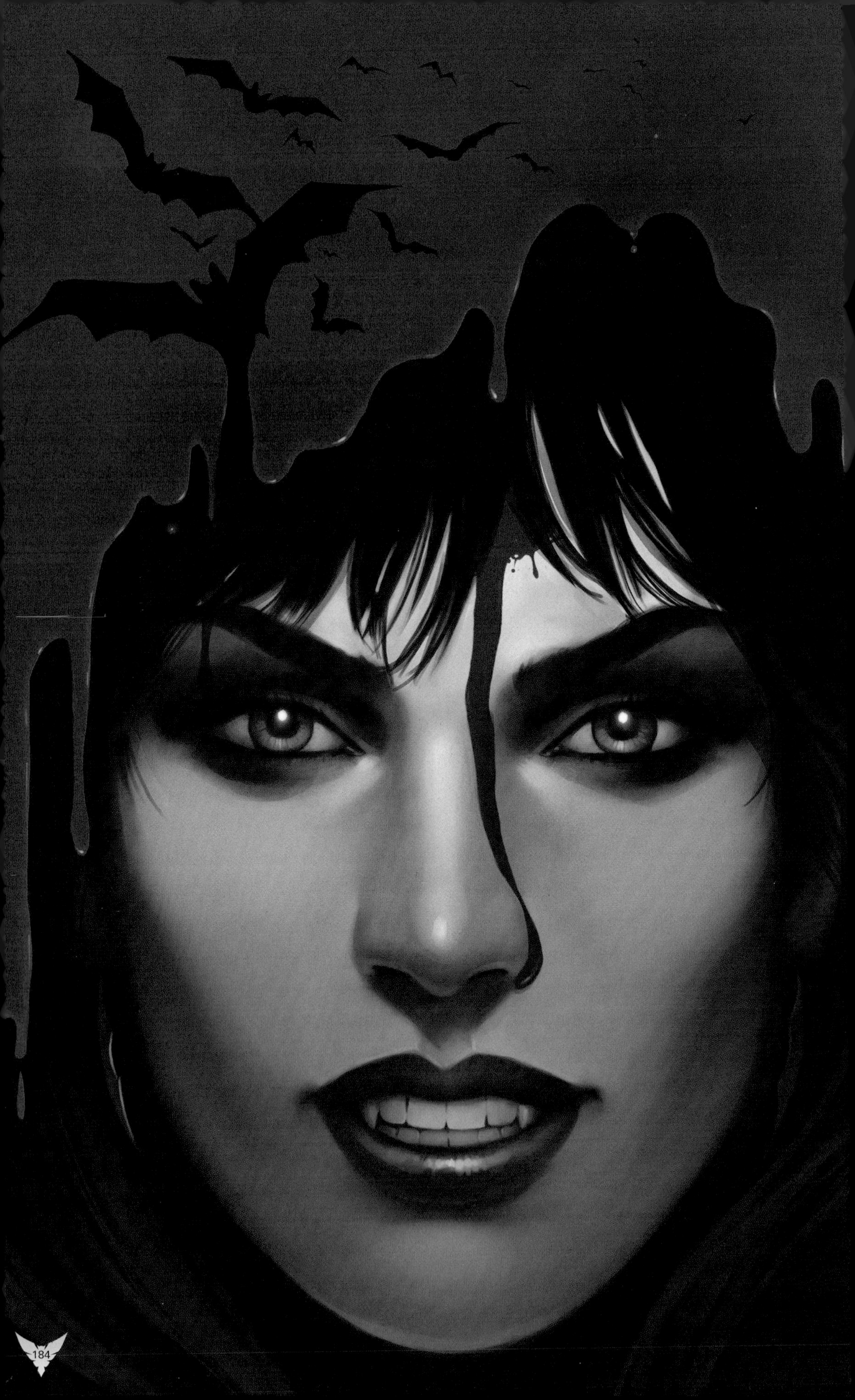

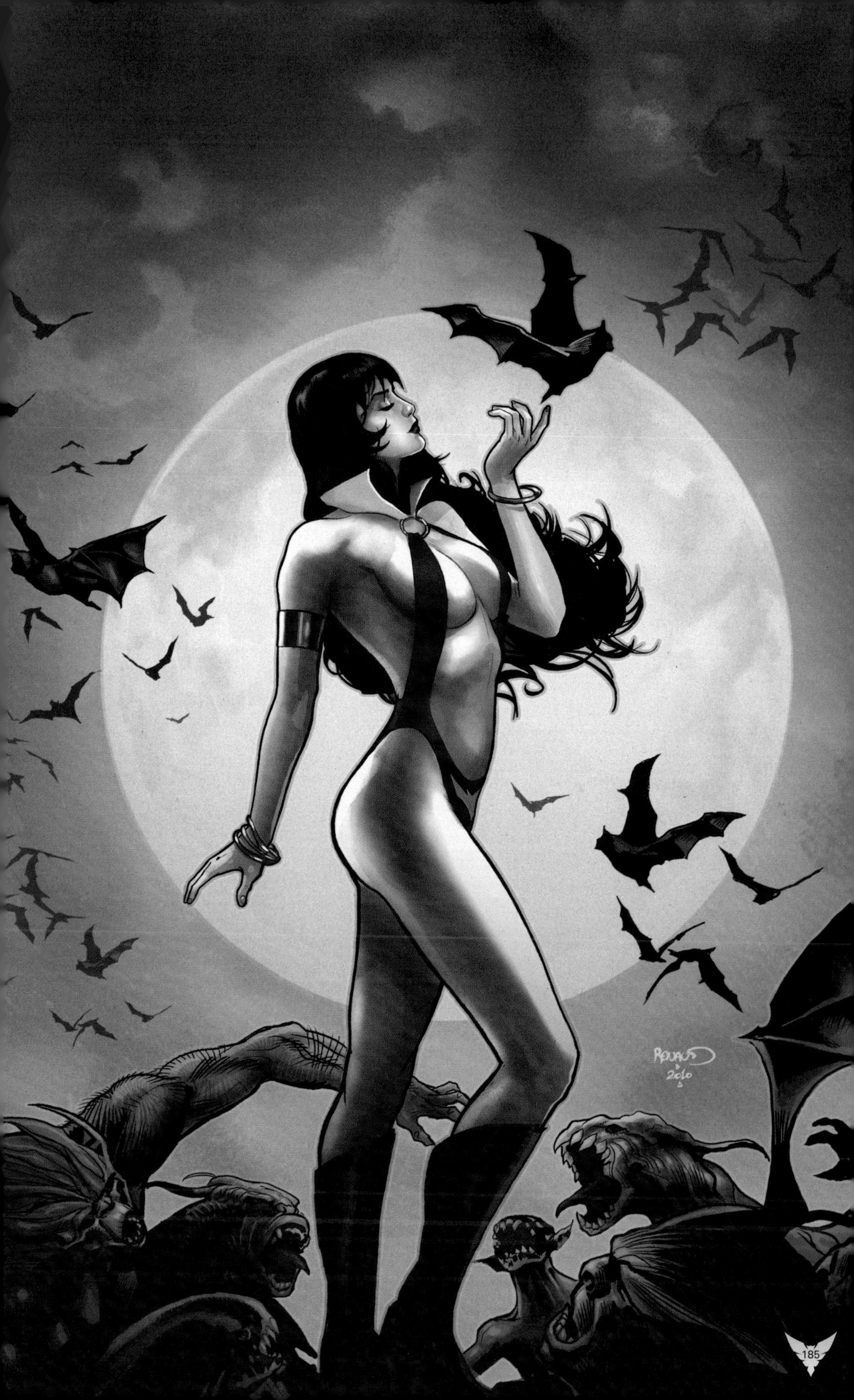

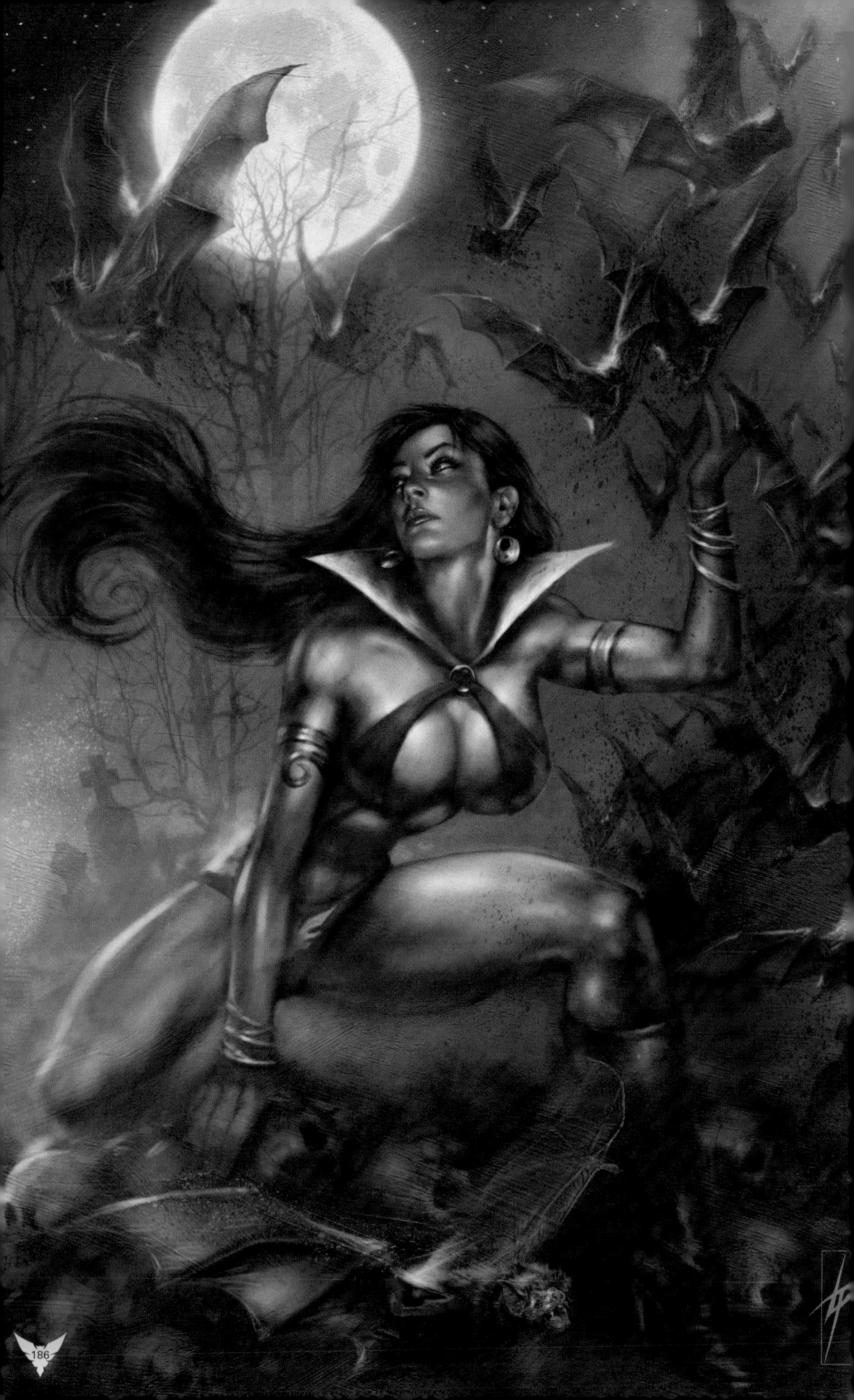

CHEN
Ivan Nunes

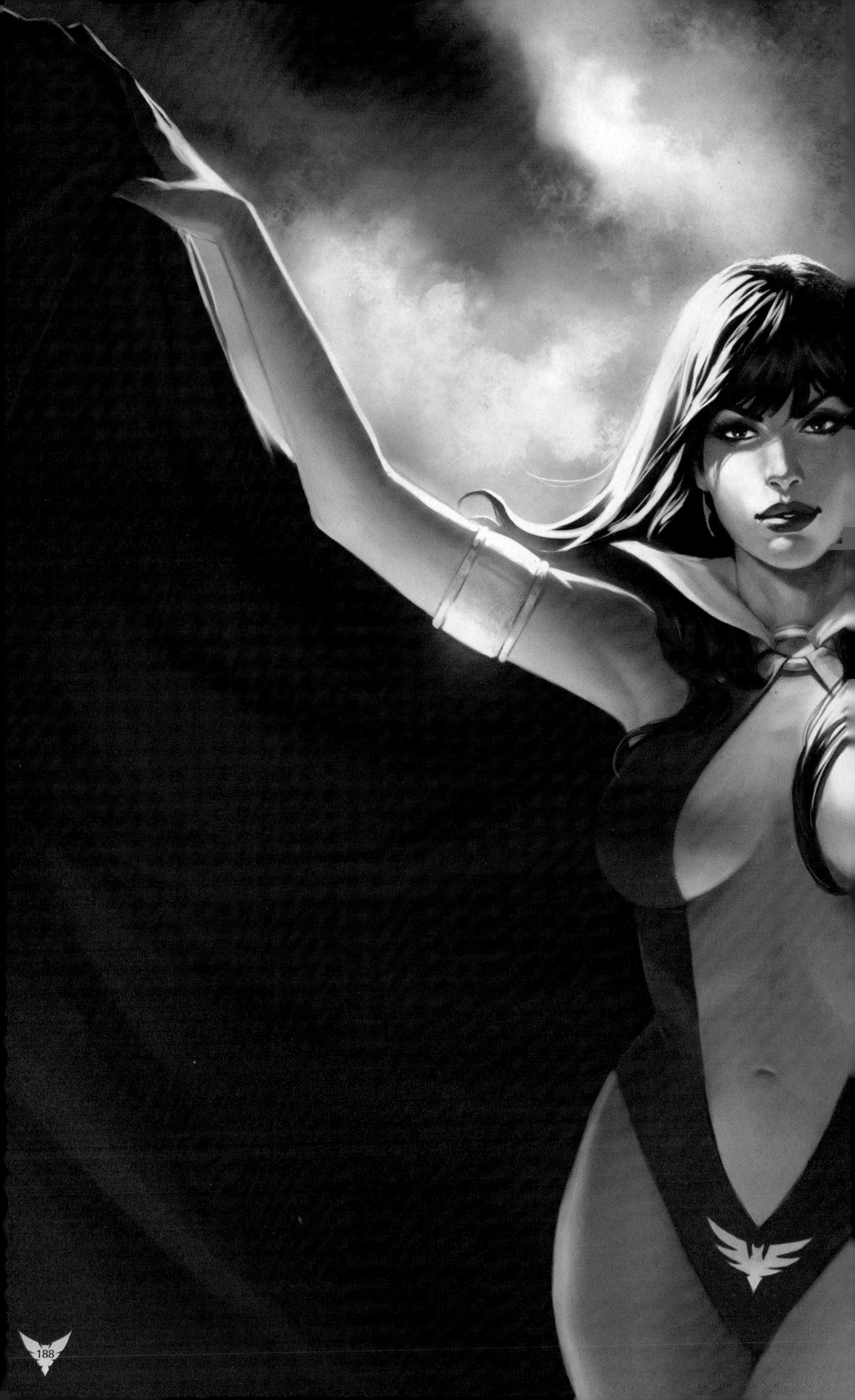

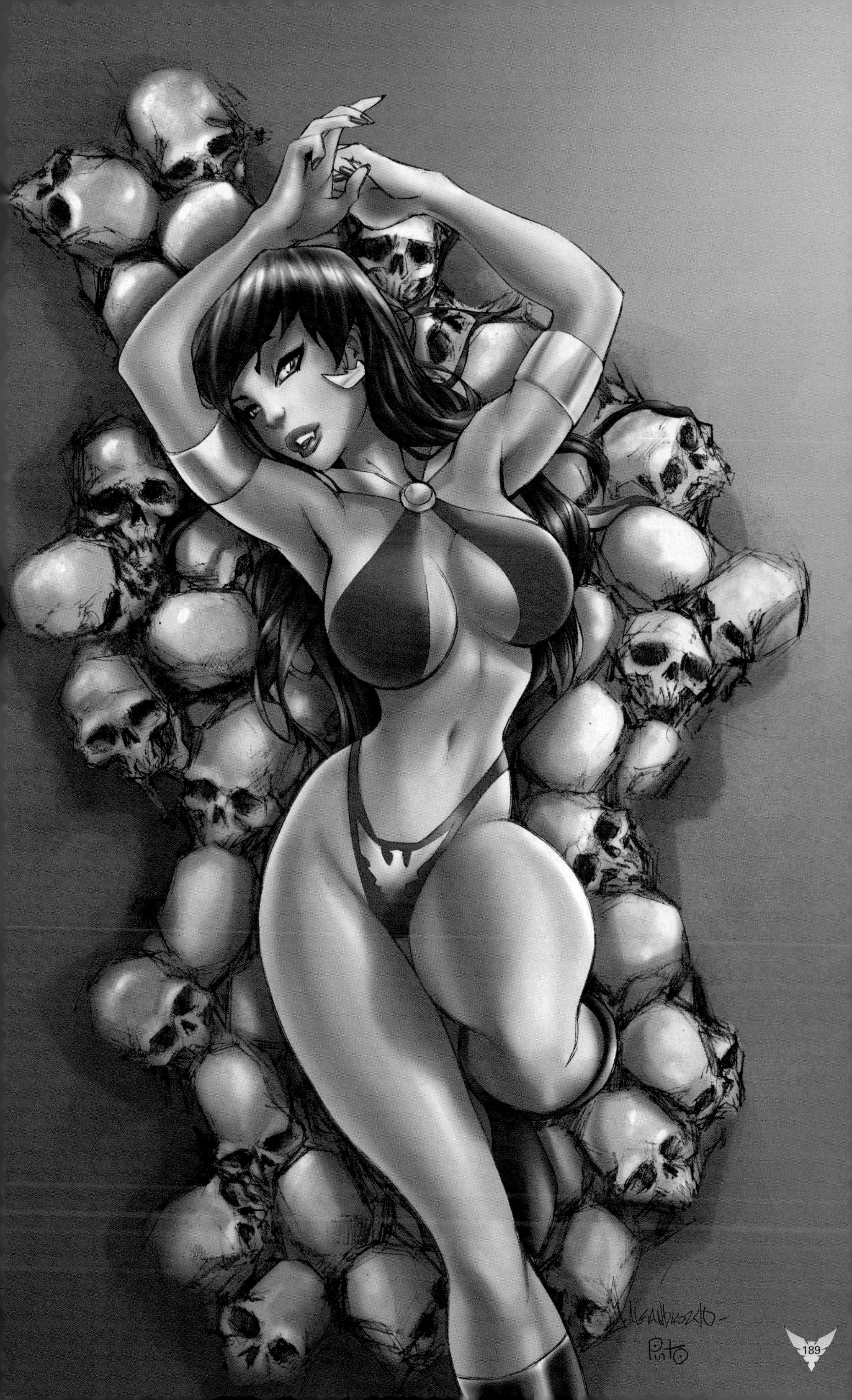
Pinto

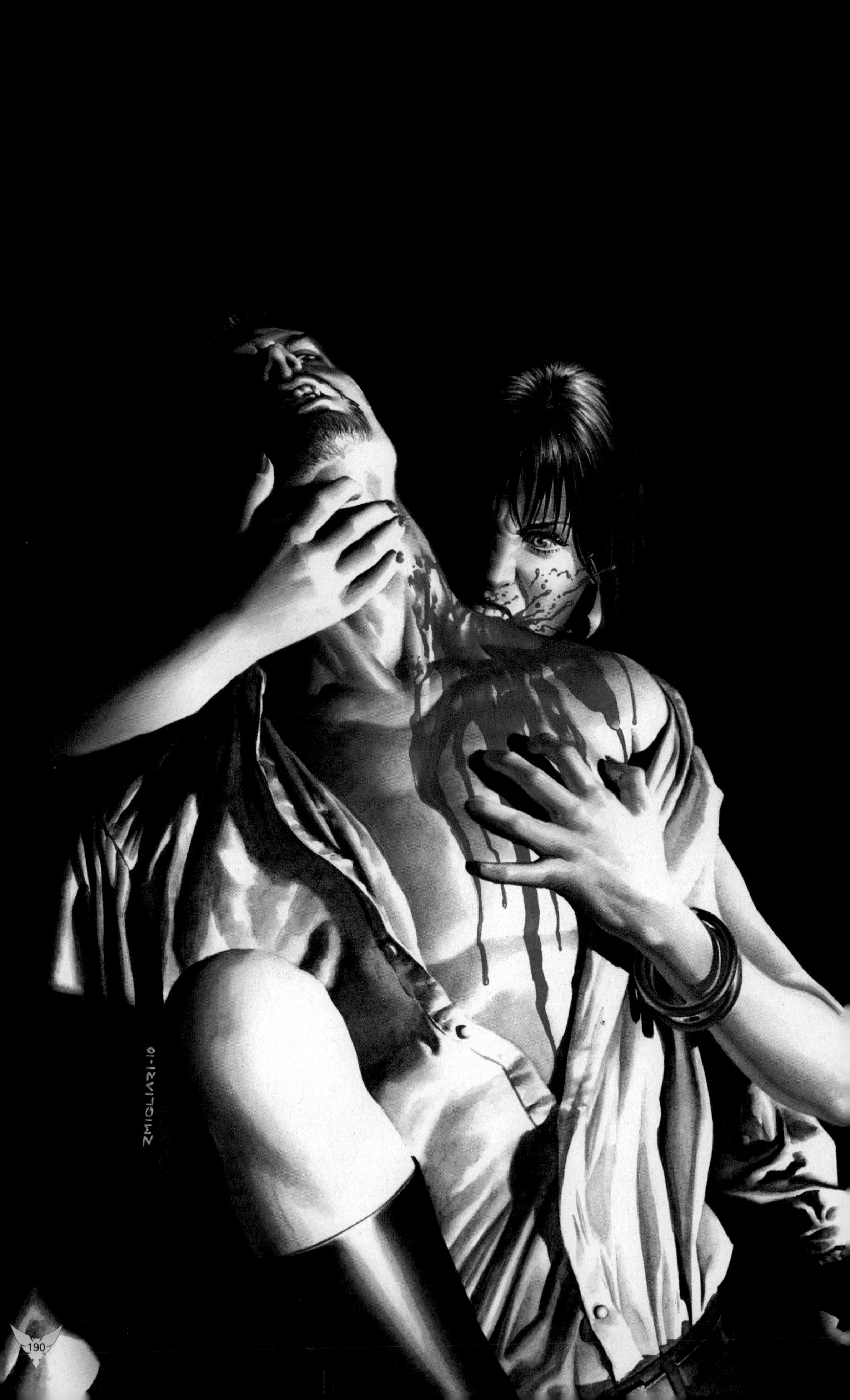
ZMIGLIARI-10

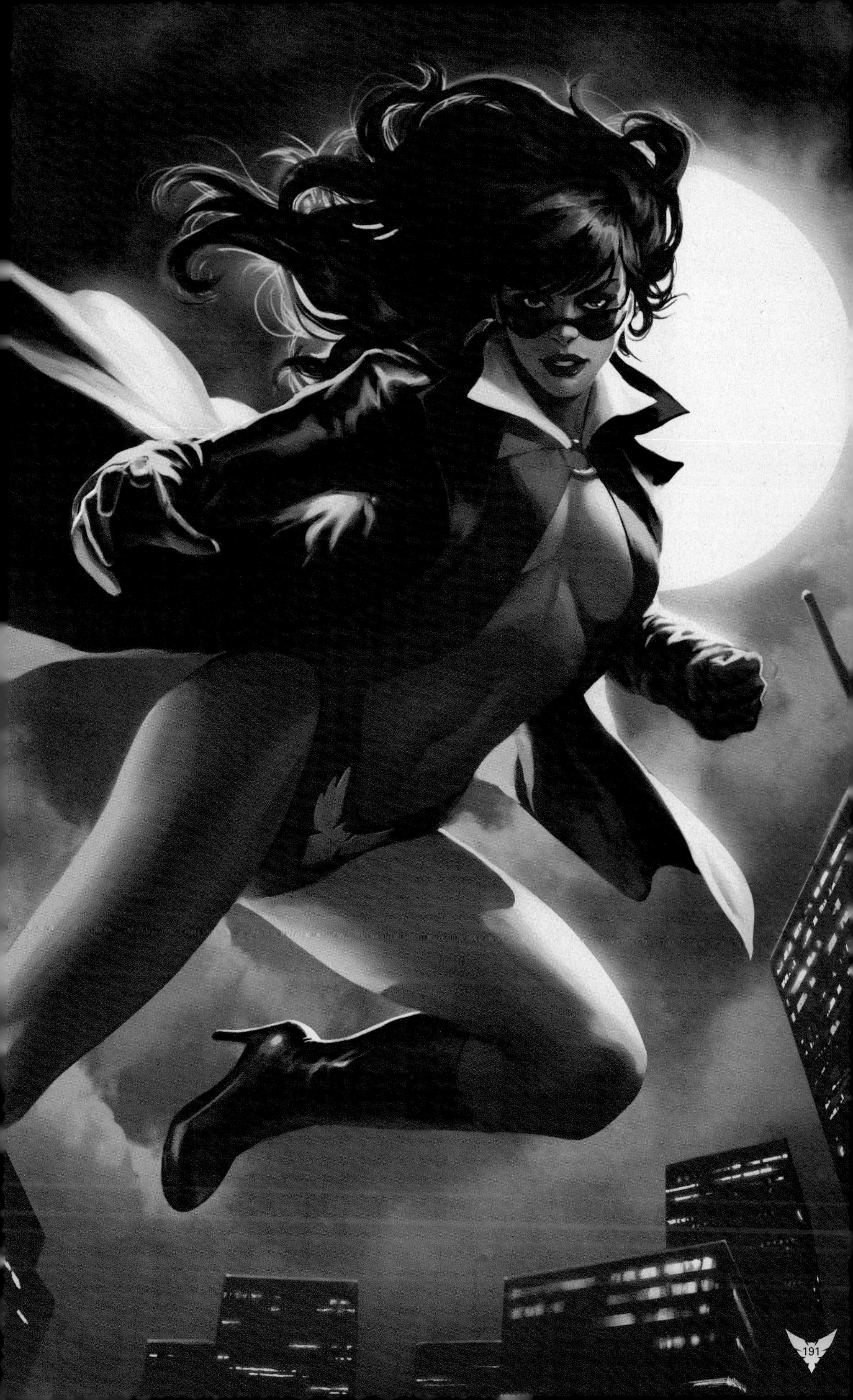

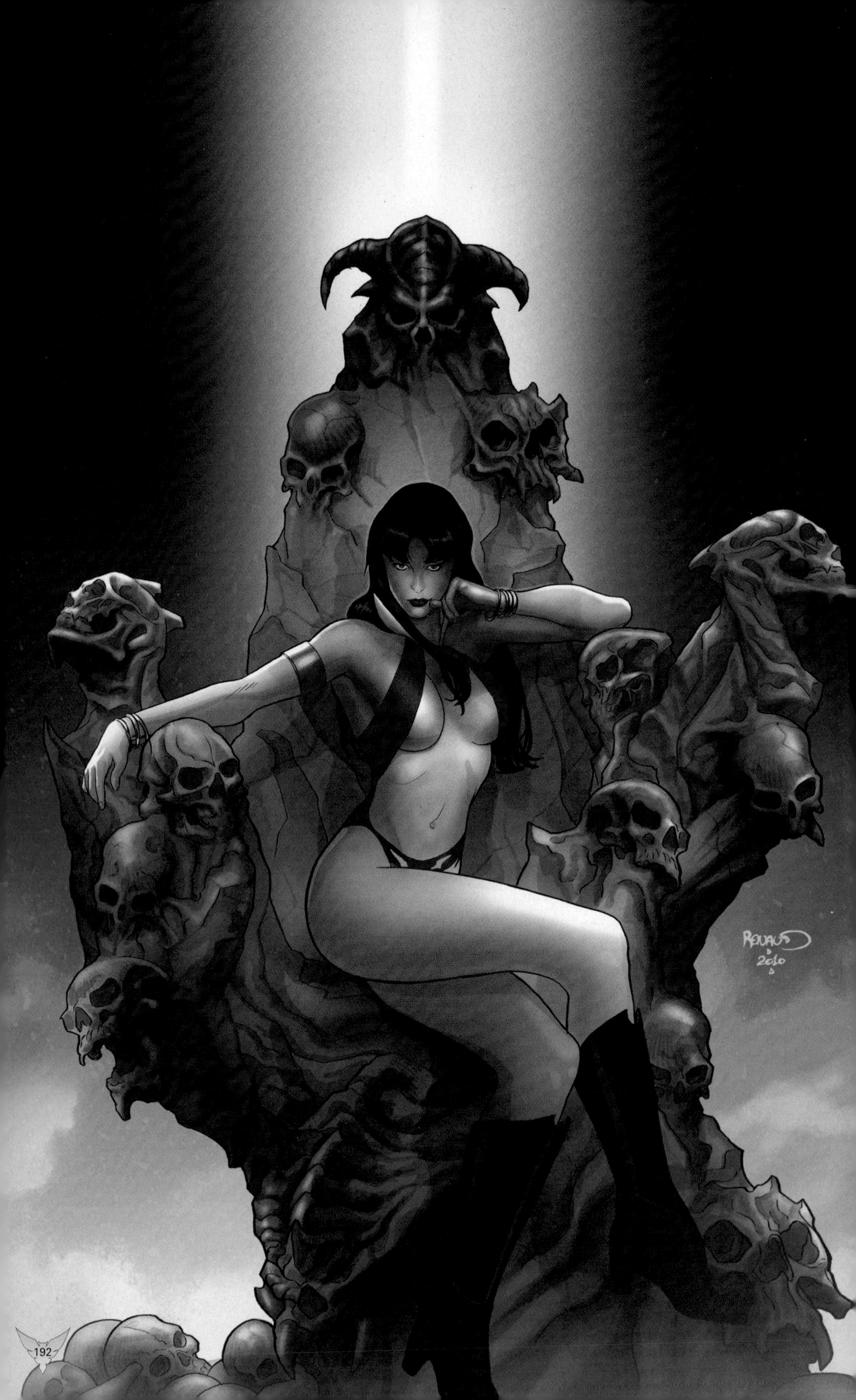

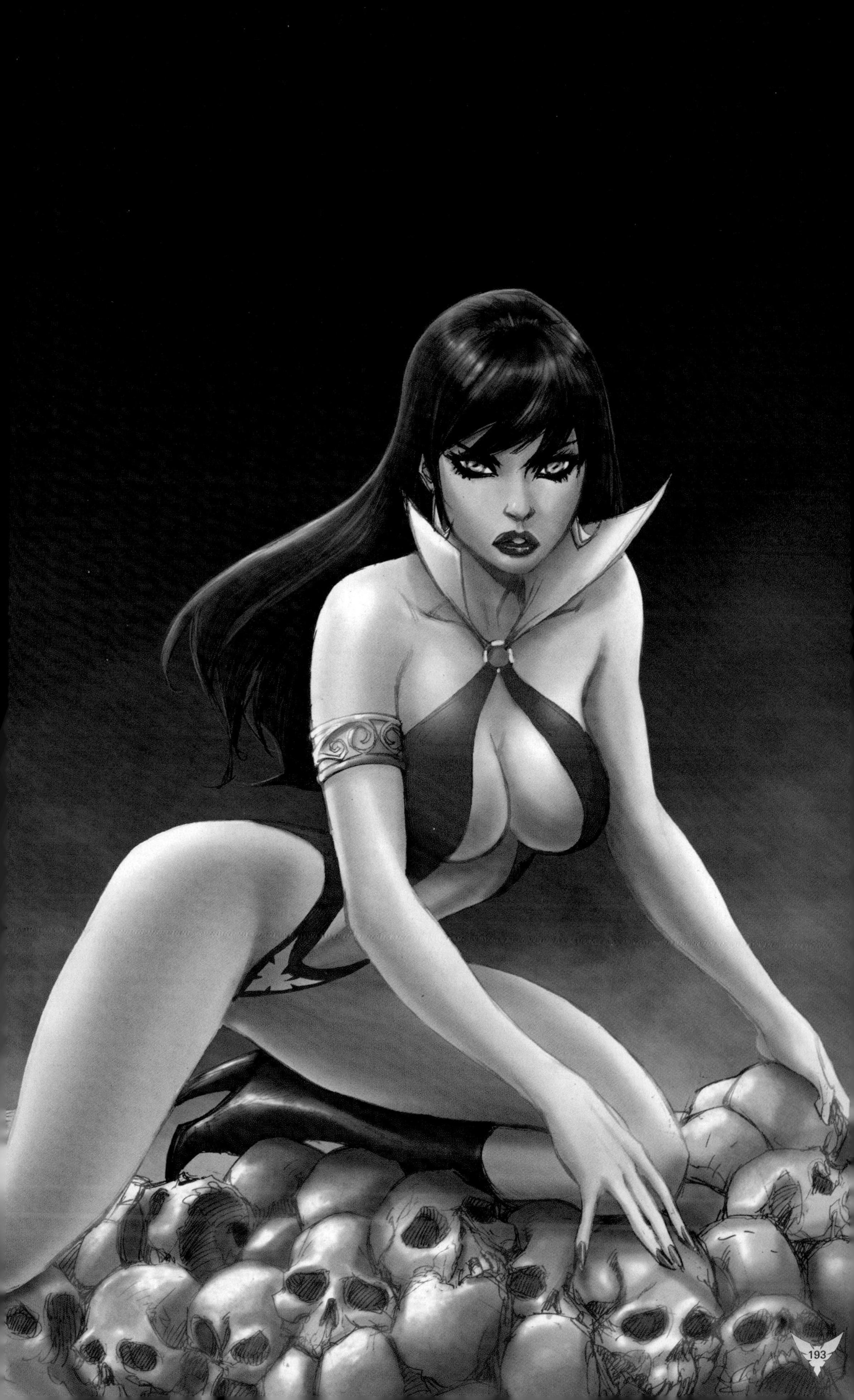

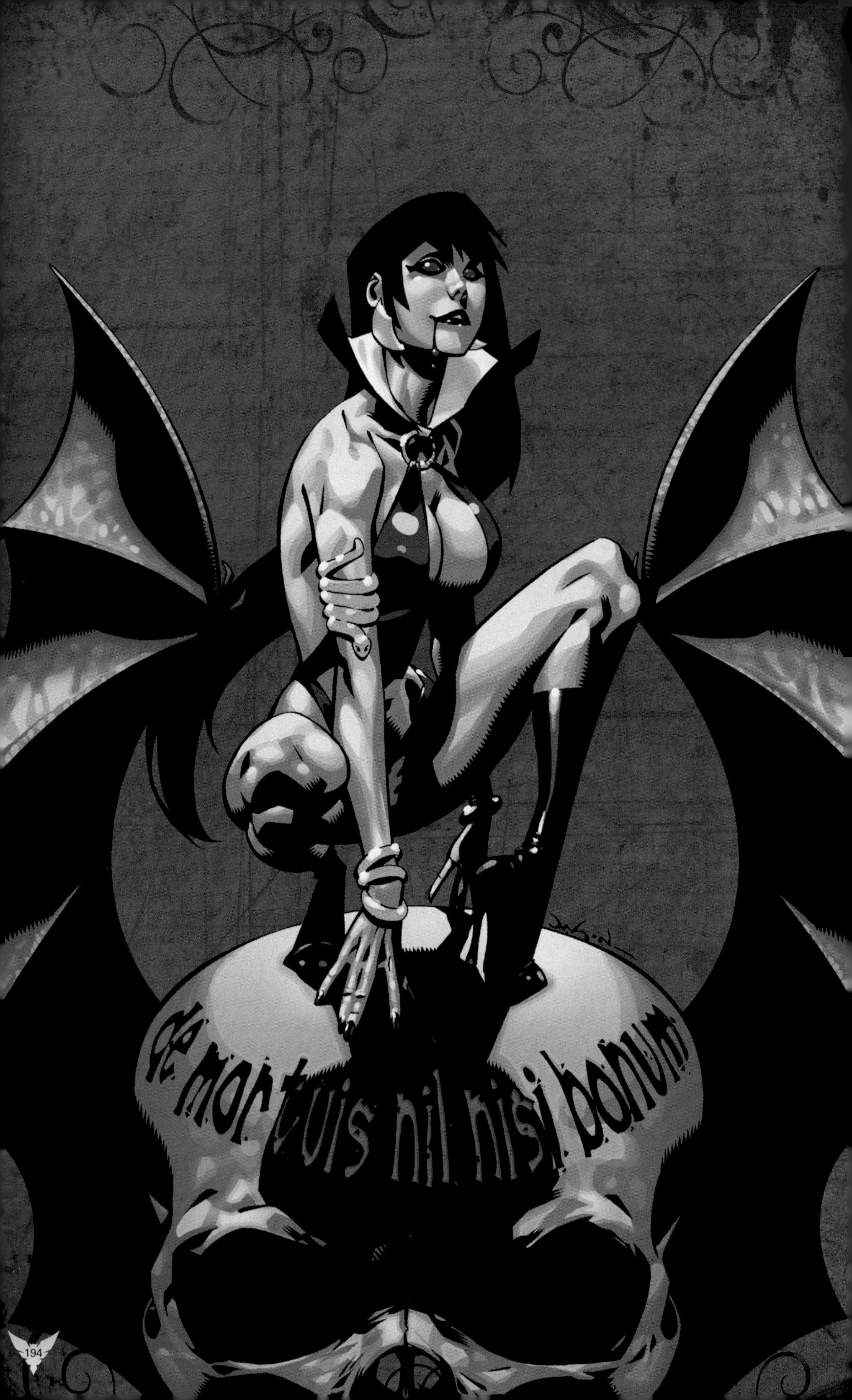
de mortuis nil nisi bonum

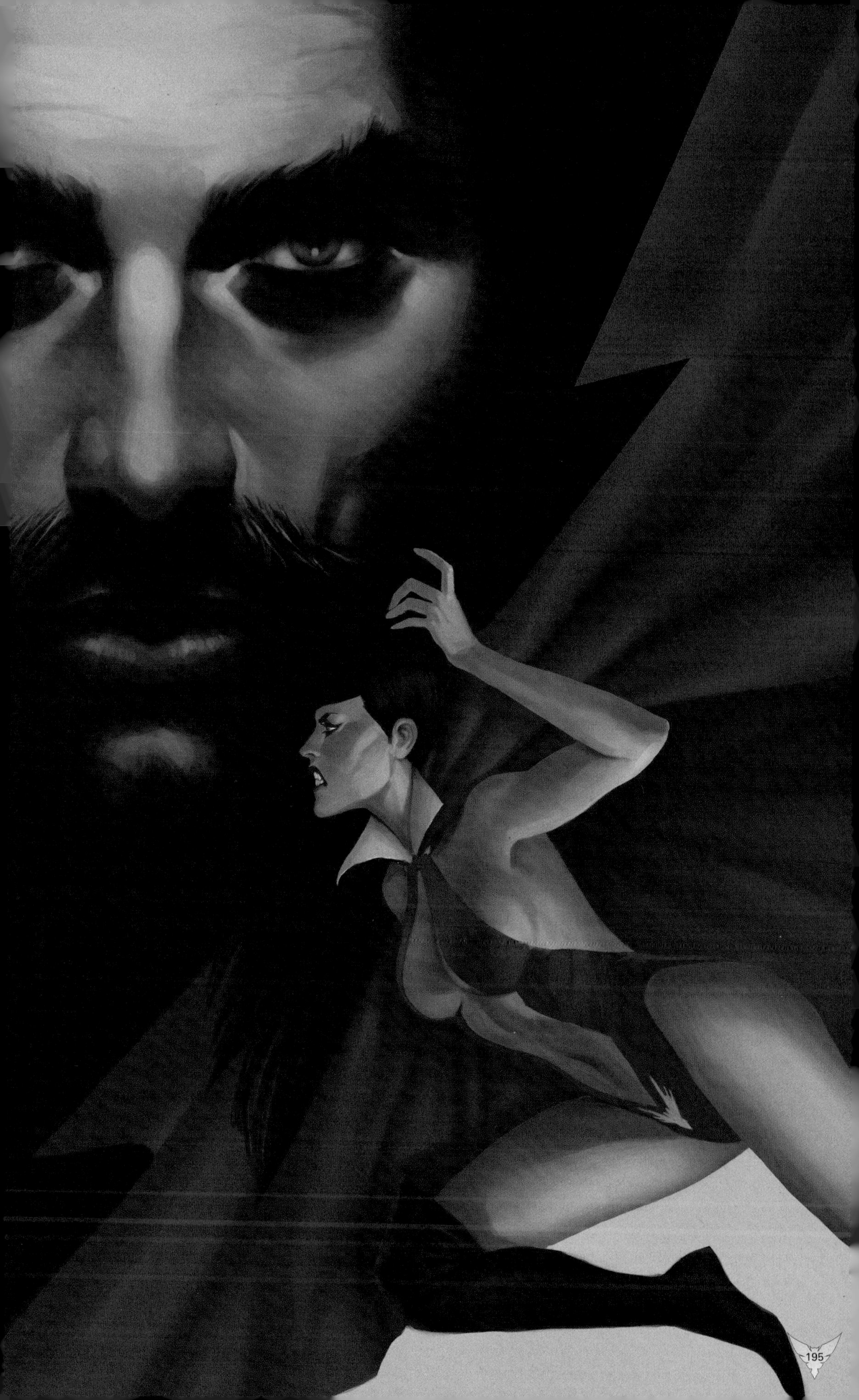

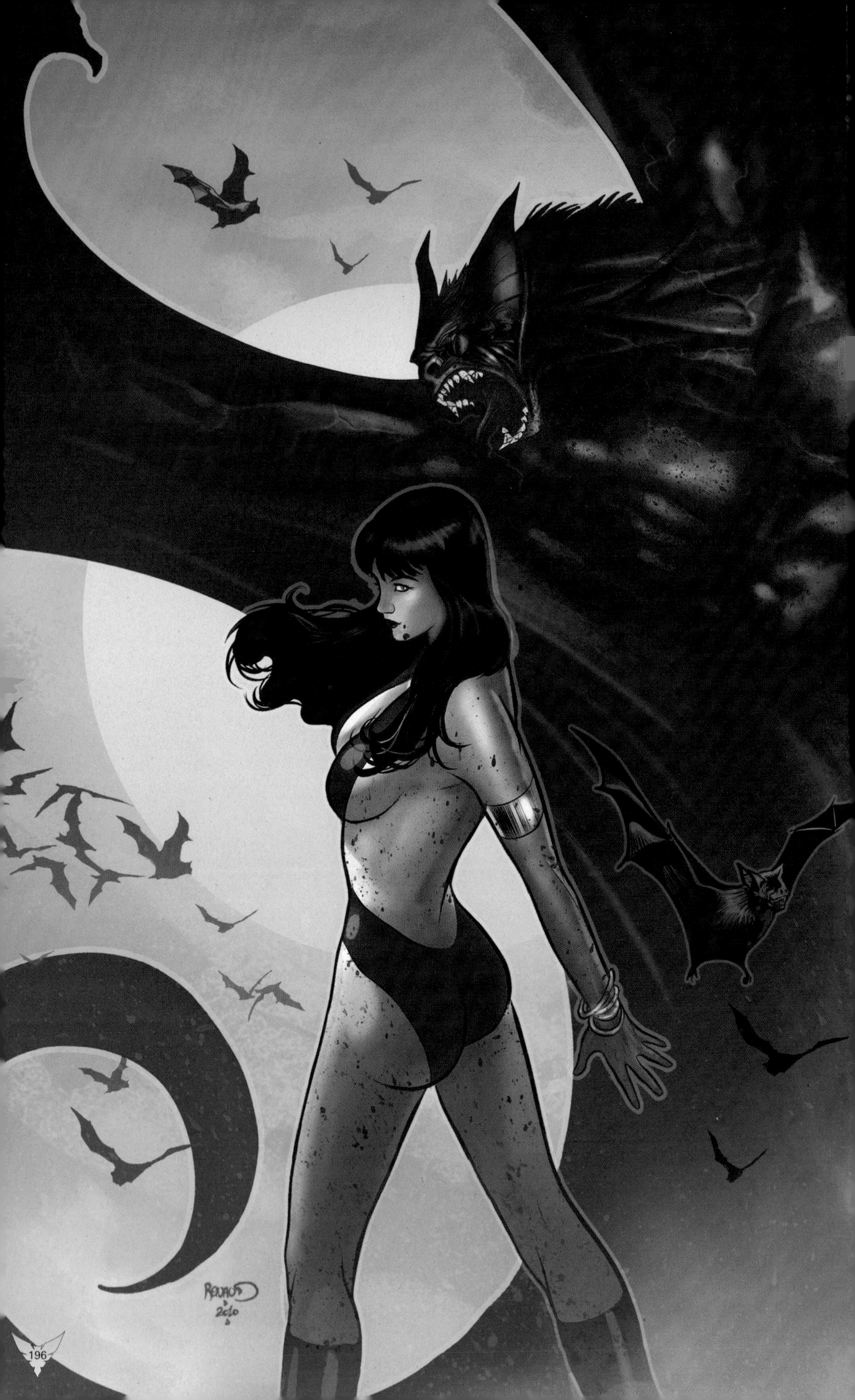

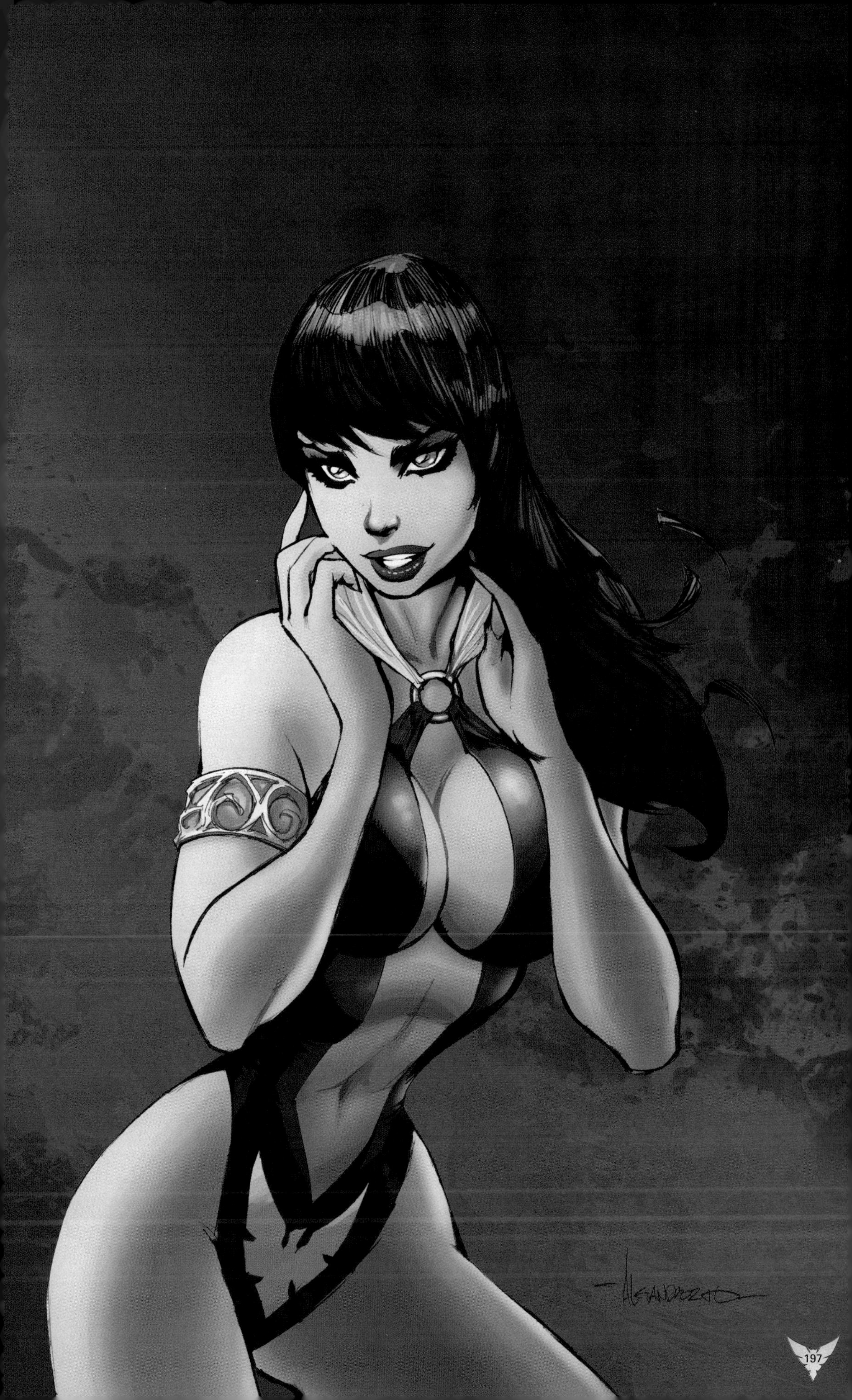

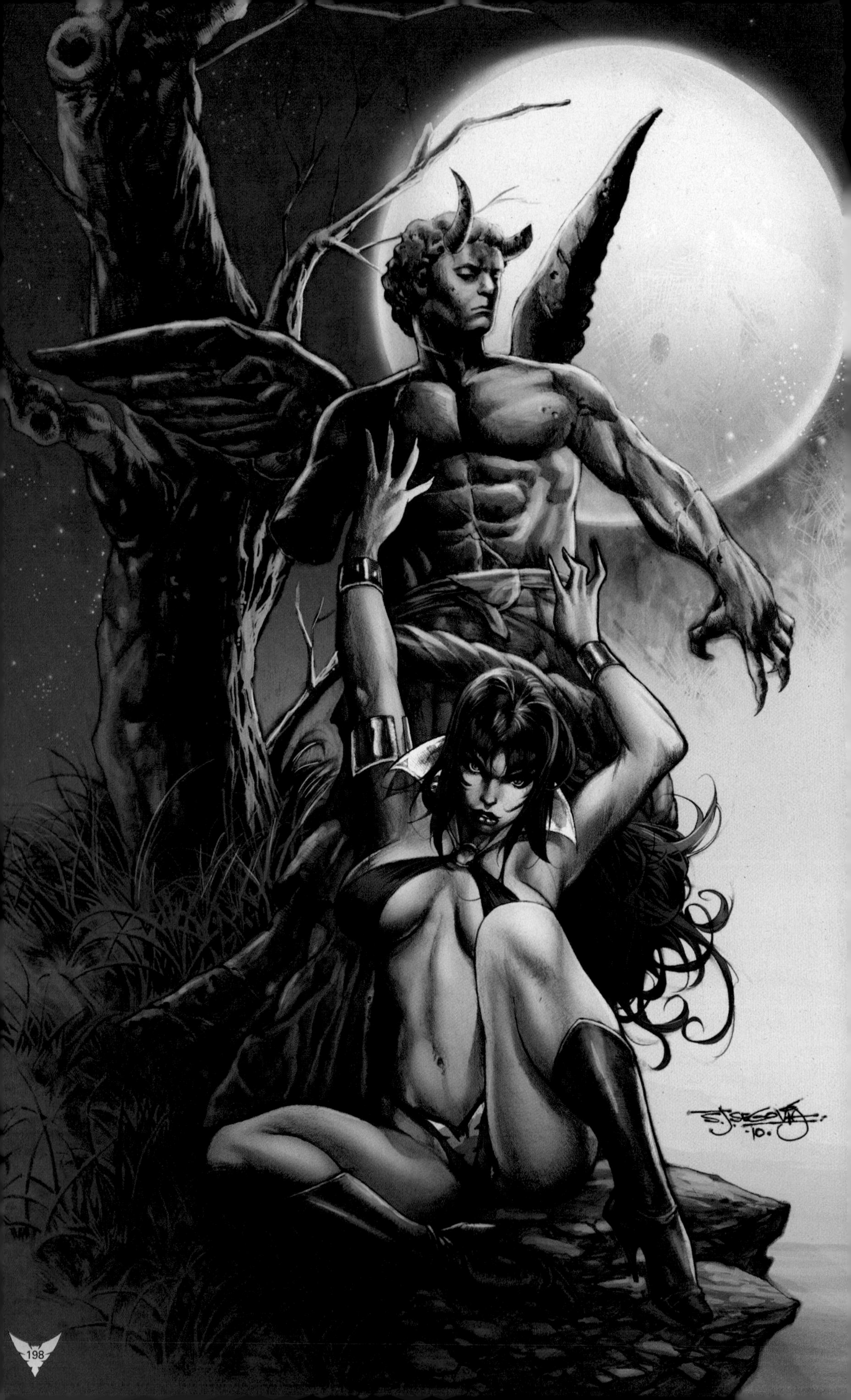

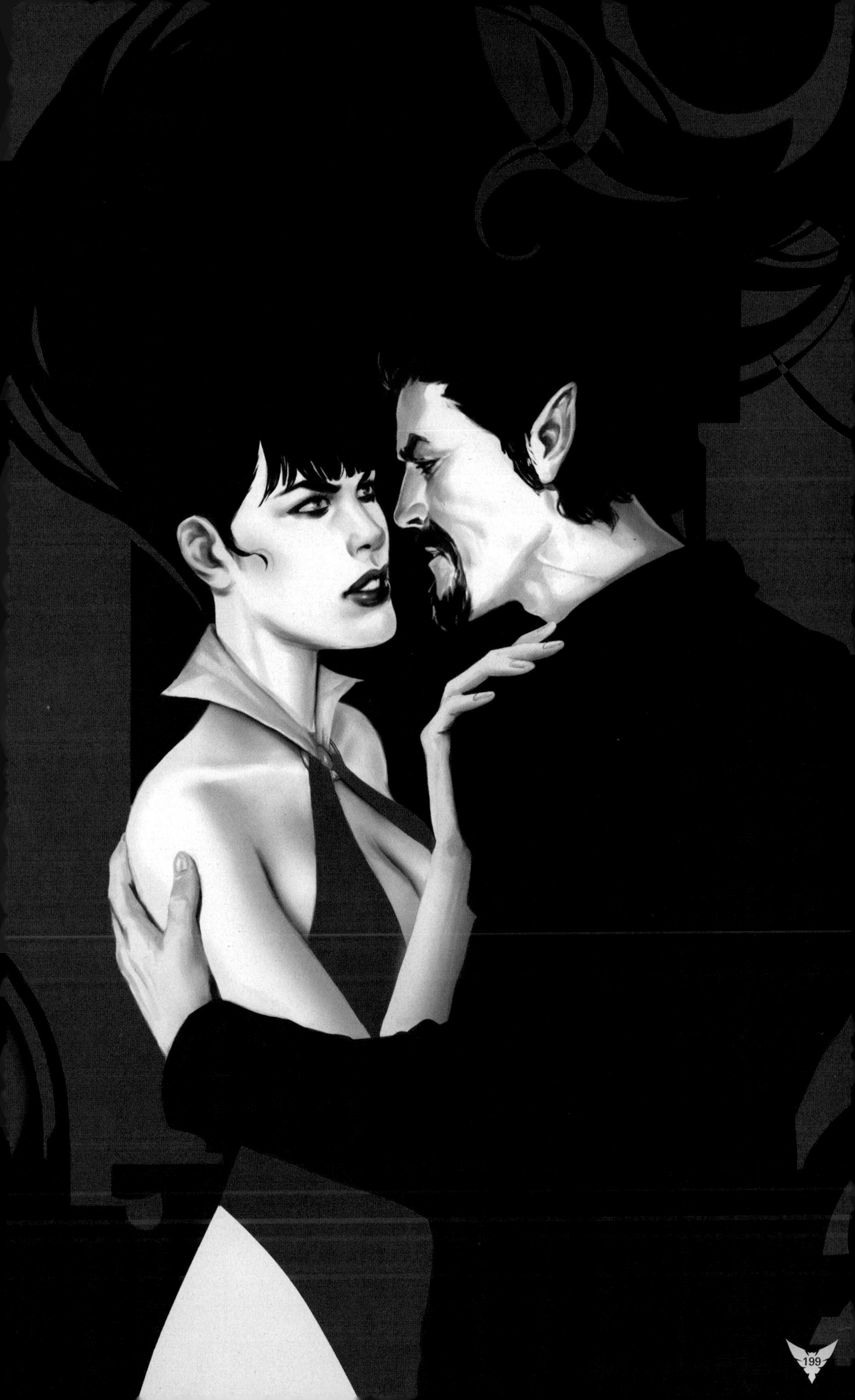

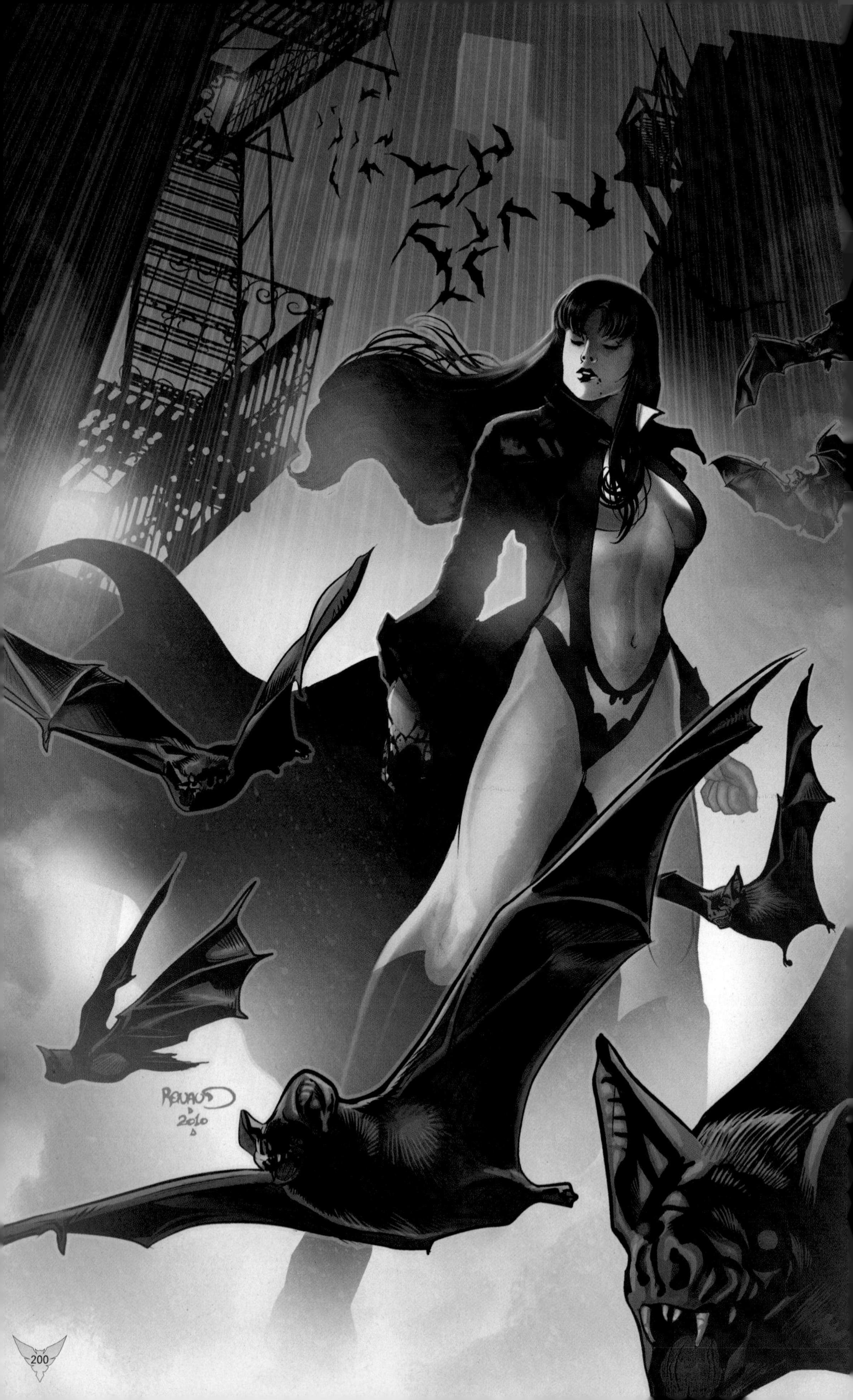

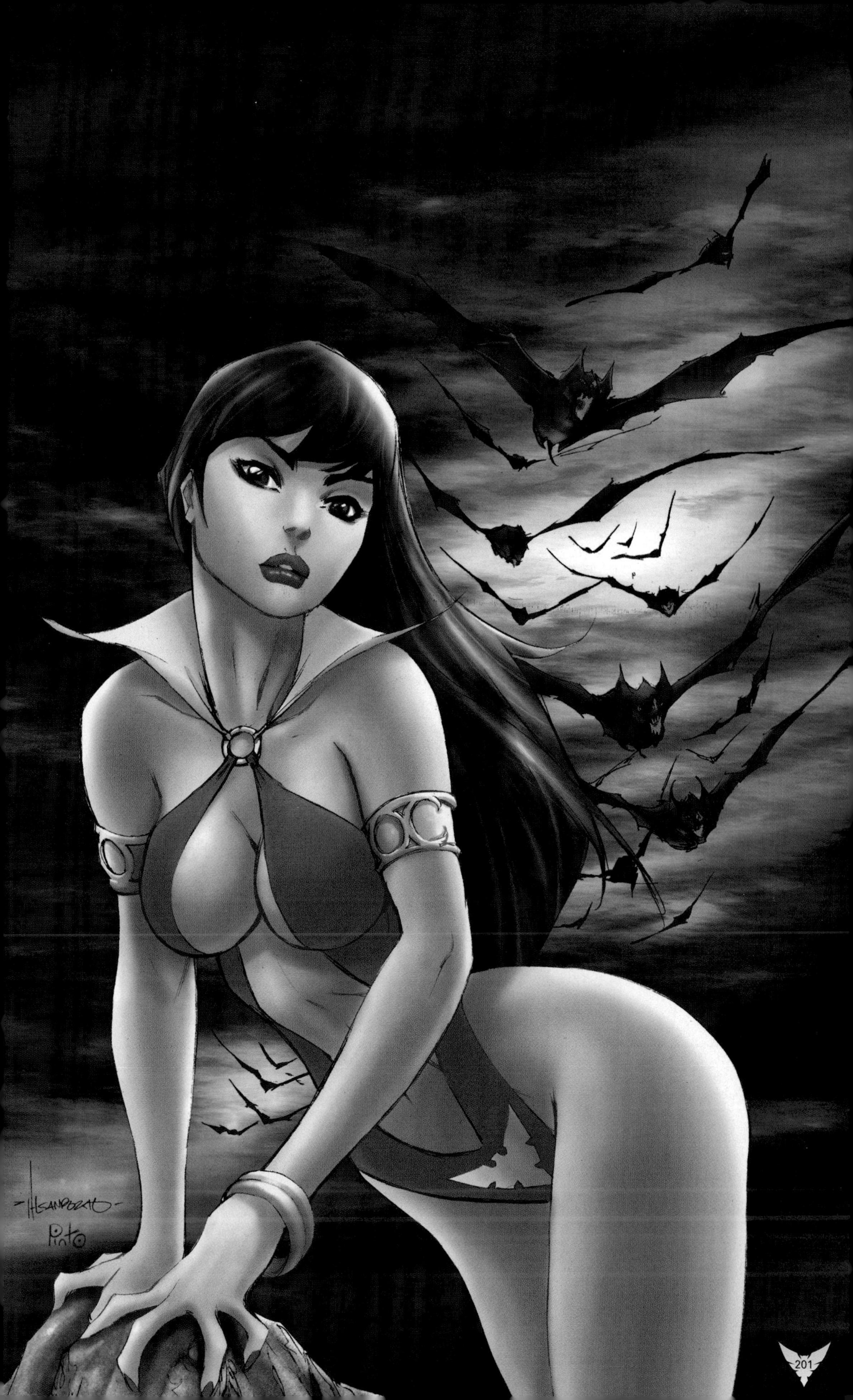

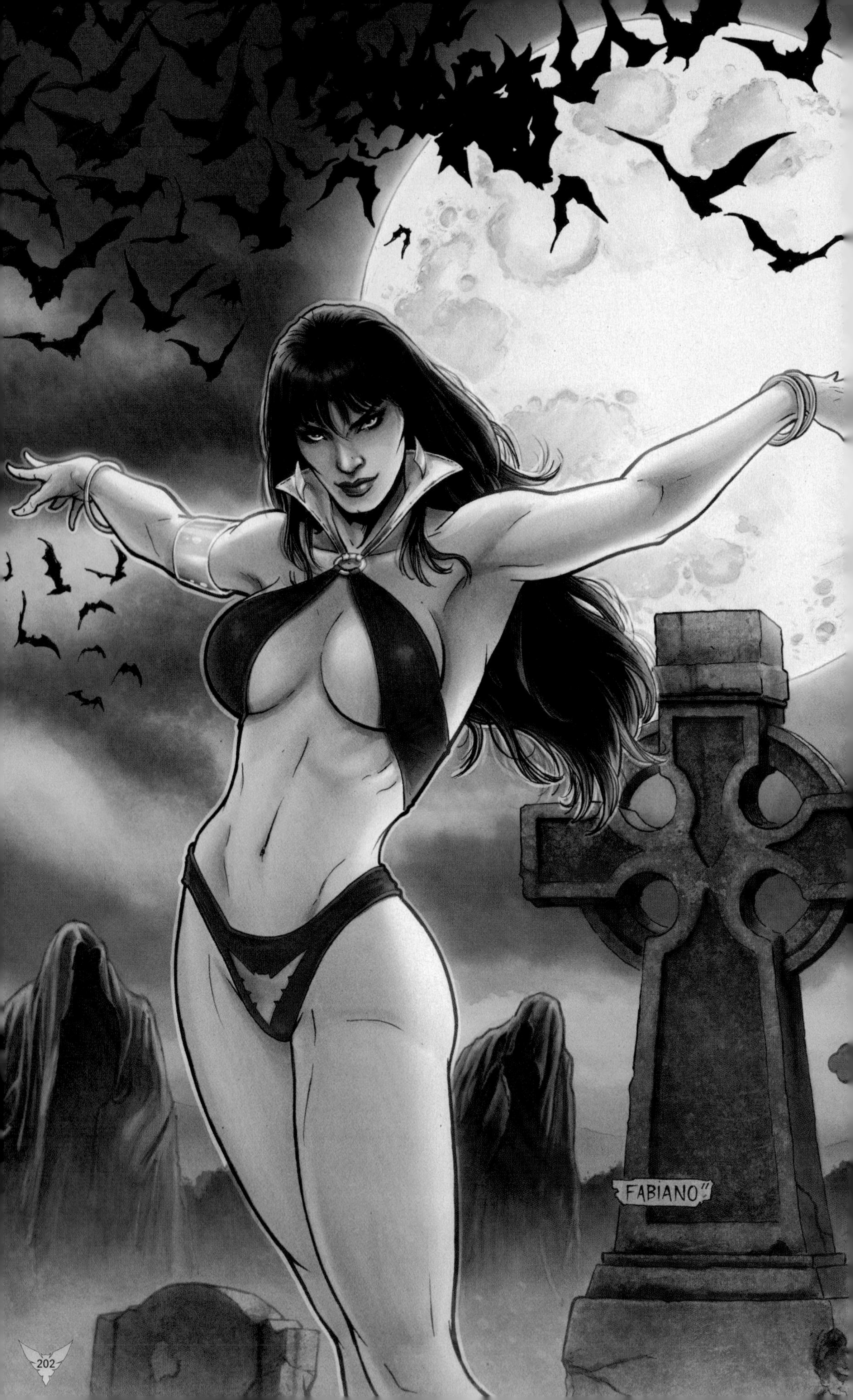
FABIANO

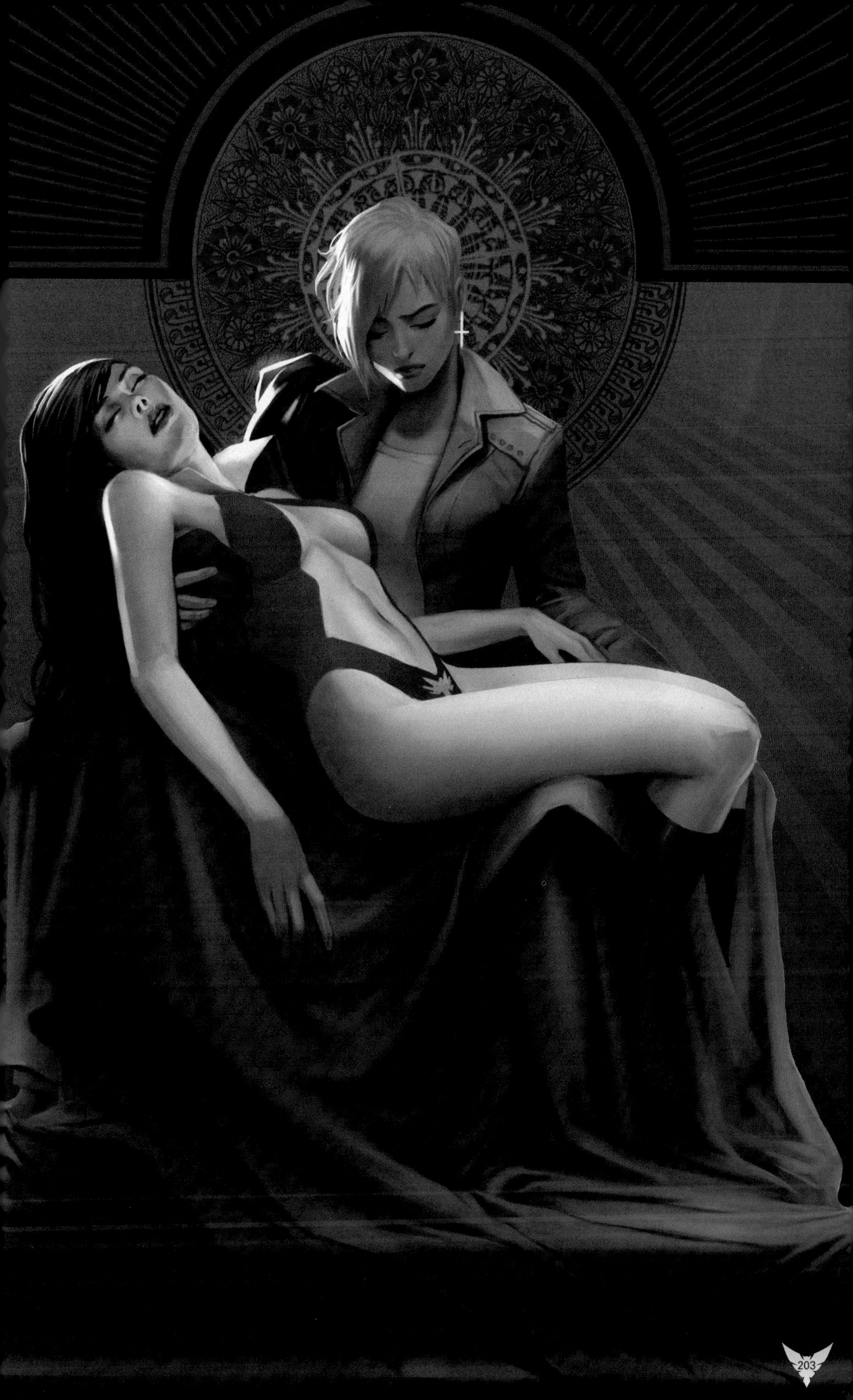

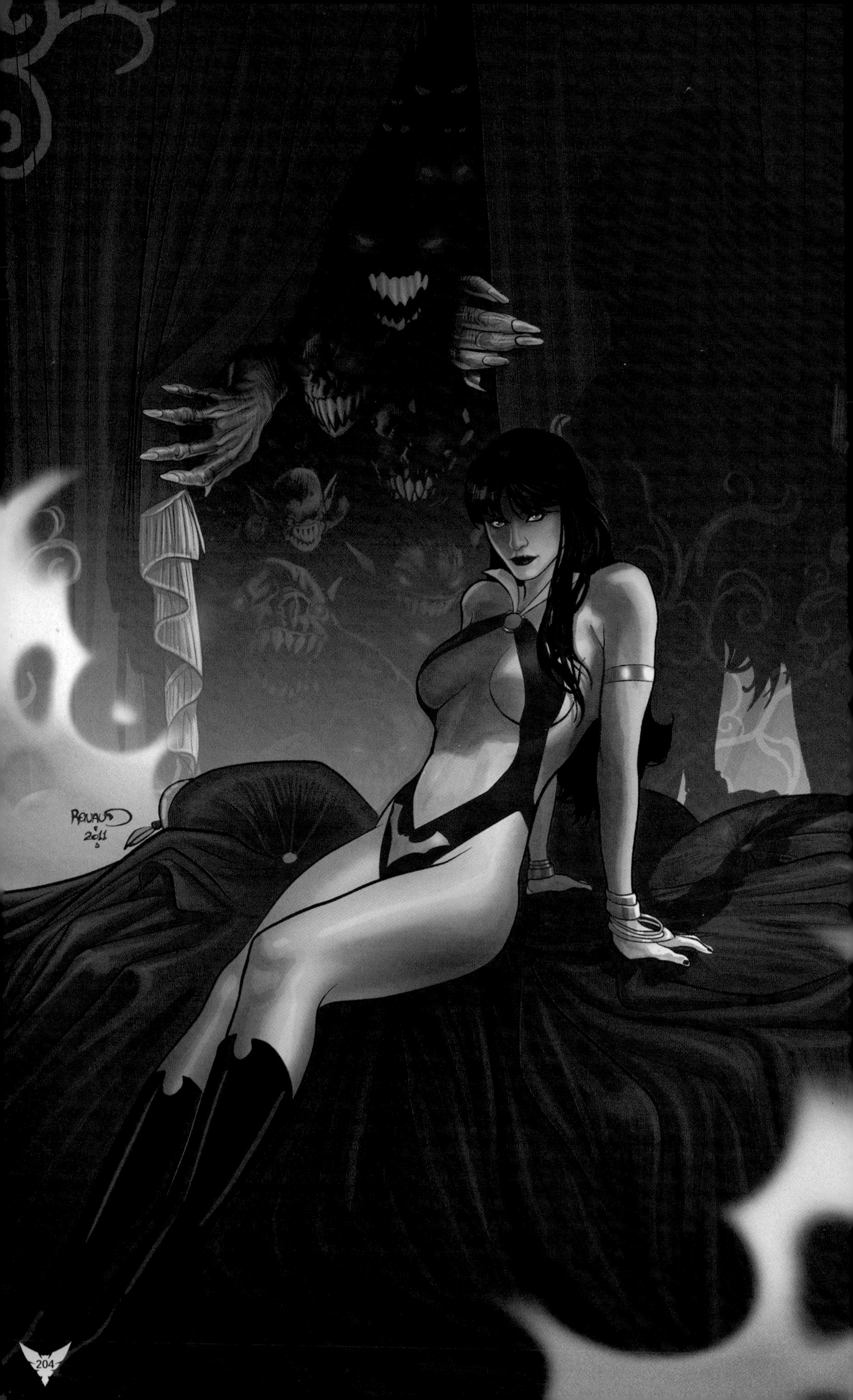
RENAUD
2011

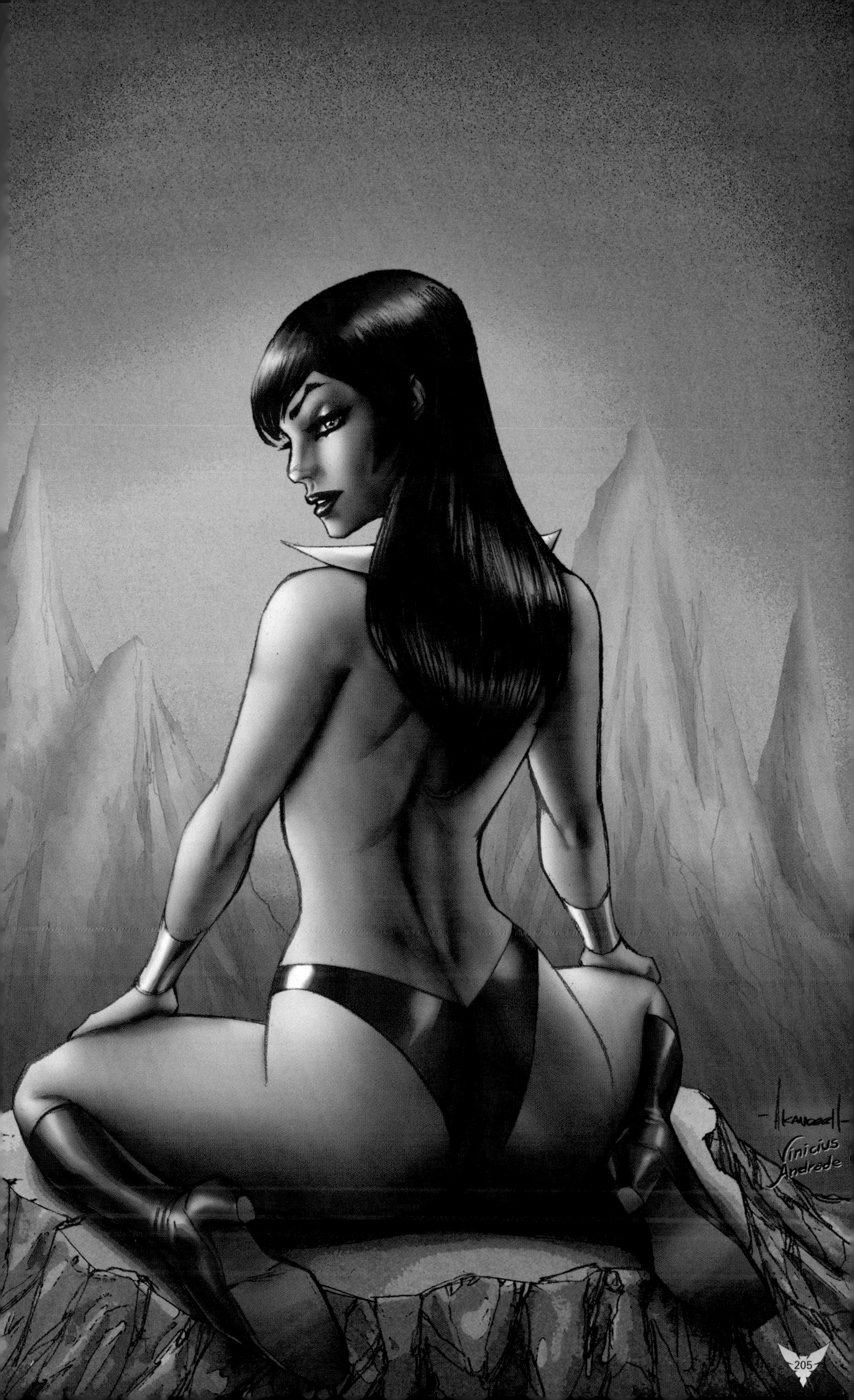
Vinicius Andrade

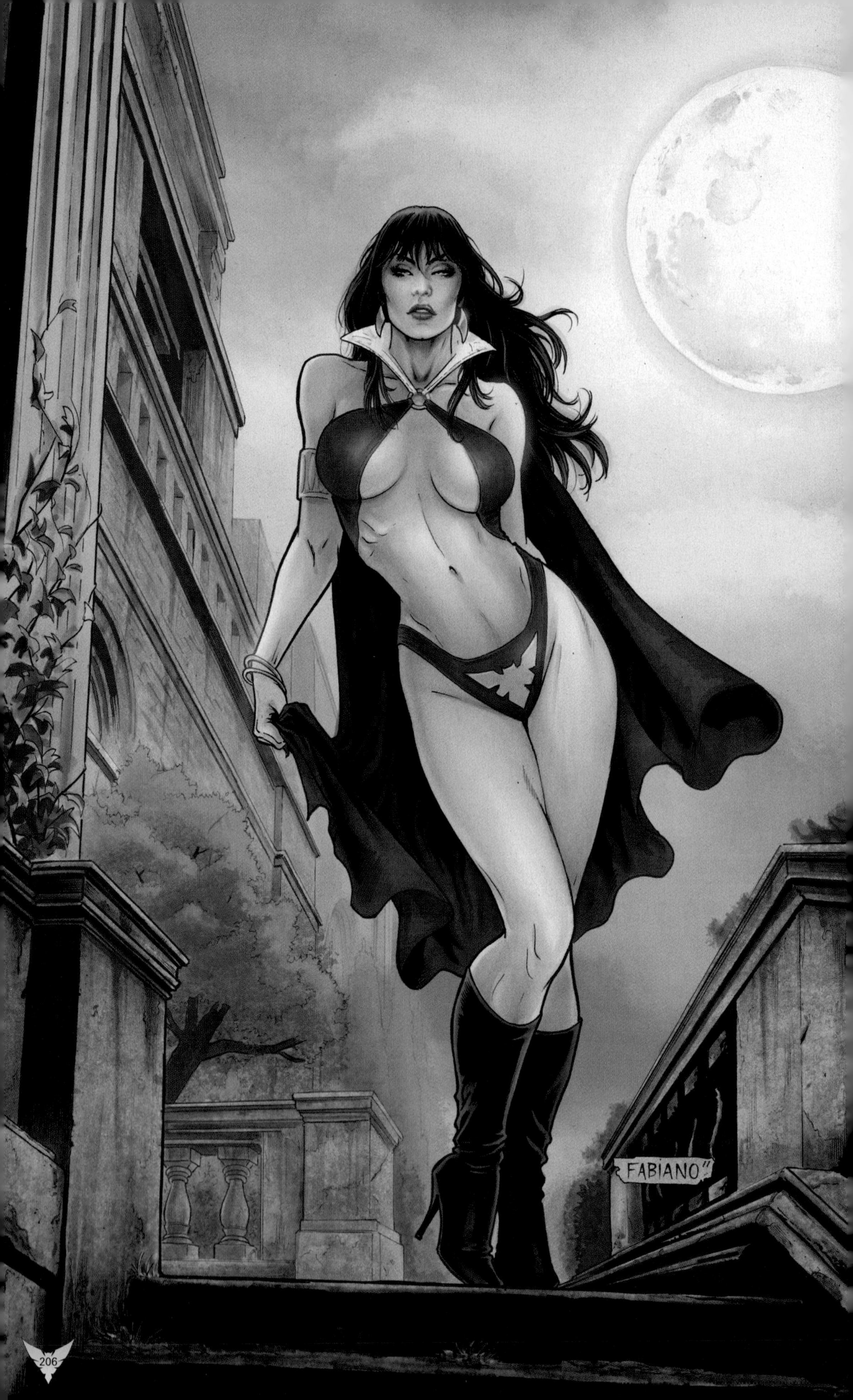
FABIANO

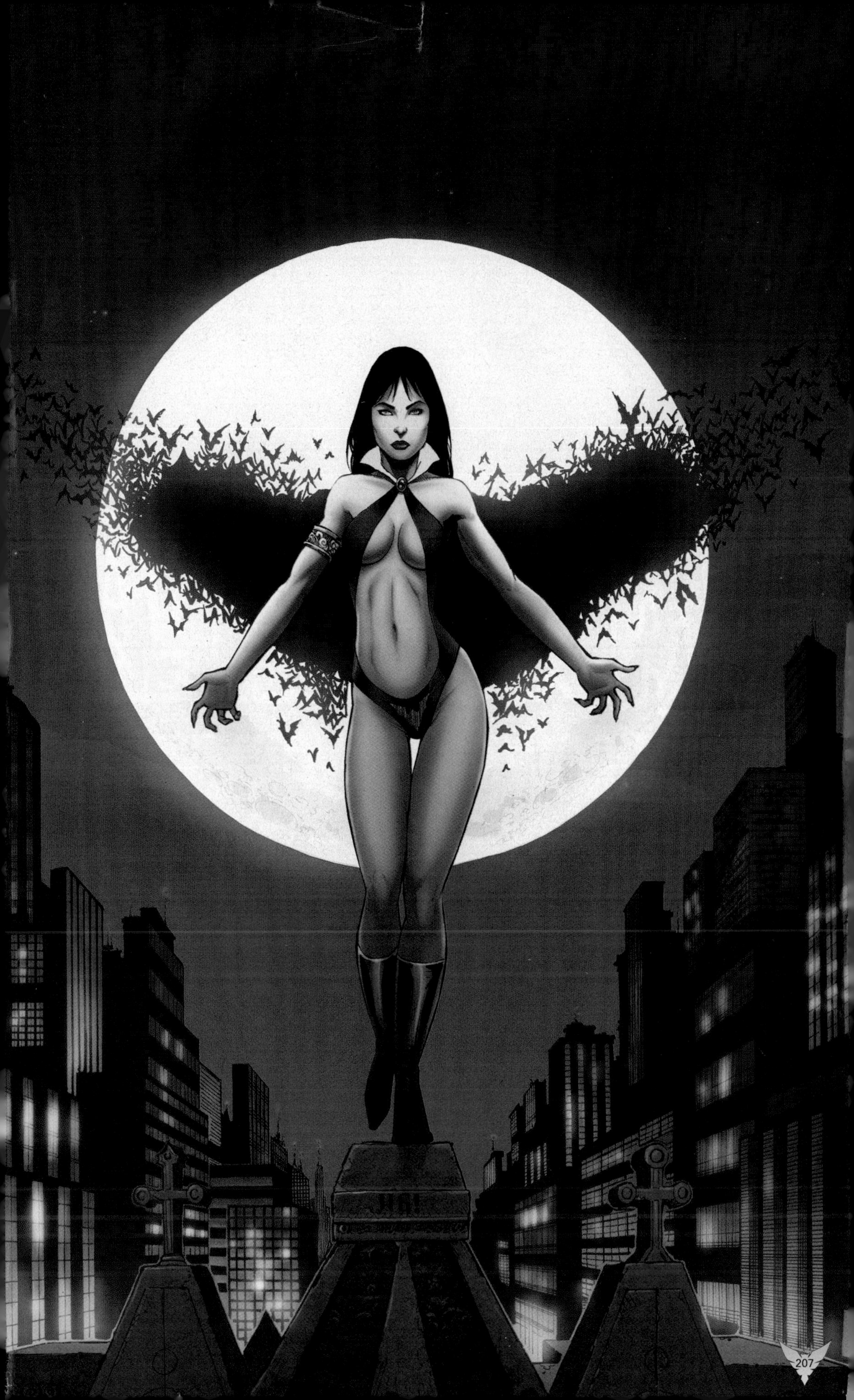

VAMPIRELLA®

CROWN OF WORMS